ITALY
IN THE MAKING
June 1846 TO 1 *January* 1848

PIUS IX

Painted while he was Cardinal Mastai (1840–46) and Bishop of Imola. This
portrait-in-oils is in the Palazzo Santa Croce in Rome, and is reproduced by the kind
permission of the Pasolini family.

ITALY
IN THE MAKING
June 1846 to 1 *January* 1848

By

G. F.-H. & J. BERKELEY

CAMBRIDGE
AT THE UNIVERSITY PRESS
1936

LONDON
Cambridge University Press
FETTER LANE

NEW YORK · TORONTO
BOMBAY · CALCUTTA · MADRAS
Macmillan

TOKYO
Maruzen Company Ltd

PRINTED IN GREAT BRITAIN

In memoriam

C. I. B.

The truth, the whole truth,
and nothing but the truth,
—with the help of God

CONTENTS

PART II

(*June* 1847 *to* 1 *December* 1847)

MAPS

PREFACE

This second volume of *Italy in the Making* deals with the period between June 1846 and January 1848. This brief space of time seems too short to require a whole book, but in revolutionary days every item is of importance; witness the crucial years of the French Revolution.

This concentration on a short section of the story offers at all events one great advantage: within such limits it becomes easier to obtain virtual certainty of the truth about every successive step forward. Apart from the knowledge acquired in the various Italian State-Archives and in the Vatican, it has been possible to verify every essential fact and opinion from the Archives of Vienna, Paris and London.

Readers will find that some of the conclusions here stated do not entirely coincide with the views in the standard histories,—even in those by Italian authors. This is regrettable: but most of those standard histories were written thirty-five or forty years ago; and certainly the statements in this volume would be more in harmony with present day Italian studies of the period, than with them. By now, of course, there are countless new documents and memoirs available; and undoubtedly moments occur when it becomes necessary to strike out a new line or else fail to state the truth.[1]

In volume I the principal hero was Charles Albert: in the present volume it is Pius IX. The latter has never received the credit due to him for his splendid effort during his first two years. And indeed, until recently, the same might be said of

[1] The chief subjects on which the more modern views are stated here are the winning of the Civic Guard, the Piedmontese Group in Rome, the "Gran Congiura" (Great Conspiracy), the Ferrara episode, and Naples. On most of these questions excellent information has been obtainable at the Viennese Archives.

almost the whole life of Charles Albert,—and about one or
two of the other princes as well.[2]

For each of the authors the Risorgimento has been a life-
study: and during those long years there have been so many
people to whom we are indebted for kind and courteous
assistance that it would be difficult to name them all.

We must make our acknowledgments once again to the
memory of the late Cardinal Gasquet for his great kindness
in discussing the whole subject, in lending us books and in
obtaining permission for us to search in the Vatican Archives.

Next, to the Countess Maria Pasolini who, out of her great
knowledge, was abundantly generous to a foreign student.
Also to her son, Count Guido Pasolini.

In Florence our warmest thanks are due to the Commendatore Dorini for all the trouble taken on our behalf in the
splendidly managed archives of the old state of Tuscany; and
also to the Marquis Degli Azzi-Vitelleschi, the author of the
well-known books *Le Stragi di Perugia* and *La Liberazione di
Perugia*, for his kind advice and suggestions.

In Rome we are indebted, firstly, to the British Ambassador
for permission to delve in the State Archives; also to Mr
Randall of the British Legation to the Holy See; also to
Commendatore Casanova, Commendatore Rè and Cavaliere
Polidori. And we owe a great debt of gratitude to Commendatore Menghini, Director of the Risorgimento Library and
editor of the National Edition of Mazzini's letters, for his
constant help and advice; also to General Ezio Garibaldi for
much extremely interesting information about the times of

[2] One reason for this is that until lately the old ruling families and
the Pope were still regarded as dangers to the unity of Italy, and
consequently they often received little sympathy from historians:
whereas now the old rulers are forgotten and the Vatican question is
settled. Moreover, as the lesser rulers were all dispossessed by the
Risorgimento, it would have damped the joy in the national triumph
to point out that in most cases this dispossession was a tragedy. Yet
that was true; but it was inevitable, if Italy was ever to become a
nation.

his grandfather. At the Vatican we owe our sincerest thanks to Monsignor Mercati, Prefect of the Vatican Library, and also to his brother, Monsignor Mercati, Prefect of the Vatican Archives.

At Milan, in the Risorgimento Library, Commendatore Monti gave us the kindest assistance.

In Paris we owe our thanks to the British Ambassador and are deeply indebted for the help afforded by the admirable organisation of the Archives des Affaires Étrangères.

In Vienna we owe an equal debt of thanks to Professor Gross for all the help given at the splendidly organised Staats-Archiv.

Finally, in London, we must acknowledge with gratitude the practical and prompt assistance which we received from all the employees in the Public Record Office in Chancery Lane.

G. F.-H. B.

J. B.

INTRODUCTION

RECAPITULATION

I

In a previous volume we began by stating that the years between 1846 and 1849 constitute the first period of trial and test in the Making of Italy, and undoubtedly mark the chief turning-point in its history. That short period is the central moment —one might call it the junction in point of time—and from all sides the important lines of development lead up to it. Then, during those three years, all the various parties and beliefs are tested in the fire of war and strife, and many of them are consumed. After 1849 those which have emerged from the furnace are welded into one single successful policy by Cavour.

The next question to decide is: what were these main lines of development that led to the making of modern Italy? In volume 1 we limited ourselves to tracing five chief factors in its advance—namely, the history of three ideas: Reaction (headed by Austria), Revolution (Mazzini) and Moderation (Federalists); and of two states, Piedmont (Charles Albert) and the Papacy (Gregory XVI). Of these, the *Reaction* meant Austrian domination, a divided Italy and no Liberal institutions. The *Revolution* was led by Mazzini whose creed was (*a*) republican and (*b*) fusionist, i.e. in favour of uniting Italy by fusing all her states into one, and not by federation. Then arose the *Moderates*, who, headed by Gioberti, favoured uniting Italy by federation. In *Piedmont* Charles Albert aimed at Piedmontese hegemony, and in case of war believed that if the rest of Italy would follow him she could drive out the Austrians single-handed (*Italia farà da sè*)—without foreign alliances. In the *Papal State* the rebellions had produced two Liberal schemes of government, namely the Memorandum in 1831, and the Manifesto of Rimini in 1845 : and these ideas, combined with Gioberti's federalism, after 1846 were to form a basis of constructive work for the Liberal Pope, Pius IX.

The present volume only covers the period from June 1846 to the end of the year 1847; but—just to complete the story of the Risorgimento—we may add that during those three years of strife and war, 1846 to 1849, the Conservative Reaction lost Metternich; Mazzini's republic was found to be impossible but his principle of union by fusion survived. The Moderates' plan of uniting Italy by federation was discredited. Charles Albert's idea that Italy could fight Austria single-handed (*Italia farà da sè*) was proved to be only a patriotic dream, but his establishment of Piedmontese hegemony survived; and, finally, as a settlement for the Papal State, Gioberti's vision of a Liberal Pope was abandoned.

Thus out of all the different schemes for the regeneration of Italy there remained, after 1849, only the Albertist claim of Piedmontese hegemony, and the Mazzinian creed of an Italy united by fusion and not by federation. To these two principles Cavour added his plan of a French alliance against Austria and then, inspired by the heroism of Garibaldi, the Making of Italy was accomplished in 1860.

II

In some works on the Making of Italy its history rather seems to have been fogged by laborious attempts to set out, not the story of the movement, but, simultaneously, the records of the eight or nine small Italian nations during that half-century. In these two volumes our aim has been to trace only the main succession of cause and effect in the national advance until each result is achieved. If we regard the whole Risorgimento as the building of a beautiful dwelling-house, we may call this period—1846 to 1849—the first floor in its scaffolding; the stage when the builders meet and exchange ideas before making a fresh start on their upward climb. The first thing noticeable in 1846 is that, of the five original factors above named, two have now coalesced. The Moderates have converted the Pope; and thus the new Pope is now a Liberal and the leader of the Moderates; so that for two years to come the Moderate movement is by far the most important in Italy. For the time being the main progress of the Risorgimento lies with them, and no longer with Mazzini or even with Charles Albert.

III

The present volume (June 1846 to January 1st, 1848) covers the first eighteen months of Pius IX's pontificate: those during which he put into practice the Moderate programme outlined in Gioberti's *Primato*.

This short period is one of great importance. Undoubtedly it constitutes a separate phase in the Risorgimento. It is the phase when agitation prepares the way for action. A period of agitation occurs in almost every national movement.

Manifestly the work of making a nation is primarily a mental process, the work of converting people to the idea; for, as soon as everyone, or even a sufficient majority of the people within its frontiers, is agreed that it is a nation, then the work is done: sooner or later that people will win its freedom. Of Italy this was exceptionally true. In that 700-mile-long peninsula, in 1846, there were nearly 24,000,000 people, and if they had all wished for a united and independent Italy—if, for instance, they had been as united as the Irish under O'Connell—they would have been irresistible.[1] But it was impossible that they all, or that even a large proportion of them, should have that feeling. They were divided by mountains, by distances, by ancient national traditions and dialects, by differences of race and cultural development.

[1] Massimo d'Azeglio said: "If everyone in Italy wanted it the thing would be done."

Most certainly it is only fair to Italians to remember these divisions, and to bear in mind that in every national uprising the gallant minority who sacrifice themselves for the rest are comparatively few in number. In Italy there were millions, especially among the peasantry, to whom the idea that they were members of the Italian nation had never been practical politics nor even clearly understood.

The case of Italy was entirely different from that of Poland or Greece or any other of the nations fighting to win their freedom. Italy was not a conquered nation; she had never been a nation at all. The problem before her sons was to convert her into a nation—a process which was only completed, most probably, by and since the Great War. To illustrate the difficulties of Italy in 1846 let us suppose that to-day, in South America, two of the states were being held in subjection by some immense world-power. The first problem would be to persuade all those neo-Latin peoples and individuals that they were part of one great nation and that it was their duty to unite against the foreigner.[2]

In Italy, of course, the dream of unity was one of old date. In times prior to the French Revolution it had existed as an idea, but as one that was in the heads of only a few exceptional individuals. Then when the Napoleonic régime arrived, bringing better roads but a constant influx of foreign armies and officials, this sentiment, that all Italians were of one stock, had been felt both more closely and more bitterly, and had come to be considered the feeling of a group. Later still, after 1815—and more especially after 1821—the desire for unity had spread until it could claim to be the opinion of a

[2] We use South America merely for illustration, *not analogy*. The cases are not analogous for many reasons; for one, because the South American states are free; they are not, as were the Italians, ruled by despots all under the hand of a foreign arch-despot: also because so far the idea of possible unity has not made any progress in South America at all comparable to that made by the idea of unity in Italy even before 1815.

small minority.[3] Finally, in 1831, the Revolution revealed its
development in most of the municipalities of central Italy;
and from that date onward the great aim of all Italian nationalists was to make converts and to turn their minority into a
majority.

Here we come to the subject-matter of the present volume;
the preparation both mental and material; the immense
Moderate movement which called for Liberal institutions,
for unity and for independence, and for the growth, through
federalism,of a sense of common nationhood. The years 1846
and 1847 are the period of a common agitation which did
more than any other movement to spread the feeling of being
one nation.

It is at this preparatory stage that a Moderate movement
is always the most useful. It makes far more converts than the
Extremists because its suggestions are practicable and the
result of reasoned thought. It introduces the phase when
irrational violence is at a discount, and when the whole
question is treated as a problem for examination, discussion
and practical suggestions. Thus, during these years, Mazzini's
schemes for winning a fused republic by violence were dis-
carded as being impossible; but the Moderate plan of uniting
all the states by federation made thousands of converts because it was constructive, and could be accepted by law-
abiding men. Consequently between 1843 and 1848 the
Moderates did more to popularise the national cause than
had ever been done before; and in 1846, when the new Pope,
Pius IX, declared himself a Liberal, they swept into their
train almost the whole of the political classes in every state
except the two Sicilies.

[3] The above is Tivaroni's view as to the progress of the idea of
unity. Pellegrino Rossi's opinion is also valuable because he was one
of the men who did most propaganda for Murat's national campaign
in 1814–15. Thirty years later he said: "In 1815 the national party
in Italy...was, as yet, merely philosophic.... It was hardly national
at all in the true sense of the word." V. Ledermann, p. 35.

IV

If we are to understand what was expected of Pius IX when he came to the throne, it will be best to give a few quotations summarising the beliefs of the Moderate writers; they were men of a particularly attractive type; thinkers and writers of exceptional ability who had devoted their brains to studying the situation and discovering a way through the difficulties and dangers which beset their country.

Their movement was primarily a reaction against the alternate horrors of revolution and reprisals, which resulted from the sanguinary conflicts between the Mazzinian revolutionists and the existing governments. Their creed has been summed up in volume 1 as follows:

They believed that small risings were useless and that large risings were impossible for the time being; that such sporadic outbursts merely resulted in bloodshed and suffering; that it was better to work peaceably and try to convert the princes to their views; to agitate, if necessary, for Liberal institutions and thus to capture and use the Italian governments instead of following Mazzini's impracticable plan of trying to destroy them all simultaneously. Once that each of the small states should be under the rule of a sympathetic prince, or else governed by the people, they could all band themselves together by means of a league or confederation; and then Austria's first moment of difficulty might become their golden opportunity....

In reality perhaps their aims may be summarised best under three headings: they wanted Independence from Austria; they wanted the Unification of Italy; and they wanted Liberal institutions within the Italian states. And most of them believed that these three aims could be achieved by introducing Liberal reforms first, and then by using the popular liberties thus obtained to unite the small Italian states into a great confederation.

The three aims, then, of the Moderates were Independence, Unification and Liberalism. But there were two main difficulties which lay across their path—problems for which they had to find some solution. Firstly, the position of the Pope: as long as the Papal State lay right across the centre of Italy there seemed no possibility of unification; it was a neutral, international state guaranteed to the Pope by the Great Powers of Europe in 1815 in order to secure his independence from outside influence. In a united Italy the Pope could not be king and he could not be a subject, and he could not be deprived of his state. Secondly, apart from the Papacy there was another impediment to unification, namely the position of the princes and the individual state-patriotisms; there was, and even now there still is, a great deal of very genuine patriotic sentiment for the old states of Italy; and it is natural —even foreigners feel it.

The Abbé Gioberti, who was the greatest of the Moderate writers, had solved these problems in the following manner: instead of uniting Italy by fusion—as Mazzini preached—he wanted to unite her by federation. He reasoned that to form a federation of Italian states would not interfere with the existing princes or state-patriotisms. Let the Pope be its president; thus his supremacy would be maintained: and Gioberti made a pathetic appeal to the future Pope—whoever he might be—to undertake this patriotic duty for the sake of Italy; at the same time he appealed to Charles Albert of Piedmont to be its shield and defender.

The other two leading writers of the Moderate school, Count Cesare Balbo and the Marquis Massimo d'Azeglio, were both Piedmontese nobles. Naturally they were Albertists. They followed Gioberti's ideas as to federation but, instead of the Pope, they wanted to instal Charles Albert as chief; and they claimed that he had the right to annex Lombardy and Venetia—if he could take them from the Austrians—and also the two northern duchies of Parma and Modena. They wanted the Kingdom of Piedmont to become a powerful state right across the north of Italy, from sea to sea; and to be the guardian of the whole peninsula against invasions.

Finally, they believed in working by open agitation, not by secret conspiracy.

V

From the very first, of course, the Moderate party aroused the bitterest opposition of the extremists on either side. Metternich hated its Liberalism more bitterly than he hated Mazzini, because he felt that if the Moderates succeeded in winning Liberal assemblies for Piedmont or Tuscany or the Papal State, he would be obliged to grant similar institutions in Lombardo-Venetia; and he knew that to start representative assemblies within the Austrian Empire would probably result in dividing it up into six or seven separate nations.

Mazzini, too, disliked the Moderates; they were taking the fire out of his movement. According to his views, these Moderate patriots were not ready to risk their lives, and they told his followers that agitation was better than risings: this policy he believed would result in the spirit of nationality dying out and becoming merely a memory. To some extent he was right, for if his outrages had ceased the authorities would soon have said that there was no need for reforms. But in any case he was opposed to federalism, because he saw that it would stereotype the existing divisions, and that in time of stress each small nation would think only of its own profit or safety. There he was certainly right; in the long run federation never could have been as efficient a solution as his plan of union by fusion. For the moment, however, fusion was entirely impossible; it meant attacking nine governments at once, including the Pope and the Austrians, and also the other Great Powers of Europe, guarantors of the Settlement of 1815; whereas there seemed to be no valid reason against setting up—without war or bloodshed—a confederation of Italian states on lines similar to those of the Swiss Confederation or the United States or the German Bund.[4]

[4] As a natural consequence the federal form of government captured the minds of that part of the nation which reflected. Tivaroni, *Domin. Austr.* III, 503. Tivaroni, however, points out elsewhere that neither side was entirely right. Mazzini's union by

Thus Mazzini was ready to encourage a Liberal Pope or anyone else who, in his opinion, would be useful towards freeing his country; but his own aims remained immutable; to oust all the existing sovereigns, including the Pope, and to unite Italy by fusing all the states into one single republic.

VI

At the beginning of 1846 every party in Italy was waiting for the old Pope, Gregory XVI, to die. Everywhere it was realised that the whole country was approaching a crisis. Hitherto Charles Albert had been the most prominent of the Italian sovereigns, but it was felt that the Papal election might have an immense influence on the future.

Gioberti's ideas were in the air. Would there be any possible chance of the cardinals electing a Liberal Pope?

For most Moderates, the whole progress of the national movement depended primarily on the growth of Liberal ideas and on the winning of Liberal institutions: and obviously no one was so well equipped for spreading Liberal ideas as the Pope. He could reply to any complaints from the Great Powers by quoting against them their own Liberal Memorandum of 1831: he alone could appeal to the mass of the people in every state and class alike; and then—when the press became free and when consequently the people were aroused and the ministers were more or less responsible, and all the state governments had moved a stage onward towards democracy—then the Austrian bureaucracy in Milan and Vienna would be publicly discredited as a despotic anachronism. In fact, for it, the advent of a Liberal Pope might be the beginning of the end.

But what was to happen to the Church?

fusion was right, but he failed to see that as yet it was entirely impossible. The Federalists' union by confederation was the farthest advance possible just then, but they failed to see that it was by no means the ideal settlement. *V.* Tivaroni, *ibid.* p. 509.

When the Moderates dreamed of a Liberal Pope they realised, though perhaps not fully, that it would be very difficult for him to grant Liberal institutions, and impossible for him to become a constitutional monarch. Manifestly it was not thinkable that he should resign full powers into the hands of ministers responsible to the people. Supposing for instance—as happened elsewhere—that they passed a measure secularising education, he might, as a constitutional monarch, be compelled to affix his signature to the act. This would make his own position impossible. It was necessary, therefore, that he should retain a right of veto. Another consideration was the question of war. Sooner or later a constitutional Pope was certain to be forced into war, and, for the Pope, every war is a civil war: he has millions of spiritual subjects on either side. He could not declare war and issue excommunications except in self-defence.

The hope of the Moderates was that, for the Papal Chair, some self-sacrificing hero might be found who would dare to break with all tradition. It meant deliberately giving up for ever most of the temporal authority which the Pope considered necessary to his sacred trust; it meant the recognition of democracy by the Roman Catholic Church in the teeth of all the governments which had hitherto been its best friends. For the new Italy the Reformers required a Pope with enlightened modern ideas, a patriot king in the truest sense; one who would introduce railways, industries, commerce, laicised administration, and, as far as possible, representative institutions. Over ecclesiastical questions and Church government he should retain supreme power—probably a right of veto. This would create a very delicate situation between him and the democracy, requiring a tactful spirit of give-and-take on either side; *but if he made these sacrifices for the sake of the people, in justice he might expect consideration from those whom he had served.*

The importance of Pius IX's election was summarised in the following words by the great historian Tivaroni, himself a republican who in 1867 fought against Pius' troops at Mentana:

Without Pius IX Charles Albert would not have dared to draw the sword, being, as he was, king of little Piedmont opposed by the colossal empire of Austria. Without Pius IX the majority of the clergy, the nobility, the countryside would not have moved; without Pius IX the active minority which started the Risorgimento would have been a much smaller minority still, and who knows what prolonged trials Italy might not have had to undergo; for it is incontestable that the numerical majority in the peninsula, especially of the rural populations, remained almost indifferent during the whole development of the history of the Risorgimento. Tivaroni, *Domin. Austr.* III, 469.

VII

This volume is divided into two parts, that relating to the period before and that after the Austrian military episode at Ferrara (July 17th, 1847).

In chapter II we review the position of the Papacy as a world-power. This chapter may seem unusual in a book on the Risorgimento, but surely it is necessary. For twenty-two months to come—a crucial period—Pius IX played by far the principal part in the national advance, and consequently it is all-important to realise his state of mind and the influences around him. And we know—though it is often ignored—that he was Pope first and foremost, and a reigning sovereign only in virtue of being Pope. That is the principal factor in the situation.[5]

For twenty-two months Rome is our centre of interest because it is there that the main progress of the Risorgimento is taking place. This is proved by the fact that some of the shrewdest judges of the situation—Massimo d'Azeglio for instance—have taken up their abode there. But at the end of

[5] In volume I, Mazzini, Metternich and Charles Albert played the leading parts and in each case a chapter was devoted to analysing their life and mission. Here, in volume II, it is far more necessary to form an accurate idea of the limitations of the Supreme Pontiff.

twenty-two months, on the day when war is declared, the leadership reverts to Piedmont.

During those two years the mentality of Pius IX is a profoundly interesting study. He is a conscientious man who is being torn in two between his conflicting duties: the call of his religion and the call of his country, the two greatest calls that a man can hear.

Threefold, in reality, were his duties: firstly to the Church; secondly to the people of his state; and thirdly to the whole of Italy. His duty to the Church was partly spiritual and partly temporal. He was the guardian of the Catholic tradition; he was responsible for the care of the great ecclesiastical organisation all over the world; and he was bound by his coronation oath to hand on the State of the Church as he had received it. Secondly, there was his duty to the people in his state; he must provide them with better government—as he believed, by granting them Liberal institutions. Thirdly, there was his duty to the whole of Italy—in his view that of uniting it, if possible, by means of a league or federation.

Inspired by these convictions he set out to save the Papal State by turning it into a modern Liberalised nation in which the ruler was assisted by a Consulta, or secondarily elected consultative assembly; that was the farthest point to which he intended to go on the path of democratic concession. It was in accordance with Gioberti's programme.

He began by issuing his celebrated Amnesty to political prisoners (chapter III) and then embarked at once on a policy of reforms within his state. He was a good man and he started on this attempt with evident enthusiasm. There is something very pathetic in the fervour with which, just before war broke out in 1848, he solemnly blessed the new nation for which so many young men were going to die. "Benedite, Gran Dio, l'Italia!" "Lord God, bless Italy." But to be a Liberal Pope was not possible; the new power which he was blessing would inevitably be built on the ruins of his own.

Certainly during those months of his reign Pius IX was a good Italian as far as that was possible for a Pope. Is this not proved by the fact that Garibaldi, fresh after his brilliant victory[6] at Sant' Antonio in Uruguay, offered to devote his sword and his glorious reputation to the service of this patriot Pope in Italy? Thus the same people who condemn —and, from the national point of view, rightly condemn— Pius IX's policy in later years should sympathise with this first great effort between 1846 and 1848. It ended in failure— humanly speaking; but for all that, it constitutes a noble episode in the history of the Papacy; and the record will remain ineffaceable. To those who assert that the Papal attitude towards the Risorgimento was always one of obscurantism and *non possumus*, the story of these first two years forms a complete reply.[7]

The most important result of Pius' work was its wonder-fully vivifying effect in the other states of Italy. It came as a stimulus to the national movement throughout the whole peninsula.

And here lies the tragedy of the situation. As the national growth became stronger Pius found himself compelled to maintain safeguards for the Church; and became aware that his own Liberals were working against him. A considerable majority of his people were enthusiastically grateful to him; whenever he appeared he was received by the whole population with acclamations, even with tears of gratitude and joy. But within the heart of that crowd there were the political organisers and their immediate followers the agitators, who were accepting each concession with enthusiastic demonstra-

[6] *V.* chapter x.
[7] The following is the opinion of Tivaroni: "All [parties] con-tributed to the great result; all united in the construction of the building, which was the supreme aim of their ideals, namely the resurrection of their fatherland; and without the tenacious belief of Mazzini, without the rough energy of Garibaldi, without the steadfast sword of Charles Albert and without the attraction of Pius IX's blessing, it would not have been attained."

tions always accompanied by demands for more. Some of these wire-pullers were genuine Moderates who understood his feeling about the Church; others wanted to drive him on until they had definitely separated him from his cardinals, and made him a constitutional monarch: and some few, chiefly Mazzinians, meant to push him on until they had made an end of the temporal power.

This policy was destined soon to become general in all the small states of Italy. At first sight it conveys an impression of ingratitude on the part of the people; but now let us look at it from the point of view of the Liberals in the nine different states.

What else were they to do? They were determined to federate and to free their country. Can anyone blame them? For that purpose they required representative institutions. This was natural: but how were they to get them? By agitation. Is not agitation the most moderate method known of winning freedom? But, always and inevitably, agitation appears ungrateful towards the few generous rulers who, like Pius IX and Leopold of Tuscany, are willing to grant concessions.

It fell very hardly on Pius because his hands were tied; he had to defend the Church: but in the other states the rulers were only called upon to become constitutional monarchs, and Charles Albert did so: and that was the next important step in the advance of Italy.

The truth is that all revolutions are hard and brutal; and any historian who omits that fact has failed in his duty. If any of the right-thinking men among the agitators of that day had been challenged on this question he would have replied: It is very sad, but there is no alternative even imaginable. The movement *must* go on. The Austrians are still there. The work of the nation *must* go forward—until we have a representative government and an armed force of our own. This is the cause of the people and the cause of Italy.

Were the peoples to remain divided for ever into nine states?

After all, they were moving by the gentlest means possible; in Rome by the *agitazione amorosa*. Compare that with the Revolution of Robespierre or of the Russian Soviets. A year later the Italian agitation became rather brutalised by war, but, even so, how moderate it appears in comparison with the others named. And certainly in 1846 and 1847 the Italian historian finds nothing that he need regret. It is the story of a great development of civic efficiency; and of great advance towards a national mentality.

At the beginning of that period of agitation—in June 1846 where this volume starts—the picture is still that of Metternich's Italy. Eight small states[8] each under an absolute ruler; eight small rulers all under the sway of Metternich. Below the surface, some Liberalism and some revolution.

At the end of this volume, January 1st, 1848, the picture is one of eight states in most of which there is a free press, a Consultative assembly and an armed Civic Guard; and all of which are on the verge of winning a parliament, and sending men to fight in the common cause against Metternich.

[8] Omitting the tiny republic of San Marino.

BIBLIOGRAPHY

LIST OF PRINTED MATTER AND MSS. CONSULTED BY THE AUTHORS

A. *PUBLISHED SOURCES*
(Books and Newspapers)

A list of the principal books[1] used in compiling this volume, which only covers the years 1846–47. Of course this list does not include nearly all the books read. And, naturally, most of these works cover a far wider period than these two years.

I. GENERAL

(not relating especially to any one state)

Anzilotti = Anzilotti. *Gioberti.* 1922.

Archivio triennale = *Archivio triennale delle cose d' Italia dall' avvenimento di Pio IX all' abbandono di Venezia.* 3 vols. 1851.

Ashley = Ashley, *Life of Palmerston.* 2 vols. 1876.

D'Azeglio, *Correspondance* = D'Azeglio, Massimo. *Correspondance politique.* 1867.

D'Azeglio, *Lettere* = D'Azeglio, Massimo. *Lettere a sua moglie.* 1876.

D'Azeglio, *Proposta* = D'Azeglio, Massimo. *Proposta di un programma per l' opinione nazionale.* 1847.

D'Azeglio, *Raccolta* = D'Azeglio, Massimo. *Raccolta degli scritti politici.* 1850.

D'Azeglio, *Ricordi* = D'Azeglio, Massimo. *I miei Ricordi.* New ed. 1910.

D'Azeglio, *a Torelli* = D'Azeglio, Massimo. *Lettere a Giuseppe Torelli.* 2nd ed. 1870.

Balbo = Balbo, Count Cesare. *Delle speranze d' Italia.* 2nd ed. 1844.

Balbo, *Sommario* = Balbo, Count Cesare. *Sommario della storia d' Italia.* Popular ed. 1933.

Berti = Berti, *Vincenzo Gioberti.* 1881.

Beust = Beust, Count von. *Memoirs of;* trans. by Baron H. de Worms. 2 vols. 1887.

---

[1] We have already commented on many of these authorities in the Bibliography of *Italy in the Making,* vol. 1; so that in the present list it has not been necessary to say anything further about them.

BIANCHI, *Stor. Doc.* = BIANCHI, N. *Storia documentata della diplomazia europea in Italia dall' anno* 1814 *all' anno* 1861. 8 vols. Vol. v, 1869. *V.* also under PIEDMONT.

BONGHI = BONGHI, RUGGIERO. *Vita e tempi di Valentino Pasini.* 1867.

BOUILLET = BOUILLET, M. N. *Dictionnaire d'histoire et de géographie.* 1908.

Camb. Mod. Hist. xi = *Cambridge Modern History.* Vol. xi. "The Growth of Nationalities." 1909.

CANTÙ = CANTÙ, CESARE. *Cronistoria.* 3 vols. 1872 *et seq.*

Carte segrete = *Carte segrete ed atti ufficiali della polizia austriaca in Italia.* 3 vols. 1851–58.

CASTELLI = CASTELLI, MICHELANGELO. *Ricordi* (1847–75), editi per cura di L. Chiala. 1888. A series of articles on leading figures in the Risorgimento by a Piedmontese friend of Cavour.

CASTELLI, *Carteggio* = CASTELLI, MICHELANGELO. *Carteggio politico,* edito per cura di L. Chiala. 2 vols. 1890–92.

CECIL = CECIL, ALGERNON. *Metternich.* 1931.

Civiltà Cattolica = *Civiltà Cattolica, La.* 1879. BALLERINI, Article "Pio IX e Carlo Alberto".

Civiltà Cattolica causa = *Civiltà Cattolica, La.* 1898. BALLERINI, Article "La causa nazionale".

COPPI = COPPI, A. *Annali d' Italia dall' anno* 1814. No date.

DEBIDOUR = DEBIDOUR, *Histoire diplomatique d'Europe.* Vol. II. 1871.

Diz. del Risorg. = *Dizionario del Risorgimento nazionale.* 4 vols.: one of events, and three of persons, the last of which is still in the press; 1931–33. A new and valuable work of reference containing articles by well-known writers on the period, under the general editorship of the late Professor Michele Rosi.

Encyc. Brit. = *Encyclopaedia Britannica.* Various articles.

FABRIS = FABRIS, CECILIO. *Gli Avvenimenti militari di* 1848 *e* 1849. 3 vols. 1898.

FARINI, *Epist.* = FARINI, LUIGI CARLO. *Epistolario,* per cura di Luigi Rava. Vol. I. 1911.

FICQUELMONT = FICQUELMONT, Count. *Lord Palmerston, l'Angleterre et le continent.* An interesting exposition of the Austrian Conservative view. 2 vols. 1852–53.

GARIBALDI, A. I. = GARIBALDI, ANNITA ITALIA. *Garibaldi in America.* 1932. An interesting account of Garibaldi's American campaigns, by his granddaughter.

GIOBERTI = GIOBERTI, VINCENZO. *Prolegomeni del Primato.* 1846. For description of Gioberti *v. Italy in the Making,* vol. i, chs. x and xi.

GIUSTI = GIUSTI, GIUSEPPE. *Memorie inedite,* edite per cura di F. Martini. 1890.

GOBAT = GOBAT, ALBERT. *Histoire de la Suisse.* 1900.

GOOCH = GOOCH, C. P. *Later Correspondence of Lord John Russell.*
Vol. II. 1926.

GORI = GORI, AGOSTINO. *Storia della rivoluzione italiana durante il periodo delle riforme* (1846 *al* 14 *Marzo*, 1848). 1897.

GRIFFITHS = GRIFFITHS, GWILYM. *Mazzini.* 1930.

GUALTERIO = GUALTERIO, F. A. *Gli ultimi rivolgimenti italiani. Memorie storiche.* 6 vols. 1850–51.

GUIZOT = GUIZOT. *Mémoires pour servir à l'histoire de mon temps.* 8 vols. 1850. An indispensable book for the relations between France and the rest of Europe during this period.

HERMAN = HERMAN, ARTHUR. *Metternich.* 1932.

HILLEBRAND = HILLEBRAND. *Geschichte Frankreichs von der Thronbesteigung Louis Philipps bis zum Fall Napoleon III.* Vol. III. 1879.

BOLTON KING = KING, BOLTON. *History of Italian Unity.* 2 vols. 1889.

BOLTON KING, *Mazzini* = KING, BOLTON. *Mazzini.* Everyman ed. 1919.

KOCH = KOCH, JULIUS. *Deutsche Geschichte.* IV. Sammlung Göschen. 1924.

LA CECILIA = LA CECILIA, G. *Memorie storiche-politiche, dal* 1820 *al* 1876. 1876. Not very valuable.

LA FARINA = LA FARINA, GIUSEPPE. *Storia d' Italia dal* 1815 *al* 1850. Vol. II. 2nd ed. 1861.

LAGRANGE = LAGRANGE, F. *Life of Monsignor Dupanloup.* Trans. Lady Herbert. 2 vols. 1885.

LEMMI, F. = LEMMI, F. *Il Risorgimento (Guida bibliografica).* 1926. *V.* also under PIEDMONT.

LE ROY BEAULIEU = LE ROY BEAULIEU. *Les Catholiques libéraux de* 1830 *jusqu'à nos jours.* 1885.

London Corr. = *Correspondence Respecting the Affairs of Italy*, 1846–49. 4 vols. 1849.

LÜTZOW = LÜTZOW, Count. *Bohemia.* 1895.

LUZIO = LUZIO, A. *Profili biografici e bozzetti storici.* 1927. *V.* also under PIEDMONT.

MARIO = MARIO, JESSIE WHITE. *The Birth of Modern Italy.* 1909.

MARRIOTT = MARRIOTT, Sir J. A. R. *Makers of Modern Italy.* 1931. A history of the whole period from Napoleon to Mussolini. Is one of the best-proportioned books on the subject; naturally can only deal very shortly with these two years.

MARTINENGO = MARTINENGO, CESARESCO. (Countess Evelyn.) *Italian Characters.* 1890.

MASI = MASI, E. *Il Risorgimento italiano.* 2 vols. 1917.

MASI, *Nell' Ottocento* = MASI, E. *Nell' Ottocento.* 1922.

MASI, *Risorg. nei libri* = MASI, E. *Il Risorgimento nei libri.* 1911.

MASI, *Fra libri e ricordi* = MASI, E. *Fra libri e ricordi.* 1887. *V.* also *Cambridge Modern History,* vol. XI : " Italy and the Revolution". 1909.

MASSARI = MASSARI, G. *Le Opere inedite di Vincenzo Gioberti.* Vols. IX and X. 1861.

MASSARI, *Uomini* = MASSARI, G. *Uomini di destra.* A cura di G. Infante. 1934.

MAZZINI, A.E. = MAZZINI, G. *Scritti editi ed inediti,* edizione diretta dall' autore. (A.E. = Author's Edition.) *Proemi,* vols. I–VIII, written by MAZZINI. Ditto, vols. IX–XII, by AURELIO SAFFI. 12 vols. 1861–89.

MAZZINI, E.N. = MAZZINI, GIUSEPPE. *Scritti editi ed inediti.* Edizione nazionale a cura di Mario Menghini. 1906 *et seq.*

MENGHINI = MENGHINI, MARIO. *La Giovine Italia.* 1902.

METTERNICH = METTERNICH, Prince KLEMENS VON. *Aus Metternichs nachgelassenen Papieren.* Vol. VII; edited Adolf von Klinkow-ström. 1883.

METTERNICH, *Mémoires* = METTERNICH, Prince KLEMENS VON. *Mémoires.* French ed. 2nd ed. 1880. *V.* also under Cecil, Herman, and Srbik.

MINGHETTI = MINGHETTI, MARCO. *I miei Ricordi.* 3 vols. 4th ed. 1899.

Nuovo Atlante = *Nuovo Atlante.* 1820.

OECHSLI = OECHSLI. *History of Switzerland from 1499 to 1914.* 1922. *V.* also *Cambridge Modern History,* vol. XI. 1909.

ORSI = ORSI, PIETRO. *Histoire de l'Italie moderne.* French trans. by Bergmann. 1911.

ORSINI = ORSINI, FELICE. *Memoirs and Adventures.* English trans. by Carbonel. 1857.

PROTOCOLLO = *Protocollo della Giovine Italia.* Appendix to the National Edition of Mazzini's works. 6 vols. 1915–22.

QUINTAVALLI = QUINTAVALLI, FRANCESCO. *Storia dell' unità italiana.* 1926.

RANALLI = RANALLI, F. *Le Istorie italiane dal 1846 al 1854.* Vol. I. 1858.

Rass. stor. = *Rassegna storica del Risorgimento.* The organ of the Società nazionale per la storia del risorgimento. Various dates.

RAULICH = RAULICH, ITALO. *Storia del risorgimento politico d' Italia.* Vol. III. 1923. A useful general history.

Revue des deux Mondes = *Revue des deux Mondes.* Janvier, 1923. Article "L'Italie libérée".

RICCIARDI = RICCIARDI, G. N. *Cenni storici intorno agli ultimi casi d' Italia.* 1849.

RINAUDO = RINAUDO, COSTANZO. *Il Risorgimento italiano.* Vol. I. 1911.

Risorgimento = *Risorgimento, Il.* The well-known review: predecessor of the *Rassegna storica.* Various dates.

Riv. Ital. = *Rivista italiana*. Nuova serie. Vol. II. 1927.
ROSI = ROSI, M. *Storia contemporanea d' Italia*. 1922.
ROSIER = ROSIER. *Histoire illustrée de la Suisse*. 1905.
SILVA = SILVA, PIETRO. *La Monarchia di Luglio e l' Italia*. 1917.
SRBIK = SRBIK, HEINRICH RITTER VON. *Metternich der Staatsman und der Mensch*. 2 vols. 1925.
STERN = STERN. *Geschichte Europas seit den Verträgen von 1815 bis zum Frankfurter Frieden von 1871*. Vols. IV, V, VI, VII. 1916.
STILLMAN = STILLMAN. *The Union of Italy*. 1899.
THAYER = THAYER, W. R. *The Dawn of Italian Independence*. 2 vols. 1894.
THUREAU-DANGIN = THUREAU-DANGIN. *Histoire de la monarchie de Juillet*. 8 vols. 1884–92.
TIVARONI, *Domin. Austr.* = TIVARONI, CARLO. *L' Italia durante il dominio austriaco*, vols I, II, and III. But in reality these are vols. IV, V and VI of his great complete work in nine volumes, *Storia critica del Risorgimento*. 1888–97, Turin and Rome. His complete work begins with vol. I: Italy before Napoleon; vols. II and III: Italy under the French (up to 1815); vols. IV, V and VI: Italy under the Austrians (up to 1849); vols. VII, VIII and IX: Italy, 1849–70.
TORELLI = TORELLI, L. *Pensieri di un anonimo Lombardo*. 1846. Described in this book, p. 138.
TREVELYAN = TREVELYAN, G. M. *Garibaldi and the Making of Italy*. 1911.
TREVELYAN, *Manin. V.* under LOMBARDO-VENETIA.
VANUCCI = VANUCCI, ATTO. *I Martiri della libertà italiana*. 1860.
Vita italiana, 1846–49 = Volume called *La Vita italiana nel risorgimento* in the series of *La Vita italiana* volumes of historical essays. Florence, 1898–1901.

II. THE VARIOUS ITALIAN STATES
LOMBARDO-VENETIA

BELGIOJOSO = BELGIOJOSO, Princess. *L' Austria e la rivoluzione italiana*. 1847.
BIANCHI-GIOVINI = BIANCHI-GIOVINI. *L' Austria in Italia*. 1847. A propaganda pamphlet.
CASATI, ANT. = CASATI, ANTONIO. *Milano ed i principi di Savoia*. 1853. A useful book, but with little matter on our period.
CASATI, CARLO = CASATI, DR CARLO. *Nuove rivelazioni sui fatti di Milano nel 1847-48*. 2 vols. 1888. A description of the revolution in Milan and the events which led up to it by one of the leaders. Somewhat biased but informative.

CATTANEO = CATTANEO, C. *L' Insurrezione di Milano.* 1849.

CORRENTI = CORRENTI, CESARE. *L' Austria e l' Italia.* 1847.

CORRENTI, *Scritti* = CORRENTI, CESARE. *Scritti scelti*, per cura di L. Masserana. 2 vols. Vol. I. 1891. Contains some sensible and practical criticisms of the Austrian régime in Lombardo-Venetia.

HELFERT = HELFERT. *Geschichte der Österreichischen Revolution.* Vols. I and II. 1907 and 1909. A valuable work.

OTTOLINI = OTTOLINI, VITTORE. *La Rivoluzione lombarda, del* 1848 *e* 1849. 1887. An interesting work by one who took part in the "Five Days".

PALLAVICINO = PALLAVICINO. *Memorie* pubblicate per cura della moglie. 2 vols. 1892–95.

SANDONÀ = SANDONÀ, AUGUSTO. "Il preludio delle cinque giornate di Milano" in *Rivista d' Italia.* January–February, 1927. A very valuable writer on Lombardo-Venetia.

SANDONÀ, *Regno lombardo* = SANDONÀ, AUGUSTO. *Il regno lombardo-veneto,* 1814–59. 1912.

TORELLI = TORELLI, LUIGI. *Pensieri di un anonimo Lombardo.* 1846.

TREVELYAN = TREVELYAN, G. M. *Manin and the Venetian Revolution of* 1848. 1923. From some points of view perhaps the most valuable of Mr Trevelyan's interesting works on the Risorgimento.

NAPLES AND SICILY

AMARI = AMARI, M. *La Sicile et les Bourbons.* Paris, 1849. *V.* also under Palmieri.

D'ANCONA = D'ANCONA, A. *Carteggio di Michele Amari.* Vol. II. 1896.

ARCUNO = ARCUNO, IRMA. *Il Regno delle due Sicilie nei rapporti con lo Stato pontificio.* 1933.

D'AYALA = D'AYALA, MARIANO. *Vita del re di Napoli* (Ferdinand II). 1856.

BELTRANO-SCALIA = BELTRANO-SCALIA, M. *Memorie storiche della rivoluzione di Sicilia,* 1848–49. Vol. I. 1933. Memoirs of a revolutionist published by his son; naturally rather partisan.

CALVI = CALVI, P. *Memorie storiche e critiche della rivoluzione siciliana.* 1851. A revolutionist, bitter and very critical of his companions, but full of information.

DE CESARE = DE CESARE, R. *La Fine di un regno. Dal* 1855 *al* 1860. 1895.

CHIARAMONTE = CHIARAMONTE, S. *Il Programma del* 1848 *e i partiti politici in Sicilia dal* 1830 *al* 1861. 1901. Perhaps the best *short* work on the period up to 1848.

COLLETTA = COLLETTA, P. *Storia del reame di Napoli.* Vol. II. Popular ed. 1861.

COPPOLA = COPPOLA, A. *La Vita di Giuseppe La Masa.* 1919. The only life of La Masa we have been able to find.

CRISPI = CRISPI. *La Sicilia e la rivoluzione.* Essay in volume on Risorgimento (1846–49) in series called *La Vita italiana.* V. under that heading.

GUARDIONE = GUARDIONE, F. *Il Dominio dei Borboni in Sicilia.* 2 vols. Vol. I. 1907.

GUARDIONE, *Confessioni* = GUARDIONE, F. *Confessioni postumi inglesi sulla violata corrispondenza dei Bandiera col Mazzini.* Signor Guardione has been writing useful books for forty years; a patriotic Sicilian, but impartial.

GUARDIONE, *Sicilia* = GUARDIONE, F. *La Sicilia,* 1795–1860. 1907.

LA FARINA = LA FARINA, G. *Storia documentata della rivoluzione della Sicilia.* 2 vols. 1851. The well-known revolutionist.

LA MASA = LA MASA, G. *Documenti della rivoluzione siciliana nel 1847–49.* 2 vols. 1851. The young hero of 1848. A useful book and gives a good many documents.

LA MASA, *Popoli* = LA MASA, G. *I Popoli del regno delle Due Sicilie ai fratelli italiani.* 1847.

LEOPARDI = LEOPARDI, PIERSILVESTRO. *Narrazioni storiche con documenti relativi alla reazione Napolitana.* 1856.

LIBERTINI and PALADINO = LIBERTINI, G. and PALADINO, G. *Storia della Sicilia.* 1933. The latest general history of Sicily from prehistoric days: very well done, but naturally can only touch shortly on our period.

MASSARI = MASSARI, G. *I Casi di Napoli.* 1849.

NISCO = NISCO, Baron N. *Ferdinando II e il suo regno.* 1884. A rebel, but on the whole surprisingly impartial.

NISCO, *Storia* = NISCO, Baron N. *Storia d' Italia dall' 1814 al 1880.* Vol. III. 1885.

NITTI = NITTI. *Sui moti di Napoli in 1848.* Essay in the volume on the Risorgimento (1846–49) of the series called *La Vita italiana.* V. under that heading.

PALADINO = PALADINO, G. *Il 15 maggio del 1848 in Napoli.* 1921.

PALADINO, *La Rivoluzione* = PALADINO, G. *La Rivoluzione napolitana nel 1848.* 1914. V. also under Libertini.

PALMIERI = PALMIERI. *Saggio storico e politico sulla costituzione del Regno di Sicilia.* Preface by Michele Amari. 1847. A great patriotic work. 1850.

PEPE = PEPE, General GUGLIELMO. *L'Italia nel 1847, 1848, 1849.* 1850.

PEPE, *Narrative* = *A Narrative of the Political and Military Events which took place in 1820 and 1821,* by General William Pepe. 1821.

ROSSI, *Storia* = ROSSI, G. G. *Storia dei rivolgimenti politici delle Due Sicilie dal 1847 al 1850.* 1851–52.

SANSONE = SANSONE, A. *La Sicilia nella storia del Risorgimento italiano.*

SETTEMBRINI = SETTEMBRINI, L. *Ricordanze della mia vita.* 1879. *V.* text, pp. 282, 283 and note.

SETTEMBRINI, *Protesta* = SETTEMBRINI, L. *Protesta del popolo delle Due Sicilie.* 1847. *V.* text, p. 280 *et seq.*

THE PAPAL STATE

Acta = *Acta Pii Papae IX.* The religious encyclicals etc. of Pius IX.

AMIGUES = AMIGUES, JULES. *L'État romain depuis 1815 jusqu'à nos jours.* 1862.

Atti = *Atti del Sommo Pontefice Pio IX.* The civil proclamations, notifications etc. of Pius IX.

D'AZEGLIO = D'AZEGLIO, MASSIMO. *V.* under GENERAL.

BALAN = BALAN, PIETRO. *Pio IX, la chiesa e la rivoluzione.* 2 vols. 1898.

BALLERINI = BALLERINI, P. RAFFAELE. *Les Premières Pages du pontificat du Pape Pie IX.* 1909. The work of a Jesuit; naturally Papal in sympathy; but the first part of his book is good and clear; he died before finishing the second part. *V.* also *Civiltà Cattolica.*

BAUDRILLART = BAUDRILLART, Mgr. *Dictionnaire d'histoire et géographie ecclésiastique.* Vol. I. 1912.

BONI = BONI DE. *Congiura di Roma.* Lausanne, 1848.

Cath. Encyc. = *Catholic Encyclopedia, The.* Pius IX. Vol. XII, n.d.

CERRO = CERRO, EMILIO DE. *Cospirazioni romane.* 1899.

Civiltà Cattolica = *Civiltà Cattolica, La.* 1879. BALLERINI. Article "Pio IX e Carlo Alberto".

CRÉTINEAU-JOLY = CRÉTINEAU-JOLY. *L'Église romaine en face de la révolution.* 1859.

DEBIDOUR, *Rapports* = DEBIDOUR. *Histoire des rapports de l'église avec l'état en France de 1789 à 1870.* 1898.

FALDELLA = FALDELLA, G. *Massimo d'Azeglio e Diomede Pantaleoni.* 1888.

FARINI = FARINI, LUIGI CARLO. *Lo Stato romano dall' anno 1815.* 4 vols. 1850.

FERRARI = FERRARI, RINA. *Il Principe di Canino e il suo processo.* 1926.

GABUSSI = GABUSSI. *Memorie della rivoluzione degli stati romani.* 3 vols. 1851.

GALEOTTI = GALEOTTI. *Della sovranità e del governo temporale dei Papi.* 1847.

GALLETTI = GALLETTI. *Memorie intorno ai fatti accaduti in Roma.* 1863.

GAMS = GAMS. *Geschichte der Kirche Christi im XIX. Jahrhundert.* 1854-56.

GENNARELLI = GENNARELLI. *La Corte di Roma.* 1866.

GIOVAGNOLI = GIOVAGNOLI. *Ciceruacchio e Don Pirlone.* 1894.

GIOVAGNOLI, *Rossi* = GIOVAGNOLI. *Pellegrino Rossi e la Rivoluzione romana.* 3 vols. 1898-1911.

GENTILI = GENTILI, FERNANDA. "La Lega doganale." An article in *Rassegna storica del Risorgimento.* 1914.

HERGENRÖTHER = HERGENRÖTHER, Cardinal. *Histoire de l'Église.* French trans. by the Abbé Bélet. 1892.

JOHNSON = JOHNSON, Rev. HUMPHREY. *The Papacy and the Kingdom of Italy.* 1926.

JOHNSTON = JOHNSTON, R. M. *The Roman Theocracy and the Republic (1846-49).* 1901.

LEDERMANN = LEDERMANN, LÁSZLÓ. *Pellegrino Rossi, l'homme et l'économiste.* 1929.

MAGUIRE = MAGUIRE. *Rome, its Ruler and Institutions.* 1857.

MANNO = MANNO. *L' opinione religiosa e conservatrice in Italia dal 1830 al 1850 ricercata nella corrispondenza di Monsignore Giovanni Corboli Bussi.* 1910.

MASI, *Vescovo* = MASI. *Il Vescovo d' Imola,* in *La Vita italiana nel Risorgimento.* Serie II. Vol. I. The volume on the Risorgimento (1846-49). *V.* under *La Vita italiana.*

MONTI = MONTI, A. *Pio IX e il Risorgimento italiano.* 1928.

MORONI = MORONI, GAETANO. *Dizionario d' erudizione ecclesiastica.* Vol. LIII. 1851.

PASOLINI = PASOLINI, G. *Memorie raccolte dal suo figlio,* 1815-76. 2 vols. 4th ed. 1915.

PASOLINI, Eng. = PASOLINI, G. The same, trans. and abridged by the Countess of Dalhousie. 1885.

PASOLINI, *Carteggio* = PASOLINI, G. *Carteggio con Marco Minghetti,* ed. Count Guido Pasolini. Vol. I. 1924.

PELCZAR = PELCZAR, Mgr. JOSEF. *Pio IX ed il suo pontificato.* Italian trans. 3 vols. 1909.

REVEL = REVEL, G. DI. *Negoziati per la lega doganale a Modena e a Napoli.* 1847.

SAFFI = SAFFI, AURELIO. *Storia di Roma.* (Vol. II of *Ricordi e scritti.* 1893.)

SILVAGNI = SILVAGNI, DAVID. *La Corte e la società Romana nei secoli XVIII e XIX.* Vol. III. 1885.

SODERINI = SODERINI, Count EDUARDO. *Il Pontificato di Leone XIII.* 3 vols. Vol. I. Milan, 1932.

SPADA = SPADA, GIUSEPPE. *Storia della rivoluzione di Roma.* 3 vols. 1868 and 1869.

TROCCHI = TROCCHI, DINO. *Pio IX e la rivoluzione romana.* 1934.
VERCESI = VERCESI, ERNESTO. *Pio IX.* 1930.
WARD = WARD, WILFRED. *Life of Cardinal Wiseman.* 2 vols. 1897.
WARD, Mgr. BERNARD = WARD, Mgr. BERNARD. *Sequel to Catholic Emancipation.* 2 vols. 1915.

PIEDMONT

ALBERTI = ALBERTI, MARIO DEGLI. *La Politica estera di Piemonte sotto Carlo Alberto secondo il carteggio diplomatico del Conte Bertone di Sambuy.* 1835–46. *V. Biblioteca storica del risorgimento italiano.* 1914–19. Vol. III.
D'AZEGLIO, COSTANZA = D'AZEGLIO, COSTANZA. *Souvenirs historiques.* 1884.
BARANTE = BARANTE, Baron DE. *Souvenirs.* Vol. IV. 1894.
BARANTE, *Revue* = BARANTE, Baron DE. *V. Revue d'histoire diplomatique.* (Reference unfortunately lost.)
BERSEZIO = BERSEZIO, VITTORIO. *Il Regno di Vittorio Emanuele II.* 2 vols. 2nd ed. 1895.
BIANCHI, *Curiosità* = BIANCHI, N. *Curiosità e ricerche di storia subalpina.* 8 vols. 1874–81.
BIANCHI, *Stor. Doc. V.* under GENERAL.
BOSIO = BOSIO, FERDINANDO. *Il Marchese Pes di Villamarina.* 1877.
BROFFERIO = BROFFERIO, ANGELO. *Storia del Piemonte.* 3 parts. 1849–51.
CIBRARIO = CIBRARIO, L. *Notizia sulla vita di Carlo Alberto.* 1861.
COLOMBO = COLOMBO, A. *Dalle riforme allo statuto di Carlo Alberto.* 1924.
C. DE BEAUREGARD = COSTA DE BEAUREGARD. *Les Dernières Années du roi Charles Albert.* 1890.
DELLA ROCCA = DELLA ROCCA. *Autobiografia di un veterano.* 2 vols. 1897–98.
LEMMI, *Carlo Alberto* = LEMMI, FRANCESCO. *La Politica estera di Carlo Alberto.* 1928.
LUZIO, *Carlo Alberto* = LUZIO, A. *Carlo Alberto e Mazzini.* 1923.
MATTER = MATTER, PAUL. *Cavour et l'unité italienne.* 3 vols. 1922.
PREDARI = PREDARI, F. *I Primi Vagiti della libertà in Piemonte.* 1860.
REVEL = REVEL, GENOVA DI. *Dal 1847 al 1855.* 1891.
RICOTTI = RICOTTI, E. *Della vita e degli scritti del conte Cesare Balbo.* 1856.
RINIERI = RINIERI, I. *Lo Statuto e il giuramento del re Carlo Alberto.* 1899.
THAYER = THAYER, WILLIAM ROSCOE. *Life and Times of Cavour.* 1911.

VIDAL = VIDAL, C. *Charles Albert et le Risorgimento.* 1927.
WHYTE = WHYTE, Rev. Dr A. J. *Early Life and Letters of Cavour.*
1925.

TUSCANY, PARMA AND MODENA

BALDASSERONI = BALDASSERONI, G. *Leopoldo II e i suoi tempi.*
1871.
BIANCHI, *Ducati* = BIANCHI, N. *I Ducati estensi dall' anno* 1815 *al*
1850. Vol. I. 1852.
CAPPONI = CAPPONI, GINO. *Lettere.* 1886.
CAPPONI, *Carteggio* = CAPPONI, GINO. *Carteggio. Lettere di Gino
Capponi e di altri a lui.* A. Carrarese. 2 vols. 1883.
GALVANI = GALVANI, C. *Memorie storiche intorno la vita di S.A.R.
Francesco IV.* 4 vols. 1847.
GUERRAZZI = GUERRAZZI, D. *Apologia.* 1851.
GUERRAZZI, *Memorie* = GUERRAZZI, D. *Memorie.* 1849.
GIUSTI = GIUSTI, GIUSEPPE. *Memorie inediti*, per cura di Ferdi-
nando Martini. 1890.
HANCOCK = HANCOCK, W. K. *Ricasoli and the Risorgimento in
Tuscany.* 1926.
HUTTON = HUTTON, EDWARD. *Florence and the Cities of Northern
Tuscany.* 1907.
MONTANELLI = MONTANELLI, GIUSEPPE. *Memorie sull' Italia.* 2 vols.
2nd ed. 1880.
RICASOLI = RICASOLI, Barone BETTINO. *Lettere e documenti*, pubbli-
cati per cura di M. Tabarrini e A. Gotti. Vol. I. 1887.
TABARRINI = TABARRINI, M. *Gino Capponi: i suoi tempi, i suoi studi,
i suoi amici.* 1819.
TOMMASEO = TOMMASEO N. and CAPPONI G. *Carteggio inedito dal*
1833 *al* 1874, per cura di T. del Lungo e P. Prunas. 3 vols.
Vol. II (1837–49). 1914.
ZOBI = ZOBI, A. *Storia civile della Toscana.* 5 vols. 1850–52.

III. NEWSPAPERS

L' Alba, Florence.   *Il Contemporaneo*, Rome.
La Patria, Florence.   *La Pallade*, Rome.
Il Felsineo, Bologna.   *La Rivista*, Rome.
La Bilancia, Rome.   *Il Popolare*, Rome.
Il Diario di Roma, Rome.
        And others of less importance.

B. *UNPUBLISHED SOURCES*

LONDON. *Public Record Office, Chancery Lane.* They are referred to in text as F.O. but the British documents of which most use has been made, and which are invaluable for the student of the period, are contained in the four volumes of Correspondence respecting the affairs of Italy: reference in text = *London Corr.* (For these *v.* Published Sources.)

ROME. State Archives (Archivio di Stato). Reference in the text = Rome S.A.

Vatican Archives. They contain invaluable material for the pontificate of Gregory XVI. For that of Pius IX they have not yet been thrown open to the public: an exception has, however, been made with regard to the "Fondo Spada", which contains a vast collection of material both printed and unprinted for 1846 to 1849. Reference in the text = Vatican Arch. *or* Fondo Spada.

PARIS. Affaires Étrangères. Reference in the text = Paris Aff. Etr. These French documents are invaluable for the years 1846 and 1847. They are the despatches exchanged between Guizot and Pellegrino Rossi, who was not only French ambassador in Rome but also a personal friend of Guizot. Being an Italian by birth and a Liberal by sympathy, Rossi soon became a close friend and adviser of Pius IX; and, of course, his own opinion was always worth having.

VIENNA. State Archives. Reference in the text = Vienna Staats-Archiv. These despatches between Metternich and Lützow, and their subordinates, afford a wonderfully vivid picture of the situation in Rome during the Liberal movement. Lützow had been ambassador there for years and his pro-Austrian views form an invaluable set-off to those of Rossi and the Italian Liberals. His despatches are mainly reports of conversations with Pius IX and his ministers, whom they seem to convert from being merely historical names into living human beings. Lützow was a charitable adviser who believed that he could save Pius from the results of his own kind-hearted folly.

FLORENCE. Here we have the documents of the state of Tuscany. Reference in the text = Florence Archives. These are very interesting for both Piedmont and the Papal State and occasionally for questions elsewhere. The Tuscan ambassador Bargagli was an efficient and interesting representative, and he was on friendly terms with Pius.

Part I

June 1846 to *June* 1847

Chapter I

METTERNICH'S ITALY, 1846

In 1846 Italy was still divided up into nine different small nations: this was how the diplomats had left her in 1815; and it was in nine parts, according to them, that she was always to remain—with her two north-eastern provinces in the grip of Austria (the Kingdom of Lombardo-Venetia).

In 1848 the population[1] of the whole of Italy totalled 24,685,000. This was more by about six million than in 1815; and this increase was one of the causes of the Risorgimento.

The following is a table of the Italian states in the year 1846:

	RULER	POPULATION
Lombardo-Venetia (Kingdom, Austrian)	The Emperor Ferdinand of Austria	5,000,000 (almost)
Sardinia—Savoy, Piedmont, etc. (Kingdom)	King Charles Albert	4,916,084*
The Papal State	Pope Pius IX (elected June 16th)	2,898,115
Tuscany (Grand-duchy)	The Grand Duke Leopold II (first cousin of the Austrian Emperor Ferdinand)	1,534,740
Modena (Duchy)	Francesco IV (an Austrian Este, grandson of the Empress Maria Theresa)	575,410
Parma (Duchy)	The Empress Marie Louise (Napoleon's widow; Austrian)	497,343†
The two Sicilies—Naples, Sicily (Kingdom)	King Ferdinand II (a Spanish Bourbon)	6,382,706 2,046,610
Lucca (Duchy)	Duke Charles-Louis (Carlo-Ludovico) de Bourbon	165,198
San Marino	Republic	7,800

* Including 547,112 in Sardinia and 564,187 French-speaking Savoyards.

† In 1851.

Thus the whole peninsula was ruled by a ring of legitimist sovereigns of varying importance and standing. In Rome, of

[1] Tivaroni, *Domin. Austr.* III, 495.

course, the Popes' temporal rule dated back to the days of the
Roman Empire, and in Piedmont the royal house could trace
its ancestry as Dukes of Savoy for seven centuries, but the
other sovereigns had a far less interesting record. In most
cases they could only claim that their families had been
established on their existing thrones for three or four generations before the Revolution; and since 1815 they relied on
force—on the force of the Austrian army. They were part of
Metternich's so-called system and he intended to keep them
where they were.

I. METTERNICH'S SYSTEM

By using them as his agents Metternich meant to assure
his possession of Lombardo-Venetia, and also the supremacy
of Austria throughout the rest of the peninsula; he would
prevent the small nations from either winning Liberal state
institutions or embarking on any scheme of Italian unity.

He had secured his position firstly through these princelets
who were bound to him by ties of relationship (an archduke
in Tuscany, another in Modena and an archduchess in
Parma), of gratitude, of self-interest and of common danger;
secondly, in a military way, by an army of 70,000 men en-
sconced within the almost impregnable Quadrilateral. The
Quadrilateral was a group of four strong fortresses and rivers,
namely Peschiera and Mantua on the line of the River Mincio
(facing west), and Verona and Legnago on the line of the
Adige (facing east); and from Peschiera to Verona the line
was partly covered by Lake Garda (north) and from Mantua
to Legnago by the River Po (south). That block of four
great strongholds enabled Metternich to defend any side of
his central position. Moreover he had troops in various advanced positions such as the Papal towns of Ferrara and
Comacchio, or Piacenza, a city within the Duchy of Parma.
Thirdly, he relied on alliances, such as those which before
the end of 1847 virtually wiped out the small states of Parma

and Modena: and lastly there was his constantly asserted right of *Intervention* (*v.* Congress of Laibach, 1821, and Meeting of Münchengrätz in 1833).

II. ITALIAN NATIONALITY

In opposition to Metternich's immense material force there had come into being several persistent ideas. This was natural. They were the inevitable outcome of the situation.

They may be summarised as a demand for independence, for unification, and for Liberal institutions in Italy.

As to independence, the demand had arisen inevitably from anger at seeing Germans holding down Italians in Lombardo-Venetia. That was oppression. Sooner or later it was certain to arouse the cry of "Fuori i barbari!" "Out with the barbarians!"

As to unification—all Italy to be one nation. This idea, too, owed much of its vitality to the presence of the Austrians, although it had existed long before their day. Many people realised that without unity it was impossible to turn out the invaders: but their difficulty was to imbue that great mass of twenty-four million people with a real desire for it: to make them feel that here was a cause for which every man should live and die. Italy never had been a nation. And in spite of Mazzinian preaching and martyrs, there were millions of people, especially among the peasants, to whom such an idea as Italian nationality had never been "practical politics" nor even clearly understood.[2] And indeed, to unite that long mountain-divided peninsula was a matter difficult of realisation before the advent of steam-power.

What was required was a national movement; an agitation throughout the whole peninsula to make all those varying types of Italic inhabitants feel that they had a sacred cause in common.

In such conditions the influence of the Pope was of incalculable value: for he alone would be listened to by every

[2] Tivaroni, *Domin. Austr.* III, 497, quoting Anelli.

class of person, in every Italian state; and he alone could reach the parish priest and the millions of toiling peasantry.

III. THE FOUR CHIEF LINES OF DEVELOPMENT

In Italy the development of nationality centred round the four lines already mentioned in volume I (v. Introduction), the Revolution, the Moderates, Piedmont and the Papal State.

(1) The Revolution was represented principally by Mazzini and his Giovine Italia. This was a world-organisation. It had been founded in 1831; but in 1846 and 1847 the Giovine Italia was in abeyance within Italy itself, temporarily eclipsed by the Moderate party and by the Albertists. This was due to the tragic outcome of most of his risings, which rather horrified ordinary men. Nevertheless, Mazzini still believed that the only way to arouse the great inert majority was by the story of Italians dying for freedom. The townsmen could be stirred by writing; but what use was writing for the millions of peasants who could not read?

In this connection we must make one other point before leaving Mazzini. He was, of course, great as an organiser of propaganda and a devoted inspirer of patriotism, but he was unskilful as a planner of rebellion. Indeed it has been said that in all his forty years of work Mazzini never planned a successful rising. This is more or less true. Nevertheless, Mazzini was a necessity. Without him there would have been no motor in the revolutionary machine. It was the constant working of the Giovine Italia and its periodical explosions— often futile in themselves—which kept the whole machine in motion.[3]

In a national uprising it is always necessary to have a Mazzini, because agitation and moderation are regarded by

---

[3] On all these points cf. Tivaroni's opinion, *Domin. Austr.* III, 445, 461, 469. On Mazzini there are scores of books, but it is impossible to understand him fully without a study of his own works, more especially the *Proemi* (forewords) prefixed to the various volumes of the *Scritti editi ed inediti* (A.E.), v. Bibliography.

a despotic government as "mere talk" unless they carry with them some threat of rebellion. In reality it hates the compromises offered to it by the moderates and would not consent to consider them at all, were it not with a view to undermining the extremists. If outrages cease, it says at once: Now we have peace. Concessions are no longer necessary.

Mazzini's activities kept the small tinselly governments in a state of nervousness, and at times even affected Metternich himself.

Thus, it is the extremists who unconsciously produce the moderates. It was the popular desire to placate Mazzini which created the demand for Gioberti and through him for Pius IX (1846). And they in turn—more conscious of what was immediately possible and therefore more constructive—initiated a Liberal agitation which spread nationalism throughout the whole people and went farther than any other movement towards arousing and uniting Italy for the wars of liberation. Ultimately of course war became necessary; for, in the end, freedom is seldom won without bloodshed.

(2) The second of our four main lines of national development is the moderate party. Its position has already been described in the Introduction. By 1846 it was temporarily predominant.

(3) Thirdly, the Kingdom of Sardinia, more conveniently referred to as Piedmont.[4] In this small but patriotic and persistent state there was a growing element of real opposition to Metternich. For fifteen years King Charles Albert had been working secretly but steadily, preparing his army and his finances to strike a decisive blow at Austria whenever the great opportunity should occur. During the last three years (1843–46) he had extended his more or less secret activities by means of agents such as the well-known Marquis Massimo d' Azeglio, and he was pushing the interests of Piedmont into Lombardo-Venetia, into Tuscany, and into the northern provinces of the Papal State. He had defied Austria over the wine duties. He dared not strike yet: but he aimed at making

[4] For authorities v. Bibliography, under Piedmont.

himself the champion of Italy, to whom at the great crisis all patriots should turn.

He was fortunate in the fact that his own interests, the tradition of his house, and the future advance of Italy, could all be combined in one cause. In his view, Piedmont was to be the leader of all the rest of Italy in a war of liberation, and was to acquire Lombardy and Venetia as soon as they could be set free. Some day perhaps the House of Savoy would rule over a united Italian nation. This was a definite aim and destined to bear its fruit: but for the moment it was beset by difficulties.

Manifestly, Piedmont was too weak to go to war alone. It was impossible for a nation numbering only 4,900,000 to attack an empire of 29,000,000. Charles Albert, however, hoped that on the day when he marched against Austria all Italy would follow him, and in that case he believed that he might be successful. His motto was *Italia farà da sè*, Italy will fend for herself. This meant that if only all Italy were aroused, then *single-handed* she could drive out the Austrians; and it was this belief, a very noble sentiment but mistaken, which differentiated his policy from that of Cavour, who perceived that a foreign alliance was necessary.

Meanwhile he had the sense to know that he must work in silence. He should make himself the chief hope of Italy, but he must not attempt actually to strike until the right moment had come. Hitherto—before 1846—not only the Austrians had been opposed to him, but the other princes as well; and the Pope, Gregory XVI, would have regarded any such attempt with profound disapproval—a fact which carried very great weight with so religious a man as Charles Albert. The position was full of difficulties. Already some of his followers were becoming impatient. Certainly it is greatly to his credit that he held everyone in leash until the very last moment.

Thus, although for years past he had had his secret hopes, before 1846 he had never been in a position to act. The

Austrians were still all-powerful and the Pope was their
friend. Gregory XVI was a strong Conservative and not
likely to forget that their troops had saved him from losing
most of his state in the year 1831. Amid such difficulties
what a relief it was for Charles Albert when a Liberal Pope
appeared on the scene!

There is one small sign of the times which we must mention
here because it was perhaps the first practical attempt at
representing, not a single state or party, but the whole of
United Italy. In the year 1839 there was held the first annual
Scientific Congress.[5] It was initiated by Carlo Bonaparte,
Prince of Canino, son of Lucien Bonaparte; he was a citizen
of the Papal State. This was the first, and perhaps the best
step in his rather blatant political career. It was held at Pisa,
by permission of Leopold II, the kindly Grand Duke of
Tuscany, who attended some of its meetings. About 400
members were present from all parts of Italy. It proved a
great success, and aroused emulation in other states. In 1840
a similar congress was held at Turin; then—in each succeeding year (1841-47)—at Florence, at Padua, at Lucca, at Milan,
at Naples, at Genoa and at Venice. These congresses soon
constituted a kind of national assembly. At first they talked
of the scientific and industrial problems of the whole of
Italy; but, naturally, before long they talked of her politics.
Who could prevent their doing so, especially after working
hours? At the last one held in Venice in 1847, there were
1478 members present, and their meetings ended amid scenes
of heartfelt nationalist enthusiasm.

Before 1846 Pope Gregory XVI had refused to allow
Scientific Congresses to be held in the Papal State and consequently was blamed by Massimo d' Azeglio, in *Degli ultimi
casi di Romagna*, for being contrary to the spirit of the age.
His successor Pius IX was prepared to allow them.

[5] There are many descriptions of these congresses: perhaps the
best short summary is that of Tivaroni, *Domin. Austr.* III, 453. *V.*
also Gori, p. 40; Cantù and others.

(4) As to the fourth centre of development, namely the Papal State, we need only say that the old Pope Gregory XVI (1831–46) was strongly opposed to all Liberal advance. He feared for the Church; and his prisons were full of rebels.

On June 1st, however, Gregory XVI died; and on June 16th, 1846, Cardinal Mastai Ferretti was exalted to the Papal Chair and took the name of Pius IX. This was a great event throughout Italy. The new Pope was by birth a provincial noble but he was known to be a Liberal and a good Italian.

Thus we arrive at the turn in the situation. The question was: What would he do? or rather, What *could* he do?

And in reality the chief question was: How would he reconcile the three conflicting duties—those of the priest, those of the king, and those of the patriot?

Perhaps at the end of this summary it is well to quote from volume I the description given there of Pius' personality. He lived to be nearly eighty-six and most of the portraits which we see represent him as an old man; but in his younger days he was exceptionally fortunate in his appearance and manner.

Cardinal Mastai was unmistakably a person of distinction; slightly above the average height, broad shouldered, and, by 1846, naturally rather tending towards stoutness; but in spite of his fifty-four years he had remained a handsome man, owing to his regular features, to his good dark eyes and more especially to the charm of his kindly half-humorous expression; he was clean-shaven of course, and consequently looked young for his age. And—perhaps for his help and consolation in life—he had been endowed by Heaven with a wonderfully attractive smile, with a gift of inspiring sympathy and happiness in those with whom he spoke, and with a sense of gentle fun; traits which, together with his cheerfulness under great misfortune, were destined, for thirty years to come, always to win him devoted friends among those around him—whether they were servitors, guests, foreign poten-tates, Papal Zouaves on duty at his Castello, or merely popolani to whom he gave alms.[6]

[6] *Italy in the Making*, I, p. 258.

A Liberal Pope had appeared in Metternich's Italy, a ruler who believed in trusting the people as far as possible. That was Pius' political creed; but primarily he was not a political ruler: he was Pope; and his unalterable duty was to the Holy See.

Chapter II

WORLD INFLUENCES. THE RELIGIOUS DUTY

In days of revolution I suppose there is hardly a priest who is not often torn in opposite directions by his religion and his patriotism. And Pius IX, when he assumed the immense responsibility of being interpreter of God's word to the whole Roman Catholic world, must have been anxious inwardly as to how this supreme mission would conflict, firstly with his duty as the temporal sovereign of his state and secondly with his hopes as an Italian. For in spite of his nationalist sentiment, there remained always before him his first and unalterable duty.[1] He was a priest. He had been a priest throughout all his working life, and was a temporal sovereign only in virtue of having been chosen by the cardinals to be Head of the Church.

As we have said, it was a threefold call; firstly for the Church Spiritual and Apostolic; secondly for the state; and thirdly there was his own love of Italy, the natural birthright of every normal Italian;[2] but how far should the patriotism of his younger days continue as a living influence in the mind of a Pope?

The Papacy is not national but international. Therein lies its greatness. It is one of the few international influences that

---

[1] "Pius IX is not merely the sovereign of a little state. He is Pope. Whatever judgment one may form as to his temporal administration, his influence as Head of the Church is great and can only increase. It is with the Church all over Christendom that he is essentially occupied. Owing to his beliefs and his antecedents, he is the Bishop rather than the King." Rossi's despatch July 28th, 1847—Paris Aff. Etr., Rome.

[2] Gualterio (1862 ed.) v, 241, says: "Deep in his soul there was rooted an undeterminate desire that Italy should be her own mistress without detriment to the lordship of the Church."

the world possesses. Manifestly, during the nineteenth century—which made nationality its religion—the first duty of
the Pope was to preserve this character of the Holy See; to
remember that the Catholics in Austria or elsewhere were as
much his spiritual subjects as those in Italy.

The importance of Pius' decision on this point may be
illustrated by the following consideration. In 1848 he was
expected to excommunicate the Austrians during the first
war of liberation. Had he complied, he could hardly have
refused to excommunicate them in the second war of liberation in 1859; and perhaps also in 1866. And a similar question
would have arisen in 1915. All these wars were wars of
liberation.

It is curious to see how often this primary condition is
overlooked by historians. In the English language there are
few, if any, books at all, which attempt to portray the constantly recurring strife in Pius' mind[3] between the call of the
Papacy and the call of Italian freedom: the two greatest calls
that a man can hear.

Thus the first problems confronting him were ecclesiastical,
not temporal; and the following is a short sketch of the
religious and ecclesiastical situation in the principal nations
of Europe in 1846. But it is impossible for a secular, non-
Catholic writer to offer more than a very brief notice of some
few among them. This mention, at all events, will recall their
existence.

It was a troubled world on which Pius looked forth after
his exaltation; in fact, he must have felt more or less in the
position of a general who is aware that all his divisions are

[3] One finds frequent proofs of it, not merely in Papal books or in
contemporary documents, but in entirely extraneous references such
as the following in *The Italian Letters of a Diplomat's Wife*, 1905 (Mrs
Mary King Waddington), p. 69: "Minghetti said that the most
absolutely Liberal man he had ever known was Pio Nono—but what
could he do once he was Pope?" The Italian statesman Minghetti
had been one of the ablest ministers in Pius IX's government and
knew him well. The Liberal programme included a federated Italy.

heavily engaged on a very wide battle front, and that he has hardly any reinforcements to send them. The Roman Church had its labourers in almost every country in the world. From our point of view, however, the most important nations were the five Great Powers; especially France and Austria, bitter rivals in Papal and in Italian affairs.

It will be seen that the Conservative powers—those most strongly opposed to Italian nationality—were usually the best friends of the Church.[4]

I. AUSTRIA

Undoubtedly Metternich had been the best friend of Pope Gregory XVI.

Since the eighteenth century, Josephism—so Cardinal Hergenröther[5] tells us—"had almost transformed the Catholic Church in Austria into a schismatic and national Church". This term refers to the doctrine of the Emperor Joseph II, who claimed that, in case of civil differences, the Church must give way to the state. To most Protestants that seems right. But it had almost resulted in cutting off the Austrian Church from the Papacy. Between the years 1815 and 1840 there had been very few instances of Austrian bishops visiting Rome, and in consequence religion had suffered. The higher clergy, we hear, were luxurious; they gave balls, and went to theatres; and ecclesiastical discipline was weak. In fact, even for the imperial government the situation had become unsatisfactory.

---

[4] At the moment the chief subjects of discussion in the Catholic embassies were the Jesuits and the Poles. Metternich had occupied Cracow, and the Poles were in a state of insurrection against Austria, Russia and Prussia. Some of the Polish priests had sided with the patriots, and Metternich had laid the matter before the Pope. Gregory XVI sided strongly with the Austrian authorities. There was some danger of the revolutionary activity spreading to Italy. All this question is dealt with in detail by Mr L. E. Woodward in his interesting work: *Three Studies in European Conservatism.*

[5] Hergenröther, VII, 329.

Metternich felt this. Only two years before the accession of Pius IX, in a report dated April 6th, 1844, he said:[6]

The suppression of these communications—those between the religious orders in Austria and their chiefs in Rome—far from being an advantage to the State has produced a two-fold disadvantage; that of demoralising the religious orders, and, for the government, that of producing an apparent schism. In this case, also, by re-establishing the natural communications between the religious orders and their chiefs, one could make an end of all inconveniences.

Metternich, then, considered that the matter had gone so far as to produce "an apparent schism".

Of all the statesmen in Europe he was probably the most genuine ally of the Papacy. As early as the year 1815 he had advised his master to open negotiations with Pius VII. Apart from religion he regarded the Holy See as the power most interested in preserving the *status quo* in Italy and thought its friendship always worth cultivating.

In the same year, 1844, he revived the idea of a Concordat. On April 6th he addressed a report to the Emperor Ferdinand in which he said, "without further delay...the rights of the Holy See with regard to Austria must be established".[7]

But there is no better proof of the genuineness of Metternich's feeling for the Church than his views, during his later years, upon the Jesuits. It was a period when that order was being furiously attacked in France, Switzerland and elsewhere; but Metternich takes quite a different view of their case.

"We", he says, "have no Jesuit question—about which there is so much to do elsewhere. They do not make us either hot or cold

[6] Metternich, *Mémoires* (French ed.), VII, 35.
[7] He then proceeded to deal with four outstanding questions on which he was ready to come to an agreement: (1) Legislation on marriage; (2) Communication between the heads of religious orders and their superiors in Rome; (3) Correspondence between bishops and their superior authority; (4) The government's interdict on the proposed German college. *Ibid.* 32–8.

and we are convinced that in this matter we are right. We either have them with us or do not have them with us, according to the wishes of our bishops, and according to the means of assuring them an establishment from funds other than those of the State. The colleges which they direct are distinguished by the spirit of order that reigns there; and, as to their studies, there is no difference between them and other educational establishments, colleges and gymnasia."

To sum up, therefore, the Papal situation in 1846: the new Pope, Pius IX, found himself in a very difficult position. Vienna and the Holy See were working together every day, and on such good terms that Lützow had remarked on it to Metternich:[8] he had pointed out that the only real allies of the Papacy must necessarily be the three Conservative powers, Austria, Prussia and Russia, and that of those three, Austria alone could be a wholehearted friend of the Papacy, for the other two were not even Catholic. Thus if Pius had been an ultra-Conservative, prepared to walk in the footsteps of Gregory XVI, he would have had a good friend in Metternich and he might have done a great work towards advancing the influence of the Church and perhaps redeeming the Austrian Empire from Josephism and its schismatic tendencies. What happiness that would have brought to the Church! And it was a matter which Pius had genuinely at heart; before three months were out he held an interview with Count Lützow on this very subject of Josephism.[9] But his beliefs as an Italian Liberal were certain to create difficulties between him and the all-powerful minister; and this must have been a great grief to him.

[8] Lützow to Metternich, May 17th, 1846. Vienna Staats-Archiv, Rome, *Rapports*, II.

[9] "It is a question of errors which were introduced during the reign of the late Emperor Joseph II. For more than half a century these dispositions have been a profound grief (*accablent de douleur*) to each successive Sovereign Pontiff." Vienna Staats-Archiv, Rome, *Rapports*, II, December 26th, 1846. Pius then raised the four points suggested by Metternich in 1844, *v.* p. 15, n. 7.

II. FRANCE

In France the Church had undergone strange vicissitudes since 1789. The French Revolution had involved not merely the overthrow of the king and the aristocracy but also that of the Church and of Christianity itself. In the place of the God of the New Testament there had been solemnly set up the Goddess of Reason,[10] accompanied by the guillotine. Then arose Napoleon, who believed in restoring Christianity and tried to establish Pope Pius VII more or less as his chaplain; and after him came the Legitimist Bourbons, Louis XVIII and Charles X, who, in spite of Gallican tendencies, were good friends of Popes Leo XII (1823–29) and Pius VIII (1829–30).

After the revolution of 1830 France became a Liberal power. Once that Louis Philippe (1830–48) had been safely installed by the bourgeoisie in place of Charles X, the relations with Rome, though at first doubtful, very soon began to improve. This was the era of the "juste milieu". The bourgeoisie feared a recurrence either of the revolution or of reactionary legitimism: they wanted a rest from revolutions, and Gregory XVI, essentially a Conservative and a believer in paternal rule, issued encyclicals urging the duty of obedience to authority. This led to better feeling between the governments; but within France itself there remained several outstanding religious differences:[11] for instance, the bitter struggle which lasted for years between the Church and the University over the education question—the Church wanted to have the power of opening Catholic schools and colleges; and secondly, the outcry against the Jesuits; and in 1846 the question of the Syrian Christians became a subject of long diplomatic controversy between Guizot and Pius IX.

[10] When the French under Berthier occupied Rome in 1798 a statue of Liberty trampling on the Papal tiara was set up in front of Castel S. Angelo. Hergenröther, VII, 131.

[11] Guizot, VII, 377 *et seq.*; Lagrange, I, 242; Debidour, *Rapports*, pp. 440–50; *Camb. Mod. Hist.* vol XI (Article, L. Bourgeois).

This, too, is the period of Lamennais (1781 to 1854). But lack of space—though not lack of interest—prevents our describing his dealings with Gregory XVI; for the aim of this work is to confine itself to the main lines-of-development in the Risorgimento.

The Jesuit question, however, was the most widespread of all the problems before the Holy See: it was a cause of controversy in France and Italy and of actual strife in Switzerland. The chief point at issue was the ingerence of the Society of Jesus in education. It became so serious that in March 1845—some fifteen months before the exaltation of Pius—Louis Philippe and Guizot sent an exceptionally able man, Pellegrino Rossi,[12] as envoy extraordinary to Rome, with orders to try and get the Jesuit organisation dissolved in France. It was a curious choice of envoy; Rossi was an Italian, an ex-revolutionist, reputed to be a freethinker and married to a Protestant wife; apparently the wrong man for the Vatican, but in reality an excellent choice. He was one of those Italian exiles who brought honour to the land of their birth. Wherever he went he was recognised as a distinguished man.

In this mission to Rome he proved successful. At first the old Pope was deeply hurt by the suggestion of dissolving the Society of Jesus in France: but finally he agreed that Father Roothan, General of the Jesuits, should undertake the matter himself. Father Roothan therefore directed that they should have no more colleges, or novitiates in France, and that those who stayed there should do so, not as an order, but merely as secular priests[13] under the bishops.

---

[12] For Rossi's career see *Pellegrino Rossi* by László Ledermann. He quotes letters from Rossi to Guizot. *V.* also Guizot's *Mémoires*, vol. VII; Minghetti, *Ricordi*, vol. I; Giovagnoli, *Rossi*.

[13] Guizot says with much detail that this compromise was what he asked for from the first. (Guizot, VII, 388 *et seq.*) On the other side this question is dealt with in Debidour, *Histoire des rapports de l'église et de l'état*, pp. 440–80. He is opposed to the clerical view.

In May 1846, in recognition of his able management of the Jesuit question, Pellegrino Rossi was accorded the post of French ambassador to the Holy See, with the title of Count. Thus the man who had left Italy a ruined exile was returning to Rome as an ambassador, a jurist of European fame, a member of the French Academy and a peer of France.

In June 1846 Pius came to the throne. During the next two years Rossi was his constant friend and adviser. And as he plays a leading part in the story it may be well to give a short description of him.

Pellegrino Rossi, says the historian Masi, was the only real statesman whom Italy produced before Cavour—or after. This, of course, is a jest, but it denotes that Rossi was one of the ablest and most interesting men of his day.

When he first returned to Italy he was fifty-eight years old —an age at which the memories of youth are often vivid and sad. Life in the Roman state, we know, brought back to him many recollections—among others no doubt his childhood spent below the white marble peak of Carrara; then his brilliant career at the Bologna University—the *laurea in utroque jure* won before he was nineteen; the several years spent at the law, during which he became known as the "avvocatino pallido", the pale little barrister whose legal knowledge and turn for sarcasm had brought him into notice, especially when defending prisoners:[14] after that came a year spent as a professor in a college.[15]

He says that the government had promised that the Jesuit houses should be closed; that the Jesuits had thirty houses in France and that they only dissolved three. But the word "house" might include, one supposes, even the smallest house: e.g. a parish served by a rector and a couple of curates living together. *V.* also Hergenröther, VII, 442.

[14] *V.* László Ledermann, pp. 27–31. He gives all necessary documents.

[15] Born at Carrara (Tuscany) July 13th, 1787, of middle class. Sent to school at Correggio; then to university, first at Pisa and then at Bologna. 1806, Baccalaureat. 1807, Court Secretary. Then practised as a barrister. 1813, Professor at a college. 1814, on

Then in 1814 there marched into Romagna the army from
the south under Murat, and with it came the call to make a
united Italy. Rossi threw himself enthusiastically into this
cause to which, perhaps, he was already bound. Murat
named him Commissario of the three departments round
Bologna—those of the Reno, of the Rubicon, and of the
Lower Po. For almost a year he was one of the most prominent men in those provinces. But in 1815 came the downfall of Murat. Rossi was ruined. The pontifical government
could never forgive him some of those vibrating sentences in
the proclamations which he had written calling on his country-
men to follow King Joachim. He was sent into exile; and,
of this short episode, perhaps the chief remaining record is a
scornful phrase in the *Auto-difesa* (Defence) which he wrote
in 1815; one that was characteristically stinging:

> To love my country and wish it to become great and happy,
> at a time when there existed people whom even this might dis-
> please,—if this be a crime, then, freely, I dispense my accusers
> from bringing any proof against me: I plead guilty; and I should
> call it an insult to be declared innocent.

Murat's first invasion Rossi was given the Chair of Criminal Law
and Procedure at Bologna University; and named Commissario (as
above). 1815, on Murat's downfall Rossi followed him.

Went to Geneva. Learnt French. 1818, won Chair of Roman
and Criminal Law. 1820, married a rich Protestant; published
studies on law. 1820, became a Deputy in Geneva. 1832, Deputy
in the Federal Diet of Switzerland; played a leading part in revision
of Swiss Constitution. Lost all his money.

1832, made a fresh start; founded *Le Fédéral*, which failed. 1833,
went to Paris to be Professor of Political Economy at the Collège de
France; and Law Professor. Friend of Guizot. 1839, became
member of House of Peers (Pairs de France). Worked on the
Revue des deux Mondes. 1844, sent to Rome as Plenipotentiary to
settle Jesuit question. 1846–48, French Ambassador in Rome with
the title of Count. Friend of Pius IX. 1848, Revolution in Paris;
Rossi remains in Rome unofficially. Friend of leading Liberals:
opposed to policy of war against Austria, which he considered
hopeless. September 6th, chief Minister of Pius IX; November 15th,
was assassinated.

His subsequent career among the distinguished men and women of Europe has been written at great length in his biographies; so here we need only describe the mental and physical characteristics of the Pellegrino Rossi of 1846 to 1848. There are several statues of him in Rome, but the best is probably the bust which Pius IX erected to the memory of his friend in the church of San Lorenzo in Damaso. He was tall for a southerner and rather thin and pale; and clean-shaven as befits a barrister; the Roman Law had left its stamp on him; in fact, with his wealth of now-whitening hair, his grey eyes deep-set but very bright, his cravat and his low-breasted frock-coat he must have looked more like a distinguished Scottish advocate of that period than an Italian exile. His face is fairly broad but sunken, as if from too much brain-work; the forehead wide, cheek bones a shade high, the nose and chin slightly hooked, and the expression rather sad. His long lips are closely compressed, and, normally, would break into a grave smile with probably a tinge of irony.

As a young man he had been full of fire; but now he aimed at convincing his audience by reason, rather than at carrying them off their feet. Guizot describes him as "in reality full of passion and authority; but these traits did not appear at first...in appearance he was cold, slow and disdainful and therefore exercised more influence over individuals than over crowds".[16] Perhaps Guizot did not remember that Rossi was always speaking in a foreign language, learnt after he was grown up. Count Lützow said "he spoke slowly, Italian transpiring through his phrases".[17] Elsewhere Guizot bears testimony that he was a steadfast friend.

He was now a Liberal and reformer, not a revolutionist.[18]

[16] Translated from the Italian of Giovagnoli.

[17] From a despatch of Count Lützow, May 5th, 1846. Vienna Staats-Archiv, Rome, *Rapports*, II.

[18] "Italy is more developed certainly than she was twenty-five years ago but still she is not in a condition to try great and perilous enterprises. She has before her two ways; one of them is covered with traps and rocks; while the other, though certainly longer, is

He believed in winning Italian freedom by working for reform in each state.

This was the man who as French ambassador was to carry on the diplomatic struggle against Metternich; and, later on, as Papal prime minister he was probably the only man living who might have saved the Temporal power.

III. GREAT BRITAIN AND IRELAND (1846)

Concerning this troubled period so much has been written that nothing new could be added in the space of a few paragraphs.

In the year 1804, says Bishop Pelczar, the English Catholics numbered only about 60,000. The long strain of a hundred and fifty years of Penal Laws had worn this minority almost to nothing. Those families which came through it must indeed have had a heroic and hereditary sense of duty; and when the struggle began for Emancipation they played their part—a greater part than is often realised.

But undoubtedly Emancipation was won by O'Connell's movement in Ireland. The story of his campaign of gigantic mass-meetings and of his final success in 1829 need not be repeated. After 1829, the Catholics were virtually free—according to the laws.

During the period 1830 to 1846 many converts were made to Catholicism, especially among the richer classes in England;

---

easy and seems to lead infallibly to the goal. What matter if the goal is not reached in our life-time?

"Let us speak plainly. Either I am greatly mistaken, or from year to year the Italian position will become stronger as opposed to Austria, whereas that of Austria in Italy will become relatively weaker...."

He goes on to say that a rebellion would be a service rendered to Austria by enabling her to arrest the present regular progress of nationalism which is assisted by the authorities on the example of the Head of the Church. In ten or twenty years every man and woman in Italy will be a nationalist. Paris Aff. Etr., Rome, 1847. Rossi, July 28th.

it is the period of Newman, Manning and Wiseman.[19] At the same time there began an immense immigration from Ireland, so that by the year 1846 the total number of Roman Catholics in England amounted to about a million: those in Ireland to 6¾ millions.

In 1846, therefore, at the time of Pius' exaltation, there were about 7¾ million[20] Roman Catholics in the British Isles, in a total population of about 28 millions. These figures form the high-water mark of progress ever reached by the Catholics, numerically. That very summer marks the beginning of the famine which was to starve or drive into exile nearly two million of the Irish peasantry within about three years.

In England, in 1843, there existed as yet no regular hierarchy. There were eight Apostolic vicars; and, throughout the country, there were about 487 churches and chapels and 624 priests.

In Scotland there were 69 churches and 86 priests, for a Roman Catholic population of about 100,000 souls.

In Ireland, in 1846, there were 4 Archbishops, 24 Bishops, 2205 churches, 1069 parishes, 2721 Catholic clergy. The best known were perhaps Bishop Cullen and Father Mathew, the Apostle of Temperance.

In 1846, at the time of Pius' exaltation, in certain Catholic quarters hopes seem to have prevailed that England might be converted and return to the Papal fold. As to Ireland there existed various outstanding subjects of disagreement, such as the lack of a Catholic university, the payment of tithes to the Protestant Church of Ireland—old sources of bitterness which concerned Pius IX in 1846 but are now forgotten.

[19] It is, of course, also the period of Pusey, Keble and other celebrated Protestants. For Catholic details v. Ward (Mgr Bernard), *A Sequel to Catholic Emancipation.*

[20] Roughly 6¾ million Irish and a million English, Scotch or Welsh. For the figures relating to the high clergy v. the *Irish Catholic Directory* for 1847. For English Catholics v. Ward, *op. cit.*

IV. PRUSSIA

About Prussia[21] there is very little to be said. Since her glorious rising against Napoleon, Prussia had lived for many years under the rule of King Frederick William III (1797–1840), the same sovereign who had called her to arms and led her during those great days. His régime was imbued with old Prussian ideas—militant Protestantism and hatred of the French—the same two which prevailed in most of England during that period. By the Treaty of 1815 he had acquired a large number of Catholic subjects, many of them Poles, and during the remainder of his life he left no device untried for converting them to his own faith. It was a long struggle, over mixed marriages, over convents and other points, but in the end the Catholics succeeded in maintaining the compromise originally proposed by Pope Pius VIII—a success which it is only fair to say was largely due to the tact and firmness displayed by Gregory XVI. At this time, however, Prussia, like the rest of Germany, was moving towards the revolution of 1848.

In 1840 King Frederick William III died and was succeeded by his son Frederick William IV (1840–61). This was the same Frederick William who was to summon the combined Diets in 1847. He was a broad-minded man, and it only took him two years to come to terms with the Holy See and to arrange an agreement on a friendly basis.

With Prussia, therefore, Pius found his diplomatic relations on a more satisfactory basis—except (as also in Russia and Austria) for the Polish question. In the Duchy of Posen and in the city of Thorn there was unrest, in which some patriot priests were playing their part, and it was expected that the Holy See would forbid their doing so.[22]

---

[21] *V.* Hergenröther, Gams, and other Catholic authorities; also Nielsen.

[22] *V.* Vienna Staats-Archiv, Rome, *Rapports*, II.

V. RUSSIA AND POLAND

Russia,[23] with a population of perhaps 60,000,000, was by far the more powerful; but of course Catholic Poland was the more important from the Papal point of view.

The history of Poland is terrible: three times partitioned—in 1771, in 1793 and 1795—and then treated as a recruiting ground by Napoleon, to whom she had sent her bravest and most patriotic sons in the vain hope of winning freedom: and finally in 1815 she was partitioned for the fourth time. But she still retained her religion and her language; and a splendid will to be free.

The czar Alexander I had hoped to conciliate his Polish and Catholic subjects by granting them a constitution as "the kingdom of Poland" and by taking their religion under his special protection. But in 1825 he died and was succeeded by his brother, Nicholas I (1825-55).

The new czar[24] was an absolutist of the iron type; like Henry VIII he meant to be his own Pope; and he had a similar predilection for monastic possessions. His basic conception seems to have been the unity and uniformity of his whole empire: one czar, one state, no parliament, and only one Church which was to be entirely at his beck and call.

Towards the end of 1830 came another rebellion: the Polish army mutinied and struck for freedom. As late as in April 1831 the Poles were still victorious; but at the end of May they were defeated; Warsaw was taken and the Polish constitution was abolished.

The persecution which followed is too long to be chronicled here. It may be divided roughly into two main phases, firstly,

[23] It is only fair to say that this short sketch of the Russian and Polish difficulties is drawn almost entirely from Papal sources. But *L'Église catholique en Pologne et en Russie* by Theiner gives all the eighty-four Ukases and other documents quoted in Gregory XVI's Allocution of July 1842; he also gives the Allocution itself.

[24] Born 1796; married 1817 to Princess Charlotte, daughter of Frederick William III of Prussia; succeeded his brother as emperor 1825; died 1855.

that directed against the Uniates; about which we need only say that it seems to have been successful, though not until innumerable martyrs had been made, including the celebrated nuns of Minsk; secondly, that against the Catholics, most of whom were Poles. Against them the campaign was carried on from 1833 to 1846, and it came to a head during the last six years. In 1842 Gregory published the Allocution *Haerentem diu*, deploring the state of the Church in Russia and defending himself against the imputation of having abandoned part of his flock. In 1845 Makryna Mieczyslawska, the heroic Mother Superior of the Nuns of Minsk,[25] arrived in Rome, and her case caused interminable discussions between the Holy See, Russia, Austria and France.

In 1845 the czar came to Rome and had an interview, which has often been described, with Gregory XVI. It resulted in negotiations for a Concordat; a commission was appointed, but a few months later Gregory died and the whole question remained over for Pius IX.

The Liberalism of Pius, therefore, was regarded with great distrust by the czar. It might set right above despotism in Russia, and it might become a call of freedom for the Poles.[26]

VI. SWITZERLAND: THE SONDERBUND

So much for the five Great Powers. But the religious-political question which most of all was troubling the statesmen of Europe at the moment was that of the Sonderbund in Switzerland: it was the only point at which there was a definite clash between Protestant and Catholic populations; and so

---

[25] "A beautiful woman, still young and proud of her Jagollen descent: with more the appearance of a grenadier than of a saint". *V. Aus nachgelassenen Papieren*, VII, 304. Princess Melanie adds that the ecclesiastical authorities were rather doubtful about her story.

[26] Gregory XVI's treatment of the Poles is the most regrettable phase in his life; at times it is heart-breaking. His Encyclical of 1832 can only partly be excused by the fact that all Europe, including the Papal State, had recently been in rebellion. This Polish question, however, does not concern our subject, the Risorgimento.

important did this controversy become that one might almost find here a turning-point of European history.

In Switzerland some 200,000 men were arming, on the verge of a religious war, for a conflict which threatened the very existence of that brave and sensible people. It was of some fifteen years standing—far too complicated to be dealt with here—one of the many quarrels between Liberal Protestants and Conservative Catholics, to which were added differences as to Cantonal and Federal loyalty. The immediate cause of strife was the question of the Jesuits. Several risings had taken place, and the Papal Nuncio—who was Monsignor Gizzi, already known[27] to us—had been obliged to fly from Lucerne.

The nation consisted of twenty-two Cantons under a Federal Diet—twenty-two little republics then bound together by a pact so loose that each one was more or less independent. The Catholics were in a minority, and they were angry because they had been deprived of four monasteries in the Canton of Argovie (Argau), and more especially because Lucerne had been prevented from appointing Jesuit professors to its University; and some of the Protestants were proposing (in the Diet) to expel the Jesuits from the whole of Switzerland. The result was that in June 1846 the seven Catholic Cantons proclaimed a defensive league called the Sonderbund; its aims were to oppose the expulsion of the Jesuits and to maintain cantonal independence by preventing the tightening up of the Federal Pact of 1815.

It was the very month in which Pius was elected Pope. Thus he found himself faced in Switzerland by bitter quarrels; Conservative against Radical; Catholic against Protestant. It was a question which was arousing partisan feeling in all the countries of Europe. In Italy, for instance, the Mazzinians

[27] For the Sonderbund v. Oechsli. Also Gobat, *Histoire de la Suisse*; Rosier, *Histoire illustrée de la Suisse*; *Camb. Mod. Hist.* vol. XI, and, of course, countless political memoirs. On the Papal side v. Hergenröther, Gams, Pelczar, etc. *op. cit.*

sympathised with the Protestants, and the Conservatives and Clericals with the Sonderbund. Charles Albert and Solaro della Margherita were on the side of the Sonderbund. As Pius was both a Catholic and also a Liberal his course was hard to steer; but his sympathies naturally went out to the seven Catholic Cantons which were arming to defend the Jesuits, and no doubt this sentiment had been strengthened by the murder of one of their leaders in July 1845: but his Nuncio in Switzerland, Mgr Macciotti, for some reason or other earned the strongest disapproval of the Austrian embassy in Rome.

Nowadays there is little sympathy with the Catholics, because it is felt that their success might have divided Switzerland and that there existed no religious intolerance so unbearable as to justify the secession of one-fifth of the population. But at the time, their Sonderbund had the support of nearly all the European governments. Palmerston was almost the only minister on the Liberal side. From 1845 to 1847 Metternich tried hard to arrange with France for a joint intervention in order to defend the Sonderbund and prevent any alteration of the Federal Constitution of 1815. He supplied arms, ammunition, and even a well-known officer—Prince Schwarzenberg—to help the Catholics, but without results. The Swiss stood firm. A year later, after very little fighting,[28] the Protestant-Liberal majority proved successful, and Switzerland remained united.

VII. THE ITALIAN STATES

It was in Italy itself that the position taken up by Pius was of vital importance, for there religion was the only influence

[28] In Switzerland I once had some conversation with an old man who remembered the days of the Sonderbund. He told me that he thought there was little bitterness throughout most of the civilian population. He himself was working for a man on the opposite side in religion and politics, and "although the soldiers marched by our house" he noticed no difference in his employer's manner to him.

that could counteract the Revolution. Consequently the
Italian princes were all well-disposed towards the Holy See;
and Pius must have seen with regret that, by embarking on a
policy of reform, he was endangering both them and also the
material interests of the Church. Liberal reform was very
difficult for a Pope—as the ecclesiastics pointed out—because
to give power into the hands of the Liberals was tantamount
to handing it over sooner or later to the anti-clericals.

Piedmont. Of the small Italian states Piedmont was the
most conservative and aristocratic; and King Charles Albert,
like his predecessors, was devoted to religion. The following
account of the situation in Piedmont is given by Gams:[29]

Up to the last years of the reign of Charles Albert, who through
ambition allowed himself to sink into misfortune and tried to
build up a firm throne as King of Italy upon the waves of the
revolution—we find the Church in the Kingdom of Sardinia in
fortunate conditions. It was perhaps the most fortunate of all the
churches, just as it is to-day incontestably the most unfortunate
on earth. An unfeigned and living piety reigned, not only in the
country districts, but also in the large towns.

He instances Genoa, Novara, Nice, Chambery and Annecy
as being specially remarkable in this sense, and also the
capital Turin "rightly known as the city of the Blessed
Sacrament", and then devotes four pages to enumerating the
charitable institutions of the Church in Piedmont, from which
description the following is an extract:

In the year 1841 the Ministry issued a statistical document
which gave the most accurate information as to the condition of
the charitable institutions as a whole, throughout the Kingdom.
According to it, there existed in the country, without counting
various small local foundations, 1727 charitable institutions of
which many were in the smaller towns—for instance Asti had ten.
Included in this total are 187 hospitals; 10 hospitals for incurables;
42 orphanages; 46 other institutions for receiving and helping the
needy; 1277 institutions for the distribution of alms to the poor;
75 ditto for providing dowries for poor girls; 26 others for helping
children by teaching them a trade.

[29] Gams, of course, is one of the chief clerical writers.

He says, too, that very good regulations were made for presenting the yearly budget for all these institutions.

Of Charles Albert himself this clerical writer has nothing but good to say, until he reaches the year 1848 (in which year Charles Albert granted a Liberal constitution):

His upright piety, his strictness in the fulfilment of his religious duties, his untiring diligence and many other things that he did after his accession in 1831, earned for him the universal respect of all right-thinking people. In the year 1841, on March 27th, he concluded with Gregory XVI a Concordat as to the personal immunity of the clergy who had been convicted of crimes; in which although the basis of clerical immunity is abandoned, yet definite outside rules are laid down which establish an unalterable limit in the matter of penalties for clerics. Count Barbaroux, who had concluded the Concordats of 1817, 1828 and 1841, worked as Minister of Clerical Affairs with notable results until his death in 1843.

Up to 1846 all had gone well with the clericals. At this point, however, it is very instructive to cast our eyes forward beyond the limits of this volume. In 1848 Charles Albert granted a popular constitution to Piedmont, and almost at once the Liberals threw themselves upon the Church. In this volume we are not discussing the question as to how far they were justified in curtailing its privileges or confiscating its religious houses; as to whether there were too many monasteries, or whether their suppression could have been carried out less harshly. Those are long controversies which do not concern us. Our point is that these actions of the Liberals prove the justice of the clerical contention and of the views of Metternich, that if Pius ever resigned his full authority he would be exposing the Church to attacks in his own state. For Pius as Pope it was impossible to be a constitutional monarch in the full sense of the term. He was compelled to reserve a right of veto in order to defend the Church. Otherwise he might have been obliged to sign, in his own state, anti-clerical measures which he was denouncing elsewhere.

Gams' highly clerical description of the events after 1848 runs as follows:

All this happened in Sardinia before the year 1848; and, since then, the one endeavour in that unhappy country has been to destroy that which a more pious generation built up with sweat and tears; and these destroyers call themselves the friends of mankind and leaders of progress. By this example of unhappy Piedmont God desires to give an example to the whole world of whither the enmity to the Church will lead.[30]

In Naples, too, the Church stood on good terms with the government: a Concordat of 35 articles had been signed at Terracina on February 16th, 1818.[31]

[30] Vide also Hergenröther: "L'Ordre (the Jesuits) fut définitive-ment expulsé le 25 Août, ainsi que les Dames du Sacré Cœur. Vint ensuite le 4 octobre, une loi sur l'enseignement, tout à fait hostile à l'Église. En 1849, commencèrent les hostilités contre l'archevêque de Turin, contre l'évêque d'Asti et aussi contre le pape. En 1850 les lois Siccardi supprimèrent les immunités ecclésiastiques; la juris-diction spirituelle fut attaquée; on emprisonna les archevêques de Turin et de Sassari, ainsi que plusieurs prédicateurs; l'enseignement théologique fut réglé par le seul pouvoir civil (1851), le mariage civil introduit (1852), l'économat apostolique complètement secularisé (1852). L'année 1854 fut marquée par les lois sur les couvents; celle de 1855 par la suppression de l'Académie ecclésiastique de Superga, et les années qui suivent 1856 par d'incessantes tracasseries contre les curés et les prêtres séculiers et par la spoliation des biens de l'Église." Hergenröther, VII, 348.

[31] The main terms of the Concordat of 1818, which aimed at clearing up matters after the Napoleonic Era, ran as follows: (i) The dioceses were to be restored to the Church; there were to be 109 of them. (ii) Church property not already sold to be restored. (iii) A fairly large number of the monasteries to be restored and also the religious orders, including the Jesuits. (iv) The Church to have the right of acquiring property. (v) The king pledged himself and his successors not to annex Church property; henceforth it was to be inviolable. (vi) Every year 12,000 ducats were to be sent to Rome out of the Neapolitan bishops' incomings. (vii) Clerical jurisdiction is restored for Church discipline and for what is described in the Tridentinum as clerical privilege. (viii) The bishops are allowed the right of censure against anyone in matters of theology, canon law, etc. (ix) The bishops to have free correspondence with the Pope; appeal to Rome is open to everyone. (x) The bishops may prevent

VIII. LOMBARDO-VENETIA

The Austrian provinces in Italy—then known as the Kingdom of Lombardo-Venetia—presented a rather curious condition; the civil authorities were all servants of the Austrian
Emperor, whereas the ecclesiastical authorities were all
responsible to the Pope. In Lombardy there was an arch-
bishopric (Milan) and seven bishoprics, Bergamo, Brescia,
Como, Cremona, Lodi, Mantua and Pavia; and in Venetia
several others. Thus when Pius, a year later, came to be
regarded as the leader of Italy against Austria, it seemed to
the Italians that in the Church they had a splendid piece of
national organisation within the enemy's camp. This was one
of the reasons why they urged Pius to proclaim a holy war
against Austria, to launch his excommunication and arouse
the clergy and peasants in every parish against the foreigner.
They felt that he alone could carry the whole population with
him in a war of freedom. But Pius knew that the Church was
an international institution and that to hurl it into a national
rebellion would be a crime.

For the smaller states—Tuscany, Parma, Modena—we
need not give details. Their rulers were all anxious to have a
Conservative Pope.

It will be seen that all the governments in Italy were good
friends of the Church. From the purely ecclesiastical point
of view, therefore, it was undesirable to initiate changes in
Italy, unless forced to do so by the Revolution.

But at the same time the existing conditions were wrong—
wrong politically: it was right before God and man that the
people should have more liberty and that the Austrian domination should cease. Yet the *status quo* could not be altered
without danger to the thrones and to the Church.

the printing and distribution of books contrary to sacred teaching.
(xi) The king shall choose the bishops; the Pope shall approve and
instal them. (xii) The bishops shall swear obedience to the king;
also not to take part in any association that might disturb the peace,
and on receiving information of any such movement shall reveal it
to the king.

It is surely to the glory of Pius that he broke through this ring, and by his reforms initiated the last phase in the making of Italy. Only two years later the Papal State, with Piedmont and Tuscany which had followed its example, were known as the three reforming states; and their movement was certainly the beginning of wisdom. But, for Pius, to whose sense of right the movement was due, it was the beginning of thirty years of sorrow, culminating at last in the destruction of the Temporal Power.

What an immense work lay before Pius IX and his Secretary of State and his foreign Nuncios at the various courts. Already the vast crisis was near at hand. Everywhere the two great principles of Conservatism and Progress were at war with one another and the decisions of the Church would bear a deep influence on the millions who believed in its guidance. With all these rulers and peoples it was his task to carry on negotiations; and not only with the countries above-named but with many others all over the world: with the Ottoman Empire for instance: with the new nations lately freed by Bolivar and other patriots in South America, concerning some of which Pius himself was considered to have special knowledge, because he had been there:[32] and with countless others. He was king only in virtue of being Pope. Yet this gigantic responsibility and its influence on his policy is seldom considered by those who write the history of the making of Italy.

[32] Pius had visited South America in his younger days on a diplomatic mission; he is the only Pope, I believe, who has ever been there.

Chapter III

THE AMNESTY

We may now return to the side of the newly elected Pope, and note his first impulse in the use of power. Perhaps the following quotation from the work of the great historian Tivaroni, a republican, will give some idea of the importance of the moment.[1]

"What would have happened", asks Tivaroni, "if Cardinal Lambruschini had been elected? Probably there would soon have been a rising in Romagna. Austria and France would have intervened as in 1831; Charles Albert would not have moved. The history of Italy would have been changed. One man is sometimes enough to alter the destinies of a people.

"It is believed that Cardinal Gaysrück,[2] who arrived the day

[1] Tivaroni, *Domin. Austr.* ii, 264.

[2] As to Cardinal Gaisruck, Italian writers believe that Metternich intended to veto Mastai's election, but his printed memoirs certainly give quite the opposite impression. Metternich, *Mémoires*, vii, 225–6. According to Monti he knew little about Mastai, and it was Gizzi whom he intended to veto, or any other neo-Guelf cardinal (Monti, p. 59).

In the Viennese Archives there is a despatch from Lützow to Metternich which throws a little light on the subject—Lützow asks whether he is to be accredited to the cardinals and to address them; and if so, "s'il serait utile que je fasse mention ou non dans mon discours au Conclave, du Secret, ainsi que je l'avais fait en 1829 et 1831; ou bien que je parle à cet égard avec franchise et en faisant connaître que ce que l'Autriche veut, doit être le but de la tâche du S. Collège, et ne saurait que correspondre au vœu général de la Catholicité entière. Pour donner à Votre Altesse une idée de la préoccupation des esprits et de la fertilité de l'imagination de ceux qui font et défont les Papes dans ces jours, il vous suffira, Mon Prince, d'apprendre que selon les mêmes nouvellistes—souvent des agens [sic] très subalternes de quelque électeur—le Cardinal Altieri serait le dépositaire du Secret de l'Autriche avec ordre de donner l'exclusion au Cardinal Gizzi:—l'un des plus dignes et des plus prudens du S. Collège." Vienna Staats-Archiv, 1846, Fasc. 73, Rome, June 10th. Evidently Lützow did not think that Metternich meant to exclude Gizzi.

after the election, brought with him the esclusiva (Austrian veto) against Mastai. Even 24 hours can sometimes have great weight on the life of the world."

As Pius IX was now elected, people began to enquire who he was; and were told that he was regarded as a good man.

During his first two or three weeks, though very busy with state functions, he began, almost accidentally as it were, to make progress with his people.[3] He had given generously to the poor, and they were grateful, although they knew of course that this was more or less customary for a newly elected Pope. It was universally agreed that he had a kindly and charming manner, and, before long, stories of his Liberal sympathies and of his previous acts of benevolence and even of his gentle witticisms[4] began to reach Rome from the provinces; then it became known that he had set apart one day in the week for audiences, and this was regarded as a welcome change from the custom of Gregory XVI, who had been almost inaccessible to his subjects. But one small episode seems to have won popular sympathy more fully than all the others: on July 2nd, the feast of the Visitation, he was seen walking almost unaccompanied to the Church of the Umiltà. This gave immense pleasure.[5] The populace was accustomed to rulers who never moved about except in a carriage surrounded by an armed guard: here, they felt, was

[3] *London Corr.* Pt. I, p. 23—Petre to Hamilton.

[4] Cf. the following extract from a letter of Charles Albert: "J'ai appris deux anecdotes qui vous intéresseront. L'une...L'autre, qu'on fit rapport au Pape que l'on avait trouvé dans les rues des cocardes tricolores, et qu'il repondit que c'était bon signe: parceque ceux qui les avaient les avaient jetées. Ne trouvez-vous point que c'est fort spirituel?" The point of this story is that the police had strewn tricolour revolutionary cockades on the ground in order to frighten Pius away from his Liberal programme; but he merely said that it was a good sign if the people who possessed them were now throwing them away. Quoted by Gualterio (1862 ed.), vol. v, Appendix, Doc. IV.

[5] *Diario di Roma*, July 4th—quoted by Spada.

a man who trusted them; and on his return journey they thronged out into the streets to greet him.

Meanwhile he had appointed a Provisional Council for consultative purposes, consisting of Cardinals Macchi, Lambruschini, Mattei, Amat, Gizzi and Bernetti, with Monsignor Corboli-Bussi as secretary—thus including in it both of his former competitors for the Papal throne, Cardinals Lambruschini and Gizzi. This council is a good example of what was by far the most insidious difficulty during his first year, namely that his personnel belonged almost entirely to the old school of Gregory XVI and hated the very idea of change or reform. Its composition aroused hostile criticism because only three of its members were considered "to inspire popular confidence". Cardinals Gizzi and Amat were Liberals, and so was the secretary, Monsignor Corboli-Bussi, a young and delicate enthusiast of good family,[6] the son of a rebel of 1831; but the other four members were cardinals of the Gregorian days. Yet these were the advisers with whom Pius was obliged to work at the great project which he designed to be the first and the most truly characteristic of his reign; in fact one might almost say, the rock upon which he would build his Church.

[6] "Of slender build and pale face, with a sustained and gentle gaze, he bore signs of the illness which brought him to the grave. His nature was candid and kindly...and as it was known that he had drawn up the proclamation for the Amnesty, he enjoyed popular favour" (Minghetti, I, 218). Born September 24th, 1813, at Urbino; died July 30th, 1850, at Rome. Of good family and position. September 1840, became a priest. 1841, appointed Consultore to the bishops and regular clergy. Consultore of Propaganda; (June 16th) Secretary of Ecclesiastical affairs; (August) Secretary of Society for Orphans caused by the cholera. 1842, refused to be Nuncio in Belgium and in Naples. 1845, Secretary of the Concistoriale. 1846, acting Secretary of State. 1847, Secretary of Eccles. affaires extraordinaires (cf. Gori, p. 131).

I. THE GRANTING OF THE AMNESTY

It has been observed by one of the most recent Italian historians[7] that the first authoritative command given by Pius IX is expressed in the word Forgiveness, and that it was from this word that arose all his subsequent troubles.

This is true. His first act as Pope was to proclaim a general Amnesty for all political prisoners throughout the Papal State, and to this edict was due both his greatness and his fall. He did it of his own determination; in fact it took him nearly a month to get the scheme through the Provisional Council because the Conservative members, though willing to agree to an amnesty, were afraid of passing a wide and generous measure.[8] They feared—and Count Lützow, the Austrian ambassador, also feared—that it would bring back hundreds of veteran revolutionists and perhaps result in the setting up of Carbonari "vendite" even within the walls of Rome. As a result of this disagreement certain limitations were introduced, but nevertheless it was felt that on all essential points Pius had accepted the advice of his three Liberal councillors. He was thought also to have listened to that of his lifelong friend the Abate Graziosi,[9] a quiet and modest old man who had been Pius' instructor in philosophy and theology some thirty years before, and was now appointed to be his private secretary.

The Amnesty[10] began by a preamble in which it said that during those days of rejoicing "it had been impossible for Us not to grieve at the thought that many families were prevented from sharing in the common joy"; and that the young people

---

[7] Masi.

[8] Paris Aff. Etr., Rome, 1847–48 (Rossi); Vienna, Staats-Archiv, Rome, 69 (Lützow). *V.* also Gualterio; Farini, I, 159, and other contemporaries.

[9] Gori, p. 130; Pelczar, I, 31, and others.

[10] *Atti*, 1846. The *Atti* were Pius' secular Acts, decrees, notifications, etc. The *Acta* were those of ecclesiastical nature. There are collections of the *Atti* in the Vatican Archives, in the *Civiltà Cattolica* and elsewhere.

had erred, through being misled rather than through sinning. Therefore "from that moment We proposed to extend our hand and offer peace, from our heart, to all those misguided sons who were ready to show a sincere repentance". Then followed the actual terms of the pardon, which were wider than those granted on previous occasions.

I. A general Amnesty was proclaimed for every prisoner willing to make a solemn declaration in writing, on his honour, in no way and at no time to abuse this forgiveness, but on the contrary to fulfil faithfully every duty of a good subject.

II. The Amnesty was to apply to all exiles who within a year made known their desire to return.

III. Arrangements were made for the rehabilitation of all those under police surveillance or disqualified from municipal office.

IV. A few names were excluded; their case was to be considered later.

V. Some exceptions were made: political prisoners against whom ordinary crimes were alleged.

This Amnesty covered almost every possible case, and spread immense happiness throughout the whole state.[11] About a thousand political prisoners were released under it— nearly all natives of the provinces—many of whom had been sentenced for life. True, it did not come entirely as a surprise: some act of clemency had been expected; but what gave especial pleasure was the tone in which it was expressed, the evident kindliness of the preamble, and the fact that Pius actually contented himself with accepting each man's word of honour at a time when political prisoners—men ready to die for their ideals—were usually treated merely as common criminals.[12] The terms of the oath were perhaps a little

[11] *V. La Pallade* (July 18th and 22nd) and other papers.
[12] The words were: "I promise on my word of honour that I will never at any time or in any way abuse such act of sovereign clemency but will faithfully fulfil every duty of a good subject." Vatican Arch., Fondo Spada, Documenti storici, 1846, No. 12.

exacting, but its wording was attributed to the Conservative councillors, and the prisoners made no difficulty about signing it. One Bolognese, indeed, a well-known lawyer named Galetti, who was serving a life sentence in Castel Sant' Angelo, was so grateful for his release that after being set free he went to thank the Pope personally, and published in the press a declaration of his gratitude and devotion. From Paris and other foreign places there soon came flocks of exiles, some of whom, like Count Terenzio Mamiani, had been lost to their homes and their families ever since the rebellion of 1831.[13]

On July 17th, 1846, at 7 p.m., the proclamation was first posted up throughout Rome for the people to see. It was a warm summer evening, so the streets were crowded, and many people were listening to a band in the Piazza della Maddalena, when suddenly the good news began to fly from mouth to mouth. It was received with an absolute transport of enthusiasm. A rush was made for the notices, and every copy of the edict became the centre of a crowd. Never probably had the old Aurelian walls seen such joy within their circle. The descriptions of eyewitnesses leave one quite astonished. "When the news of the pardon was spread in Rome and the kindly words were read, it seemed as if there had suddenly descended on the town a ray of divine love", says Farini; and Spada tells us how citizens embraced one another as brothers, and "some were so much intoxicated with joy that without exaggeration it bordered on delirium". Count Gualterio, also a contemporary writer, speaks of "such joy as had never before been seen".[14]

Everywhere the people broke out into shouts of "Viva Pio

[13] Mamiani remained in Paris for some months to come, and refused to take the oath required; but he wrote so touching a letter of gratitude to Pius that he was allowed to return without actually binding himself.

[14] Farini, I, 163; Spada, I, 55; Gualterio (1851 ed.), I, *Le Riforme*, Pt. II, p. 63, and many other books, newspapers and pamphlets.

Nono", that cry which soon was to awaken the Italian nation and indeed to arouse the sympathy of the whole world.

Later in the evening the news went around that a set of young men with torches had made their way up on to the Piazza del Quirinale, the square in front of the Quirinal palace, and that the Holy Father had blessed them from the loggia above the gate. Instantly, although the hour was about midnight, an immense concourse set out, together with the band whom they forced to accompany them, and surged up on to the piazza in front of the statue of the horse-tamers, calling aloud for His Holiness; and when he appeared on the balcony, they threw themselves on their knees and received his blessing in profound silence. Soon afterwards they were succeeded by an even greater crowd, estimated at about thirty thousand people, and, for the third time that night Pius bestowed his blessing. It was one of those scenes of genuine gratitude and goodwill which show human nature at its best. Many of the people were moved to tears.[15]

The enthusiasm of these kneeling thousands was not due merely to a momentary outburst of excitement. On the following day the only topic of conversation in the houses, in the squares, in the streets and in the places of public resort was the solemn demonstration of the previous evening, and there was a general determination "to immortalise the memory of July 17th, 1846". On the 18th and 19th there

[15] Pellegrino Rossi, the French ambassador, tells us that he himself shared the emotion; a profoundly tragic statement when one remembers that in that same piazza only two years later the Roman crowds were to howl blessings on the hand that had stabbed him. His description runs as follows: "Bientôt en effet le balcon s'est ouvert et le Saint Père en robe blanche et mantelet rouge apparut au milieu des flambeaux. Que Votre Excellence se répresente une place magnifique, une nuit d'été, le ciel de Rome, un peuple immense ému de reconnaissance, pleurant de joie, et recevant avec amour et respect la bénédiction de son pasteur et de son prince, et elle ne sera pas étonnée si j'ajoute que nous avons tous partagé l'émotion générale et placé ce spectacle au-dessus de tout ce que Rome nous avait offert jusqu'ici." Paris Aff. Etr., Rome, 1845–46.

were illuminations. Nor were the rejoicings confined to Rome; a great wave of enthusiasm swept over the whole state. Even Bologna and the rebel towns of the north were half mad with joy; they wreathed the edict with flowers, and they organised feasts and torchlight processions in which there appeared in letters of fire the motto "Nova incipit aetas". It seemed as if by one single act Pius had won back Romagna. And from the Roman state the wave of rejoicing spread into Tuscany and Piedmont and far and wide throughout Italy.[16]

On the 19th,[17] Pius had arranged to drive to the church of the Missione at Monte Citorio, to celebrate the feast of St Vincent de Paul, and he started very early so as to avoid some of the demonstration. But the crowd had been in the streets since sunrise. The houses were all decorated with rich tapestries, the balconies and windows were full of people and the ladies were throwing flowers as he passed: his whole progress was a procession between flags and vivas. And on his return journey a hundred youths of good Roman families insisted, in spite of his unwillingness, on taking out his horses and on themselves dragging him back to the Quirinal in triumph.[18] There the thousands of people around him knelt and received his blessing. Pius was profoundly affected by these expressions of gratitude; and he issued a notification thanking the people in affectionate terms: at the same time, however, he gently suggested their now suspending the demonstrations.[19]

Similar scenes continued for some time to come, while the

---

[16] The *Felsineo*, July 24th: it was the principal Bolognese newspaper. *V.* also *London Corr.* 1, 24 (Consul Moore). Naples was the only state in which the enthusiasm for Pius made little progress at first; the authorities succeeded in keeping it out for about eight or nine months.

[17] *La Pallade*; Spada, 1, 56; and other authorities.

[18] Besides the Italian authorities *v.* Vienna Staats-Archiv, Rome, 69; and Paris Aff. Etr., Rome, 1846.

[19] Vatican Arch., Fondo Spada, 1846.

Romans were preparing for their great celebration of September 8th.

Thus on June 17th, the day when he was first proclaimed Pope, the name of Cardinal Mastai Ferretti had been received in dead silence by a people which knew nothing of him and had little enthusiasm left for the Papacy. But on July 17th, only one month later, he, His Holiness Pope Pius IX, had risen to heights of popularity probably unequalled in Papal history.

One may well ask why this was so; why his simple act of pardon should have gone straight to the heart of his people.

The truth was that it was not merely an act of pardon, and that it was not regarded by the people only in that light; the actual freeing of the prisoners would not have affected the Romans so deeply, because the men released nearly all came from the provinces.[20] But it was regarded by them as a great

[20] With two exceptions, the prisoners were all provincials. Rome had always remained loyal. Zellide Fattiboni, the daughter of an old Carbonaro in Cesena, gives the following account of the feeling there: "The day after the proclamation of the Amnesty...bands were playing and the air echoed with thousands of Evviva for Pius IX. No sovereign has ever been more cordially acclaimed. One wanted to invent new words in order to magnify this magnanimous act which had given peace to his peoples. The political prisoners were returning to their homes, those who had been condemned long ago were coming back, and so were those still under trial, and those who had remained lost in foreign countries, exiles since 1831. To see them again was a joy, an unspeakable, supreme emotion!" (Fattiboni, II, 63).

A year later Pellegrino Rossi wrote to Guizot that Pius' exaltation had aroused a two-fold expectation: firstly, would he be a reformer within his own state; secondly, would he stand for Italy against Austria?

"The election of Mastai was greeted as a victory because he was known to be the candidate of those Cardinals who were most strongly opposed to Lambruschini, and to the Gregorian, Austrian and Jesuit party: in the popular opinion all these were synonymous.

"It was a serious moment. Pius IX replied to this double expectation by a solemn and decisive act, the General Amnesty." Paris Aff. Etr., Rome, 1847–48.

revulsion of feeling, a complete change in the outlook of the Holy See: at last they had a Pope who would stand for the people and for the national cause. And to them—especially to many thousands who were sincerely religious—this feeling brought unimaginable joy.

It must have seemed to some of them as if the chief anti-national stronghold of their opponents—the state guaranteed forever by the five Powers and the whole Catholic world—had suddenly hoisted their own tricolour. The great difficulty in the path of Liberalism had been the princes; the great difficulty in the plans of the nationalists had been the Pope. But now they had a Liberal prince and, so they hoped, a nationalist Pope; and his immeasurable influence throughout Italy would compel the other rulers to follow in his train. This might well be the first step towards achieving a great *débâcle* of their opponents. They did not realise in the least how fatally a Pontiff was tied by his duty as high priest of a world-religion. They saw in him only the good Italian patriot whom they wanted. In some places the cry had already gone up "Viva Pio IX, re d' Italia! Morte ai Tedeschi", "Long live Pius IX, King of Italy! Death to the Germans!"[21] The dream of Gioberti, they thought, was about to come true; a patriot Pope might be turned into a patriot king.

To some extent they were right. It was, already, a great moral victory for them. It gave a kind of sanction to Liberalism, especially among the always timorous "respectable" people. They said to themselves: If the Pope can be a Liberal, anyone can be a Liberal.[22] And, indeed, it was soon to become the deciding influence with King Charles Albert and his Piedmontese army; without Pius' action in 1846 Charles Albert would never have moved in 1848.

[21] Gori, p. 134.
[22] "The Liberal and national party, without seeming too bold, can raise its eyes even to the Pontifical throne and find there, if not a leader properly so-called, at all events an indulgent judge and a kindly adviser." Pellegrino Rossi, Paris Aff. Etr., July 28th, 1847—on the results of the Amnesty.

II. RECEPTION THROUGHOUT ITALY

Throughout all the other Italian states except Naples Pius'
movement was felt at once as a new influence, and as one
with national tendencies.[23] In Tuscany, for instance, the
kindly old Grand Duke Leopold II viewed its advent with a
good deal of uneasiness. Before many weeks were past several
hundreds of the poorer Amnistiati (amnestied men) came
flocking through his country to return to their home in the
Papal State, and a *national* subscription was raised for them
by Professor Montanelli: Liberals were collecting for it in
Tuscany, Piedmont, Genoa, Lucca and elsewhere, and demonstrations were being held in Pius' honour. In September
Leopold decided to establish a Tuscan embassy in Rome, for
hitherto Tuscany had been represented only by Austrian
diplomats in Rome and elsewhere. What a striking proof does
this afford of her subserviency to Metternich!

In Piedmont[24] Charles Albert had received the Amnesty
with joy. Henceforth he was no longer alone in his ideas:
the Church herself was shedding the light of her approval
upon them. From the first he seems to have been anxious to
help and develop the Liberal movement in Rome.

On July 25th he wrote to Villamarina: "A war of national
independence which united us all in defence of the Pope
would be for me a piece of great good fortune." And in
August when he heard of Gizzi's appointment, he wrote:
"Blessed be Pius IX; this means that he is undertaking war
against Austria." But, to his annoyance, his old Conservative
minister Solaro della Margherita decided to go to Rome to
see for himself how matters stood. Through him Charles
Albert sent a letter to Pius in which he said:[25] "I beg you to
believe that in any circumstances that may arise Your Holiness

---

[23] For all this paragraph *v*. Montanelli, I, 179, 182–3; Spada, I,
79; Orsini, p. 57; Balbo, *Sommario*, p. 435. Besides these contemporaries *v*. the general historians, Raulich, III, 85; Gori, p. 146;
Masi, *Risorgimento*, II, 122; and others.

[24] Gualterio (1862 ed.), V, 15 (numbered in error p. 343).

[25] *Civiltà Cattolica* for 1879, p. 264.

will find in me an unshakable attachment and I shall be happy to give proof of it with my blood."

Della Margherita,[26] however, made his own enquiries among old friends of the Gregorian type, "various cardinals of the Diplomatic Corps", and found them all of one opinion, namely that "the Revolution is no longer a thing of the future but is already accomplished".

They were not entirely wrong. Already Pius' Amnesty and the measures which followed it had started a wave of enthusiastic Liberalism throughout Italy. On September 9th at the Agrarian Congress of Mortara, in Piedmont, the patriotic enthusiasm for Charles Albert was, for the first time, coupled with joyful references to the Pope.

Only five days later, from September 14th to 19th, there assembled in Genoa the Scientific Congress of all Italy, the eighth of these annual congresses, each held in a different city. This was a great historic meeting.[27] It might almost be called a national assemblage. A thousand members were present, delegates from every state, including Lombardo-Venetia; and for the first time, by Pius' permission, the Papal State was among those represented. The presence of the pontifical delegates headed by Prince Canino, a nephew of Napoleon, was regarded as a victory and "as evidence that the new times had already begun". They were questioned with avidity, "to make certain of the truth of this unexpected phenomenon, namely that the banner of freedom was waving above what was usually regarded as the strongest trench of despotism". In the debates, and more especially in the private conversations, every side of the Italian question was discussed and new friendships were made. The two principal themes were Charles Albert's resistance to Austria over the salt question and wine duties, and the splendid Amnesty granted by the new Pope, Pius IX.[28]

[26] Della Margherita, *Memorandum*, p. 381.
[27] Gualterio (1862 ed.), v, 111; Farini, i, 173; Minghetti, *Ricordi*, i, 202–5; Rina Ferrari, p. 19. [28] Gualterio (1862 ed.), v, 114.

Gualterio makes rather a pertinent observation in connection with this congress. He says that henceforward Rome became the centre of the national movement rather than Piedmont, and he regards that as having been a mistake.

III. RECEPTION IN AUSTRIA

But the question remained to be answered: How would the news of the Pope's movement be received by the world-powers? Firstly, would the diplomats of the Holy Alliance combine to arrest it? Secondly, how would it be received by Mazzini's revolutionists and by the more violent section of the Moderates? Those were the two great principles between which the work of Pius was destined in the end to be crushed as in a vice: on the one side Conservatism represented abroad by Austria and in Rome by the old Gregorian party: on the other side the Revolution and the Agitators.

Prince Metternich was now a veteran in his seventy-fifth year, whose old age could find little repose. He was troubled by the discontents and risings in Poland, Hungary and Bohemia, as also by the Sonderbund question in Switzerland; of recent years, too, he had been living in a state of considerable resentment at the advance of Liberalism in Italy, especially in Piedmont. On all sides the foundations of his life's work were being undermined; and finally, as a serious, though not unexpected blow, there came the death of his best ally, Pope Gregory XVI.

On receipt[29] of the news he had written a most sincere letter of grief, assuring the cardinals of his support and offering troops if necessary; also sending a special message to Lambruschini, his former protégé,[30] who seemed almost certain to be the next occupant of the Papal throne. And on June 5th an Austrian frigate appeared before the port of Ancona.

[29] Metternich to Lützow, June 9th, 1846.
[30] *London Corr.* I, I.

On Pius' election, however, Metternich wrote a most courteous and complimentary letter[31] of congratulation on "the good news", rejoicing for several pages over "this most striking proof of the wisdom of the cardinals", and again offering his support to the pontifical government. In his next despatch[32] he sent a long paper concerning four main projects which Pius had named to the Austrian ambassador, Count Lützow, and tendering his advice on each of them. Concerning the first of them, namely the construction of railways, he had already expressed his views. The other three were the following:

(*a*) The form of government. On this he wrote two pages recommending a Council of State consisting of heads of departments: in fact a bureaucracy! No doubt this advice would have been accepted if Lambruschini had been elected Pope.

(*b*) The Amnesty. For the name Amnesty he preferred to substitute the name Pardon, so as to remind the released prisoners that they had been guilty. "The power of the sovereign is only an emanation of the divine power, and clemency in the sovereign is only an emanation of the divine goodness and mercy. God does not grant amnesties."

(*c*) Concessions. These he opposes. They cannot be recalled. For a sovereign, concessions are tantamount to spending his capital, in which he has in reality only a life-interest.

The Amnesty evidently did not meet with his approval. On August 6th he wrote to Count Buol at Turin:

Will this act of kindness bring peace to the State of the Church? I dare not hope so. With a few exceptions the men pardoned will be the incorrigible promoters of the movement whose aim it is to overthrow all order legally existing.

As usual, Metternich was right. Instant advantage was

[31] Metternich to Lützow, June 28th, 1846.
[32] Metternich to Lützow, July 12th, 1846.

taken of the Amnesty, even by Mazzini, to re-establish his agents within the Papal State.[33]

Metternich had good reason to be anxious. His empire was a giant but its feet were of clay; already the rising of the Poles had demonstrated that fact to the world:[34] and now—though no one could foresee it—through one simple act of kindness, Pius had definitely started the movement which, by the swords of Charles Albert and Victor Emmanuel, was destined to culminate in the freedom of Italy. For Austria this was the beginning of the end.

IV. RECEPTION IN FRANCE AND ENGLAND

There remained the Liberal powers, France and England.

During these early days there was one ambassador, at all events, who had spoken out well in favour of the Amnesty, namely Count Pellegrino Rossi, representing the government of France. Beneath all his honours he remained devoted to his native land; he and Pius would often discuss its affairs together, in their own Italian tongue; and consequently he soon became the *bête noire* of Metternich.[35]

[33] Mazzini, E.N. xxx, 94, 98, 106, etc. This is a point on which Mazzini does not come out very well. He said that he himself would never have accepted the oath of allegiance to Pius which accompanied the Amnesty: but when his followers accepted the oath he took advantage of their doing so to re-establish them as his agents in the Papal State. At the same time, in the *Edinburgh Review* he had an article condemning the Amnesty because "we fear there will be too many examples—it is offering a premium to perjury: it is substituting—and this is the custom of the Roman Church in everything—the dead letter for the life". Mazzini, E.N. xxxiv, 256.

[34] Metternich himself said that the scheme of revolution had been organised on a vast scale; that the rising in Poland had been intended to keep Austria, Russia and Prussia occupied internally, while Italy rose in rebellion. Metternich, *Mémoires*, vii, 227. Letter to Count Buol at Turin, May 29th, 1846.

[35] In a letter dated August 6th, 1846, Metternich refers to Rossi's appointment as being one of the principal causes of revolution. In one of October 7th, 1847, he says: "One cause of the eminently dangerous situation in which the State of the Church is placed, lies

Before the election Guizot had written to Rossi that his ideal Pope would be[36] one who would remember to live on harmonious terms with the other sovereigns, but was independent in character and devoted to the independence of the Italian states. No doubt Guizot meant one who would start Liberal reforms and would not allow Austria to intervene. Consequently he received the Amnesty with genuine satisfaction. But although Guizot favoured the independence of the small states—especially from Austria—he said nothing about the unification of Italy. That was quite another matter.

Pellegrino Rossi, however, was delighted with the kindliness of Pius' greeting. At his first official reception the room was crowded, but the Pope himself asked that way should be made for the French ambassador to approach him: at their first private audience Rossi addressed him in French, but Pius replied in Italian.[37] This was a compliment, because Pius could speak French fluently—and indeed Spanish as well—although "not like one who thinks in that language". This official audience took the form of an interview in Italian during which Pius spoke to Rossi of the great problems before him; of the "fearful" mission that God had imposed on him, and of the fact that "he was passing suddenly from private life to so high and difficult a position, and that he must, of

in the selection of M. Rossi as French representative at Rome. During all his embassy this former chief of the Carbonari has stirred the masses, caressed his former brothers and friends and exalted the hopes of the faction." Metternich, *Mémoires*, VII, 342.

Rossi had also his enemies among the Italians. The Jesuits naturally did not like him as he had been instrumental in dissolving (nominally at all events) their organisation in France: the cardinals could not forget that he was an ex-revolutionist, an exile, a Liberal and a freethinker. It was against the wishes of Cardinal Lambruschini that he had been appointed ambassador; the Papal Secretary of State objected to Rossi's having a Protestant wife. Guizot, VII, 456; and Lützow's despatch.

[36] Paris Aff. Etr., Rome, June 8th, 1846.
[37] Paris Aff. Etr. (Rossi), July 18th, 1846.

necessity, be allowed time to obtain some knowledge of public business".

In this way Pellegrino Rossi became Pius' friend and for the better part of two years to come was one of his ablest advisers.[38] His despatches to Guizot give us perhaps the best picture that exists of Pius during this early period. At times the experienced lawyer and diplomat, whom success had made a little didactic, seems to have looked on the Pope almost as he might on a younger brother.[39] He realised the immense difficulties of the task which Pius, with no political experience, was undertaking, in trying to reconcile two almost irreconcilable lines of development. He sympathised with his efforts and took pleasure in his successes. After the Amnesty he wrote to Guizot: "Peace is now signed...between the Holy See and the populations of its states. Yesterday I said to a Cardinal with perfect sincerity, 'To-day I know of only one person who could make the whole of this country rise like one man: it is Pius IX.'" A wonderful change; only a month had passed since the days of Gregory XVI!

Of the Protestant powers Great Britain was by far the most important. Fortunately at this moment the Whigs were just coming into office under Lord Lansdowne, and their opinion as expressed by Palmerston (Foreign Office) was fairly definite and outspoken during this first year of Pius IX's pontificate.[40] It can be stated under three headings: England was a strong

[38] Paris Aff. Etr. (Rossi), July 27th, 1846, and following despatches.

[39] Later on, for instance, he wrote about Pius and Corboli-Bussi: "Although the Pope has been compelled to remove him (Corboli-Bussi) from the office of the Secretary of State he is very fond of him. These are two natures which suit each other, two spirits which, under forms that I might almost call soft and flexible, have more firmness and perseverance in their ideas than is generally supposed." Evidently Rossi became greatly attached to Pius: after a year's knowledge of him he wrote to Guizot: "As Pope, or not as Pope, he never abandons a friend." Despatch of July 28th, 1847, Paris Aff. Etr. 1846–47.

[40] *London Corr.* I, 80 (Palmerston, August 12th, 1847) and also p. 115.

supporter of Liberal reforms within each Italian state; she was an equally strong supporter of the Treaty of 1815, and consequently would do nothing to help on Italian unity; thirdly, though not hostile to Austria, she gradually became an opponent of Metternich's aggressions and, diplomatically, a defender of Charles Albert and the Pope.

For the time being, therefore, she received the news of Pius' election with genuine approval.[41] Palmerston suggested to the French ambassador that they should give their joint support to the Amnesty and to a policy of reform embodying the Memorandum of 1831.

The British government had no ambassador with the Holy See; but it had a representative in Rome, Mr Petre, and a consul, Mr Freeborn. In all the other Italian states there were ministers, and their despatches, duly collected and published under the name *Correspondence respecting the affairs of Italy*, form perhaps the most valuable source of all on this period.

The Amnesty, we fear, has been dealt with at rather considerable length, but this was necessary because it marks a turning-point in modern Italian history. It inaugurated a new phase in the Risorgimento. For the next two years Pius IX was considered the leader of Italy.[42] It was not until Pied-

[41] *Ibid.* Despatch to Cowley, July 21st, 1846.

[42] It may seem unnecessary to lay so much stress upon the wave of enthusiasm for Pius. But the truth is that one feels how very few people realise—and it is impossible to do so, until after wading through seven or eight thousand newspapers and documents of the period—that during these first two years before the first war of independence, the name of Pius IX became a power and a rallying cry all over Italy, never equalled by any other name except that of Garibaldi in 1860. The sentiment is often similar. In 1860, for instance, whenever one reads in a Pontifical newspaper or police report of even a small disturbance crushed by the Gendarmes, one usually hears that the rebels were shouting "Viva Garibaldi!" Similarly in 1847 and the beginning of 1848, whenever the crowds attacked

mont declared war in 1848 that the hegemony passed definitely
to Charles Albert.

It was a dramatic situation. Pius had led his people into a
movement which placed them on the way of ultimate triumph,
but which, inevitably, would result in his own downfall; for
the temporal power of the Popes would not continue to exist
in a united Italy. It is hard to say how far Pius foresaw this
danger. He certainly hoped to save the temporal power, but
he must have known that he was risking many of the great
and sacred interests entrusted to him. Nevertheless he was
manifestly right in taking such a risk. And in the course of
time, such right actions bring their reward. The merely
temporal power of the Popes has gone; but owing to Pius'
action there remains to the Holy See, in the record of those
critical years, the undying honour of having sought the way
of justice.

But no foreign writer can deal with the subject half so
vividly as an Italian historian. It is best therefore to close the
chapter with a translation from Masi's work, *Nell' Ottocento*,
which contains the most accurate and at the same time the
most powerful pages that have been written on the
subject.

By good fortune he (Pius) had the help of two advisers who
recalled to his mind the inspirations and counsels of the Pasolini:
namely Canon Graziosi and Monsignor Corboli-Bussi: the first-
named a learned and enlightened priest; the second of such ardent
disposition that, according to Minghetti, he would nowadays be
called a Catholic Socialist. It was they who (next to the Pasolini)
were the inspirers of the Amnesty of July 16th, 1846, which made
the *Bishop of Imola* the beginner, in order of facts, of the Italian
political risorgimento; and it was Monsignor Corboli-Bussi, moreover, who drafted the great act in whose magnificently rounded
Giobertian sentences a pardon was extended to all political
prisoners. At that moment who could trouble about any of the

the Austrian or loyalist soldiers anywhere in Italy, they did so with
shouts of "Viva Pio Nono" and singing Pius' hymn. These acts of
violence caused some distress to Pius.

restrictions or safeguards or even threats in the decree? One single word of kindness and pardon, sent down from that throne which had so often issued anathemas or condemnations, had sufficed to fire in one instant the whole of the inflammable material that had been accumulating for years. That immense concourse of people collected from every corner of Rome and guided by Ciceruacchio ...that immense concourse of people, I repeat, which comes up each evening to greet and thank Pius IX on the Quirinal, is in reality the advance-guard of Italy,[43] and of the world; for the word of Pius IX spreads abroad, rapid and clear as a flash of lightning and moves Italy, and the whole world; just as though it had in itself the miraculous power of redressing all wrongs, of avenging all injustice, of pacifying all hates and of healing all human sorrow; of casting the mighty into the shade for ever and of raising the oppressed.

There are few such hours in history; perhaps none entirely equal to it. And if it was, in reality, an immense, universal and almost inexplicable illusion—well, so let it be!...

From that moment until the day when Pius, standing on the balcony of the Quirinal, raised his arms to heaven, while a ray of sunlight fell upon his forehead and the crowd prostrated itself before him weeping, and called aloud in his sonorous voice, "Benedite, gran Dio, l' Italia"; until that day, the delirium aroused by the Amnesty grows, expands, rises and finally overwhelms like a whirling wave, everything and everyone, including the Pope himself....

But meanwhile, Viva Pio IX! Long live Pius IX, will be for a time the cry which in Italy and throughout the world represents every shade of meaning; the watchword of every revolt and of every movement in the country. To its sound Palermo will rise against the Bourbons; Naples and Calabria will go through their terrible agitation; and Milan and Venice will drive out the Austrians. It will be heard on the barricades in Paris; it will echo in the valleys and mountains of free Switzerland against the League of the Sonderbund; it will resound in the ears of Metternich as he flies before the revolution in Vienna. With this shout on their lips the soldiers of Charles Albert will cross the Ticino, and the volunteers of central Italy will cross the River Po to fight in the first holy war of Italian independence. For some of them the cry will mean liberty, for others it will mean the conciliation of their reason with their belief, and for yet others it will mean the universal

[43] The Italy that was yet to be made.

brotherhood; but to all of them it will speak of their native land and their national resurrection. At that moment the country was emerging from darkness. Viva Pio IX! was the cry of the future. But of what future? No one could tell—least of all Pius himself![44]

NOTE ON THE AUTHORITIES FOR CHAPTER III, THE AMNESTY

There is some difficulty in selecting authorities for the period of the amnesty because it is described by almost every writer on the Risorgimento, and there are no important points of difference between them.

The diplomatic despatches of all the ambassadors contain interesting accounts or references relating to it; especially those of France, Austria and England.

Of documents the best collection is the Fondo Spada in the Vatican Archives. Spada, of course, was a Papal writer; but in this collection there are many contemporary pamphlets and documents of all sorts.

For contemporary books:

On the Papal side one has
    Spada, Cantù, Ballerini (1867);

On the revolutionary side
    Mazzini's writings, La Farina, Gabussi, Aurelio Saffi and Zellide Fattiboni;

On the Moderate side
    Farini, Gualterio, Pasolini, Montanelli, Minghetti and others.

But these are only a few out of many contemporary writers who might be named.

Newspapers: as Pius had not yet granted his press law there were not very many in existence.

Coming to the modern Italian historians, perhaps the best descriptions are to be found in Masi's *Nell' Ottocento*, and in Gori; of the general historians Tivaroni is the best; but Raulich is also useful. *V*. also Monti's life of Pius IX. On the Papal side there is rather an interesting life of Pius IX by the Polish Bishop Pelczar (Italian translation).

[44] Masi, *Nell' Ottocento*, p. 163. It will be remembered that Professor Masi was the Italian historian invited by the Cambridge University Press to write the article on this period in the *Camb. Mod. Hist.* vol. xi.

Chapter IV

CHRONOLOGICAL SUMMARY OF THE SECULAR REFORMS OF POPE PIUS IX DURING HIS FIRST YEAR

We now come to the great work of Pius' first years, namely his endeavour to reform the old Papal institutions. It is certainly one of the most remarkable attempts at constitutionalism of all the numerous schemes undertaken during the nineteenth century. He had before him a wonderful ideal: that of founding a Liberal Papacy, within an Italy federated and free, and, from Rome, extending its supreme guidance to two hundred million spiritual subjects all over the world. A Liberal Papacy was perhaps impossible;[1] but, most undoubtedly, the fact that he tried it will be the main justification before history of Papal policy during the nineteenth century. For two long years he worked unceasingly among the medieval institutions and dignitaries around him, trying hard to evolve a modern, up-to-date pontifical government. And before abandoning this hope and finally relapsing into the traditional groove of the old-time Popes, he made certain, at all events, of having given Liberalism and nationalism every possible trial: no stone had been left unturned.

He very soon gave evidence of his intentions by appointing Cardinal Gizzi to be Secretary of State. This selection shows a laudable absence of jealousy with regard to his popular rival, and was received with keen satisfaction by the Liberals both in Rome and Turin, as foreshadowing a policy of reform. Most probably Gizzi was the best man obtainable. He was fifty-eight years of age—nearly three years below the average

---

[1] In a very interesting conversation with the late Cardinal Gasquet he expressed to me the opinion that the Liberal Papacy had been an impossibility.

age of the cardinals—able and experienced; a Liberal whose prestige would carry a matter through. Unfortunately he suffered from attacks of gout and throughout his year of office was often ill.[2] What Pius required among his senior officials was a greater number of comparatively young ministers, endowed with business capacities, prompt, resourceful and able to cope with unscrupulous men; and it was a type of person very difficult to find in the Papal entourage.[3] During his first year Pius' difficulty lay not so much in preparing his actual reforms, as in the slow and heart-breaking task of forcing his ideas gradually upon the circle

[2] Mr Bolton King states Gizzi's age as "nearly 90". This is a strange mistake because Gizzi's career is extremely well known; and, apart from that fact, he would hardly have been the candidate for the Papal throne favoured by the adventurous Massimo d'Azeglio (he was known as d'Azeglio's Pope) if he had been nearly ninety. Nor would Charles Albert, when Pius appointed Gizzi to be State Secretary, have welcomed a nonogenarian with the cry: "Blessings on him! He is undertaking a campaign against Austria. Evviva!" (Gualterio (1862 ed.), vol. v, Doc. IV, gives this letter of Charles Albert.) "One whose statesmanlike views, liberal opinions, knowledge of foreign states, and steadiness of conduct had succeeded in inspiring...an affection and respect, etc." was the opinion of the Hon. R. Abercromby, British minister at Turin, when Gizzi retired. *Correspondence*, p. 63. "His mind was cultured, but not like that of a statesman", says Gualterio (1862 ed., v, 81). Life: Gizzi (Pasquale). Born September 22nd, 1787, at Ceccano; died July 3rd, 1849, at Lenola. Of a Papal titled family. After taking holy orders he became (1819) an avvocato in the Court of the Santa Ruota. 1820, went to Lucerne as Uditore of the Nuncio, and there began his diplomatic career; 1820–27, he was Uditore; 1827–28, Internuncio; 1829–35, Chargé d'Affaires at Turin; 1837–39, Delegato at Ancona; 1839–40, returned to Switzerland; 1841–44, Papal Nuncio in Turin. He had also served for short periods in Bavaria and Belgium; in 1844 he became a cardinal and from 1844 to 1846 was Papal Delegate at Forlì, where he distinguished himself by his broad-mindedness, and in Rome was the centre of hope of the Liberals for the Papal Chair.

[3] The lack of suitable men was dilated on again and again by Pellegrino Rossi, d'Azeglio, Lützow, Gizzi—even by Pius himself: to say nothing of contemporary historians such as Gualterio, Farini, and others.

of often kindly, but usually unwilling, old princely ecclesiastics, who filled all the highest offices of state. Consummate
tact was required, for he could hardly have continued his life
as Pope if all the clergy had believed that he was betraying
his sacred trust. And they were supported by a bureaucracy
which was equally difficult to move.

The following description gives an idea of the situation:

Where the Pope's good will met with almost invincible opposition was in the Roman bureaucracy. The arts of the Sanfedisti
were known to him—at all events in part; but of these deeper and
more hypocritical methods of the Roman bureaucrats he had no
knowledge. These arts centred in the Ministry of the Interior....
I have spoken elsewhere of the organisation of the Ministry of the
Interior, and especially of a so-called commission of employés
which formed, as it were, the centre of this wretched bureaucracy;
here I cannot refrain from saying that these people, being more
seriously threatened by reform than any others, opposed the
greatest resistance to the Pope's intentions from the very first.[4]

In this connection it is well worth noting the opinion of
Sir George Hamilton, British minister in Florence:

At Rome the Pope has to contend with great difficulties, and I
understand that His Holiness bitterly complains of the want of
men capable of assisting him in his moderate reforms. Another
danger to be apprehended is from the violence of the ultra-liberal
party, who are calling for measures which it would be impossible
for the Pope to adopt, and to which, I understand, they are pro-
pelled underhand by the powerful party consisting of some of the
chief personages of the State most adverse to reform. Their
reasons are too obvious to render it necessary that I should point
them out to your Lordship.

Pius began his work by appointing commissions[5] to collect
information about all the administrative branches, and to

---

[4] Gualterio, Pt. II, vol. I, p. 16. Gualterio was a reformer, but he
was by no means a blind partisan of Pius, whom he blames more than
once: and these opinions were shared by scores of observers. Count
Lützow wrote again and again to Metternich about Pius' difficulties
with his Gregorian entourage.

[5] The first of these was appointed on June 30th, a fortnight after
his election, to enquire into the administration of justice; the others
at various dates during the next few months.

present schemes of reform. Immediately there arose complaints that they contained many members of the Gregorian type; but this was inevitable at first. Before the end of the year, however, Pius arranged for the retirement of three cardinals of the old school: Cardinal Vannucelli, Legate at Bologna, Cardinal Ugolino, Delegate at Ferrara, Cardinal Della Genga, Delegate at Pesaro; and also of Monsignor Marini, governor of Rome. Their places were filled by men more in sympathy with his ideas; Cardinals Amat, Ciacchi, Ferretti and Monsignor Grassellini respectively. Of these appointments the first three were extremely popular: and, at first, Grassellini was successful.[6]

Certainly no time was wasted before setting to work. He had been elected on June 16th, and crowned on June 21st. On June 30th he appointed his first commission of enquiry. On July 17th, after much discussion, he proclaimed the Amnesty. On August 22nd he named a commission to report on a scheme for the construction of railways, and two days later he began to consider the problem of unemployment.

On August 24th he issued a warning circular to the Papal Delegates and heads of provinces, reminding them that the true cause of crime is usually unemployment; and directing them to make every endeavour to find work for the people either in agriculture or industry, and to unite the clergy with the employers in establishing Sunday schools and evening schools. He also foreshadowed a scheme for bringing young men to an institution in Rome, where they should be taught a trade and receive some military training, so as to become fit, either for civil employment or, if in the army, for promotion to non-commissioned rank. This was his first attempt at alleviating unemployment and in promoting education, and it was only tentative; he returned to the subject on various other occasions;[7] but as yet he could only work in this way

[6] *V. Felsineo*, January 6th, 1847, for Amat's reception in Bologna.
[7] On October 8th he sent out another circular, saying that the money collected for banquets in his honour should, instead, be

through his provincial delegates, because he had not had time to establish any local body to keep him in touch with his people. But this circular was an intimation, at all events, to his officials as to the manner in which he desired to be served.

One notes that it was received with warm approval by the chief Bolognese paper, the *Felsineo*, which printed a good article by Minghetti on this subject.[8]

At the end of the circular there comes rather a striking statement as to his general policy. It proves that before he had been on the throne ten weeks he was already warning his people that the Pope could have nothing to say to the Revolution.

His Holiness purposes to promote the real, positive and practical good of his State, and of his well-beloved subjects...convinced that by these means alone his people can derive their prosperity, and not by adopting certain theories which in their very nature are inapplicable to the situation and to the character of the States of the Church; nor by associating themselves with certain tendencies to which His Holiness is entirely opposed. Both these theories and tendencies are disapproved by many people of experience (*savi*) and manifestly would compromise that internal and external tranquillity necessary to every government which desires to procure the well-being of its subjects.[9]

This statement is highly important because it shows that, from the very first, Pius laid down his position quite clearly: he was not a retrograde but, equally, he was not a revolutionist. It is intended to reassure the old Conservatives and at the same time to convey a definite warning to the extremists, that it was impossible for the State of the Church to go to the utmost length on the path of democracy. For the agitators it is a very important indication of his views. It reminds them that he is the Pope; that he can be a reformer but that he

saved for the poor during the winter, as payment for works of public utility. On October 10th he directed the Delegates to organise public works during December and January.

[8] *Felsineo*, September 18th, 1846.

[9] Gizzi's circular of August 24th, 1846.

cannot be a revolutionist; and it is the earliest of the series of reminders (often omitted by historians) which he continued to address to them through the whole of his reign.[10]

Just a few of the extremists read this warning as a denial of the programme of Rimini.[11] But Pius' popularity remained undiminished. The rejoicings over the Amnesty had hardly died away in the provincial towns, when the Romans began to organise a fresh demonstration in his honour, for the Nativity of our Lady, September 8th, 1846, in the Piazza del Popolo. It was extremely successful.[12] An inscription on the triumphal arch announced: "He conquered discord by clemency; he conceded public audiences; he made preparations for railways; he disclosed a fount of civilisation and riches; Applaud, ye nations. Pius is the beloved name which will be blessed by all centuries." Pius was doubtless touched by this appreciation of his efforts, but he had already issued a Notification asking the people to moderate their demonstrations, and afterwards issued further protests on the subject.[13]

For the railways, he had, in the words of the inscription, "made preparations" by appointing a commission of enquiry. By November 7th it handed in its first report, as Pius says, with laudable promptitude, and the Papal government published the following resolutions:

Art. 1. The principal lines were to be

1. Rome to the Neapolitan boundary near Ceprano.
2. Rome to Porto d'Anzio.
3. Rome to Civita Vecchia.
4. Rome to the most populous places in Umbria, as for instance Foligno. Also by the valley of the Potenza to Ancona; and thence to Bologna following the old Via Flaminia Emilia.

[10] Gori, p. 135.
[11] *Italy in the Making*, I, 225–8.
[12] It is more fully described in chapter v, where its political significance is dealt with.
[13] *V. Atti*, July 19th, 1846.

If these lines were successful, it was proposed to make one from Foligno towards Perugia and Città di Castello. Unfortunately this report caused some differences of opinion and two of the commissioners resigned.

The construction was to be entrusted to private companies, and rules were laid down as to business details, guarantees, time, capital, completion, interests of landowners, etc. A gold medal worth 1000 scudi (about £200) was offered as a prize for the person who should select the easiest and cheapest passage across the Apennines[14] between Umbria and the Marches.

On November 24th Pius issued a circular Order making certain reforms in the criminal law courts. This was a very complicated work, and is far too long to be included in this short account. But briefly; he began by abolishing two criminal courts (those of the Uditorato della Camera and the Tribunale Del Campidoglio or Capitol), and consolidated their business under the government court (Tribunale del Governo); it was henceforth to consist of two chambers (*turni*). At the same time he placed the provincial criminal courts under the supervision of the Sacra Ruota, in Rome; it was to be their supreme court.[15] Other reforms followed. Having thus centralised the organisation, he instituted tests to improve the

[14] The construction of railways was delayed by the fact that Prince Conti and Co., who first undertook it, had formed a national scheme which proved to be impracticable. *V.* Spada, 1, 82 *et seq.*; also p. 112. There is a prospectus of the Company which took over this scheme in the Spada Collection (Vatican), vol. 1, No. 54. For the Report *v. Atti*, Notificazione of November 7th. *V.* Paris Aff. Etr., Rome, 1846, Broglie, November 11th. For the appointment of the commission on railways *v.* the *Diario* of August 26th, 1846.

[15] Ordini Circolari of November 24th, 1846, January 1st, 1847, January 30th, 1847; *v. Atti*. This measure was well received according to Spada, 1, 176. Pellegrino Rossi, himself a distinguished lawyer, says that the multiplicity of overlapping courts was one of the greatest evils in the Papal State: that this measure of Pius was a step in the right direction, though a very slight one: that it had been received with satisfaction as being a beginning. *V.* Rossi's despatch, January 8th, 1847, Paris Aff. Etr. 1847.

standard of the personnel: young men were encouraged to join the profession provided (1) that they had a satisfactory record at school and had reached the philosophy course; (2) that they had passed in Law at a university in the Papal State, and had obtained an M.A. degree. They were then received on trial, for two years, before being finally accepted. Pius seems to have been anxious to introduce this trained legal element into his administration; one notices, for instance, that whereas the titular president of the court, being also Governor of Rome, was and had always been an ecclesiastic, henceforth an Uditore, a trained lawyer, was included on the list in order to give assistance to the secretary. All this was a step in the right direction; but one is inclined to think that the old complicated system of courts required more drastic and fundamental changes than these.

Another important legal reform: by a circular order, every tribunal was directed to send in, before the 5th day of each month, a list of all cases begun or pending, an account of the prison visitations giving lists of the prisoners detained, their country, age, description, etc., of the court in which they had been tried, and of the *material state of the prison*.

In a despatch to Metternich, Count Lützow reports that while carrying out these measures, Pius was perfectly horrified at finding in the prisons some men who had never been tried or even examined for trial.[16]

Shortly afterwards a commission was appointed to undertake the troublesome task of reforming the Code itself. Eventually its suggestions were adopted. Whether they were successful or not is impossible for a layman to decide.

On December 1st, 1846, Pius was faced by another difficulty—the price of wheat. The protective tariff had not been

[16] "Ces dispositions...expriment l'effroi dont Sa Sainteté avait été saisie en trouvant les prisons remplies et d'avoir trouvé des accusés détenus pendant des mois sans que leurs causes ne fussent, non pas jugées, mais pas même acheminées—examinées." Vienna Staats-Archiv, 1847, Rome, January 5th.

altered by government since the year 1823, when prices had
been high. In the tariff reform question Pius had to think on
both sides—like many another statesman since.[17] There had
been two bad harvests in succession, and he was very anxious
to lower the price of food so as to relieve suffering among the
poor. On the other hand the country-bred population in his
state outnumbered the townsmen by about five or six to one,
so that the interests of the producers were of supreme importance. He decided therefore to lower the tariff on imported
corn, maize and flour, but only by two scudi per rubbio, or
about eight and fourpence per 300 litres. This, he said in his
edict, would cheapen food while still protecting the farmers.
But the harvest was bad and even at this lower price distress
ensued. On January 3rd he forbade the export of corn. This
order was well received; but the dealers retorted by forming
rings to keep up the price. Finally, on February 20th, in an
edict which showed some signs of indignation, he declared
that speculators, especially on the Adriatic sea-board, had
been trying to prevent the free circulation of wheat, so that
there was a danger of shortage in some districts and over-
abundance in others.[18] He ordered therefore that, from
March 1st to the end of June, corn and maize should be
admitted into the state free of duty, and he also intimated
that the government would proceed against anyone preventing
the free circulation of wheat, and especially against "extor-
tioners and monopolists". To us, nowadays, these regulations
may seem rather over-paternal, but one must remember that
a small territory, in which the chief means of transport were
ox-carts, would have been a very easy prey to food speculators.

[17] The Papal financial system and policy stood in crying need of
reform (Farini, I, 133, and other writers), but accurate details were
as yet unobtainable. In July 1845, a year before Pius' accession,
Cardinal Antonelli had ordered Angelo Galli to compile a balance-
sheet for the ten previous years: this work could not be completed
until December 31st, 1847. Spada, I, 162.
[18] V. Atti, Notificazioni of January 3rd and February 20th, 1847.
V. also Diario of February 23rd.

During the winter food riots took place in a large number of the Papal towns, but in many cases they were due in reality to political causes.[19]

On March 4th Pius authorised a society of five hundred annual subscribers at five scudi each to found an Agricultural Institute.[20] Its aims were (1) theoretical: to collect statistics, study problems and give advice: (2) practical: to keep in touch with the government and with commerce; to improve methods of cultivation and of raising live stock; to repopulate the Agro Romano; start model farms, new plantations and cattle-breeding establishments; educate the unemployed and start rural infant schools; organise exhibitions, shows (of cattle, horse, sheep and agricultural implements), competitions and prizes for the best field, best fruit, etc.; and perhaps start a periodical. If the society should prove useful the government proposed to help it with funds.

On March 9th Pius paid a surprise visit to the night schools in the region of Monti;[21] and this practical way of showing interest in them won him great approval.

On March 10th the government ordered the construction of an establishment for distilling gas outside the town. This was to be the first step towards lighting Rome by gas, "a completely new enterprise for our city and one which contributes not only to the beauty and splendour of our streets but also to the safety of the citizens".[22]

March 15th, 1847, is a very important date for all Italy; on that day Pius granted freedom to the Press.[23] He issued an

[19] It is difficult to know the truth about this matter. Apparently some of these riots were started for political ends; others merely for plunder. In Gualterio, *Gli ultimi rivolgimenti* (1851 ed.), 1, 562, there is a very instructive government report on this problem. *V.* also chapter XI of this book.
[20] Vatican Arch., Fondo Spada, II.
[21] Monti is one of the fourteen regions of Rome.
[22] *Contemporaneo*, May 1st, 1847. *V.* also *Atti*, Notificazione of March 10th, and *Diario*, March 13th.
[23] *Atti*, Edict of March 15th, 1847.

Edict setting up a Council of Censors. It was to consist of five members, of whom four were laymen presided over by an ecclesiastic; and henceforth the former ecclesiastical revisers were to send all purely political matter to this new authority. The institution of an almost lay censorship, whose number was later increased to seven, formed a distinct advance on anything that previously had existed in the Papal dominions. The subjects censorable were, broadly speaking, any writing in contempt of religion or the Church, or its ministers, anything against the honour of public or private people, any speeches that bring the acts or the forms of the Papal government into hatred, that foment faction or excite popular movement against the law. It may be added that the greater freedom allowed to his people was taken advantage of, and very soon used against him by the revolutionary party—as perhaps was to be expected.[24]

There were very few branches of administration to which Pius had not devoted his attention during the first nine months of his reign. Nevertheless his people were beginning to become a little impatient. This was because as yet he had not established any machinery for democratic government. Here of course lay his true difficulty; how could the old Papal régime ever be democratised? It was evident that he must find some method of introducing the representative element into the government without endangering his authority as Head of the Catholic Church, and that his people were already being worked upon by the revolutionists to clamour for some step in that direction. At this point Pius arrives at the threshold of his constitutional experiment. He was face to face with a very difficult problem, and he meant, therefore, to begin tentatively and thus gradually to bring his old eighteenth-century régime into touch with modern political ideas.

---

[24] At first there was some disappointment because this concession did not go farther; but Massimo d'Azeglio wrote a long letter in its favour pointing out Pius' difficulties, and this produced an excellent effect. V. also Fattiboni, II, 67; Farini, I, 188; and others.

Thus April 19th, 1847, is another very important date. On that day Pius issued a circular to his delegates in the provinces informing them that he intended to summon one of his subjects from each province to come to Rome for a period of two years in order to give his advice as regards the better regulation of communal councils, and other local matters.[25] With this end in view, he directed the Delegate in each province to furnish him with two or three names from which to choose. This circular contained the germ of his Consulta di Stato or Consultative State Council, which was to be the leading feature of his constitution.

Small as this advance may seem to us now, it was a great step forward for the Papal government, and indeed for almost any government in Italy in 1847; and it was received with the most heartfelt gratitude by the people because they regarded it as the first step towards a larger grant of self-government, and at the same time they felt that their Pontiff was on the way to diminish his own temporal authority. It seemed to them that the wonderful dream of Gioberti, the vision of a patriot Pope becoming a patriot king, was now about to be realised. They were more grateful than ever they had been since the day of the Amnesty, and determined to express their joy in a fitting manner; and owing to their now excellent organisation they were able to do so at a day's notice.

For this demonstration of April 22nd the meeting place was, as usual, the Piazza del Popolo.[26] There, at Ave Maria, about sunset, the nucleus of the procession started along the Corso, some two or three thousand strong, carrying torches and accompanied by bands. The well-known leader of the people, Ciceruacchio, was their standard-bearer, but instead of a banner he bore a great sign-board on a wooden staff, with Gizzi's circular inscribed on it in large characters. On the way the demonstrators were joined by many thousands

[25] Circular of April 19th, 1847, Vatican Arch., Fondo Spada, VII.
[26] Spada, I, 203. *V.* also Bargagli's report, Florence Arch., Despatch of April 23rd, 1847.

of others until they formed an immense crowd, perhaps forty or fifty thousand strong, which moved along the Corso between the lines of illuminations, raising enthusiastic cheers for Pius, and finally wound its way up into the piazza outside the Quirinal. There, that whole great concourse of people came to a halt beneath their torches, and received Pius' blessing on their knees and in dead silence. This demonstration was undoubtedly one of the most heartfelt that had ever taken place.[27]

On May 11th Pius issued an edict regulating the growing of rice.

On May 12th he issued a circular regulating procedure in case of debt.[28]

During this period Pius also carried out one of his best reforms, namely that of freeing the Jews in Rome from various unjust and humiliating regulations. In future they were to be allowed to share in Papal charities; were dispensed from bringing tribute publicly at Carnival time; and were no longer compelled once a week to listen to a Christian sermon. They were permitted to summon a Rabbi from Jerusalem. On the 13th July their representatives paid a formal visit of thanks to Pius and presented him with an ancient urn. (*V*. Pelczar, I, 296.)

On June 14th[29] he established a Consiglio dei Ministri, a Council of Ministers, to act more or less as a cabinet; the heads of the state departments were to meet in one assembly. This, for the time being, formed his governing body.[30] It consisted of his seven chief public servants, who were thus centred round his Secretary of State. Each was to bring his

[27] For a different view of their demonstration *v*. p. 114. Mr Freeborn speaks of it as "a procession of more than 20,000 people". Perhaps he did not include the onlookers. *London Corr*. p. 40. *V*. also d'Azeglio, *Lettere*, April 28th, 1847.

[28] *Atti*, Edict of May 11th and Circular of May 12th, 1847.

[29] Dated June 12th on one copy that I saw; and also by Gori.

[30] For this measure *v*. Paris Aff. Etr., Rome, 1847, Rossi's despatch, June 18th.

most important business, including the estimates, for common discussion. Its work would extend to initiating new laws, and giving rulings or making appointments, but none of them would be valid until they had been approved by the Pope. This Consiglio was received with disapproval by the people, mainly because it was manned entirely by ecclesiastics. The Liberals naturally wanted some lay ministers and made little allowance for Pius' difficulties in getting his reforms into being. But we need not discuss the Council of Ministers any further, because, before the end of the year, it was increased and improved when he produced his constitution.[31]

June 17th, 1847, was the anniversary of his accession. It was celebrated by an immense procession with banners, bands, Ciceruacchio and fifty thousand people to receive the Papal blessing—all of which we need not describe again. Its most satisfactory feature was that the city of Bologna sent a splendid standard in token of loyalty—a very different greeting from those under Gregory XVI. And on the lofty Roman banners were inscribed the words: Amnesty—Codes—Railways—Municipal government—Deputies—Education.[32]

At six o'clock, in the Church of Santa Maria degli Angeli, the Barnabite friar, Padre Gavazzi—destined only two years later to proclaim revolution far and wide throughout Italy—preached for an hour and a half to an immense crowd which "hung on his ringing words while he exulted in Pius IX as a miracle of Providence, of clemency, and of union. This was succeeded by a *Te Deum*, a thanksgiving to the most High for having granted to the Church so great a reforming Pope."[33]

Another and more celebrated Barnabite orator, Ugo Bassi, afterwards the devoted disciple of Garibaldi, wrote a poem for this occasion, pouring out blessings on the mother of

[31] *V*. Petre to Hamilton, *London Corr.* I, 50.

[32] One item was omitted, most significantly; the motu-proprio of June 12th established the Council of Ministers. Pellegrino Rossi reported this fact to Guizot. Paris Aff. Etr., Rome, 1847–48, Rossi, June 18th.

[33] Vatican Arch., Fondo Spada, vol. VII, No. 53.

Pius IX. One wonders whether either of these two friars would have started on the line which they afterwards followed, had it not been for Pius' Liberal movement.

Near the balcony of the Casino there stood a great inscription: "To Pius IX from his people in gratitude for the past, and confidence for the future." This was the work of a very different type of man, namely, the Piedmontese artist-writer-soldier, the Marquis Massimo d'Azeglio.

Most assuredly Pius had a great year of work to his credit: a wonderful year when one remembers the small numbers of his genuine helpers, the unwillingness of the old Gregorian cliques, and the fact that he himself was a country bishop suddenly called on to revolutionise a state of three million people. Indeed, one may well ask whether any one of our modern statesmen, if he were suddenly transplanted into the dead-alive, eighteenth-century organisation and atmosphere of the Papal government in 1846, without railways, telegraphs or statistics, with very few up-to-date men and (as far as could then be discovered) only a minus quantity of money, could have achieved any results as good in the course of his first twelve months. This was constructive work; so he was obliged to clear the ground and study it before starting to build.

It is difficult to imagine the impression created by a Liberal programme such as this suddenly projected into Metternich's Italy.

At the same time Pius evidently realised that his main difficulties were still before him. He was a good patriot at heart; he had worked well for his people, and he was incomparably popular not only in the Roman state but all over Italy, and had won the approval of the most enlightened men in Liberal France and even in Protestant England. But there hung over his head the sword of Damocles. He was not merely a temporal sovereign like the others. He was Pope, the head of a gigantic world-organisation. And now, when once he should start upon the problem of organising a modern

democratic government, how could he satisfy the aspirations
of his supporters? Had he been merely a secular ruler it
would have been easy for him to resign his will to that of the
people, and to found a constitutional monarchy which would
have been considered a model of enlightenment by the
Liberals all over Italy. But as Pope it was impossible for him
thus to resign his personal authority and leave the Church at
the beck and call of the state, because the results might have
proved disastrous. Many Liberals were anti-clericals, so it
was impossible for him to place his conscience in their hands.
He could never resign his ultimate authority, or—as he felt—
his right to have the final say in defending the heritage of the
Church entrusted to him by a Higher Power, for the purposes
of His work on earth.

On June 22nd, 1847, five days after the anniversary rejoicings, he began his second year by directing Gizzi to issue
a Notificazione in which his feelings on this subject were
frankly expressed.

His Holiness is firmly determined to progress on the way of
improvement in every branch of public administration that may
require it. But he is equally determined to do so only by wise and
carefully considered steps, and within those limits which are essentially in accordance with the sovereignty and the temporal government of the Head of the Catholic Church. To it certain forms
cannot be applied because they would undermine the existence of
the sovereignty itself, or at all events would diminish its intrinsic
liberty and independence in the exercising of the Supreme
Primacy; for the sake of which liberty and independence God
disposed in his profound counsels that the Holy See should
possess a temporal principality. The Holy Father cannot forget
the sacred duties which bind him to maintain intact the trust that
has been confided to him.[34]

[34] The *Felsineo*, the organ of the Bolognese Liberals, was perhaps
the most sensible of the newspapers in 1847. From it, therefore,
one may learn their opinion of Pius' position at the end of his first
year. They were rather alarmed by Gizzi's Circular of June 22nd,
because they feared that it foreshadowed an end of reforms. In
an able article on July 1st, Montanari, the editor, expressed his full
understanding that Pius, as Pope, was compelled to keep his reforms

This Notificazione of Gizzi on June 22nd, 1847, is very important. It soon became a turning-point in the story.

within the limits possible for the Head of the Church. But, he added, the reforms for which they hoped did not overstep those limits: he considered that it was Pius' duty to continue with the reform of the finances, of the codices, and of public instruction; and with the establishment of communal Councils, of the Civic Guard and of a Consultative assembly. These were the measures which Pius proceeded to carry out during the next six months.

Chapter V

THE PARTIES IN ROME DURING PIUS' FIRST SIX MONTHS (JUNE 1846 TO JANUARY 1847)

A. THE PARTIES IN ROME.

It has already been shown that when Pius first launched his policy of reform, it seemed rather like a small vessel between two immense contending waves. On one side of it was European conservatism, as typified by Austria; on the other side of it was the Revolution with its world-wide net-work of committees, mainly directed by Mazzini from London or Paris.

These two were the world-powers.

But more insidious and far harder for him to meet were the parties within the Papal State itself; on the Conservative side the old Gregorian ecclesiastics and bureaucrats; on the Liberal side the Esaltati and, eventually, the Piedmontese Albertists.

Pius' most dangerous opponents were to be the Esaltati, or violent Moderates, because they were nominally on his side.

The following table aims at giving an idea of the various parties during his first year; but we must remember that everything was in a state of flux.

I. THE CONSERVATIVE REACTION
Led by Austria.
Within the Papal State, headed by the Gregorian ecclesiastics and bureaucrats.

II. THE MODERATES
(a) Genuine followers of Pius IX. Liberals; Federalists: ready to work through the government and to preserve Pius' supreme authority; to follow his programme.
(b) Esaltati; violent Moderates. Agitators. These men too were Liberal Federalists, but within the Papal State they wanted to compel Pius to go farther than he intended. They used street agitation in order to force democratic concessions from him. Their chief representatives were Dr Sterbini, Prince Canino and Ciceruacchio.[1]

[1] During the year 1847.

III. THE REVOLUTION

Mazzinians; fusionist-republicans. They wanted to overthrow all nine governments in Italy and (1) unite Italy by fusion, (2) establish her as a republic. They were temporarily in the background.

IV. THE PIEDMONTESE ALBERTISTS

A small but select party in Rome; they were working for Piedmont and were in touch with Charles Albert. The best-known among them was the Marquis Massimo d'Azeglio; and, later on, General Giovanni Durando, Colonel Count Casanuova and Dr Pantaleoni.

It must be remembered that at first these headings apply more to the party organisers and their immediate followers than to the people in general. The majority of the people in the towns were greatly attached to Pius, but easily led: and the majority of the peasants were little influenced by the agitators.

It was the Esaltati party which—during the course of the next two years—gradually drove Pius from pillar to post; first they forced from him a constitution (March 1848); then they called on him to declare war, and because, as Pope, he could not do so, they virtually drove him from his state. Looking back on the scene to-day, we perceive that they were entitled to a constitution; and that, as the Pope could not declare war except in self-defence, he was thereby disqualified from possessing a state. From the experience of 1848 it could be claimed that Italy would never be able to exert her full strength against the Austrians as long as there existed a pontifical government in Rome.

Certainly it seems to be true that in 1848 the existence of a Papal State within united Italy was proved to be impossible.

On the other hand it was proved, equally, that from the start Pius had done his best: and had received enthusiastic gratitude from the bulk of the people at first, but very little indeed from the agitators. It was his own Liberal-mindedness at the start that made possible the agitation which eventually overthrew him. Moreover here, as in all other countries, some of the methods of agitation were not beautiful; still less so some of the men. Several of the leaders who overthrew Pius in 1848 were Amnistiati of July 1846—men who would still have been in prison or in exile but for his pardon.

I. CONSERVATIVES. This party included the great majority of the ecclesiastical hierarchy, and virtually all of the established bureaucracy; an immense body of genuine disapproval, and an immense body of vested interests.[2] The old cardinals and bishops who were Pius' contemporaries or seniors were perfectly genuine in fearing that his Liberalism would lead to the ending of the Papal State and to the disendowment of their Church—though no doubt their own personal life-interests could be safeguarded.

Still more recalcitrant were the civil bureaucrats. "Your Holiness should clear out the Secretary of State's office even down to the cats" was a saying attributed to Cardinal Micara. How far the offices were corrupt it is hard to say, but they were certainly incompetent and haters of the new ideas.

Comparatively small as it may appear, this Gregorian ecclesiastical-bureaucratic party was a constant drag on progress and reform; because it lived within the gates and claimed to speak in the Church's name, and indeed, for the welfare of religion itself. It was a tacit reproach to the conscience of Pius: we elected you Head of the Church and how are you treating the Church? He was a man of very sensitive, in fact of over-sensitive conscience, especially in matters of religion;

[2] Everybody agrees that it tried to thwart Pius, but one does not know how far the stories are true. Gori, for instance, says that the old employés in the provinces temporarily suppressed the Amnesty, and delayed and harassed the returning exiles; that at Sinigaglia and Faenza the priests preached against Pius as heretical and unlawfully elected, etc. And these instances are mentioned by Mazzini. Of course all the Moderate writers complained of this opposition, Farini, Minghetti, Gualterio, Pasolini, etc., etc.

Bianchi says of the Gregorian party: "It had let no time pass before conspiring to upset the works of the new Pontiff. And when these people had then seen the alterations in the ordini statuali become genuine, firm and fruitful, they had let themselves run to extremes, giving manifest signs of their desire to start civil discords."

a man who would spend hours in prayer, who acted always from a sense of duty and to whom religion was the first call. Such men are in great trouble when, as happened daily in his life just then, their duties come into conflict with one another.[3]

II. THE MODERATES, in Rome, may be classified roughly into two sections: the genuine Moderates; and the Esaltati (Enthusiasts) or violent Moderates.[4]

(a) The genuine Moderates, or Liberals, wanted reforms within the Papal State; this was the creed of Gioberti which Pius was trying to translate into action; their first ideal was a modern enlightened government under the constitutional rule of the Pope; and some of them were perfectly satisfied with this alone. But most of them had far wider hopes than mere state reform; they might be called neo-Guelfs; in their view the first step was that the people should win a pre-dominating power in every government; this power would be used in turn to promote a league or federation of the small states of Italy, under the Papal ægis; and some day this league or federation would either edge out or drive out the Austrians. So their joy in Pius' reforming policy was due, not so much to the actual improvements effected, as to the hope that it was binding together the ruler and the people, and

[3] Before six months were gone his policy had alienated the cardinals—which must have been a great grief to him. In the Vienna Archives there is a despatch from Count Lützow to Metternich in which he says: " It is regrettable to have to confess that there is little sympathy between the Sovereign Pontiff and the Sacred College, between the elected and the electors; nor even with the Prime Minister of his Holiness."—Count Lützow goes on to speak of "the difficulty, in fact, the impossibility—even if he summons the Cardinals to his assistance—of finding capable men when a post of any importance falls vacant. The Cardinals on their part complain of being neglected, set aside, not consulted." Vienna Staats-Archiv, Rome, December 26th, 1846. See also Capponi, *Lettere*, p. 252 *et seq*.

[4] Thus the whole body of Nationalists in Rome would be divided roughly into four sections: the genuine Moderates, the violent Moderates, the Mazzinians and the Piedmontese Albertists.

fitting them both for the supreme work of national regeneration.

As a rule, however, they did not want to force Pius to go farther than he was willing to go.

(*b*) The Esaltati. Violent Moderates. Agitators. This section of progressives soon became the real danger to Pius. They wanted to force him to go beyond his programme. Certainly some of them secretly were little else but republicans within the Papal State. They believed in agitating by means of street demonstrations. Whereas the genuine Giobertian Moderates, such as Orioli, Silvagni and, in Bologna, Minghetti, wanted to preserve the sovereign power of the government and to work through it, these Esaltati were democrats; they wanted to work through the people towards popular government, and would expect the Pope to adapt himself to it. Their exact aims are hard to describe because they were not clearly defined at first, and because they became more extreme as time went on. The best known among them were Prince Canino, his young secretary Dr Luigi Masi, Dr Sterbini and Angelo Brunetti, better known as Ciceruacchio. These men were federalists (during this period) and worked by agitating, and therefore were distinguishable from the party-of-action (Mazzini), which was fusionist and worked by rebellion. But in reality many of the Esaltati must have had very similar sentiments and objectives to those of the Mazzinians. Indeed Sterbini had been a prominent member of the Giovine Italia since 1840, and Ciceruacchio was an ex-Carbonaro.

III. THE REVOLUTION. Mazzini's extremists (fusionist republicans). In 1846 and 1847 they were far less numerous[5] than the Moderates. They cared little for reform[6] and dis-

[5] "The Moderate Liberal party now absorbs everyone over there, and everywhere; just look round and see who remains to us." Protocol of the Giovine Italia, v, 19.

[6] Mazzini feared reform. "The Pope—whose intentions seem to be really good—what can he do? Take from the national movement

approved of federation, either as a league of princes or a league of peoples. They were opposed to both Pius and Charles Albert. Their own creed was the "democratic universal republic" of Mazzini, and their method of obtaining it was to be an armed rising *en masse*. Avowedly this would mean the abolition of the Temporal Power. Now at this period of the story they saw plainly that if Pius were successful as a Liberal Pope, he would be able to save the Papal State; they intended therefore that Pius' reforms should be a failure.[7]

IV. THE SMALL PIEDMONTESE GROUP headed by Massimo d'Azeglio. This party will be dealt with in a separate chapter.

There were some cross-currents: and there were some of the extremists who had become Moderates since Pius' accession, and were temporarily[8] his supporters, notably the young Dr Masi.

---

that district in Italy upon which we could count most, owing to its local interests and hopes. This danger is more serious than is generally thought. Woe to us if our princes ever entered upon the way of material and administrative improvements...the sense of duty, of having a mission, and of national unity would evaporate." Mazzini, E.N. xxx, 142, September 3rd, 1846, and xxxiv, 284.

[7] This is admitted by Lamberti in a letter to Mazzini, January 31st, 1847.

[8] "Our Italy might also rejoice if she knew the spirit of the Pope, for he is by no means submissive to her mortal enemies. Pius IX will not grasp the Guelf sword; he will not fulminate the great Bull [of excommunication] but from any act of abject vassalage and from any astute intrigue he will keep himself religiously distant. And that is enough for the present! Consequently all the manifestations of enthusiasm are not always adulatory.... As long as (*take good note of this condition*) our most kindly Pius proceeds upon this path of regeneration we shall be for him, his guardians and his supporters." Extract from a letter of Masi to Montanelli, December 31st, 1846, *v.* Montanelli, I, 191.

This letter shows that Masi and his circle never expected Pius to declare war or excommunicate Austria; whereas most of the revolutionary writers afterwards justified Pius' overthrow on the ground that he refused to declare war in 1848. Cf. Capponi, *Lettere*, pp. 245, 252; Farini, I, 190; and other authorities.

Subsequent history has shown that both of the schemes I and II were unsatisfactory. Concerning scheme I, experience was shortly to prove that it was virtually impossible for the Pope to become a constitutional monarch, and that in any case a federation of the smaller states was only a frail defence against Austria. Still, in 1846, this federation was the only scheme of unity that could be called "practical politics".[9]

On the other hand, the other alternative, Mazzini's ideal of fusing all Italy into one single republic by means of a rising *en masse*, was absolutely impossible in 1846, and as long as it was tied to republicanism it always remained so. This, too, was destined to be tried soon afterwards during Garibaldi's glorious defence of Rome, and to prove a failure.[10]

Parenthetically one must admit that both Pius and Mazzini failed to see the whole of the situation. Pius evidently did not realise how many of his best followers regarded the reforms as a prelude to war. Reforms within the Papal State might have satisfied them if the Austrians had not been so close at hand, holding down two splendid Italian provinces only just across the river Po, and forming a standing menace to the rest of the country. But as long as the foreigners were in Italy, any grants of popular institutions would probably lead to war; and Pius as Pope could not declare war unless he were first attacked.

Mazzini, on the other hand, could see nothing but his own ideal. And so it was necessary that Italy should try both schemes and pass through a period of suffering, before she

[9] *V. Italy in the Making*, I, 19.

[10] This sentence, I hope, will not be misunderstood. Garibaldi's defence of Rome was undoubtedly a step forward towards the unity of Italy, because owing to the heroism of the defenders it spread greater self-confidence and a greater desire for unity among the Italian peoples, and aroused their enthusiasm and the sympathy of Europe. But at the same time it showed the impossibility of the system adopted; and from that time onwards Mazzini and the republicans began to lose ground in the estimation of practical men. Mazzini, of course, was perfectly aware of the fact that the defence had no chance of success.

realised that fusion, as preached by Mazzini, was essential for her perfect safety, but that his republicanism and the rising "*en masse*" were only a dream.

B. PIUS' POSITION

The question for Pius was—and Pellegrino Rossi saw it plainly—would he succeed in establishing his Liberal Papacy before he was overwhelmed?

From the very earliest moment the more extreme Progressives intended to capture Pius' movement: but in the opinion of the present writer, during the first twelve months the Progressives were not personified by Mazzini; in fact the Mazzinian method of action was temporarily in abeyance. Our documents show that so far from directing the Moderate movement, he disliked it because it substituted state federalism for fusion; that he cared little for any reforms unless they were political and included such measures as the secularisation of the Roman government and the reform of convents; that he regarded the Papal movement as purely local and temporary—not national; that he believed in exaggerating the popular expectations about Pius in order to increase the greatness of his fall;[11] and that already he was preparing propaganda, agents, and a national fund, so as to take advantage of the reaction which would ensue. It was certainly not he who led the movement to capture Pius; it was the local men in the Papal State.

[11] "If you have anyone re-entering...the tactics to be carried out are the following: without antagonising or betraying hostility, to push the hopes founded on the Pope to their extreme limit; to attribute to Austrian influence anything left undone by him; to introduce cautiously, as far as possible, a political and national character into the demonstrations of enthusiasm; to manage that Austria may become more and more alarmed, may send notes and make claims until Pius draws back and thereby reveals his impotence. And people's minds will be in condition for a violent reaction which will be anti-Austrian and consequently national." Mazzini, E.N. xxx, 194, Letter September 29th, 1846; *v.* also p. 238.

From his home in London Mazzini meant, if possible, to get the pontifical blessing on his cause[12] and then, when necessary, to overthrow the pontifical government if it impeded the unifying of his country—which was inevitable.

At Rome during Pius' first six months (June to December 1846) the Progressives showed no apparent signs of hostility to his movement. They did not want to check it or to kill it, but rather to encourage and assimilate it. But during the next six months they began to press for political concessions as distinct from reforms and, led by the Esaltati (agitators), they became more violent. As yet all was done with every mark of enthusiastic loyalty to the Pope, and up to the end of 1847, most probably, the mass of the people remained genuinely loyal; but by that time they had been imbued by the agitators with the idea that Pius would lead all Italy in a war of liberation against the Austrians.

C. METHODS OF AGITATION

The methods employed by the Esaltati to capture Pius' movement were rather curious. One might classify them roughly under four headings: namely those of the crowds and of the banquets during the first six months; to which, in 1847, were added those of the press and the clubs. After Pius relaxed the Censorship (March 15th, 1847) they were able to capture the press and to found political clubs. But these last two methods belong to chapter VII.

Firstly: *The crowds*. Pius, of course, was worshipped by the crowd, and wherever he went there was a demonstration. The agitators perceived, therefore, that it was necessary to dominate the crowd and to direct the demonstrations, but without appearing to do so. This could be done by various means, but the most usual methods were: by introducing organised bodies of young men here and there among the people to lead the cheering, and to raise such cries

---

[12] *V*. Mazzini's letter to Pius a year later, September 8th, 1847.

as might be ordered, either of praise, or later on, of disapproval.[13]

By this means they turned the demonstrations of gratitude
into a kind of out-door tribunal for Pius; he was received
with joy or with coldness according to the particular edict
that he had issued. If the latest reform was not considered
good enough, this fact could be made known by cries raised
or by inscriptions on the banners. By this system they intended to push him onward step by step until they had got
every possible concession.

That this was their system is fully admitted by the agitators
and revolutionists.

Moreover in 1872, when Pius was a saddened and rather
embittered old man of eighty years, he described these early
scenes of his pontificate in the following terms:

The crowds came to honour the Pope and to show him
respect; and to pay him the homage of their open-hearted affection.
But alas! These crowds were not, like those described in Holy
Writ, brought up in faith and uncorrupted living. Many came. I
am convinced that they came in good faith. But even then from
the deepest abysses of Hell, even then there was being prepared
a way to overturn the world. And while these processions were
becoming too numerous, and while I was urging, commanding
and wishing for them all to return to their own daily work, the order

[13] Maguire (Papal), p. 55: "The plan of promoting demonstrations was systematically persevered in; and thus cunningly devised
a kind of out-door tribunal, to which the daily course of the government was submitted and by which its particular acts were applauded
or condemned."

Castelli (a friend of Cavour), *Ricordi*, p. 237: "Here began the
demonstrations, that is to say the meetings arranged by the people,
with aims either defined or undefined—the system which proved so
efficacious a method for the Liberal party. On each new act of
Pius IX the Roman people ran to the piazza and held a demonstration to glorify the reforming Pontiff;—by that means pushing him
further and further forward.... At Rome every day the matter
became more serious. Pius IX began to perceive that through the
frenzy of acclamations and enthusiasm he found himself engaged in
a path of which he had never dreamt."

For other authorities *v.* Appendix.

of the day sent out from Hell was this: Agitate and go on agitating always, because in troubled waters we may obtain our objects.[14]

The banquets. The second method employed by the Progressives to capture Pius' movement was that of arranging public banquets in honour of each reform, and using them as an opportunity for making violent speeches, thus spreading extreme ideas, and, as it were, including Pius in the revolution.

This method of organising great political banquets with guests numbering anything between a hundred and a thousand or two, ostensibly to express gratitude for Pius' last reform, was exceedingly ingenious and successful, because it enabled the organisers to keep the whole direction of the demonstration in their own hands. When the wine had flowed freely the speakers became bold and the audience enthusiastic. It was a system already becoming known in Paris and was partly responsible for the fall of Louis Philippe in 1848.

D. THE CHIEF DEMONSTRATIONS DURING THESE SIX MONTHS OF 1846

Before six weeks were past the government had begun to realise that there was a percentage of political agitators amid the thousands of genuine thanksgivers. In July the rejoicings over the Amnesty had been so delirious that, on the third day,

---

[14] De Franciscis, 1, 368. This is one of Pius' Discorsi which Don Pasquale de Franciscis wrote down verbatim to form part of his huge collection of Pius' sayings after 1870.

Gizzi told Bargagli, the Tuscan minister in Rome, that the government was perfectly aware that the demands [of the agitators] were insatiable. That they want to drag it beyond its fixed limit and compromise it with the interested foreign powers. That if this resulted in a general Italian conflagration, then these same people who are now exalting Pius IX would be the first to declare themselves the common enemies of the Germans and of the established Italian governments. Florence Arch., Dept. Est. 1846–48, Busta 2956. Bargagli reported this to his government on January 24th, 1847. We know from the Viennese documents that Gizzi often spoke in a similar strain to Lützow.

the government had issued a notification[15] asking the people, most kindly and tactfully, to moderate their expressions of enthusiasm. Then followed the rejoicings in the provinces. Then on September 8th came the great thanksgiving for the Amnesty, and this may probably be described as the first *organised* demonstration, and, at the same time, as the last in which the true outburst of gratitude was actually spontaneous. It was artificially prepared; but the joy was genuine.[16]

This great thanksgiving of September 8th, 1846, has remained celebrated.[17]

There is certainly something touching in the heartfelt sentiment of the people and their great efforts to do honour to their prince. In the Piazza del Popolo, at the entrance to the Corso, they had raised a magnificent triumphal arch which was an exact reproduction, in size as well as in detail, of the arch of Constantine. It was made of wood, paper and gesso, and, says Spada, who was in Rome at the time,

the gradual completion of the arch, of the emblems composing the bas-reliefs of the inscriptions, and above all of the statue of the pontiff, kept the Romans occupied for nearly a month.... Along the Corso for about a mile were planted stakes surmounted by two

[15] On July 19th, three days after the Amnesty. "His Holiness is keenly touched by the spontaneous demonstrations of filial affection which the inhabitants of this, his city, have offered him on the previous evenings. He cannot but express his complete gratification. As, however, the quality which increases the value of every beautiful thing is moderation, thus the setting a limit to these extraordinary signs of rejoicing would convey to the Holy Father a fresh proof of the docility of his Roman people, for whom every wish of the Chief Pontiff is always a command." Cardinal Santucci's Notificazione of July 19th, 1846.

[16] Spada and Lützow were of opinion that it was entirely engineered by the revolutionists. But the people were certainly very much in earnest in their expressions of gratitude. *V.* Lützow's despatch of July 31st, Vienna Staats-Archiv, Rome, 69.

[17] Spada, 1, 94 and many other authorities. He speaks of the new caffè, but perhaps he means the Caffè Nuovo which, according to Lützow, was becoming a great meeting-place for revolutionists.

small banners with the motto *Viva Pio IX* (Long live Pius IX), linked to one another by garlands of myrtle and wreaths of laurel. Above each of them there would be a lighted torch aflame in the evening. Every balcony, every window attracted attention by the variety of the emblems and inscriptions, by the rich and many-coloured hangings, as well as by the splendour of flowers, ornaments, decorations of every sort, whose descriptions would fill a large book. The inscriptions in the new caffè were read with attention and reported in many of the papers. They were composed by my brother Francesco Spada.

Thus the brother of the Papalist banker assisted in the work; but one of the principal organisers was the cheery Trasteverine wine-cart driver Ciceruacchio, who was already a popular leader of the mob.

According to our friend Spada, the population of Rome had almost doubled itself for the occasion. And—he tells us —as Pius moved slowly along the Corso, with his *treno nobile*, giving his blessing on either side with dignified and at the same time smiling aspect, the enthusiasm for him surpassed all bounds.

To describe the applause, the shouts, the blessings invoked on him, the flowers, and even the tears which welled from the eyes of many, is simply impossible. It was the apogee, the culminating point, the superlative moment of the triumph of Pius IX over the hearts of Rome.[18]

The arch bore the inscription:

Honour and glory to Pius IX, for whom one day sufficed to bring happiness to his subjects and to bespeak the admiration of the world.

That evening when all Rome was a blaze of illumination the people again gathered in thousands before the Quirinal to receive the Papal blessing. They bore a standard with the inscription: "Eternal fidelity to Pius IX."

On October 8th Gizzi was obliged to issue a second order within the two and a half months since the Amnesty—this

[18] Spada, I, 94.

time a circular[19] urging that the festivities should be curtailed and that the money collected for them should be spent on the poor in winter, in return for works of public utility. By that date the government had fully realised that the demonstrations were being used as a political weapon.[20] At all events the circular produced a curious result: on the 14th and the 21st of October, Pius, returning from Tivoli and Frascati respectively, was greeted with the usual ovations: but on November 4th, the feast of S. Carlo Borromeo, when his movements were known beforehand, he was received in dead silence. Rightly or not, this "glacial" reception has been attributed to the agitators and revolutionists. It is thought that, since their agitation for political concessions had been countered by Gizzi's circular, they regarded themselves as discovered and wished to give some sign of their power. It was the first attempt at controlling the Pope, and, says Spada, "it made many people open their eyes".

The government very stupidly replied by what looked like a concession;[21] it increased the number of laymen on the commission revising the legal code. Pius ought to have prevented this.

Banquets. Meanwhile the feasts continued. On November

[19] Gizzi's Circular, October 8th, 1846.
[20] *V.* Paris Aff. Etr., Rome, 1846 (Broglie, November 8th), and also Vienna Staats-Archiv, Rome. As early as August 21st, 1846, Lützow had written to Metternich: "The Pope and his chief minister [Gizzi] know their position and are perfectly aware that they have as much to fear from their pretended friends as from their political adversaries. His Holiness understands to-day the value of this enthusiasm-to-order.... They both know what account to make of the protests of gratitude and filial affection which are the prelude for further demands and other claims; claims perhaps of a nature that can never be regarded as admissible." Lützow of course speaks bitterly: "enthusiasm-to-order" is not a fair description. The enthusiasm and joy were genuine, but at the same time there was the aiming, especially by wire-pullers, at obtaining further concessions.
[21] Paris Aff. Etr., Rome, 1846 (Broglie, November 8th).

11th[22] there was an immense banquet at the Alibert Theatre, given mainly by Amnistiati (men pardoned under the Amnesty) to celebrate the new life in Rome. This dinner was certainly intended to include Pius as a sympathiser with the Amnistiati. About a thousand guests attended and about a thousand spectators. The theatre was a blaze of light. Between intervals of military music, speeches were made full of enthusiasm for Pius and of stirring allusions to the nationality and independence of Italy; and loud cheers were given for their well-beloved Pope by the two thousand men and women present. A colossal bust of Pius overlooked the scene; and it must have had every appearance of approving the warlike sentiments.

On December 4th another banquet was given at Castel Sant' Angelo, and about two hundred and fifty soldiers were present, invited there probably for political ends.

On December 5th[23] there were patriotic feasts in various Italian towns to celebrate the centenary of a gallant feat by the Genoese populace, when in 1746 they rose and drove the Austrians from their town—a triumph now chiefly remembered by the name of the boy Balilla. That night, dotted at intervals all along the mountain slopes of the Apennines, there were bonfires blazing up furiously, in clear view of one another from height to height for hundreds of miles. In fact a flame of patriotic triumph flashed right down the centre of Italy. No one could tell the originator of this touch of genius.

---

[22] On this day Pius issued an Encyclical attacking "modern progress" and evidently designed to reassure the Papal world as to his position with regard to spiritual matters. In it he declares himself definitely on the side of Conservatism in all matters of dogma and faith, and makes it clear that he will not sanction any attacks on Catholic dogma in the name of modern progress or reason. His view—as far as it may be understood by a Protestant layman—is that the Tradition is a matter settled once and for ever. Of course this is entirely contrary to Protestant, or agnostic creeds: but it is futile to attack Pope Pius IX—as has been done—for expressing these beliefs of his Church.

[23] *V*. Vatican Archives for local papers of this period.

It was said to be the idea of the exiled Count Terenzio Mamiani; the Moderates knew nothing about it.

At the end of 1846 the mental atmosphere in Rome was evidently febrile and disposed to exaggerated demonstrations —the very atmosphere that precedes an outbreak. It is well known that a town consumed by political excitement is apt to believe a hundred wild reports and to repose a hasty confidence first in one man and then in another more extreme. Pius of course was still regarded as a Messiah—"Homo missus a Deo"—and almost everyone professed himself a Liberal, but at the same time the Amnistiati, or pardoned rebels, were treated as heroes. Meanwhile, the followers of the old régime and the more thoughtful of the Moderate party went about in silence wondering whither Pius' policy would eventually lead him. "Quo vadis?" was the question constantly in their minds. They realised plainly enough that the path on which he had started must inevitably lead to the precipice. The moment must necessarily arrive when he would be asked: "Is it to be a constitutional government and war to the knife against Austria, or is it not?" As Pope it seemed impossible for him to accept either of these demands. Perhaps it is not surprising that in December Count Lützow, on his return to Rome, after a ten weeks' holiday, noticed that the strain of the agitation had told, visibly, on the Holy Father.[24]

[24] "J'ai vu avec bien de la peine que l'amertume qui se trouve dans le calice presenté de nos jours aux souverains...n'a laissé que de produire de l'effet sur le physique du Saint Père: ce n'est pas moi seulement qui aurait fait cette observation." Vienna Staats-Archiv, Rome, *Rapports*, 1, December 12th, 1846.

NOTE TO END OF CHAPTER V

Tivaroni, the great historian (republican), *Domin. Austr.* III, 472: "The republican party...were disposed to accept [the reforms]...to push them, to accept, to lead on from reform to reform right up to the possible and the impossible. In this way, one result had been obtained by the work—that of leading the lazy and the indifferent into the movement."

Gualterio (Moderate). "Some [of the extremists] who had remained faithful to the bonds of their secret societies (*setta*) although they had returned to the state in virtue of the Amnesty, others driven by individual ambition and natural tendency to agitation, and many of these irritated at seeing the common hopes betrayed [by Gizzi's moderation], formed the design of leading hypocritical support to the prince and fighting the government, by making the tumultous popular movement rise to its culminating point, and then organising it.... They fomented the enthusiasm of the people by every possible means, and tried to discipline it, by placing as directors of its movements men who were dear to the people and knew how to talk its language," namely Ciceruacchio: "who had the reputation of being the chief and almost the Gracchus of the Roman plebs, whereas he was nothing more than a docile and passive intrument in the hands of shrewd agitators."

Gualterio (1862 ed.), V, 95. See also Saffi, *loc. cit.*

Chapter VI

THE MOVEMENT TO WIN ARMS
CRITICISMS OF PIUS IX'S WORK

THE CIVIC GUARD

Amid all this turmoil of rejoicing we must devote a few paragraphs to tracing the beginning of what was by far the most important item in the national advance of Italy during this period, namely the movement to win arms for the people. That was a matter of life and death for Italy—and unfortunately equally so for Pius.

Of course the possession of arms is the turning-point in every revolution. An unarmed movement may be scattered by a hundred policemen; but once armed, the men become a power in the state. In the earlier stages agitation is necessary in order to obtain a united outlook, but once that agitation has created a sufficiently widespread unanimity, then the moment comes when talking and writing must be backed by force, or else the movement will die.

The nationalist method of winning a concession of arms was as follows. In most of the towns the police system had broken down: the policemen were old Gregorians who now could no longer browbeat their political opponents. The Liberals retaliated. Rows, crimes and even murders were frequent. In many places the citizens were organising Civic Guards for their own protection: namely corps of citizens armed and drilled for purposes of public order. And by this means too they hoped to have the basis of a national guard. Each of these units would consist of some hundreds or even thousands of volunteers, raised primarily to keep order, but also—as foreseen by the wire-pullers—to defend the Liberal concessions and prevent their being revoked by any succeeding Pope. And, thirdly, here would be a nucleus of soldiers for a war of liberation against Austria.

For Pius, however, another question came first: in these revolutionary times, would the Civic Guard become a danger to the Temporal Power?

It is strange to think that already he was approaching the end of his great effort at compromise, and also indeed the beginning of the end of the Temporal Power; for manifestly this concession would mean handing over the armed authority to the people. In most places the Civic Guards would far outnumber his police and army, and might easily use their muskets not merely to defend his Liberal grants but also to claim further concessions. The Civica was neither police nor soldiers; it was a specimen of that somewhat precarious southern institution, a popular armed guard—usually without much discipline, and liable to be swept by every gust of political passion.

Nevertheless the people were right in feeling that it was the only way of getting arms and military training for the coming war of Liberation.

Most probably Pius was hoping not to have to grant the Civica, but he was not bitterly opposed to it. Gizzi, however, was prepared to retire rather than accept it; and the Austrians regarded this movement simply as a threat to themselves. They followed it diligently, as we can see in their official reports.

Already[1] on October 3rd, 1846, the Chevalier Ohms (the Austrian Chargé d'Affaires), during Lützow's absence on a holiday, reported to Metternich that the chief aims of the Liberals were to make the troops appear useless in the eyes of the public: they do this, he said, either by reviling them or else by fraternising with them, while at the same time setting up a "quasi-national guard". Cardinal Gizzi, he adds, told him that the government could not cut short this movement for fear of popular exasperation, but would work for the gradual disappearance of the guards. On October 17th, 22nd

[1] Vienna Staats-Archiv, Rome, *Rapports*, I, contains all the above letters.

and 31st, and November 7th and 14th, Ohms sent in similar reports to Metternich and on December 26th Count Lützow, on his return to Rome, reported that the revolution had gained ground and was now claiming the national guards.

In this connection the movement had already achieved its first success. In Bologna there had been disorders and even murders. The populace was lawless, the Gregorian policemen were sulky and the Liberals complained that both they themselves and even the Liberal reforms required protection. The Civic Guard was a necessity. In September, forty nobles and citizens sent up a petition. Gizzi refused; but on December 1st the Provincial Council of Bologna drew up a formal programme of necessary reforms including the Civic or National Guard, and stated openly that it concerned not only their own interests "but also in part those of Italy". This was undisguised Italian nationalism: but so large a town as Bologna could not be denied a perfectly reasonable request. Pius granted it; and Gizzi, when in conversation with Lützow, defended it on the ground that it was an old privilege of Bologna, and would never be taken as a precedent. Gizzi was a fairly strong and sensible man: nevertheless the hard fact remained that this case in Bologna was at once taken as a precedent and became the first step towards winning a Civic Guard everywhere.[2]

CONTEMPORARY CRITICISMS OF PIUS' WORK TO END OF 1846

During these harassing times Pius' chief friends were his old confessor, the Abbé Graziosi, and next to him Cardinal Falconieri, who has been called "the saintly and learned prelate of Ravenna", and the Piedmontese Cardinal Amat;

[2] Vienna Staats-Archiv, Ohms to Metternich, October 22nd and 31st, 1846; Lützow to Metternich, January 9th, 1847; Gualterio (1851 ed.), I, 169: he gives documents; Minghetti, *Ricordi*, I, 210. V. also Farini, I, 204. Civic Guard is the official name: but throughout the state it was often called the National Guard.

the first-named, I think, of humble origin, and the other two
of rank similar to Pius' own. He was also on terms of friendship with his cousin Cardinal Gabriele Ferretti, the hero of
Rieti in 1831; and among the younger men, Monsignor
Corboli Bussi—delicate, intellectual, able and witty. Of laymen, Pellegrino Rossi, Pasolini and no doubt others. These
names we get mainly from the despatches of Count Lützow,
who had a warm admiration for Pius and continued to send
wonderfully favourable reports to Metternich, even after
Pius' Liberalism obviously became pain and grief to him.
Lützow regarded the Liberal Pope rather as a true-hearted
innocent whom we must try and prevent from committing
political suicide.

Among contemporary writers, the Moderates, such as
Farini and Gualterio, say many kind things about Pius in their
histories, but on a few points they offer adverse criticism.
They are rather disposed to blame him for being slow in
starting on the political side of his reforms; and for not dis-
missing the existing administrators at once and appointing
Moderates and laymen in their place.

Farini says:[3]

The government, which moved slowly in everything, moved
very slowly in the matter of changing officials, and seemed more
preoccupied with the strange idea of pleasing everyone and
offending no one than with that of making its reforms possible.

Gualterio expressed opinions more or less similar to those
of Farini as to changing officials, and he took the rather
strange view that Pius would have done well to publish beforehand a programme of his projected reforms.

One must remember that both Farini and Gualterio were
Moderates, and that after their movement had proved useless
as a bulwark against the Revolution, they, and others as well
—even Pellegrino Rossi—were rather inclined to make Pius
a scapegoat. Gualterio, for instance, says that in December

---

[3] Farini, I, 178.

1846 Pius' commissions "had not even begun their work and seemed to be set up only to gain time". This is not the case: it is simply an untrue statement.[4]

No one with any experience whatever of constitutional changes would have expected a new constitution in less than a year or eighteen months; least of all in the Papal State, where there had been no annual budget for ten years.

The more extreme political section, however, was gaining ground daily; it meant to catch up the Reform movement and sweep it along with it. One asks oneself: What ought Pius to have done? and the answer is very hard to find. Pellegrino Rossi held that Pius must at once set up some Liberal and laicised form of government sufficiently popular to satisfy —and more than satisfy—the Moderates: the whole people, he held, was advancing towards revolution; let Pius throw out a concession well in front of them, something rather better than they expected; something too good to be neglected. Let him set up some Liberal institution that would be joyfully received and manned by the Moderates, and so would become a government stronghold against the revolutionary demands of the extremists. And he wanted it to be in perfect working order before the Revolution could arrive at maturity.

In Paris there is a despatch from Pellegrino Rossi to Guizot in which he describes a remarkable interview with Pius on November 29th, 1846:[5]

[4] Neither Farini nor Gualterio nor any of the leading Moderates complained *at the time* (1846). *V*. Farini's letters during Pius' first year: again and again he expresses himself satisfied with the progress that Pius is making; so did d'Azeglio; so also did Gino Capponi. *V*. Farini, *Epistolario*, vol. 1; d'Azeglio, *Lettere a sua moglie*; and especially his letter of April 12th, 1847 (Rendu's *Correspondance politique de Massimo d'Azeglio*, p. 3). *V*. also Minghetti, *Ricordi*, vol. 1, and Carrarese, *Lettere di Gino Capponi*. Others could be cited. During the first year the Moderates were more than satisfied with Pius' progress; and, indeed, he could hardly have achieved more in the time. *V*. also Predari.

[5] Paris Aff. Etr., Rome, November 29th, 1846.

I found him, just as in the first days of his reign, quiet, resolute and anxious to carry out his views gradually, and with all consideration (perhaps too much consideration) for individuals and for their private interests. He complained of the opposition which he was encountering, and said that it could not be overcome by kindness: he added with an expression of modesty which was perfectly simple and natural, not seeking for a denial or a compliment, that—apart from this opposition—within the administrative machine there existed wheels of which he had no knowledge.

I said to His Holiness that one could only congratulate him on his wise perseverance in his projects of amelioration and reform; that apart from the real need for them in the country, there existed a general expectation which could not be disappointed without danger—and imminent danger; that—as must be clear to all sincere friends of the Holy See and of the policy of conservation and peace—these ameliorations were the only sure and legitimate way of removing this country from the hands of intriguers and revolutionists: that the country asked only for regular administration and for reforms which would not touch in any way the bases of the pontifical establishment....

Rossi then told Pius that he had received countless letters, remonstrances and schemes from all parts of the country and that they "asked for nothing that was incompatible with the constitution of the Holy See, or could reasonably give umbrage to anyone". Pius replied that he was greatly rejoiced to hear this, and that it was fully confirmed by other informants:

He then reverted to the obstacles which were being raised against him more especially by persons who ought to have aided and seconded him: he said that, unfortunately there had been an undue multiplication of official functions and positions, and that consequently the posts were poorly salaried and filled by men who were incompetent and badly paid: that it would be hard treatment to dismiss them without a pension, but that to pension them all would be ruinous for the Treasury.

This statement is confirmed a hundred times by Lützow, Gizzi and others.

In reply Rossi urged him to be firm in this question of the employés; it was, he said, "the capital" question.

Rossi's next paragraphs show firstly how Pius' policy was thwarted even by his own police, and secondly that he (Rossi) was rather anxious at Pius' not having any salient *political* reform to show: he foresaw that the era of his great popularity would pass.

He begins by describing how the police—enlisted under Gregory XVI—caused a riot in a theatre at Bologna; and then he continues:

At Bazzano, near Bologna, a banquet under the presidency of the district authorities was being held to celebrate in a perfectly inoffensive manner the succession of the new Pope and the Amnesty. No doubt people were shouting at the top of their voices, but most certainly they were only calling out "Pius IX forever". The Carbineers came in; raised a quarrel and killed two of the guests.[6]

What could I not tell you, M. le Ministre? In the very anteroom of the Pope the prelates on duty railed against His Holiness and his principles of government as soon as they thought they had a sympathetic audience. That was what was heard—to their profound surprise—by the attachés of the new Belgian Legation on the day when the Prince of Chimay presented his letters of credit.[7]

These are the instruments which the Holy Father has given himself by deciding, out of kindness, to preserve the personnel of the preceding pontificate.

To all this, one must add the fact that, after all, nothing has been accomplished yet; that hitherto there have been only promises, projects, and commissions which do but little work, and one will not be surprised to learn that the country is beginning to be distrustful and irritated. As yet it does not accuse the Pope of duplicity, but it suspects him of weakness.

[6] Minghetti had an audience with Pius at about this period and he confirmed this opinion as to the moderation of the reforms demanded. Pius replied: "Yes, but we require time and quiet." And soon afterwards they too spoke of the "horror" over the events at Bazzano, and of the necessity of changing the personnel. *V.* Minghetti, I, 215.

[7] These stories are included here because it seemed necessary to give this despatch almost in full: as a general rule only the last paragraph given above is quoted—out of its context—and consequently it conveys a wrong impression.

His Liberal friends were asking too much of him. The joint suggestions of Farini and Rossi would have signified the immediate initiation of three immense changes: the substitution of lay personnel for the clerical which would involve the sudden dismissal of a large number of pontifical administrators simply because they were clerics: also a more or less democratic constitution and an anti-Austrian policy.

Such sweeping changes were unimaginable in his first six months. The bureaucrats and the clerics (if they had the desire) could have made government impossible for him throughout the state, because he had no trained men to put in their place. In after years they said he had moved too slowly. But on the other hand two of the ablest clerics of that day both thought, afterwards, that he had moved too rapidly. Monsignore Pecci (afterwards Pope Leo XIII) said, later on, that Pius had advanced too fast in 1846 and had gone back too fast in 1848. Cardinal Antonelli agreed with the first part of this opinion, but not with the second.[8]

There was one Liberal at all events who greatly feared that Pius was being hurried by the people. On October 2nd, 1846, Massimo d'Azeglio had already published a pamphlet-letter (*Lettera a Sig. N.N.*) in which he urged the people to trust Pius and to give him time:

I see him with a rapidity which reminds one of the sure method of the greatest men, grant in the space of a few days the Amnesty, the railways, the infant schools, the public audiences; restrict the expenses of his court, and, amid general approval, either give or withdraw rewards and appointments.... I say that such a man as this has done more for Italy in two months[9] than all the Italians together have done in twenty years.

As to hurrying on Pius to grant self-government to his people, Massimo suggested the following analogy. Take the case of a man who is dying, after a long illness, owing to lack

[8] Soderini, *Il Pontificato di Leone XIII*, p. 177. We may note that in reality Pius could not be said to go back at all in 1848.

[9] In reality it was 3½ months after Pius' accession. Sig. N.N. was Minghetti.

of skill on the part of his doctor. He gets a new doctor, both expert and prudent, who gives him hope of recovery. Would it be wise for him to get up and start his everyday life and food at once? Would not the doctor be right in using force to prevent his patient's doing so?

At that time no one could foretell whether the revolution was really coming or not—and it did not actually break out in Paris until February 1848. Surely, therefore, the wisest course for Pius to pursue was that on which he had started: namely the appointment of commissions to enquire as to how matters really stood; and more especially to report the exact amount of the annual revenue and annual deficit. After that he would be in a position to introduce reforms which would gradually lead to a freer type of government without causing internal convulsions. It was evident that there must be no false moves on the part of the Pope, for even if all went smoothly, it would be an extraordinarily delicate undertaking to reconcile the Church institutions and dignitaries with the new Liberal ideas.

It was towards the end of March 1847 that he sent for his old friend Pasolini to come and see him in Rome, and on April 6th received him in an audience.[10]

"He was kind enough", says Pasolini in a letter to Ravenna, "to remind me of the days when I used to see him as Bishop of Imola, and of the talks that we had. From what he said I gathered that he has a very accurate idea of the actual circumstances all over the country, and was determined to achieve its good in spite of all the resistance that he meets, to which he opposes an admirable spirit of courage and hopefulness. I will not conceal from you that during all that long audience he seemed to me greater than I had known him, and I wished myself better qualified to talk with him. On Friday he again received me, with my wife, and again showed himself most courteous and kind."

[10] Pasolini, I, 81.

Chapter VII

1847, JANUARY TO JULY. ROME AND THE AGITATORS

To obtain a clear skeleton outline of the whole year of 1847 we will begin by saying that the agitation in Rome led the way for the rest of Italy, because the Pope was ready to grant its demands as far as his sacred calling would permit; so in the Papal State the advance was rapid; and almost at once the other princes were compelled to follow in his footsteps.

In Rome the three principal objectives aimed at by the agitators were the Press Law, the Consulta and the armed Civic Guard. The Press Law was granted on March 15th, 1847, the Consulta was promised to them on April 19th, and the Civic Guard was conceded—unwillingly—on July 5th. Thus in Rome the three main objectives were secured, we may say, within the first half of 1847.

But in the other states of Italy, generally, the advance followed upon that of Rome: their agitation aimed, during the first half of 1847, at winning the Press Law; and during the second half at winning the Consulta and the Civic Guard.

Of all these concessions the right to have an armed Civic Guard was by far the most important.

In Rome during these six months (January to July 1847) the Nationalists of all types become more aggressive in their attitude towards Pius: and it is often hard to keep a well-balanced opinion as to their motives.

The standpoint of the Progressive agitators may be described perhaps as follows. Here they had a magnificent opportunity: they had a Pope who was a genuine Liberal ready to make all possible sacrifices for the people. They must not lose this chance. They must praise him, encourage him or even drive him forward. They must make the very most of his movement: otherwise he would stop short, and then their wonderful, unparalleled opportunity would be lost. They knew that he was being held back by Gregorians: down with the Gregorians, Austrians, Jesuits and the like! This time we will not be put off with mere administrative or industrial reforms: we will take a genuine step forward towards political freedom and Italian independence, and we will establish an armed Civic Guard to see that the next Pope does not go back. Then, when every town has a Civic Guard, we shall be an armed nation; and to be armed is to be free!

The crucial point for everyone lay in the question: How far, exactly, can one expect the Pope to go? And each person fixed the limit according to his own opinion; we have already described the views of various parties.

In Rome, says Spada the Papal historian, the Revolution[1] had been a baby in 1846, but in 1847 it was in the flower of its youth; he then proceeds to tell us that it was to reach maturity in 1848 and to die of its own lack of control in 1849.

During the earlier half of 1847 we find the agitators using the same methods as before, but with greater boldness: firstly and secondly, directing the crowds and organising banquets as heretofore; thirdly, they are founding newspapers, both clandestine and legitimate; and fourthly, starting clubs. Of these methods, the two latter weapons could be worked most effectively in combination with one another, especially after Pius had relaxed the Censorship (March 15th, 1847). In the provinces they were already advancing towards the possession of armed Civic Guards.

I AND II. CROWDS AND BANQUETS

The banquet which took place on New Year's Day is another example of innocent enthusiasm on the part of the people and careful organisation on the part of the wire-pullers. Evidently it was regarded by the latter as more or less a trial of strength between the genuine Moderates and agitators.

---

[1] Spada called it the Revolution. He thought Mazzini was the prime mover; but this, as we have seen, was a mistake.

In the morning there was a great meeting in the Piazza del
Popolo, of students, Amnistiati, frequenters of the Belle Arti
Caffè and some of the Trasteverine populace.[2] From thence
they defiled, about five hundred strong, marching in fours
along the Corso,[3] headed by Ciceruacchio bearing a banner on
which were inscribed certain reforms that they wanted. As
they moved onward they were joined by large numbers of
citizens, until they formed the centre of an imposing crowd
which wended its way up to the Quirinal to offer Pius its New
Year's greetings. This morning's work is apparently regarded
by Gualterio as the beginning of a new phase:[4] "The people
were no longer merely *applauding*, but *demanding*", he says,
and the same idea struck Bargagli, the Tuscan minister in
Rome. Certainly, on this day, it was from the crowd and no
longer from the prince that came the suggestion of new
reforms. But in reality it was not the people who were
demanding, though it had the appearance of being so, but
merely the revolutionary section of the crowd headed by the
five hundred men drilled and organised by Ciceruacchio and
his leaders. The majority of the Roman citizens had come out
merely to wish their sovereign a prosperous New Year.
Presently they sent in a deputation, to whom Pius made a
suitable reply; and then, as he appeared on the high balcony
of the Quirinal palace he was received with a thunderous
shout of "Viva Pio Nono!" and, as usual, he blessed the

[2] Vatican Arch., Fondo Spada, 7. Also Gualterio and others.
[3] The *Contemporaneo* (January 9th, 1847) describes it as follows:
"When the singing ceased, with that same wonderful order with
which the feast had been inaugurated there moved off along the
Corso that immense tide of nobles, citizens and populace all turned
into brothers by the great sentiment which they held in common:
and it was astounding to see how they all moved in long files of eight
[of eight lines of fours?] keeping perfect order, without the slightest
confusion." The *Contemporaneo* of course was a sympathiser with
the movement and made the most of the scene. *V.* also Vatican Arch.,
Fondo Spada, Relazione Mathey.
[4] Gualterio (1862 ed.), v, 154; Florence Arch., Dip. Est., Busta
2956.

thousands of people below. By now they had received blessings on many occasions, but on this, the New Year's morn, it was taken to be an omen that, as he stood there looking down upon that great concourse, said to number as many as sixty thousand, a ray of sunlight suddenly broke through the clouds and fell upon his face, and that a dove— whether released by chance or by some enthusiastic supporter one cannot say—flew hither and thither close over the heads of the people.

In the evening came the celebration by the Moderates and reactionaries.[5] A cantata in praise of Pius, written by the poet Marchetti and set to music by the famous Rossini, was given in the great senatorial hall of the Capitol. There were about twelve hundred people present, including thirteen cardinals, and various distinguished foreigners such as the Count of Syracuse (brother of the King of Naples), the Princess of Saxony and the Duke of Devonshire. It was organised by two hundred and fifty shareholders, "people of consideration", and paid for mainly by Prince Torlonia, the head of a new and wealthy Roman family of bankers.

One point is absolutely certain; that the democratic morning demonstration under Ciceruacchio was far more suitable for party propaganda than the evening entertainment. The agitators were now no longer merely leading the crowd. They had got to the point of training, and even drilling them; and it was their policy to encourage such demonstrations. Their guiding principle, culled perhaps from Mazzini, was "Associate".[6] They believed that by accustoming the crowds to assemble, they could train them to make their will bear on the sovereign—and that of course is the object of every

[5] *Contemporaneo*, January 9th, 1847; *La Rivista*, January 11th, 1847.

[6] That this was the policy of the republicans is admitted by writers of all shades of opinion. Gabussi, for instance (*Memorie*, 1, 56), writes as follows: "Thus the right of association, so necessary to a people on its forward path, was, I might almost say, conquered by the Romans, although never actually consecrated (*consacrato*) by

agitation. Each reform in turn was to be loudly cheered and
to be received as being the prelude to something more extreme; the revolutionary bodies were to join with such
enthusiasm in the popular rejoicings that no one would doubt
that Pius was on their side. Already it was constantly stated
that he had given his blessing to the Revolution; soon he
would be unable to withdraw from the situation without being
regarded as a traitor who had broken his promises.

And, if rebellion against the Papal government should
eventually become necessary, this system of gathering huge
crowds for thanksgiving and thus teaching them to act in
unison would produce invaluable results. To the leaders every
crowd was a weapon: it could easily be inflamed to anger;
and in those days, anger might mean revolt. "By means of
gatherings of the people the demonstrations were started;
and by means of these demonstrations was prepared the
revolution", says Spada, who lived in it. "From flowers they
could pass to arms—as actually happened."

The great majority of the people were still devoted to Pius;
but that this was the deliberate policy of the organisers is not
denied by them. Gabussi, for instance (*Memorie*, 1, 58),
himself a strong republican, tells us that the enthusiasm of
the people was encouraged by the agitators, and that its
demonstrations would not have reached so exuberant a pitch
if they had not been

egged on with unflagging zeal by the press, and received the very
warmest encouragement to give to the acts of the Pope a greater
importance than they actually deserved: a course which I personally do not disapprove, which in fact I am ready to praise:
because—if we wanted to prevent the Pope from coming to a halt,

the permission of the sovereign; and this was done under pretence
of celebrating the glories of the Pontiff and exalting any act of his.
But at these gatherings the pensiero italiano (thoughts of the Italian
ideal) would fall from people's lips and they began to unite the name
and glory of Pius with the name and glory of Italy, and to form hopes
that, arising under the shadow of the Cross, our country might
recover her ancient splendour."

and to avoid offering our enemies a chance of slandering us, and above all to produce a great moral effect on the outside world—if we wanted these things, it was necessary that the people should pretend to be pleased with every reform and every new concession, and should not appear too hard to satisfy. Therefore the people manifested their gratitude to their worthy Pontiff both by words and by applause; some of them from sincere conviction, and others because they thought that their act would pave the way to genuine and radical institutions.

The government, and especially Pius himself, disliked these demonstrations[7] and was aware that these ovations, though in themselves fundamentally genuine, were being used by the politicians to represent the Pope as an extremist. In any case Pius would have preferred to work quietly at first so as to avoid arousing the Conservatives against him. He determined therefore to make another and more striking expression of his wishes on the subject.

On the evening of January 13th he presented himself, un-expected, at the church of S. Andrea della Valle, and, to the surprise of Padre Ventura, expressed his intention of preach-ing. Then in the course of his sermon, he asked the people to abstain from further scenes of enthusiasm. Count Lützow reported to Metternich that this unexpected protest created a notable impression.[8]

III. NEWSPAPERS

Before the end of the old year 1846 the Progressives had made a fresh and really important advance by founding a newspaper of the modern political type. This marks a step forward in the Risorgimento. It was called the *Contempo-raneo* and achieved a success so rapid that the whole of its first issue was sold out, and it was obliged to print a new one to satisfy the general demand.

[7] Florence Arch., Dip. Est., Busta 2956, January 4th, 1847: Bargagli to the Tuscan government.

[8] Bargagli reported about this to the Tuscan government, just as Lützow did to Metternich, *v.* Florence Arch., Dip. Est., Busta 2956, January 16th, 1847, and also Vienna Staats-Archiv, Fasc. 76, January 16th, 1847.

It was a good newspaper for those days. It consisted of
four large sides which appeared weekly at first and afterwards
daily, and cost the subscriber 3.60 scudi or about fifteen
shillings a year. Its articles were long for modern taste—often
they contained as many as three thousand words—but they
were well written, and covered almost every kind of intellectual interest. Its politics were progressive but moderate;
at first they consisted chiefly in praising the Pope and his movement, and in showing respect for religion. In its earlier numbers
reform was mentioned only in the most guarded terms, but
before very long the paper became more extreme and its
hostile criticisms were regarded by the Papal authorities as an
ungrateful misuse of Pius' concession of freedom to the press.

On April 29th, 1847, another important newspaper[9] made
its appearance, namely the *Bilancia* (the Balance or Weighing-
Machine). It was started partly as a set-off against the
increasingly progressive views of the *Contemporaneo*. Its
guiding spirit was Professor Orioli, and his programme was
"slow and pondered progress". This too was a good newspaper and a credit to the movement: but the *Bilancia* was
soon followed by the *Contro-Bilancia* or Counterbalance,
started by certain strong Liberals who were alarmed at the
moderate views of the *Bilancia*. Thus, before long, newspapers
were springing up like mushrooms. Under Pius' relaxed
censure there must have been nearly a hundred of them in
Rome during the years 1847 and 1848.

In connection with the press the government showed itself
extraordinarily ignorant of the art of popular administration.
The ministers were doing their best to carry out a very
delicate policy, and therefore they ought at all costs to have
secured a strong and interesting press to hammer in their
views and prevent misrepresentation. For any ruler to try
to negotiate a peaceful upheaval of the people, without
newspapers, is obviously as foolish as to start galloping a
horse without having any reins. In this respect the *Contem-*

[9] For its Prospectus *v.* Vatican Arch., Fondo Spada, 7.

poraneo very soon taught the government a lesson. So rapid was its progress (so it claimed) that on March 6th, 1847, it had established agencies for collecting subscriptions in Bologna, Ancona, Florence, Lucca, Turin, Genoa, Milan, Venice, Lugano, Naples, Palermo, Messina, Paris, London, Madrid, Vienna, Berlin, St Petersburg, Constantinople, Egypt, Smyrna and New York. Its first four directors were men of singularly different types; Monsignor Carlo Gazòla (a Liberal priest), the Marquis Ludovico Potenziani (a Moderate and a political economist), Count Federigo Torre (a young Beneventan who afterwards turned republican) and Dr Luigi Masi (the young poet of the movement): but all these were soon to be overshadowed by Dr Pietro Sterbini who, during the next eighteen months, became editor and then owner of the *Contemporaneo*. He was a middle-aged Mazzinian and one of the ablest journalists in Rome. The first article from his pen appeared on April 1st, and at once it seemed to introduce a note of more extreme opinion.

IV. THE CLUBS

During these months of April and May 1847 there was initiated the last of the four principal developments of Mazzini's doctrine of association: three clubs were opened— the Circolo Romano, the Società Artistica and the Casino dei Commercianti. This was a very important step; in times of unrest all clubs sooner or later turn to politics, and in Rome before long every political question was discussed and settled at the Circolo Romano; eventually, in fact, matters reached such a pass that plans of agitation were arranged even before a measure had been published. Spada complains that during the year 1847 the Circolo Romano[10] ruled Rome—as Metternich also remarked; and in 1848 a far more democratic club,

[10] At the beginning of May there were 309 members in the Circolo Romano. The most prominent were princes of the oldest families in Rome. At the same time there were members of the type of Massimo d'Azeglio and Pantaleoni; and—which is more surprising—it also included Esaltati such as Sterbini and Masi.

the Circolo Popolare, took its place under the guidance of
Sterbini.

THE PRINCIPAL AGITATORS

When Pius was a very old man he once remarked gaily that
he thought that he himself and Garibaldi were the only people
who had made nothing out of the Risorgimento. This jest may
perhaps have been due to recollections of certain of the new
and ambitious characters who began to appear in Rome during
the spring of 1847. Some of them—as Metternich had
prophesied—were Amnistiati, now turned agitators: most of
them were of the Esaltati type.

We will begin with the highest in point of rank, namely
Carlo Bonaparte,[11] Prince of Canino. He was a true Bonaparte by blood, being the son of Lucien, Napoleon's brother,
by his second wife Alexandrine de Bleschamps; born at Paris
in the year 1803, the eldest of nine. In the same year the
family was exiled because Lucien refused to give up his wife;
but the Pope received them kindly and gave them a villa at
Frascati. In 1808 they were driven from there; they set sail
for America; were captured by an English frigate; were
landed in Malta and then interned in Wales until 1814. At
last on the fall of Napoleon they returned to Rome, where
Pope Pius VII again received Lucien with great kindness and
created the Principality of Canino for him. Prince Carlo was
educated at Pavia, Padua and Bologna; in 1822 he married
his first cousin (Princess Zenaide, daughter of Joseph Bonaparte) and then emigrated to the United States. While there
he was able to pursue his favourite study, Natural History,
and in 1832 published at Philadelphia a work called *An
American Ornithology*, said to be of some value.

In 1837 he returned to Europe, at the age of thirty-four,
and five years later published a book which earned him a

[11] *V.* Giovagnoli, *Ciceruacchio*, p. 218; Farini, 1, 173, 174;
Minghetti, 1, 203; Ferrari (Rina), *Il Principe di Canino*. He is
described by almost everybody who knew him.

definite position in the scientific world, namely the *Iconografia della Fauna italica.*

To look at he was short, fat, rubicund and spectacular,[12] but of smart appearance, and usually dressed in black; his biographer says that he had the strange notion "of always, at any time of the day, wearing black evening clothes". His face was rather of the Napoleonic type—and so were some of his tendencies. He was a revolutionary politician, of the ambitious variety: noisy, restless, vain, a fiery orator with a sonorous, Bonaparte voice, and rather given to rodomontade; his best quality, that he was a good father; his most sincere belief, perhaps, that in democracy. The story is told of him that being the owner of a fine property and a Roman prince-dom, he had sold the estate for a hundred thousand scudi and the title for a halfpenny (one soldo) and had had both bargains entered in the deed. No doubt the story is untrue, for he certainly continued to be known as Prince Canino, and in Roman society he was a person of some standing owing to his friendly relations with his two old uncles, Louis the ex-King of Holland, and Joseph the ex-King of Spain to whose daughter he was married. However, as a republican and an atheist (like many scientific men at that time) he was not on the best of terms with the Papal Court.

The shrewdest piece of work in his life was his founding of the annual Scientific Congresses for all Italy.[13]

[12] Minghetti, I, 203.

[13] In *Wanderings in South America*, by the English naturalist Charles Waterton, there occurs an anecdote which, if accurate, is also greatly to his credit. It rests on the authority of Mr J. G. Wood, the editor of the book. He describes how Waterton was on board a vessel named the *Pollux* bound from Civita Vecchia to Leghorn, when it was run into on a starlight night and almost cut in two by a steamer named the *Mongibello*. "As is too often the case under similar circumstances the officials on board the offending vessel lost their presence of mind and were actually sheering off from the wreck. Had it not been for the courage and skill of Prince Canino (Charles Bonaparte) the loss of life would have been very great. He was a passenger on board the *Mongibello,* knocked the steersman off

Dr Luigi Masi, his private secretary, was a far better man than Prince Canino himself. He was a young Perugian,[14] an enthusiastic Italian nationalist, a doctor of medicine, a journalist, a poet and an orator. He seems to have had a wonderful gift for improvising verses, and was constantly called upon to recite or speak at the banquets and political meetings during this period. But he was not merely a talker: he was a genuine patriot, always ready to put his life in the balance for his beliefs. When war broke out in 1848 he volunteered for it, and was taken as private secretary by General Ferrari. In the following year he served as colonel of a battalion under Garibaldi during his defence of Rome; in the next war, ten years later, we find him again to the fore, commanding a battalion in 1859; and in 1860 he raised the Cacciatori del Tevere (Chasseurs of the Tiber), at whose head he seized the towns of Orvieto and Viterbo. At the time of his death he was a general in the Italian army; but he seems to have been at his best when commanding irregulars, and to have had a talent for inspiring them with his own enthusiasm.

A very different character was Dr Pietro Sterbini, who was destined to be, very shortly, one of the most powerful men in Rome.[15] Within about eighteen months he became editor and then owner of the *Contemporaneo* and also President of the Circolo Popolare, the club which ruled the government in 1848. He was the journalist-organiser of the *Esaltati* section.

Born in Lazio in 1798 he had studied medicine at the Roman University, and had started in life as a medical practitioner, as a conspirator of Carbonaro tendencies, and as a poet. After the rebellion of 1831 he fled to Paris, and thence

the wheel, took the helm himself and laid the vessel alongside the sinking *Pollux*. Only one life was lost, that of a man who had a large sum of gold sewed in a belt round his waist and was drawn under water by the weight." *V.* p. 26 of Waterton's *Wanderings in South America*, edited by the Rev. J. G. Wood.

[14] Born at Petrignano in 1814. Giovagnoli, *Ciceruacchio*, p. 103. *V.* also Minghetti 1, 204.

[15] Giovagnoli, *Ciceruacchio*, p. 100.

went to Marseilles, where in 1840 he joined the Giovine Italia, and worked as its local agent there for the next six years.[16] In August 1846 he and several others were pardoned under Pius' amnesty and returned to Rome without notifying the revolutionists; by that time he was a man of forty-eight and apparently rather embittered by fifteen years of poverty and exile.

Outwardly he was not attractive; a somewhat coarse, spectacled face, a thick-set body and a harsh voice rather in consonance with his looks. But what strikes one most is the general bitterness against him, among his contemporaries. They evidently regarded him as an unscrupulous mob-organiser; and certainly, later on, appearances were against him. Perhaps he deteriorated during the course of the next two years.[17]

Although Sterbini was one of the earliest "Amnistiati" or pardoned men, nevertheless in January 1847 he had already started a secret newspaper, *La Sentinella*. It was said to be harmless, but, as Pius was displeased, Sterbini abandoned it. He was then enabled to obtain a post on the *Contemporaneo* and for perhaps a year his newspaper articles were well studded with compliments[18] to Pius, probably because he believed and intended that the agitation should carry Pius with it. It is very difficult to write with perfect confidence of Sterbini's motives, but a long perusal of his articles gives one

---

[16] *Protocollo*, IV, 116, 123.

[17] The common belief is that Sterbini was the man who organised the murder of Pellegrino Rossi; and that the actual blow was struck by a son of Ciceruacchio. As to his appearance it is only fair to add that the only picture that I have seen of him was more complimentary than the descriptions. Tivaroni describes him as "thin", but his portraits do not suggest it. (Tivaroni, *Domin. Austr.* II, 354.)

[18] "Sterbini is composing sickening (*stomachevole*) adulations to the Pope", Lamberti to Mazzini, October 3rd, 1846, *Protocollo*, IV, 157. Gualterio (1862 ed.), V, 342 (or 13) note says that "several witnesses of good faith" had seen reports in Sterbini's writing to Del Carretto, head of the Neapolitan police. This is perhaps the worst accusation against him: but it cannot be tested.

an impression that there existed genuine feeling at their back. Assuming that this was so, one can say about him: that he was an advanced democrat; that he received the first concessions with apparently genuine expressions of gratitude, and was ready to accept the idea of a federated nation with the Pope as president; that he wanted Italy to be free from the Austrians and the Five Powers; that his patriotism was unscrupulous; and that if the Pope or any of the Italian princes failed him they would find no more callous or hard-bitten revolutionist in all Italy than Sterbini. When Pius had served his turn Pius could go. This actually occurred in 1848.

Farini has written of him that he was "ignorant of everything except the history of Ancient Rome and the phrases and facts of the French Revolution". But imperial Rome and the French Revolution were powerful themes in 1847—especially as a contrast to Papal Rome; and Sterbini was not ignorant. He was an able, thoughtful, even powerful journalist, with an excellent gift for clarifying people's ideas on current topics, and catching their interest by an arresting phrase. His articles made the *Contemporaneo* a power. Moreover he was a poet of some merit—as poets went in 1847; during the next few years Sterbini's hymn was received as the national anthem.

But literature is only one side of a progressive movement; the other is agitation: and during the coming year Sterbini undoubtedly controlled the shouting populace of Rome by means of his influence over Ciceruacchio, who seems to have regarded him with the deep respect sometimes exhibited by an uneducated man for what he regards as a master-mind. Moreover, a year later, Sterbini acquired a third source of power, as founder and president of the Circolo Popolare.

The last of the politicians who need be described is Ciceruacchio, the leader of the Trasteverine populace, that is to say, the inhabitants of the poor quarter on the far side of the Tiber; and to him at all events there is a statue beside that river.[19]

[19] On Lungotevere Arnaldo da Brescia, close to Ponte Margherita.

It commemorates the fact that he took part in Garibaldi's defence of Rome, was one of the last men with him during the retreat, and finally was captured and shot by the Austrians. His name suggests the following picture:[20] a popolano, a man of the people; a cheery loud-voiced Trasteverine wine-carter with a great flow of talk, but nearly all in dialect, not in Italian; above middle height, robust, with broad shoulders and a thick throat, muscular legs, largish face, blue eyes, very light chestnut hair, and a pink and white skin. His dress, in which he affected a certain elegance, was the dress of his class; in style perhaps it had a faint suggestion of a London coster—a short jacket usually of velvet, over a short waist-coat, trousers tight at the knee but swelling out into a bell-shape at the ankle; a large silk scarf round his waist, a flowered silk handkerchief about his neck; on his head a hat "a cenceo" rather high and tapering, "almost like a Calabrian hat".

"Ciceruacchio" was merely a nickname given to him as a baby on account of his rotundity. His real name was Angelo Brunetti. He was a wine-carter, and the son of a blacksmith, so his education had gone no farther than reading, making up accounts, and writing; we put the writing last because it was his weak subject. But he had done well in life. He was full of vitality and courage: the man with the quick intelligence and the loud voice, the same man whom we find all over the world, taking hold of a situation and pushing it through. He had made his way from small beginnings; buying a fresh horse and cart when his savings permitted, carrying hay when the wine trade was slack; then, as his connection increased, he showed an increasing capacity and power of organising. Soon he had a wine business of his own. But he was a politician.

He was, in fact, an old Carbonaro of the year 1830 if not earlier, and a member of the Giovine Italia since 1833.

[20] Giovagnoli, *Ciceruacchio*, pp. 76, 77; Masi, *Nell' Ottocento*, p. 163. *V. Dizionario del Risorgimento* under "Brunetti" for a rather adulatory article on him.

In 1837, during the epidemic of cholera, he distinguished himself by his good work for those in suffering, but in the same year he became implicated in a political plot. In 1846 we find him still a member of Mazzini's society, and—as he was a good organiser, well-off, and immensely popular among his own people—rapidly becoming one of its leaders. He knew how to sway the Trastevere: at quite a short notice he could call out his men by the hundred.

For the time being Pius' personality and his liberal policy had won over Ciceruacchio to his side; but he remained a republican, and his lack of education, which made him shy in the presence of educated people, also made him very susceptible to the influence of men such as Sterbini, who used him freely to put their schemes into practice. Other agitators thought out the plan of action, and then got Ciceruacchio to lead the mob.

THE PROGRESS OF THE AGITATION (JANUARY TO JUNE 1847)

These four men, and others of the Esaltati type (violent-moderate), soon began to take the lead in the agitation. The aim was to keep Pius moving forward; to give him no respite until the political aims were secured.

It would be impossible to follow or describe all the demonstrations and banquets that took place before the end of Pius' first year. The agitators certainly showed a marked improvement in organisation as the weeks went on. It was said that they proposed, when the crisis arrived, to make each demonstration follow on top of the one before, and never to let popular excitement abate. Meanwhile on February 10th a banquet was given to Massimo d'Azeglio,[21] and another to

[21] On this occasion he made an excellent speech urging moderation, and was received in audience by Pius on the following day, and is said to have been greatly touched by the kindness of Pius' greeting (v. Contemporaneo, February 20th, 1847). One notices, however, that throughout all this period Massimo d'Azeglio seems to be working with Ciceruacchio, and it is hard to say exactly what that means.

Richard Cobden; and on the 23rd Ciceruacchio gave one which was attended by d'Azeglio. But, for the moment, the agitators contented themselves mainly with influencing the popular demonstrations which followed each reform by Pius.[22] His censorship law, passed on March 15th, was not considered quite sweeping enough, so at the next demonstration the crowd, while still cheering him to the echo, mingled with their applause such cries as "Viva Pio Nono *solo*. Coraggio, Santo Padre!" "Long live Pius IX *alone*. Courage, Holy Father."[23] The organisers imagined that he was being held back by the old Gregorian party, and as yet it was against that party that their anger was directed. By these cries they were urging him to act on his own initiative; and according to Spada, Ciceruacchio was leading a special band of cheerers, who, by means of short cuts, made their special cries heard at three different points along the line.

Gualterio tells us that Pius was greatly discouraged because he saw that his reforms would be misrepresented to the mob to make them ask for more. Certainly it was hard for him to distinguish the false from the genuine approval. On March 4th, for instance, Gioberti wrote him a touching letter of admiration: "Within a few months you have achieved more good for religion, by far, than some of your predecessors...in many years."[24]

At the end of April 1847 the government made another determined attempt to put an end to this agitation by banquets and by demonstrations. It was time; on three days running there had been immense political assemblages; on April 20th Ciceruacchio had given a banquet, for no very definite

[22] Not only on some special occasion, but every day "they aroused the people in tumult to be an arbiter and a tribunal before which every act of the government was brought up for judgment. By these beginnings they were preparing the reign of anarchy". Gualterio (1862 ed.), v, 268; *v*. also Spada, I, 195.

[23] Spada, I, 195; Gualterio (1862 ed.), v, 267–9.

[24] Vatican Arch., Fondo Spada, 7, and also 2, No. 29A.

reason,[25] to about two hundred people at the "Quercia di Tasso" (Tasso's Oak), up on the Janiculum hill. One is surprised to hear that some of the most distinguished people in Rome accepted his invitations. Old Prince Corsini presided, and among the guests were Massimo d'Azeglio and his co-nationalist the Marchese Pareto, Piedmontese minister in Rome.

On April 21st there was another and far larger political banquet for the annual feast in honour of the foundation of Rome. Near the Baths of Titus on the Esquiline hill tables were laid in the form of a star with seven points—to commemorate the Seven Hills. Massimo d'Azeglio was principal orator and spoke with eloquence about the ancient glories of Rome soon to be renewed under Pius IX; the Marchese Dragonetti, a revolutionist from Naples, and Dr Sterbini also made speeches, and nearly nine hundred people attended. On this occasion Sterbini's hymn to Rome was sung for the first time.

On April 22nd there took place the last great demonstration before the end of Pius' first year, the most heartfelt of all— the thanksgiving for the Consulta.

This has already been described as a genuine act of gratitude for Pius' first step towards resigning some of his own authority in favour of some form of national representation; but it was also a triumph of organisation for the extremists.[26] They prepared it in the following way:

From their two headquarters the orders were sent out to

[25] Count Lützow (Austria) says "a banquet of over 160 people... on the rather specious pretext of the Pope's arrival at the Vatican where he only spent four days". As to the banquet on April 21st, he says there were 900 guests, and "about 4000 spectators of either sex and every class, admitted by ticket". Vienna Staats-Archiv, 1847, *Rapports*, 1, April 23rd.

[26] Of course there are many descriptions of all these banquets, but perhaps the most impartial accounts are to be found in the despatches of Bargagli, the Tuscan minister to the Holy See. *V.* Florence Arch., Dip. Est., 1846–8, Busta 2956; especially those for April 22nd and April 23rd, 1847.

the heads of each of the rioni (fourteen in number) in Rome. Each head of a rione sent his orders to his capi-squadra (heads of squadrons) and each capo-squadra brought his followers. Bands played and Ciceruacchio was standard-bearer. In fact they now had everything necessary for capturing the government except arms and uniforms, and these they had long been calling for on the pretext of raising a civic guard.

The secret intentions of the organisers were becoming plain even to outsiders such as Count O'Sullivan, the Belgian minister, or Mr Petre, the British representative in Rome. When writing to Sir George Hamilton on June 23rd, 1847, about Gizzi's notification forbidding these demonstrations, Mr Petre said:[27]

As to these public meetings and processions it was certainly desirable that they should be put an end to. No longer, as at the beginning of the Pope's reign, a spontaneous outbreak of enthusiasm...they were gradually getting under the management of two or three hundred individuals, some perhaps with no very peaceable designs. They would, there is little doubt, have attempted sooner of later to dictate to and overawe the government.

Count Lützow[28] also—for about the twentieth time—expressed similar views to Metternich (despatch of April 23rd), and on June 18th Pellegrino Rossi[29] wrote in like terms to Guizot.

One fact was assured—that Pius would persist in his endeavour to save the Temporal Power and the prestige of the Holy See by establishing it on a modern basis. After an interview with him on March 13th the Tuscan minister, Bargagli, reported to his government in Florence:[30]

He realises his independence both political and religious; he believes that God has committed to him the mission of contributing to his subjects' happiness by re-uniting Religion and Civilisa-

---

[27] *London Corr*. Pt. II, p. 53.
[28] Vienna Staats-Archiv, Rome, 1847, *Rapports*, I.
[29] Paris Aff. Etr., Rome, 1847–48.
[30] Florence Arch., Dip. Est., 1846–48, Busta 2956.

tion to one another. And when have religious convictions such as these ever been changeable?

This opinion is also confirmed in Lützow's despatches.

PIUS' POSITION IN EUROPE AT THE END OF HIS FIRST YEAR

In Rome, though no longer on very safe ground, Pius was still immensely popular with the bulk of the people. So great was the anxiety for his health that in the beginning of June he received a petition, signed by thousands, begging him not to give up his usual visit to his country house at Castel-Gandolfo. As it was known that his motive was economy, the signatories asked to be allowed to defray the expenses. The loss, after 1870, of these annual visits to the Campagna must have been a serious matter for the Popes.

On May 13th, Ascension Day,[31] which happened to be his name-day, he drove in state to the Lateran, and the whole way, especially on his return journey, was lined with people who had come once again in their thousands to greet him. It is said that when he appeared on the balcony there were forty thousand people kneeling to receive his blessing. "A new and touching feature", said the Tuscan minister, "was the immense quantity of flowers that were thrown towards the pontifical terrace."

Outside the borders of Italy Pius' movement had won an almost universal approval.

In France his progress has been described as follows by Guizot, a Protestant:[32]

At each step taken by the new Pontiff upon his path of innovation, each time that he appeared in public the crowds assembled and received him with the most effusive expressions of satisfaction and gratitude. "*Corragio, Santo Padre!*" a whole nation cried aloud. And to the popular acclamations of the Romans were soon joined the parliamentary acclamations of Europe; "*Courage, Saint Père!*" from the French Chamber of Deputies.

[31] Vatican Arch., Fondo Spada, No. 41.
[32] On February 4th, 1847; v. Guizot, *Mémoires*, VIII, 340.

In England—so said the Roman people—he was gaining ground. It was the era of Newman and Manning; and great hopes were aroused in Rome by a reply of Lord John Russell with reference to re-establishing diplomatic relations with the Holy See: he had said that, as Pius IX had shown such liberality of opinion, it was desirable that these relations should be revived.

We are told too that the Roman populace was much flattered by the fact that during the course of the year he had been visited by members of nearly all the royal families in Europe. In August by the Prince de Joinville, son of Louis Philippe; in October by the Queen of the Netherlands; in November by the Princess Mariana, consort of Prince Albert of Prussia, also by Prince Maximilian, heir apparent of Bavaria, and by Prince Leopold, Count of Syracuse, brother of the King of Naples; in February by the Duc de Valentinois, heir of Monaco; in March by the prince royal of Sweden and Norway; in April by the Infante of Spain and in June by Queen Christina of Spain. A galaxy of royalties! Their visits may have denoted political purposes, or they may, in many cases, have been mere politenesses on the part of those who happened to be visiting Rome, but in the eyes of the people they were a mark of appreciation extended to their Holy Father in honour of his great work.

Perhaps the most singular acknowledgment[33] of Pius' prestige throughout Europe was furnished by the arrival in Rome of Chekib Effendi, the Turkish ambassador at Vienna. Chekib Effendi expressed himself in the most complimentary terms: he said that the Sultan wished to associate himself with the world-wide satisfaction at Pius' accession by establishing a direct relationship. He added that the position of his master, as ruling over subjects of many different types, "all of whom he loads with equal benefits", would be better appreciated by His Holiness than by anyone else. After one

[33] *Contemporaneo*, February 27th and March 6th, 1847; also Spada and others.

of these audiences Chekib was seen walking in the street with
a portrait of Pius in his hand, and tears of emotion running
down his cheeks. It seems that Pius, unable to confer on him
any pontifical order because they all contained crosses or
Christian emblems, had solved the difficulty by presenting
him with his portrait. In Turkey this would have been considered the highest honour that the Sultan could bestow; and
that same evening Chekib Effendi, when dining at the
Austrian Embassy in the Palazzo Venezia, rather irritated
Count Lützow by claiming that he had received a decoration
from His Holiness.[34] It was to meet this difficulty that Pius
revived the Ordine Piano, or Pius' Order, which had existed
in the eighteenth century.[35]

[34] Vienna Staats-Archiv, Rome, 1847, *Rapports*, II, March 2nd.
[35] Gualterio (1862 ed.), v, 214. At this moment Pius was in
negotiation with Guizot over the Christians in Syria. Hitherto they
had referred their difficulties to the French consuls, but he had some
idea of establishing a Papal consular service for them. *V*. Paris Aff.
Etr., Rome, Rossi, February 18th, 1847.

Chapter VIII

THE MODERATE MOVEMENT OUTSIDE THE PAPAL STATE (JUNE 1846 TO JUNE 1847)

I

Outside the Italian peninsula Pius IX's Liberal movement had been received with mixed feelings; with dislike by the Mazzinians, Gregorian ecclesiastics and reactionists all over the world,[1] but on the other hand with a great deal of sympathy and approval by Liberals—even by the Liberals in Protestant England.[2] Although we may despair of ever being able to gauge its exact importance in the European movement, we know that Metternich, at all events, was deeply impressed by its character.

Within Italy, however, it had come as a fresh inspiration; in each of the small states it had marked a new and more vigorous phase in the movement towards nationality, and it had brought great joy to all patriots. When, again and again throughout that first year, the news had arrived of some fresh reform granted by this benefactor of his people, and received by immense concourses kneeling in silent gratitude, in all states alike people felt as if there were more human kindliness

[1] By Metternich. See his letter to Dietrichstein of August 2nd, 1847 (*London Corr.* I, 78) and Cowley's letter to Palmerston of July 17th, 1847 (*ibid.* p. 20). See also Abercromby's letter to Palmerston, July 24th, 1847 (*ibid.* p. 68) and Napier's letter to Palmerston from Naples, July 25th, 1847 (*ibid.* p. 75).

[2] On September 13th, 1847, Sir George Hamilton wrote to Palmerston: "The spiritual power of the Pope is an element of the utmost consequence in this universal movement in Italy, and if his influence is properly directed, he may almost make himself the only controlling power, and arbiter of the political fate of every State in the Peninsula." (*London Corr.* p. 135.) Numerous English Protestant opinions could be cited.

in the world than they had yet known, and more hope of good will among men.

At the same time this improvement had produced one rather strange result; although, as yet, Pius had not proposed any scheme of Italian unification, already he was becoming the representative of Italian unity[3]—in the following manner: he had granted his Amnesty to the rebels in his prisons, thereby showing that after all he did not consider them very wicked: he had conceded to his subjects the same Liberal reforms for which the Progressives in every state were longing; moreover, he was Gioberti's Pope, soon, perhaps, to be President of the whole Italian Confederation. In fact, throughout the length and breadth of the land, he and he alone represented the wishes of millions of law-abiding people who cared for their country and who cared for progress; and felt that they might all become his followers without having to join a secret society or to hate one another. The cause which he personified was simply that of justice. Thus he was regarded as the leader of a great Moderate movement which was sweeping over all parts of Italy: and the year 1847 was the period when the Moderate party reached its zenith.

II

The present chapter only covers the twelve months from June 1846 to June 1847; but for clearness we may begin by a summary of the progress of the Risorgimento from the death of Gregory XVI (June 1846) to the beginning of 1848, that is

[3] Cf. Gori, *Storia*, p. 145: "Rome, after so much opprobrium, was becoming the centre of Italian hopes; and with all her provinces gravitating towards her in the name of Pius, Italy was beginning to reconstitute herself morally as a nation. If to non-religious people, Pius seemed a miracle...much greater still was the effect produced on those who regarded the restoration of religious beliefs as the supreme need of the century." Masi, *Il Risorgimento*, II, 158: "The figure of 'the great Pius', redeemer of his people and symbol of the Italian fatherland, seemed as it were a giant, and idealised itself in the hearts of all, collecting their sentiments into one spiritual and patriotic union...." Cf. also Castelli, *Ricordi*, pp. 236–43, and many others.

to say, to the end of the present volume. The period is short but critical: and during those eighteen months the leading force in the advance towards nationhood is the movement in Rome. As it marches forward it compels the rulers of the other states to follow in its train. For eighteen months all the small governments are borne along by it; and undoubtedly, without this Liberal advance, Italy in 1848 might have achieved no more than Italy in 1831.

This becomes evident from the following considerations. Firstly, one feels that probably it contributed to the downfall of Metternich: but apart from that, within Italy itself it transformed an almost helpless population into one with an incipient power of organised resistance. In each state the new freedom of the press, copied from Pius' measure, made the Progressive sections both articulate and independent; the Civica, or National Guard, gave them arms; and the setting up of the Consulta gave them a central assembly, which in the beginning of 1848 was easily turned into a free parliament. And this led to the invaluable parliamentary development under Cavour. Unfortunately the Paris Revolution of 1848 and the war of liberation came upon the small states long before they were ready. In that war they had very little chance of success. They required another five or ten years in which to prepare for action. Nevertheless it found them far more nationally minded and ten times more capable of fending for themselves than ever they had been before Pius' campaign of Liberal reforms.

III

At the same time, although there was a general advance throughout Italy, in reality each small state was developing on its own lines and working out its own destiny.[4] Almost

---

[4] It is these small state careers which are being traced in this volume as far as the beginning of the year 1848. That is why I begin by summarising them. Each small state was rapidly working up to a crisis: it makes the story clearer if we begin by pointing out the *dénouement* towards which each of them was tending.

every single one of their governments was marching to its destruction. Thus, the Pope, after leading the way for nearly two years, was destined to have a constitution forced on him in March 1848, and eight months later to be driven into exile because he refused to declare war; after which, for six months Rome would be a republic under Mazzini and Garibaldi. Similarly in Tuscany the Grand Duke would be compelled to grant a constitution in 1848; and in January 1849 he would be driven out of the state for six months. In Sicily the people were beginning to work up for their rebellion against Naples (January 12th, 1848) and in Lombardo-Venetia for their rebellion against Austria (the Five Glorious Days in March 1848, and the siege of Venice). The Neapolitan sovereignty was to lose Sicily for a while, but, nevertheless, to survive until 1860. Thus, of all the royal houses of Italy only one was fated to come forth stronger from the years of trial: Piedmont, though twice defeated by Austria, would emerge, in 1849, a free nation under a constitutional monarchy; in fact the only real nation in the peninsula.[5]

As already related, during the first half of 1847 most of the states were occupied in winning the freedom of the press;[6] in the second half of 1847 they were each agitating for a Civic Guard and a Consulta.

In this chapter we deal with their progress only up to the end of June 1847.

PIEDMONT

In Piedmont was Charles Albert, tall and pale and sad, "the knight of the closed vizor"; he was still preparing for

[5] This chapter only takes the story of this Moderate and Liberal movement as far as the middle of 1847, the end of Pius' first year. At that point we reach the occupation of Ferrara, which rather changed the character of the movement.

[6] Not in Piedmont. In Piedmont Charles Albert had already granted Conservative reforms and at first the Liberals did not exert such pressure upon him as they did on the sovereigns in other states. It was not until October 1847 that his reforms were granted.

the great day. He has been called the "Re Tentenna", the vacillating king; but surely much of his apparent vacillation was due to the lesson learnt in 1820: namely that with a nation of under five million souls he could not possibly fight against the Austrian colossus with twenty-nine million. If he quarrelled with Metternich his throne was not worth a year's purchase. Yet he kept his end in view and his people in leash for eighteen years until the right moment came. And he worked secretly, as the following letters will show.

On August 8th, 1846, Count Lützow reported to Metternich that he had received a letter from a traveller in Piedmont. This traveller said that Liberalism had made great strides there. But that Charles Albert had said to him with a scornful laugh that some people thought him (Charles Albert) an avowed revolutionist—they must be mad! And, when asked about the medal with the motto *J'atans mon astre*, he had replied that it was merely an old seal of the House of Savoy and had no connection with present-day politics.[7]

Yet inwardly he was chafing at his position. Here was a brave man, prepared only a year later to ride out at the head of his army—the first captain of Modern Italy! With the above statements compare the following letters of his.

In May 1846 he wrote to a friend:

Ce que je désire le plus après le bien que je désire de procurer de toutes façons dans notre Patrie, c'est de voir s'y développer l'esprit de *dignité et d'indépendance nationale* qui nous donnera une force immense si jamais nous serons assez heureux pour être appelés à défendre notre nationalité....

Votre ami,
C. ALBERT.

On May 6th, 1846, he wrote to explain his having countermanded a field-day:

Neuf heures étant sonnées et n'ayant reçu de vous rien, ami... je vous préviens qu'ayant reçu de nouveau plusieurs avis qui sont

---

[7] Vienna Staats-Archiv, Lützow to Metternich, August 8th, 1846. It was perfectly true that Charles Albert hated the Revolution.

indubitables que l'on devait faire des cris de *Roi d'Italie*, j'ai contre-mandé la manœuvre. Les chefs d'ateliers avaient donné vacance à leurs ouvriers à cette fin; les étudiants, une immense foule devait se rassembler. Que l'on dise ce que l'on veuille sur moi: j'ai cru devoir faire ce sacrifice à la tranquillité et au bien du pays. Quand le temps sera venu, au lieu de crier, qu'ils viennent alors verser leur sang avec le mien pour la patrie.

Votre ami,
C. ALBERT.

Since Pius' arrival he was no longer alone.[8]

The most significant events of this year in Piedmont were the following:

In August 1846 was held a meeting of the Council of the division of Vercelli, in Piedmont. This was one of the districts which had suffered owing to the Austrian reprisals over the wine duties; and consequently the councillors took this opportunity of thanking the king for his noble attitude as opposed to the foreigners, and expressed their readiness to stand by him in any such resistance.

On September 9th was held the Agrarian Congress at Mortara. It was a Piedmontese agricultural society; but its annual meeting breathed patriotic politics. Some of its members were Lombard landowners who owned property in Piedmont. "They came", says Gualterio, "in order to say to one another 'Speriamo', Let us hope; and—looking back on it years afterwards—how unwise we thought it to speak in the same breath of 'Charles Albert' and 'Italy'."

"The enemies of the (national) movement, while professing to be the guardians of every moral idea, were obliged to proscribe the most generous feelings and condemn ideas, principles and affections considered holy in all ages even among the savage peoples".[9]

How universally true are those sentences!

The meeting was a great success; at the banquet toasts

[8] For these letters of Charles Albert v. Gualterio (1862 ed.), v, Docs. IX, X and XI. They show that he was working secretly for a war of liberation.

[9] Gualterio (1862 ed.), v, 109.

were proposed to the king, and before it broke up the secretary, Lorenzo Valerio, said openly that Charles Albert was aiming not only at a scientific union of Italy, but also—and better by far—at a political union. As this was said in reply to a Lombard, amid all the anger over the Austrian wine duties, it created a good deal of sensation.

On September 15th was held in Genoa the Scientific Congress of all Italy, already described.

But apart from congresses Charles Albert was more or less secretly at work everywhere.[10] In Rome and in Florence he had his trustworthy men. In Lombardy he was introducing arms. And in Switzerland at Capo Lago on Lake Lugano, only just over the border, there was a printing-press hard at work under a man called Ciani. Hundreds of brochures were being smuggled over into Milan.[11] True, Ciani was a Swiss, so that many of these works were republican: but they were not Mazzinian; Mazzini was discredited. And even to-day it is common enough for students of the Risorgimento to find Capo Lago printed on the book that they are reading.

TUSCANY

For years Tuscany with its beautiful capital city of Florence had been a sort of sanctuary where men of all political creeds might meet in safety. In that way it had been the chief preserver of Liberal ideas. That was its contribution to the Risorgimento; and for so small a country this was a far more useful work than could have been achieved by force of arms.

The main reason for our analysing the Tuscan situation in 1846 is, firstly, to obtain some idea of the men and parties whose names afterwards became famous; and secondly, because its political progress follows that of Rome almost step by step, and shows us plainly how difficult it was, when one of the princes granted a Liberal measure, for the neighbouring

[10] V. Casati, A., *Milano e i principi di Savoia*, pp. 144–6; for the Lombard's attitude to Piedmont v. Vidal and others.
[11] Gualterio (1862 ed.), v, 248.

rulers to refuse to allow a corresponding concession.[12] Thus, by the beginning of 1848 all the Italian rulers found themselves involved in a sort of ding-dong race until finally they had nothing left to concede. Then came the democratic constitutions.

In 1846 the ruler of Tuscany was the Grand Duke Leopold II and the president of his ministers was the Consigliere Cempini.

Leopold II, a man full of kindliness and beneficent schemes, was torn in two opposite directions. He was anxious to be a good Italian ruler, but he was constantly being reminded by Metternich that he was an agnate of the Imperial House of Hapsburg, and that Austria had a reversionary claim on his state.[13] His minister Cempini had been a loyal servant for many years; he was now an old man and greatly attached to his sovereign.

The government was purely paternal. There was a Consiglio, or Council, consisting of the Secretary of State, and the other ministers, heads of departments; and there was a Consulta which the Grand Duke could consult on important matters. He had also his own private secretary's office through which he dealt with the others. This grandfatherly régime, of course, was very little in harmony with modern Liberal ideas.

Already, at the time of Pius' accession, there existed a certain amount of Liberal agitation in Tuscany, and before the end of the year it was being fostered and spread by means of a particularly noxious system, started by Professor Montanelli, namely the clandestine press.[14] Secret newspapers

[12] *London Corr.* I, 37, Scarlett's letter to Palmerston, April 17th, 1847.

[13] At this moment he was still unpopular because of his surrender to the Pope's authorities of a rebel named Renzi. Zobi, IV, 526, says that a permanent cause of evil existed in the rivalry between the ministers and the courtiers—the latter headed by Carlo Felice, the Grand Duke's private secretary: "A most pernicious dualism between the Palazzo Vecchio and the Palazzo Pitti."

[14] Baldasseroni, *Leopoldo II e suoi tempi*, V, 210. Baldasseroni was one of Leopold's ministers.

were widely read and on one occasion they were even show-
ered on the people's heads in a theatre. Responsible Liberals
began to perceive that this agitation might become a danger
not only to the government but just possibly to the reform
movement all over Italy. They determined to warn
Cempini.

They were not all of the same shade of opinion. During
the first half of 1846 there were two main groups of Progressives in Florence, firstly the older and more moderate men,
under the Marchese Gino Capponi, and secondly the younger
men, the Arditi under Carlo Fenzi. And then, early in 1847,
Capponi's group divided itself into two: the more contented
remained with their leader, but some of the others, headed
by Baron Ricasoli, by an able lawyer named Salvagnoli and by
Raffaele Lambruschini, took a distinct line of their own as
active Moderates. This cleavage was inevitable. The Marchese
Capponi was blind: he was honourable and disinterested and
everyone loved him—indeed Massimo d' Azeglio used to wish
that he could give him one of his eyes—but for active leadership he was no longer able.

In Tuscany therefore, in February 1847, the Liberals may
be classified as (1) the Moderates who were divided into (a)
the passive Moderates under the Marchese Gino Capponi and
the Marchese Cosimo Ridolfi; and (b) the active Moderates
under Baron Ricasoli, Salvagnoli and Lambruschini. Their
aim was identical; they wanted a greater freedom for the press.
At that moment Liberalism was rampant and was disseminat-
ing hundreds of discreditable clandestine productions, simply
because there existed no other means of expression. The only
possible cure was greater liberty of the press.[15]

Of all these men Ricasoli was the most remarkable. He
was a landowner of the feudal type, the celebrated "Baron of
iron" who in 1860 was to lead Tuscany into the half-unified
Italy. Clear-headed, practical, resolute. "His conceptions

[15] Gualterio (1862 ed.), v, 175–7; Gori, p. 195; Raulich, p. 168.

did not wander through imaginary spaces but always sought the concrete."[16] In Tuscany he was the man of the future.

At the moment, however, the best known of the Progressives was a man rather outside the political groups, namely Professor Montanelli, the professor of Commercial Law at the University of Pisa. He was a person of versatile talents but without much ballast. At the age of thirty-three he had been a student of medicine and law; was devoted to music; a mystic who was said to have gone the round of several religions, and he had achieved some success as an advocate. In 1843 he had founded the Fratelli Italiani, an association for regenerating the individual, and in 1845 he had helped to write the Manifesto of Rimini; he was the originator in Tuscany of the clandestine press; he had been a Mazzinian but now was becoming an enthusiastic supporter of Pius. Owing to his kindliness he had, at the University of Pisa, a following of students who almost adored him; and it is greatly to his credit that when war broke out he led a company of these boys against the Austrians.

During the first quarter of 1847 the Liberal agitation had gained so much ground that Gino Capponi approached Cempini with a view to obtaining leave to found a Moderate newspaper: but he found that Cempini had already been approached by Ricasoli,[17] and had promised him a far more drastic concession, namely a press law. This was a great step forward; so great that at first the Grand Duke and his other ministers refused to sanction it; but on March 15th, 1847,

[16] "Similarly his will was strong enough to incarnate them and bring them to a successful conclusion." Gualterio (1862 ed.), v, 177.

[17] Ricasoli had approached him with a petition. This Memoria is an important document in the history of Tuscany. Zobi gives a copy of it, vol. v, Appendix 1. On the Tuscan progress v. also Ricasoli, *Lettere e documenti*, I, 123 *et seq.*, and the general historians Raulich, III, 170 *et seq.*, Gori, Tivaroni and others.

Pius granted a press law to the Papal State and on April 23rd he promised a Consulta. At the end of April the great English free-trader, Cobden, arrived in Florence and was received at a banquet by the Accademia dei Georgofili (May 2nd). The Tuscan government gave in. On May 6th it conceded a press law to Tuscany and on May 31st another edict promising to enlarge the powers of the already existing Consulta.[18]

Thus Tuscany had been drawn into the Liberal and Moderate movement which was sweeping over Italy; and there was also another lesson that it had learnt from the Papal State: Montanelli tells us that his policy was "to take these reforms on account; to praise them more than they deserved, and to hold as virtually accomplished things which did not enter into the government's intentions, in fact to exert every endeavour to wring from them the utmost liberty possible". (Montanelli, *Memorie*, p. 275.)

PARMA AND MODENA

In the two small duchies of Parma and Modena the new movement had aroused both interest and enthusiasm. In Parma on June 16th, 1847, the anniversary of Pius' accession, the townsmen decided to illuminate their city in his honour. Certain people, however, refused to do so and some stones were thrown, accompanied by a good many jeers, at their houses. The soldiers retaliated with unnecessary violence. That evening when, owing to the lateness of the hour and the falling rain, the crowd was peaceably retiring, it was suddenly charged both by cavalry and by infantry. The unarmed

---

[18] He also appointed a Commission for reform of both the Penal and the Civil Codes—Gualterio's opinion about these concessions runs as follows: "The Roman press law and the other laws promulgated by the Pontiff persuaded the Tuscan government that it was time to do something; but, on the contrary, the time had almost gone by.... The crowds were full of unrest, the extremists were quivering (with anger), the Moderates were grieving at not having been listened to, the ministers were temporising and the prince was dumb." Gualterio (1862 ed.), v, 273; *v.* also Zobi, v, 56, 68; Ricasoli, *Lettere e documenti*, I, 203, and others.

citizens resisted. The affair became serious. There were about eighty casualties; and from that time onward Parma was in a condition of suppressed indignation.[19] When one of the prisoners was asked in court why he was so anxious to honour Pius, he replied: "In order not to do less than the Protestants and the Turks."

LOMBARDO-VENETIA (The two Provinces under Austrian Rule)

How seldom people realise what this kingdom looked like, and what its severance meant to a dreamer after Italian unity! These are the most fertile provinces in Italy, and probably among the most beautiful in the world.[20] Imagine them in summer when the corn stands six feet high and the luxuriant green water-meadows can be cut four or five or even six times before the vintage; or when, as autumn approaches, the maize ripens and the bunches of grapes are hanging in festoons between the long pergolas of elms or planes or mulberry trees. The peasants are a fine race; the Lombards the more go-ahead, but the men and women of the Venetian mainland are perhaps the best looking in the whole peninsula. In Lombardy there are ancient castles of the days of the Sforza; and in Venice, in 1846, the old people could still remember the last years of their ancient republic.

RECAPITULATION: 1815–46

In 1815 these were handed over to Austria and placed under a bureaucracy. For these two historic Italian states the

[19] For the small states of Parma and Modena during this year I have relied chiefly on the general histories and on such books as Bianchi, *I Ducati estensi*.

[20] "Ces magnifiques provinces qui sont certes un des plus beaux fleurons de la couronne d'Autriche et qui contiennent en elles-mêmes tant de sources de prospérité se trouvent à présent dans un état de bien-être matériel auquel je crois qu'elles n'étaient jamais parvenues jusqu'ici." Sambuy, Confidential despatch of December 1st, 1842. He was Piedmontese minister at Vienna.

Austrians set up a new piece of administrative machinery: its chief was the Emperor: next in order of rank, a resplendent Austrian Viceroy in Milan; then, below him, two Governors, one in Milan and the other in Venice, each assisted by two Senates (one political and the other camerale for finance). These bureaucrats in Milan and Venice were the supreme authority for each territory.[21] But of course they were subordinate to the Aulic Dicasteries, and the bureaux in Vienna;[22] and the higher appointments and salaries were fixed in Vienna. Thus the Administration consisted of Austrian offices subordinate to Viennese offices. Many of the employés of course were Italians.

Each of the two Governi (the Milanese and Venetian) were divided into provinces; the provinces into districts; and the districts into communes.

At the same time, by way of representing Italian feeling, in each capital city there was set up:

(*a*) A *Congregazione Centrale* or Central "Congregation" (assembly), in Milan consisting of twenty-nine members, and in Venice of twenty-five; their presidents were the Austrian governors of Lombardy and Venetia.[23]

(*b*) Below these there were to be Provincial Congregazioni or assemblies; one for each province (nine in Lombardy and eight in Venetia). President: the Austrian Delegate of the province.

[21] Broadly speaking, over all administration of the existing laws. "All matters requiring government vigilance or direction" (cap. I, clause 8 of the Regolamento: *v.* also the long lists in cap. II). But no new laws or appointments were made without sanction of the Viennese bureaux (cap. II, clause 2 of the Regolamento).

[22] Sandonà, *Regno lombardo*, pp. 74–80, gives a documented description of the bureaucracy, including a copy of the Constituting Act of April 7th, 1815. He says: "Proposals from the two governments of Milan and Venice passed through the Chancellery of the Viceroy who affixed his Visto and forwarded them to Vienna." In Vienna they were each allotted to the special dicastery (department) dealing with such matters.

[23] Sandonà, *Regno lombardo*, pp. 96–110, gives the documents.

(c) Below these were the Communal Councils, big and small; 2247 of them.

In England this arrangement would correspond, quite roughly, to our Privy Council, our County Councils and our Parish Councils. But in Lombardo-Venetia there was very little real representation.[24]

The members of the two Central Congregazioni (assemblies) were elected and selected on the following system. The numerous Communal Councils each sent up a list of three names to its Provincial Congregazione; each Provincial Congregazione was entitled to have two members to represent the province on the Central Congregazione (one noble and one non-noble). So they each selected six of the names sent in by the Communal Councils (three names for each place to which they were entitled) and forwarded them to the Central Congregazione. The Central Congregazione made its comments on them and forwarded them to the Emperor. The Emperor selected the members from these lists of three, and so the central assembly was formed.

---

[24] *The Provincial Councils.* Their members were selected by the Authorities from *terne* (lists of three names for each vacancy sent up by the Communal Councils). The president was the Provincial Delegate (an Imperial official). Their numbers varied.

The Communal Councils. In those with less than 300 proprietors all the rate-payers met in "convocation", usually twice a year, and elected a "deputation", namely officials to administer the Commune. The leading Deputy (renewable every three years) was to be one of the three biggest rate-payers. In the 34 larger Communes they elected a Consiglio or Council of 30 members, namely 20 out of the 100 largest rate-payers and 10 chosen from Commerce and Industry. That formed the Communal Council and it elected the Communal officers. Torelli (Un Anonimo Lombardo), *Pensieri*, pp. 205–9, says that this resulted in the Communes being administered by three of their leading men. He says that these parish councillors might have done patriotic work, and blames the richer people for looking down upon it. One-third retired each year and the Council co-opted twice that number. From this double supply of names the Provincial Council and its Delegato (an Imperial official) selected those whom they preferred (*v.* Tivaroni, *Domin. Austr.* I, 331; Torelli (Un Anonimo Lombardo), *Pensieri*, p. 215).

This Central Congregazione was presided over by the President of the Governo (an official of the Austrian government). Its powers were consultative; and, in finance, extended to expenses not fixed by the existing laws.

To all appearances, therefore, the principle of popular election was not entirely excluded. True, but it was carefully counteracted by a system of vetoes. Elaborate provision was made to prevent anything like a political movement. At each turning-point there were government officials—the Delegato of the province and others—who could interfere; if a Liberal came up, they could "catch him young" and cut short his career at its very earliest stage.

Suppose, for instance, that a young Liberal wanted to become one of the officials of his commune; in a small commune he might be elected by the "convocation" or meeting of the rate-payers; but the government had power to annul the election and themselves appoint a council—and Torelli says that they often did so (p. 216). In a larger commune he would have to be one of those co-opted, and also to be approved by the Delegato; and no meetings were legal without the presence of the government's District Commissario, whose reports could be kept secret.[25]

Suppose, however, that our young Liberal succeeded in getting onto the Communal Council, and then wanted to get into the Provincial Congregazione. His name might be sent up in the *terne* (lists of three), but from them he would have to be selected by the Authority.

Finally, supposing that he has managed to become a

[25] Count Luigi Torelli says about the Commissario: "One cannot understand why the affairs of a commune...must pass through another office [the Commissario's], which merely causes confusion and delays. They are placed there as mediators between the Communal deputies and the Delegates, but it is seldom that they do not subject to criticism the appeals despatched through their channels to the higher authorities." He adds that these "satellites of tyranny" added secret notes to the appeals sent up for decision. *Pensieri sull' Italia*, by Un Anonimo Lombardo (Torelli), p. 213.

provincial councillor, and now wants to get into the Central Congregazione, he might possibly get himself selected by his Provincial Council and approved by the Central Congregazione and finally nominated by the Emperor himself. At last he has reached his goal! But even the Central Congregazione itself was entirely under control. The Austrian governors in Milan and Venice could summon or dismiss it at will; they presided at the meetings and they drew up the agenda. It had no power to refuse taxes.

These Central Congregazioni were manned almost entirely by Italians, but of course only by Italians who had passed the Austrian scrutiny. Ostensibly they were appointed according to a system of secondary election, but in reality every provision was made to prevent their meddling in politics.

Nevertheless, judged by the standards of 1815 the administrative machinery was fairly good.[26] Although not allowed to legislate, a Central Congregazione had some administrative authority. Its powers extended to the apportioning of any ground-taxes; the supervision and making rules for the accounts of the communes, the distribution throughout the country of charges for the army, care of bridges, river-banks, high roads, charitable institutions; and a consultative vote on the levying and administration of all money for expenditure not previously fixed by law.

All this machinery was turned to some account, but, according to Torelli and others, its higher grades were manned to a great extent by Austrians;[27] that is to say by men who, as long as they were paid by the hour and promoted up to date, did not care whether the country prospered or merely vegetated. They were efficient enough, but it was a government without a soul.

Most important of all was the decree of April 24th, 1815, whereby the two Central Congregazioni were empowered

[26] V. Tivaroni, *Domin. Austr.* 1, 330.
[27] Torelli (Un Anonimo Lombardo), *Pensieri*, p. 217; Masi, *Il Risorgimento*, 1, 354, and others.

"humbly to bring the needs of the nation to the knowledge of the Emperor". This concession to the humbly brought needs of the nation ought surely to have provided an excellent opening for agitation.

In fact, seeing how wide were these administrative powers, we are tempted to ask: If the Lombardo-Venetians really wanted to edge out the Austrians, why did they not convert the whole machine into a system for blocking every imaginable measure, and thus win for themselves grants of self-government? As matters turned out, this was the course which was finally pursued during the last few months before the revolution of 1848. But before that last year 1847 agitation was useless. In early days the Venetian Congregation had raised some protests, but in 1840 both the Centrali (Central Congregazioni) were almost negligible quantities. The truth was that after the conspiracy of 1821 the educated men saw, just as Charles Albert and the Neapolitan Liberals saw, that there was not the slightest chance of success against the Holy Alliance. Among the poor peasants national feeling hardly existed;[28] in the city of Milan there might be vague reminiscences of the Sforza and Visconti; and in Venetia they remembered the great republic: but those ancient traditions were not "practical politics"; and, as yet, the new patriotism,

---

[28] Torelli (Un Anonimo Lombardo), *Pensieri*, pp. 38–48; Sambuy, *ibid.* and many other authorities. Writing in December 1842 Torelli says that in case of war these populations would remain neutral. Gualterio (1862 ed.), v, 243, writes: "The people had few national memories and those only of the Napoleonic epoch which were partly odious to them. . . . But they understood better the religious idea, and through it they felt a reinvigorating of their natural and traditional hatred of the dominating foreigner." "The Austrians in Lombardy and Venetia, and the old dynasties in other parts of Italy . . . were received with no great repugnance by the people. Those who disliked the restorations (in 1815) were in the minority. The French Revolution had produced in Italy effects which were too sudden and unexpected, and the people had felt the shock more than the advantage." Bonghi, *La Vita e i tempi di Valentino Pasini*, p. 173.

the hope of uniting Italy, had hardly any definite existence, whereas the Austrian Empire was a working reality.

On the whole the Austrians were successful; for thirty years they deprived the Lombardo-Venetians of their right to self-government, while achieving for them enough show of prosperity to claim efficiency for their administration: but, of course, it was a success that was dearly bought and could only be temporary.

At first there was some opposition, notably the celebrated conspiracies with the trial, lasting two years in all (between 1821 and 1824), of Silvio Pellico and Count Confalonieri and their numerous friends. These were cases of real martyrdom for the sake of freedom; a record of sufferings which can never be forgotten. Count Confalonieri, for instance—a man distinguished among the Milanese nobles—had risked everything that he possessed in the cause. Undoubtedly he had plotted and enrolled members in the Federati Society and bound them by an oath "to employ all my strength even to the sacrifice of my life to redeem Italy from the foreigner": but he had gone no farther than conspiracy. He was sentenced to death; then reprieved; and then he passed

thirteen years in a prison eight yards long by four wide under a massive vault; one single opening with double bars of iron admitted a weak ray of light; from sunset to sunrise there was no light; for bed he had a bench; a counterpane to cover himself, a jug to drink from, a wooden spoon to eat with, and that was all his furniture. In coarse rough clothing with their sides shackled with irons weighing eight pounds, supplied with insufficient and nauseous food, they could take their daily exercise only on a platform. They were compelled to remain idle unless they made lint; books were forbidden.[29]

While he was in prison his wife died of grief.

During the next nine years—from 1822 to 1831—there was tranquillity in Lombardo-Venetia, mainly because rebellion

[29] Tivaroni, *Domin. Austr.* I, 377.

was entirely hopeless. Everywhere these were the years of reaction after the Napoleonic wars, and there was a deadweight of popular opinion, including all the Italian princes, and all the Great Powers, absolutely determined to have peace. In a general way throughout the whole of this period up to 1846, one may say that the tides of nationalism followed those in the rest of Italy: but they had less effect because the Austrian government was all-powerful.

Thus in 1830 there came the revolution in Paris, and in Italy Mazzini's early activities (1830–34). In Milan the Giovine Italia began to make converts; in 1833 there was another crop of arrests and trials; after two long years' waiting, in 1835 between twenty and thirty people were sentenced by the Emperor Francis II, then on his death-bed, to various terms of imprisonment. All death sentences were commuted.

Probably the Austrian government could claim that it was not so severe as Charles Albert in 1833: though he, of course, was dealing with mutiny. Nevertheless, in such unfavourable times, it was an act of heroism for men to join secret societies whose mere membership rendered a man liable to such sentences as these.

The years between 1833 and 1846 were also tranquil but not without political progress.

In 1833 Silvio Pellico published his reminiscences of the Spielberg and this, says Tivaroni, did the Austrians "more harm than a lost battle". It drew tears from thousands of readers all over the world.

In 1838, apparently, are to be found the first signs of anti-Austrian feeling. In that year the new Emperor Ferdinand I, a man not quite normal in brain, came to Milan to be crowned with the iron crown of Lombardy. He was given a great reception by the nobles—but not by the people. Moreover, in that same year the two Podestà of Lombardy and of Venetia petitioned Vienna for more extensive powers in administration, and their petition was refused: in 1838, too, the released heroes of the Spielberg were publicly feasted. Here then we have three indications of the beginnings of a more independent spirit.

In 1843, Gioberti's *Primato* appeared and with it began the Campaign of the Moderates.

In 1844 the Scientific Congress was held at Milan and Prince Canino made a speech in which he spoke openly of "freeing the Lombards from slavery".

By this time the Lombard nobility, Count Casati and others, were beginning to visit Piedmont and to look to Charles Albert as their leader.

In 1846 there appeared a book[30] called *Pensieri sull' Italia* by Un Anonimo Lombardo, an anonymous Lombard whose real name was Count Luigi Torelli. This book is said to have been of assistance to the Italian cause in Lombardy. And by this time the Capolago press was in full activity and scores of patriotic societies were in existence.

Nevertheless, at the beginning of 1846 no one dreamt of any action against Austria. Quite a tangible proportion of the population favoured Austrian rule; the government employés for instance; about half the nobles; the higher clergy; and the peaceable section of the population; and in the country districts the peasants only wanted to be left alone. On the Nationalist side the chief strength was to be found in the middle classes and the town artisans.

Suddenly there appeared on the scene an entirely unexpected figure: a Liberal Pope. The advent of Pius IX to the throne produced little less than a reversal of the balance of power which we have described. His sympathies, both real

[30] This book (already mentioned in vol. 1, p. 151) contained an attack on the Papal government of Gregory XVI and advised the Pope's territories being reduced to Rome and Elba. Consequently it was forbidden the state by Pius: but the really important pages are those which tell us of the Austrian rule in Lombardo-Venetia, as Torelli knew it. Its suggestions are not nearly so practical as the works of Gioberti and Balbo.

and supposed, very soon began to bring over to the national side many of the hitherto conservative nobles; also, of course, the higher clergy; [31] and finally most of the peasants and their priests, who henceforward were drawn towards nationality by the very sound of his name.[32] At this moment in Lombardo-Venetia there begins the movement which eventually leads to the Five Glorious Days of Milan and to the still more glorious siege of Venice.

The Austrian army was there under Radetzky; but it was more isolated than ever before, in these Italian provinces of the House of Hapsburg.

Unfortunately divisions existed among the nationalists: some were Mazzinians, others Albertists, and there was a group of federal republicans under Carlo Cattaneo. Still as long as the Austrians remained in Milan they could all unite against them, as they were destined to prove during the coming two years. And it was not long before there was held the first great political demonstration, which happened to be of a singularly touching nature. In December 1846 news arrived of the death of Count Confalonieri, the "martyr of the Spielberg". Since his release he had been living in exile, until at last the story of Pius' movement came to fill him with renewed hope and with a longing to see his native land once again. He started for Italy, but the journey proved too much for him. He reached the foot of the St Gothard Pass almost in sight of the frontier, but there his strength gave out. "He died", says Gualterio, "blessing the reforms of Pius IX but

[31] Gualterio says they were already influenced in this direction by the writings of Rosmini. *V*. Gualterio (1862 ed.), v, 243.

[32] Consul-General Dawkins to Palmerston, June 27th, 1847, *London Corr*. II, 58. A year later Cesare Correnti wrote: "For good or ill the feeling of national dignity and the hatred for the foreigner were increasing; and we had to confess that in fifteen years we had not succeeded in propagating political passion in any except the studious young men: in the real people—never." *V*. Cesare Correnti, *Scritti*, II, 4. The first sign of the storm was the movement of the poor country people in the spring of 1847. Cesare Correnti, *ibid.*

invoking their benefits for the whole of Italy." And when the news reached Milan there swept through every class a great wave of sorrow for their patriot noble. His funeral was held at San Fedele, on January 14th, 1847, and was attended by an enormous crowd, which was all the greater—we are told by one of those present, Count Visconti Venosta—because poor Confalonieri had been libelled by the Austrian police. Apparently that was their duty to diminish the prestige of Italian patriots. Another crime against the light! and surely the most ungentle of all those upon their record!

At that point we must leave Lombardo-Venetia.

[NOTE. *This chapter VIII leads up to chapter XVI. If read consecutively, these two chapters supply a summary of the history of the lesser states during this period.*]

Chapter IX

THE PIEDMONTESE GROUP
IN ROME

One of the most peculiar elements in Rome among the several factions which were trying to capture Pius was the small Piedmontese group. Hitherto we have spoken of the old Gregorian party; the Esaltati; and the Mazzinians: this fourth unit is much harder to visualise.

As already stated, Charles Albert himself had been delighted at the line taken by Pius. In reality, however, their views did not coincide. Pius was trying to put into practice the ideas of Gioberti, which differed fundamentally from those of the Piedmontese. Gioberti, in the *Primato*, had suggested a federation of the existing states of Italy under the presidency of the Pope; as their boundaries were not to be altered, his scheme would not destroy the balance of power within Italy: and he had not made any definite statement as to what was to be done with Lombardo-Venetia or its Austrian rulers. As opposed to this suggestion the Piedmontese ambition—*Italia farà da sè*—was that their army should lead all the rest of Italy in a war of liberation against Austria; and as a reward for undertaking the fighting, they were to appropriate Lombardo-Venetia (if not other territories as well) and form a powerful kingdom under the House of Savoy right across the north of Italy. This scheme would destroy the balance of power in Italy: it would make Piedmont predominant; and the other small governments were afraid of it. But now we know that it was the only practicable plan for attacking Austria.

Looking back on the scene after a lapse of nearly ninety years, we see that there was an element of state ambition in the Piedmontese views. But anyone who is not blind to the world around him must admit that their ambitions have been justified by results—a hundred times justified. They have made a great nàtion; and *without Piedmont it would not have been made*. Its complete superiority over the other states was abundantly proved during the years 1848 and 1860: and before achieving the liberation of 1860 the Piedmontese had to declare war against Austria on three separate occasions. With a population of less than five millions they attacked a nation with over twenty-nine. Even allowing for Viennese revolution during their first two campaigns and for French help during the third that is a piece of history that should be remembered for ever. And when one reflects that they also joined in the Crimean campaign, one feels that they gave proof of a determination and pertinacity of which there have been few instances during the last hundred years.

In 1847, however, the union of Italy by fusion was not yet possible; but, unconsciously, Pius' movement was a step in that direction.

Thus there existed a centre of Piedmontese influence within Rome itself, and in the long run their aims would not be those of Pius. The policy of their state was to bring the Papacy and all the rest of Italy to follow Charles Albert in his war of liberation. In this way they were a danger to Pius, because, before long, they began to combine with the elements among his subjects who wanted war: and, as Pope, he could not declare war except in self-defence.

This Piedmontese group was both shrewd and capable of taking the lead. It was represented by a small circle of gentlemen, all of them of some standing, who were in touch with Charles Albert, and at the same time in a position to convey their ideas to Pius. They were well known to the general public, but the really effective part of their work was done quietly. The most prominent among them was our old friend the Marquis Massimo d'Azeglio, and with him Dr Pantaleoni (who was a Papal subject, not a Piedmontese), the Marquis Pareto (Piedmontese ambassador), and later on, in the month of September 1847, General Giovanni Durando and the Marquis Casanova. Usually they met at the house of Dr Pantaleoni.

Massimo d' Azeglio seems to have been the founder of this group; Dr Pantaleoni was a medical man who had a widespread practice among the rich foreigners dotted about everywhere between Rome and Nice.[1] He acted mainly as d' Azeglio's representative—at all events at first; but he was an able man and ended his career as Senator of the Kingdom of Italy. Pareto, of course, being the ambassador, was in constant touch with Turin; General Giovanni Durando, an exile aged only forty-three but covered with honours and glory from the wars of Portugal and Spain, had come to Rome by permission of Charles Albert to advise on military matters;[2] and so, apparently, had the Marquis Casanova.

[1] These are the limits given by Faldella, but, if true, his patients must have come to him, not he to them. Pantaleoni was born at Macerata in the year 1810; he studied medicine in Rome and in foreign universities. In 1816 he returned to Rome and set up practice there.

[2] Charles Albert also had officers in Tuscany to train the Tuscan army. General Giovanni (John) Durando must not be confused with his brother General Giacomo (James) Durando. Piedmontese by birth, Giovanni began life as an officer in the Cacciatori (Chasseurs) of Charles Albert; Giacomo was brought up an avvocato (lawyer). In 1831 they were both implicated in the political troubles. Giovanni had to resign his commission and they both went into exile. The next twelve years were spent in military service in Belgium, Portugal and Spain. In 1843 Giovanni returned to Italy with three wounds, a breast-full of medals and the rank of Brigadier-General to his credit. He had been a soldier of fortune in quarrels that did not concern him, but now he returned to serve his own nation. In September 1847 he arrived in Rome to train the Papal army, by arrangement with Charles Albert.

Giacomo Durando had an even more arduous career abroad because he had to enlist as a private. He, too, served in Belgium, Portugal and in Spain and emerged with the rank of Colonel. In 1844 he was allowed to return to Piedmont. He is best remembered for his rather strange book, *Saggio politico e militare della Nazionalità italiana*, published in March 1846. In 1847 he had not yet obtained military employment, but, apparently, was on the look-out for it.

V. Dizionario; under Durando (Giovanni).

Massimo d' Azeglio,[3] the fourth son of a Piedmontese Marquis, had begun life in a cavalry regiment, but had left it in order to become an artist and a writer. His first popular success had been a novel called *Ettore Fieramosca*, but the book which made him famous was *Degli ultimi casi di Romagna*, which was a scathing criticism of the Papal government in 1845. Handsome, cheery, well-bred—what a charming companion he must have been! But the true secret of his popularity lay in his outspoken patriotism.

Ettore Fieramosca, for instance, was about a genuine historical episode in which thirteen Italian knights were victorious over an equal number of French knights who had insulted them; in his book d' Azeglio made his hero tell the foreigners that they "lied in their throat". That was what people wanted to read in 1840. Latterly he had been working more or less in connection with his king, Charles Albert. His presence in Rome was very significant; it meant that, by enthusiasts for the Risorgimento, the main stream of progress was considered to be no longer in Piedmont but at the Vatican; and this was also the opinion of Mr Abercromby, the British minister at Turin: "From all that has been passing in Italy during the past twelve months it is clear that Rome has become the centre of action: from thence spring the hopes of one party, and there the other will concentrate all its powers to counteract and destroy them."[4] Until March 1848 this remained true.

These Piedmontese gentlemen were genuine Moderates and consequently of special danger to Pius because in a general way they viewed the existing situation exactly as he did. They were sensible Liberals, just as he was, and not likely as yet to ask him for a Constitution; for Charles Albert could not grant a constitution in Piedmont. They were opposed to the idea of a republic and they wished to preserve

[3] For Massimo d' Azeglio's previous life *v. Italy in the Making*, vol. i, ch. xii.

[4] *London Corr*. p. 69, Despatch of July 25th, 1847.

the existing orders of nobility, citizens and people; whereas extremists such as Sterbini most probably were secretly democratic republicans.

In reality d'Azeglio's allegiance, one might say, belonged only to the Moderate movement. He was its chief founder. He had brought Charles Albert into it, and now he hoped to bring in Pius. His political campaign in Rome during the year 1847 is very interesting, and gives abundant proof of his manifold abilities.

On February 8th, 1847, he arrived in Rome. He knew the ancient city well—indeed twenty years earlier it had been the scene of his greatest love-affair;[5] but when he arrived at the Porta del Popolo he must have felt that he was entering a town where he had plenty of enemies. The old Gregorian Conservatives naturally hated him as the author of *Degli ultimi casi di Romagna*; while on his part he had never loved priests. And the Gregorian régime had been rather a target for the cheerful breezy Massimo, who was, in reality, an agnostic and used to say that he believed in complete freedom for himself as well as for his country. Nevertheless, he was a man with a deep and unswerving principle of life, namely his devotion to the cause of Italy, which, he perceived, was primarily that of Piedmont. For that cause he was ready to sacrifice the Pope and the princes, the bonds of strict veracity and, if necessary, his own life on the field of battle.

[5] With a Roman countess. It had lasted about seven years and produced a daughter. In 1829 he married Manzoni's daughter Giulietta. In 1832 she died. In 1835 he married Luisa Blondel, widow, a Swiss Protestant, but this marriage proved a failure: in 1843 they agreed to separate and each to lead their own life; but they always kept up a friendly correspondence, which is invaluable to students. Anent this second marriage—to a Protestant—there had been a very unfortunate incident. He had been unable to get a dispensation in Italy, and, after six months waiting, had been obliged to go to Klagenfurt in Austria to be married. It has been suggested that this very regrettable occurrence may have been partly responsible for his bitterness against Papal officialdom when he wrote *Degli ultimi casi di Romagna* (*v*. Vaccalluzzo, pp. 314, 315).

Thus, on one hand, the old Gregorians hated him, while, on the other, the Mazzinians regarded him as "blowing cold", and turning their physical-force men into passivists. The Moderates however received him in triumph, and he set himself at once to win the confidence of Pius. His aim was to keep the Pope in the national movement at all costs; but he wanted to bring him in on Piedmontese lines as a helper against Austria, whereas the revolutionists were thinking not of Piedmont but of their own democratic aims.

Massimo began by a most tactful display of moderation. A reception had been arranged for him on his arrival, but he had it cancelled. On February 9th he was the chief guest at the Casino dei Nobili and proposed Pius' health in an excellent little speech preaching moderation from start to finish.[6] Then, to avoid publicity, he refused two other invitations to dinner.

A day or two later he was invited to an audience fixed for February 13th, and this interview with Pius has sometimes been compared with his celebrated meeting with Charles Albert in 1845. Of course its importance is infinitely less, but still there is a certain interest attaching to it.

On the evening in question Massimo left his dinner at 6.30 and went up to the Quirinal Palace, and after a long wait was at last shown in:

The Pope, who was dressed in white, was sitting in an armchair of red leather, under a baldacchino, in front of a writing-desk on which was piled up a mountain of cards, a brochure with his glasses upon it, and two candles with transparent shades of coloured design. He is a man of handsome and vigorous presence like his portraits, strongly built with a serene and composed glance

---

[6] "The opinions which my friends and I have tried to spread, aim at leading us to improvement by the way of moderation and of the personal reform of every individual." He ended by saying: "The only way to reform the nation is to reform ourselves individually, and to keep within the bounds of moderation." Vaccalluzzo, p. 382. As to his studied moderation v. d'Azeglio, *Lettere a sua moglie*, February 15th, 1847.

and aspect, and an easy and cordial manner, in the true degree of a
"gran signore" who knows how to bear himself as such. He talks
well; always finds the most suitable word without hesitation;
expresses himself with good taste about trivial matters and with
simplicity upon the more important topics, without a shadow of
affectation. I have never seen a man whose whole ensemble is
more pleasantly harmonious than his. And he has a very rare
gift—and the best of all for a prince—namely so great and
manifest a sincerity in his glance, in his face and in his words,
that it convinces one and removes even the possibility of a
doubt.

Massimo was evidently much taken with Pius and they had
a long and friendly conversation. On Massimo's side the
chief points made were: that, although he had written against
Gregory XVI's administration, he was not an enemy of the
Holy See; that he had never been a member of a secret
society; that all the evils of Italy came from Austria. On his
part Pius admitted that the "Gregorian system could not
continue unchanged". He complained also about the difficulties raised for him by the constant ovations. To this
Massimo replied that efforts were being made to curtail them,
and that Balbo had already written a letter for that purpose.
Pius asked him for a copy of the letter, and then made some
enquiries as to the conditions in Piedmont; and Massimo
said that "at home we were astonished that in so short a time
he (Pius) had accomplished so much...and he answered
modestly, without affectation".

The interview itself was not politically important, except as
starting Massimo on his career in Rome. But his letter describing it to Balbo proved a great success.[7] "Many copies of
it were circulated from hand to hand, from one province to
another, some falsified and some even parodied"; and the
idea went forth that Massimo d'Azeglio was now guiding the
Pope upon his leading-rein, just as he had previously been
guiding the king. The composition of letters such as this one,
for the purpose of influencing Charles Albert, had been

[7] Vaccalluzzo, p. 118.

reduced to a science by the Piedmontese literary coterie in Turin. On this point Predari says (p. 187):

Nothing pleased him (Charles Albert) better than to read what the most influential men in the various provinces were writing to one another; so much so that many letters were dictated with this end in view, and in those very terms which were considered at the moment the best calculated to influence his mind. The secret transmitter of these letters was Dom Promis, or oftener the Cavaliere Canna. Some of the letters of Massimo d'Azeglio trace their origin to this special purpose. The letter which I quote (Massimo's letter about Pius above described) had great influence in persuading the King that Pius IX was to be imitated, and that the moment had come for reforms on a more ample scale than that hitherto adopted.

From this time onward Massimo developed great energy; he was, as we know, an effective agitator and a clever wire-puller, and, like many men of that type, was ready to die for his convictions—as he proved in the following year. He worked both openly and secretly; openly, according to his doctrine of public agitation—making speeches at banquets and helping to found clubs and societies; and secretly, by sending anonymous articles to newspapers—to some in Italy, and also, Pantaleoni says, to *Le Siècle* and *The Times*:[8] by having his own letters and copies of them disseminated; by forwarding information to Balbo and Charles Albert; by writing manifestos and by directing Ciceruacchio's plans for

[8] Sending articles to foreign newspapers had been reduced to a regular system by the Piedmontese agitators, for the purpose of influencing Charles Albert. Count Balbo had first suggested it; it was carried out by Predari, by the poet Cicconi, Count Pettiti and others, and by their agent in Paris, Massari. They had articles in the *Débats*, *Gazette du Midi*, *L'Alliance* and *Le Correspondant*. They claim that on one occasion they were able to persuade Charles Albert that an article in the *Débats* was by Guizot, whereas it was merely by Cicconi: and that on another occasion an article of theirs in the *Univers* was attributed by the king to Montalembert. *V.* Predari, p. 112 *et seq.* During all this period Predari and Balbo were hard at work publishing propagandist matter in the *Antologia Italiana*.

the populace. And so, after all, it is not very surprising that Massimo d'Azeglio, with his title, with his unmistakable air of breeding, his gifts as a speaker and a talker, his charm, his shrewd common sense, his breezy humour, his friendly manner with all classes and his genuine devotion to his cause, soon became an influential personage in Rome,[9] and undoubtedly the leading figure in the Piedmontese group.

[9] The following are some, though not all, of Massimo's public engagements during this period: they are taken mainly from documents in the Vatican Archives.

1847

Feb.	8th.	Reaches Rome.

Feb. 9th. Banquet at the Casino dei Nobili. Proposes Pius' health in speech urging moderation.

Feb. 13th. His audience with Pius.

Feb. 23rd. Ciceruacchio gives a banquet to Massimo d'Azeglio.

Mar. 10th. Another interview with Pius.

Mar. 28th. His letter to Orioli approving of Pius' new censorship regulations. In this letter Massimo writes very much in Pius' favour and urges the people not to hurry him. During this month he founds the Concordia society to do good and to promote concord: by legal and public means only.

Apr. 7th. Banquet. Massimo's speech at the Casino Artistico: "Let us all follow...guided by the Pontiff whom God has sent to dry so many tears."

Apr. 20th. Banquet. Massimo is the guest of Ciceruacchio at the Quercia di Tasso.

Apr. 21st. Banquet on the Esquiline for the foundation of Rome. Massimo's most successful speech; he was encored, he said: "Just like Pius IX or Fanny Cerrito the dancer." The following were the final sentences: "Not my weak effort, but the powerful right hand of Pius will tear aside the veil that hides the future; he has made himself the prophet of his people, and not of them alone but of all Christian civilisation.... From Rome God has not yet withdrawn His Countenance nor the treasure of His Power; Rome still remains the city which will never die."

Apr. 22nd. Banquet. Demonstration for the Consulta.

May 11th. Massimo publishes his pamphlet *Sulla Nobiltà* to prove that there is no real cleavage between the nobility and the citizens. This pamphlet was a pre-arranged

He himself was delighted with the progress of the Moderate movement:

Think of two years ago and think of to-day. Think that Italy is at last united in a concordant majority and that public opinion grows and spreads with a rapidity that is not merely double but quadruple of that in former days. Another step and this opinion of ours will overwhelm everything like a torrent.... It will beat down the furious Mazzinians, the shameful Austro-Jesuit-Gregorians, our enemies within and without. I see the day not far distant... when, not to think as we do, will seem so monstrous as to be impossible. Why is it that the Inquisition and torture would be impossible nowadays? Because they are considered monstrous by everybody.[10]

Throughout his campaign there are several features that strike one: firstly, that he made a point of preaching moderation—especially during the early months; secondly, that he wanted to win the confidence of the Pope—in fact he even wrote against the ovations. Thirdly, that he seems to be in close and constant touch with Ciceruacchio—an ex-Carbonaro, a strange associate for him. Fourthly, that his moderate views evidently did win the confidence of Pius, with whom he appears to be equally in touch; although in reality Massimo d'Azeglio's ultimate aims were Unity for the purpose of winning Independence. Fifthly, that in his writings and speeches he always represents Pius as being the real protagonist of the views expressed; one might almost suppose Massimo to be merely the mouthpiece of the Pope.

Take for instance the dinner for two hundred people given

> reply to a letter from Farini; d'Azeglio, being a noble, championed the democratic side; Farini, being a man of the middle class, defended the nobility. The publication of such outspoken criticism was considered a triumph over the Piedmontese censorship (Predari, p. 158). The old Conservatives regarded Massimo as "the precursor of the Anti-Christ".

May 16th.   Banquet at the village of Zagarolo.

[10] D'Azeglio to Minghetti, March 2nd, 1847; Minghetti, *Ricordi*, I, 234.

on May 16th at the village of Zagarolo, about twenty miles outside Rome.[11] Massimo was in the chair, and Ciceruacchio was banner-bearer, and toasts were drunk to Gioberti, d'Azeglio and Ciceruacchio—an absurd trio. Massimo's speech preaching unity among Italians in order to win peace for Italy, assumed that the Pope was entirely in sympathy with his own views. It was an eloquent effusion and was afterwards circulated as a leaflet:

Consider what we were; consider what we now are. Truly the dry bones have heard the word of God; truly the sepulchre has opened and Lazarus has come forth. It was the voice, the powerful voice of Pius which aroused the queen of the nations from her age-long lethargy...and set her again upon the path of honour and virtue.... Let us be obedient and faithful to Pius; let us cleave to one another with a lasting bond of fraternal affection; for we are seeking the right, and we shall attain it.

With the month of July 1847 we come to what is perhaps the best of all his writings, a pamphlet called the *Proposta*,[12] a programme for the national opinion of Italy. This brochure is excellent; but it has never been so famous as *Degli ultimi casi di Romagna* because it did not form a turning-point in the story of the period. He begins by saying that, for years, moral force has been taking the place of mere physical force; by moral force he means public opinion; that the Moderates are better qualified than the Extremists to appeal to public opinion because they injure fewer interests, and that consequently the Moderates have been gaining ground among the educated classes; more especially since Pius IX's accession which brought in many converts previously estranged by their religious scruples. Thus he always keeps Pius in the forefront of the movement. And he adds that the Moderates are so numerous now that they may be called the national opinion of Italy.

In their name he draws up a national programme divided

[11] Vatican Arch., Fondo Spada, 7.
[12] D'Azeglio, *Proposta di un programma per l' opinione nazionale italiana.*

under nine headings. The following is a summary, in several paragraphs, of his forty-five splendid pages.

Independence is the great aim. In order to win independence we must have Unity:

(1) between the princes themselves,
(2) between each prince and his people.

This will lead to the union of all Italy against the foreigner.

To obtain unity between the princes themselves and between each prince and his people, there must be give-and-take on either side: on the one hand the princes must grant moderate reforms, and, on the other, the people must give up revolutions.

This leads us to a time when in each state there will be moderate opinion established in the government; then all the governments will act in unison to win Independence.

It is noticeable that in capitolo VI, in which Massimo inveighs passionately against the Treaty of Vienna and foresees a league of Italian states for the defence of Italy, he proclaims Pius IX as the founder of the movement: "the immense influence" which has "established the principle of justice in the public spirit". "The influence of a true virtue united to an enlightened reason is always great upon men: it is immense when that virtue and that reason are found on a throne, and on the pontifical throne."

Strange is history! Within sixteen months Pope Pius IX was in exile; within thirty months King Charles Albert was dead; and Massimo d'Azeglio was Premier of Piedmont.

Chapter X

PIUS IX'S HARBOUR CONVENTION
GARIBALDI'S FIRST TRIUMPH

During these months all the leaders of Italian nationalism were working for their cause, each in his own way.

Pius was well started on the path which might perhaps have led to uniting Italy by federation.

Charles Albert was continuing his activities already mentioned and was watching the development of the Moderate movement with the keenest interest.

During this summer of 1847 Pius' government negotiated a convention with that of Charles Albert, on lines which in normal times might have produced far greater results. It was a treaty of reciprocal freedom of commerce and navigation, and might reasonably be expected to lead to closer relations later on. The inhabitants of each nation were free to go and live and trade in the other, as if they were its subjects (Art. I). Papal vessels entering Sardinian[1] ports were to pay no more dues than Sardinian vessels, and vice versa (Art. II). All differential tariffs set up by Sardinia against the Papal States were abolished, and in return the Holy See made notable reductions on Sardinian goods crossing the Papal dazio (local customs) lines (Art. VIII). Any special favours granted in future by either power to the subjects of other nations were *ipso facto* to apply gratuitously to the subjects of the now-contracting parties (Art. XI).

These were obviously the right lines on which to lay the foundation of a close union with the north Italian power; in fact the only lines possible at that time. And the news was received with widespread satisfaction.[2]

[1] Sardinian is of course the official name; but modern writers generally refer to the kingdom in question as Piedmont.

[2] This harbour convention was an entirely different matter from the Customs League concluded later on.

Meanwhile Mazzini[3] and his republicans were at work in England: on April 28th he solemnly inaugurated the Peoples' International League, a Society with the following aims:[4]

1. To enlighten the British public as to the political condition and relations of foreign countries.

2. To disseminate the principles of national freedom and progress.

3. To embody and manifest an efficient public opinion in favour of the right of every people to self-government and the maintenance of its own nationality.

4. To promote a good understanding among the peoples of all countries.

This league—which apparently grew out of an influential meeting held on December 16th, 1846, to protest against the occupation of Cracow—was opposed by *The Times* but favourably noticed elsewhere, and soon developed various activities both in England and on the continent. Its ruling council of twenty-four members was entirely composed of English people. One notices that although Mazzini was constantly comparing his own position to that of O'Connell he refused to have any Irish because that would have brought up the question of Repeal, which would have proved fatal to the society.[5]

[3] Mazzini, E.N. XXXII, 82 note.
[4] Mazzini, *Letters to an English Family*, I, 50.
[5] This point is mentioned because it was considered worthy of special attention by Mr Bolton King, who, however, did not know the true cause of Mazzini's views on Ireland. Mr Bolton King has the following paragraphs in his *Life of Mazzini*, p. 107: "The business of the League brought one of the very few occasions on which, as far as is known, he expressed his views on Ireland. Some Repealers complained to the League that it had omitted Ireland in its report from the list of nationalities of the future; and Mazzini was asked to draft an answer to them. His argument was addressed to Separatists but it would apply almost equally to Home Rulers; it proves how radically he misunderstood the Irish movement, and he seems to have felt himself on unsafe ground. He regarded the Irish demand as at bottom one for better government only; and he had every sympathy with their 'just consciousness of human dignity

Throughout 1847 Mazzini was also trying to raise an Italian fund.

And at the same time he had been working at a matter of far greater importance: namely the sword of honour to Garibaldi: and with the mention of this sword we come to a new phase in the story. It is the first sounding in Italian ears of the Great Appeal which was presently to make all other national efforts seem insignificant.

At this point we reach the first scene in the Garibaldian epic—the glorious battlefield of Sant' Antonio: that is the first occasion on which Garibaldi's heroic feats make their appeal to all Italy. The second occasion is the defence of Rome; and the third is the expedition of the Thousand. Upon this great story, undoubtedly, was built the tradition without which the new nation would have been still-born. It was this epic which was to become the real inspiration of the future, because it spoke straight to the heart of the people. No other influence is comparable with it. To the populace, Charles Albert, for instance, and Cavour were mainly identified with Piedmont; Mazzini, of course, had preached the creed of the people, but

claiming its long violated rights', their 'wish to have rulers, educators, not masters', their protests against 'legislation grounded on distrust and hostility'. But he believed that the nationalist movement was not likely to be permanent, and he refused to see any elements of true nationality in it, on the grounds that the Irish did not 'plead for any distinct principle of life or system of legislation, derived from native peculiarities, and contrasting radically with English wants and wishes' nor claimed for their country any 'high special function' to discharge in the interests of humanity. On which it may be noted that the first objection shows Mazzini's ill-acquaintance with Irish life and feeling, and that the second involves a condition, which save in his own theories has not been asked of any nation." Bolton King, *Life of Mazzini*, p. 107: quoted by Commendatore Menghini in Mazzini, E.N. xxxii, 65.

This was the view of Mr Bolton King, but now we know that in a letter written during March 1847 to Giuseppe Giglioli, Mazzini gives his real reason: "We have no Irish on the council, because that would bring up the question of Repeal which would be fatal to us." Mazzini, E.N. xxxii, 65.

he was unskilled in action. Pius' movement had aroused universal enthusiasm, but as Pope he could go no further: when in the early days of 1848 he stood on the balcony of the Quirinal with tears in his eyes, and solemnly blessed Italy, it was in reality his farewell; on that day his national mission was fulfilled. By that time the movement was calling for a fighting leader and a fighting tradition. It was Garibaldi who was to found this tradition; not by victories—for at first victory was impossible—but by an example of incomparable daring, disinterestedness and self-sacrifice.

In a subject people it is not the resentment against material oppression that is dominant, for, as a rule, there is little violent oppression. It is the feeling among the masses that they can take no pride in their native land and that they may be regarded as lacking in courage. In 1849 Garibaldi showed the world that there were Italians who were ready to fight against any odds; and in 1860 he achieved feats of which any nation would be proud. To men striving after nationality this is the supreme appeal, compared to which agitations, conspiracies or federations are as nothing. Rightly or wrongly a man who sees his fellow-countrymen fighting for freedom will regard all else as child's play.

It has been suggested that even without Garibaldi the Kingdom of Italy might still have been formed by the genius of Cavour. This seems unlikely.[6] But even if it had been joined together by some touch of diplomatic genius it would have been merely a work of art or of statesmanship; a beautiful creation but not, as it is, a living being, and personified as such by the romantic patriotism of the people. Some cold-blooded solution of the question was what Mazzini had always feared.

In 1847 it was some thirteen years since Garibaldi had been driven from Italy, a rebel condemned to death by Charles

---

[6] Cavour died in 1862, so that without Garibaldi's help he would hardly have had time to complete the unity of Italy and it would probably have been delayed for years to come.

Albert in 1834. Since then he had led a life of wonderful adventure in Brazil, Uruguay and the Argentine republic and had become famous as a leader both by sea and by land.[7] But he remained Italian, heart and soul; always in touch with Mazzini and with the agents of the Giovine Italia, whose net was spread all over the world.

The dream of his life was unchanged—to free Italy from the Austrians; and with him it was more than a dream.

In 1843 he founded the Italian Legion, that is to say the original Redshirts. It was formed to defend the Republic of Uruguay against an overwhelming invasion from the Argentine Republic, but Garibaldi intended it to be a national Italian corps; by defending freedom abroad it should learn how to win freedom in Italy. These legionaries were colonial democratic fighting men and—most valuable of all—they looked to the whole of Italy as their native land, not merely to one of her states. Such a corps was ready to die for the national honour, and after one single preliminary failure it went from victory to victory. So fine was the record[8] of the legionaries that on January 30th, 1845, the president of the Republic of Uruguay made a formal donation to them of certain lands and buildings in recognition of their services to the state: but, in the name of his officers and men, Garibaldi declined these gifts, and refused, in dignified and grateful terms, to accept any reward for having defended freedom.

This gesture aroused admiration in Europe; in England Mazzini described it in *The Times*.

---

[7] For the battle of Sant' Antonio I rely principally on Garibaldi's own description in his Autobiography; and also on that of his grand-daughter Signorina Annita Italia Garibaldi in her wonderfully interesting little book *Garibaldi in America*. She has spent several years in South America and has collected some thousands of documents on her grandfather. Her brother, General Ezio Garibaldi, tells me that this is the latest publication on the subject. Other volumes consulted were those of Jessie White Mario, of Gualterio, Bersezio and other historians.

[8] Mazzini, E.N. XXVIII, 279.

A year later they reached the zenith of their glory at the battle of Sant' Antonio, fought on February 8th, 1846, and this far-off engagement produced so inspiring an effect in Italy that it claims a description. On that day Garibaldi, who was being besieged in the town of Salto by the Argentine invaders, marched out to join hands with a relieving force. He had with him only 186 Italian legionaries and about 100 non-Italian[9] horsemen. His first halt was on a hill called Tapera de Venancio, about six miles from the town; and while his men were piling arms, there suddenly came in sight, on the nearest hill, "a forest of lances, close squadrons of cavalry with colours flying, and a body of mounted infantry— double the strength of his own". He had been trapped by a hostile force of 900 horsemen—some said 1200—and 300 mounted infantry. It was a desperate position against such odds, but Garibaldi made up his mind to fight. He thought it hopeless to try and retire for six miles surrounded by so greatly superior a force of horsemen, and with the hostile infantry driving his men from point to point with the bayonet all the way. He must await their attack where he stood. It was their infantry that he feared. If once he could succeed in crippling their infantry he would only have to deal with the wild riders, who would cause no great anxiety to his disciplined Italian legion.

The position in which he had halted his men possessed some advantages. It was an eminence upon which there stood the remains of a ruined *estancia* (farm or country-house). Around it there was a line consisting of "a certain number of wooden posts" formerly the uprights of a wooden wall or palisade: behind each of these he posted a legionary. Of the house itself there remained a good brick wall—the northern wall of the building—which still protected a space of ground "like rooms capable of holding thirty people". Behind this wall he placed three sections in reserve, almost completely under cover.

[9] Garibaldi does not specify their regiment.

There remained his cavalry, about a hundred strong: he posted it on his right flank, and dismounted those who had carbines—those armed only with lances remained on their horses.

His aim was not merely to repulse but to cripple the attacking infantry; so he ordered the redshirted legionaries not to fire a shot until the enemy was on to the muzzles of their muskets, so that every single one of them should bring his man down.

But there was little time for making plans. The attack was already in progress—though, as Garibaldi afterwards observed, it had not been thought out with much skill. Instead of massing their superior numbers to break through at a given point, the Argentine light infantry rode forward to a distance of about two musket-shots, and then dismounted and advanced in one line—a line of two ranks, no doubt, and shoulder-to-shoulder. In this formation they left the opposite hill, crossed the stream and began to mount the near slope; and as they approached their objective they came on very rapidly with fixed bayonets and the drums beating the charge. But when they were within a few yards of the Italians, suddenly they halted and fired a volley, no doubt to prepare the way for their final rush. This halt was their undoing. They hit a good many of the defenders, but at the same time they allowed themselves to be caught standing out in the open, in close order at only a few yards' range. The Redshirts seized the moment. They raised their muskets and poured in a fire of which hardly a bullet went astray. The attack was shattered; and when the three reserve sections of Italians dashed out and charged in mass formation, they swept the assailants right off the hill with fearful slaughter. Garibaldi's object was achieved. The enemy's infantry was crippled for the day: "and now", he continues, "I encouraged myself with hopes of safety".

As he looked up, however, he perceived that all his cavalry had vanished except five or six men.

It had been about mid-day when the action began. For nine hours to come the fight continued. From time to time the enemy dismounted some of their horsemen and attempted another assault, supported by cavalry movements "which made the ground tremble"; and throughout all those hours men were falling. But the Italians remained unshakeable, fighting for the honour of the name; and the enemy's dead were far more numerous than theirs. The scene near the line of posts must have resembled a shambles.[10] At nine o'clock in the evening Garibaldi decided that he could retire. He had lost 36 men killed and more than half the remaining 154 were wounded, and his cavalry was no longer there to protect the retirement, but he formed up the unfortunate wounded and bleeding men—some of them had horrible wounds—in the centre, and as rear-guard and flankers he placed his un-wounded men with fixed bayonets to guard them like a con-voy. His chief difficulty was that some of the wounded men could not keep up with the others, and one or two of them had to be left behind to their fate.

All around them bodies of wild horsemen were swirling about and everything depended on the tired defenders re-maining steady. But, continues Garibaldi, "the little column —I recall it with pride!—was admirable". So cool and con-fident were they that when they saw the charging horsemen suddenly wheel off, under their fire, they would shout derisively in Spanish "Ah che no?" (Aren't you coming on?); and thus their retirement continued until at last they were in safety.

On the following day the invaders departed, leaving the field of Sant' Antonio covered with their dead. The siege was at an end.

[10] "We were standing in the midst of a barricade of corpses" was Garibaldi's description of the scene at the end of the fight. I see that Signorina Garibaldi gives the Italian casualties as 30 killed and 53 wounded, and says that the enemy "had 120 killed besides the wounded."—Annita Italia Garibaldi, *Garibaldi in America*, p. 147.

The Uruguay republic was saved, and once again its president proposed rewards and honours to the Italian legion, and again they were refused by Garibaldi in suitable terms. But there was one reward which he was able to accept, namely, the sword of honour offered to him in 1847 not only by Mazzini, but by Massimo d'Azeglio and by many of the best known among his fellow-countrymen.[11]

A wave of joy and pride had surged up all over Italy; and a feeling of confidence in their own powers. Many Italians, too, were wondering whether they had found a national leader.

During the next year Garibaldi kept his eyes fixed on Italy, and after the Ferrara episode in July 1847, he offered himself and his legion to serve in Pius IX's army against the Austrians. He evidently believed, like most other Italians, that the Pope would be the national leader in the coming war.

As if to remind us of the true mission of the Papacy we find, on the anniversary of the battle of Sant' Antonio, the Holy Father himself receiving a deputation craving help in the most fearful national disaster of the century. It was the first period of the Great Famine in Ireland. Already thousands of peasants were dying of starvation and fever, although these were only the early days of that disaster—unparalleled perhaps in modern history—which resulted, directly or indirectly, in the reduction of the population from nearly $8\frac{1}{2}$ millions to $6\frac{1}{2}$. When the news of this appalling suffering reached Rome, Pius started a subscription to supply relief work, sent 1000 scudi out of his own "peculio", and ordered a solemn Triduo to be held—three days during which sermons were to be preached and public prayers offered up; and, in an encyclical of March 15th, he[12] "aroused the charitable zeal of the

[11] V. Protocollo IV, p. 182 note, 201, 209, 210, and others; also Mazzini, Scritti (E.N.), XXX, 271, 272; XXXII, p. 105, and elsewhere.
[12] Contemporaneo, January 30th and April 17th, 1847.

bishops and of the faithful to help the Irish who were tor-
mented by hunger and worn out by pestilence".[13] Under his
auspices the great Liberal preacher Padre Ventura—a Sicilian
patriot—exerted the utmost of his eloquence in arousing
enthusiasm for a relief fund. On Sunday, January 24th, 1847,
he preached a passionate sermon in the church of St Andrea
della Valle, voicing the past sufferings of Ireland and the
horrors of the present Famine in one great call for help and
sympathy.

Further assistance came from many people, especially
among the English-speaking population in Rome, both
Catholic and Protestant. The "deputation of the English
residents in Rome" which waited upon Pius to thank him[14]

---

[13] Vatican Arch. Fondo Spada, 120. For the purpose of raising
a relief fund, a pamphlet entitled *Breve notizia dell' attuale Carestia
in Irlanda* (Brief notice of the present famine in Ireland) was issued
in 1847, dealing with the months of November and December 1846
and January 1847. It begins by saying that the facts are known to
all, and that the measures adopted by the British government and
the large sums collected in charity have only been able to do a little
good; then it gives letters and extracts from articles in an English
paper of which the following are the first two:
"1. Dunmanway, Monday, January 4th, 1847. Arrived at 10.
Met four corpses being carried to cemetery. Misery all around. At
Skibbereen there are men digging graves all day, and carpenters are
working at coffins day and night. Ballydehob (?) the most pitiful
sight. The people are skeletons. In neighbouring parish of *Skull*,
18,000 souls, the deaths of the last fortnight have been ten a day.
People living on seaweed, and such beasts as they can catch."
"2. Tobermory, January 10th, 1847. Hundreds in village without
a mouthful of food. Several two days without any at all. One family
of four had had nothing to eat in one day but a small piece of black
bread between them. There is no food and no work. The meat sent
by M.N. saved 20 families from dying of starvation. The snow is
making the situation even worse for it has stopped such little work
as there is. The thing is to try and find work for the women as they
can nearly all sew, knit, spin and weave. But it must be quickly for
it is a case of life and death. The people are naked as well as starving
for they have sold their clothes to get food."
[14] *V. Contemporaneo*, January 23rd, 1847. The members were
Messrs ffolliott, M.P. (of the Sligo family, I believe), Blancy (?),

was introduced by Dr Cullen (afterwards Bishop Cullen), the Rector of the Irish College, and by Dr Kirby, the Vice-rector. Pius replied to them in heartfelt terms.

Some three months later news arrived from Genoa that Daniel O'Connell had died there on May 15th. The Liberator had started from Ireland, worn out and heart-broken at the misfortunes of his people, but earnestly hoping that he might live to reach Rome. In Paris he was received with great honour. When, however, he realised that his hope would not be fulfilled he expressed a wish that his heart, at least, should be buried in the City of the Church.[15] In Rome, therefore, Pius ordered a great Requiem service to be held in his memory, and Padre Ventura preached his funeral oration.

This funeral oration for O'Connell is described in all Italian histories, partly on account of its eloquence, but more especially because in it Padre Ventura made the first definite public reference to the Roman agitation in progress. He was a devoted priest but a convinced Liberal, with Giobertian ideas, and believed that the Church could be saved by being Liberalised. In the course of his sermon he said that as Ireland had used a legal agitation to win the reform of the law,

Balfour, Whiteside (the celebrated preacher), Ross of Bladensburg, Jones, Colonel Bryan, Captain Jenkinson, Captain Patterson, the Rev. Dewedney, the Rev. Richards, Messrs Smart, Gurney, Tilt, and Mr Harford, the well-known English archaeologist, president of the Committee, v. Spada, 1, 182.

Pius replied to them in heart-felt terms: "For me it is a great consolation to see so many kind gentlemen from every part of the British realm gathered together to carry out an excellent work of charity by using every endeavour to arrest the havoc of the famine, and alleviate the fearful misery of their brothers in Ireland. If the means at my disposal were greater I should not limit myself to the small amount that I have done for a cause to which I am so strongly drawn. To supplement this want I will pray with all my fervour to the Almighty that He may deign to turn a compassionate glance on this people and remove the scourge that is upon them and presently vouchsafe them peace, happiness and abundance."

[15] He left his body to Ireland, his heart to Rome and commended his soul to God.

so Rome might use a loving agitation with her Pontiff, who himself "was all love for his people"; and hence this term "agitazione amorosa" or loving agitation has become historic among writers on this period. Moreover, the sermon itself seems to have been a splendid effort. Padre Ventura, says Spada, spoke the second portion of his funeral oration before one of the most imposing congregations ever seen, "and it is related that his listeners could hardly restrain themselves, despite the sanctity of the place, from breaking out into applause". Pellegrino Rossi, though no longer a Catholic, describes it in the following terms:

I made a point of seeing with my own eyes and hearing with my own ears what took place at the Church of St Andrea della Valle when Padre Ventura preached the funeral oration for O'Connell. He was obliged to divide it into two separate addresses—so widely and with such boldness of thought and expression had he developed his double thesis, namely that religion needs liberty in order to prosper and that liberty grows and fortifies itself through religion. What a concourse of all classes! How persistent and full of emotion was their attention. One could not detect a smile or the slightest symptom of irony on the mobile and expressive faces of these men who as a rule are so much given to mockery and epigram. Paris, Aff. Etr., Rome, 1847–48.

Perhaps the most striking proof of the universality of the sympathy for Ireland is the fact that the two men who represented the extreme opposite poles of political thought, Mazzini and Metternich, were both touched by it. In his letter of January 23rd, 1847, Mazzini wrote to his mother: "The misery here and elsewhere is a revolting spectacle. And then they can come and tell us that it is a well-ordered state of society in which, for lack of a few potatoes, thousands and even millions are reduced to starvation."

And rather later on, when in exile, old Metternich wrote:[16] "'Irland wandert auss.' Ireland is passing forth. It is wending its way to the North American States...to ask for an empty space of ground."

[16] *Aus nachgelassenen Papieren*, VIII, p. 577.

In Ireland itself Pius' acts of kindness naturally spread a deep and permanent feeling of gratitude: and thirteen years later, when all Europe was ringing with the triumphs of Garibaldi and his Thousand, and the Papal State was invaded by the Piedmontese, among the most determined defenders of Pius was a battalion of Irish volunteers.

Part II

June 1847 *to* 1 *January* 1848

Chapter XI

METTERNICH AND THE REVOLUTION

We now return to the world-conflict between the forces of Conservatism and the Revolution. We are approaching the immense crisis of the year 1848.

In 1847 Metternich and the revolutionists were at hand-grips in almost every civilised country: in Austria, in Germany, in Italy, and, generally speaking, throughout all the highways and by-ways of European diplomacy.[1] He was making every effort to strengthen his position, so as to be able to maintain the political *status quo*. "Metternich's system", he wrote afterwards, "I have proclaimed aloud to the whole world in one short sentence, 'Strength in Right', a motto for myself and my successors." In spite of his efforts however, during the second half of 1847, the Revolution was gaining ground very rapidly: and during the struggle between these two huge waves of antagonistic mentality, Pius IX's Moderate movement was on the verge of being annihilated.

A. METTERNICH IN 1847

Undoubtedly there is an element of tragedy about these last days of Metternich. By then he was a man of seventy-four years, partly blind of one eye and rather deaf; and he was beginning to feel weary, *lebensmüde*, but his letters reveal few, if any, signs of diminished energy.[2] He still remained as capable as ever of forming an exhaustively reasoned opinion

---

[1] These four headings are the main subjects of this chapter.

[2] "Ich binn so lebensmüde", he said to the Princess Mélanie, who adds: "This utterance cut me to the heart." *Aus nachgelassenen Papieren*, p. 304. His biographies speak of him as being mentally and physically devitalised; but he lived another twelve years, to be eighty-six. *V. Metternich*, by Arthur Herman (English translation, 1932), pp. 216, 225, etc. Also Srbik.

on any of the innumerable questions laid before him. It is true that his ideas did not advance with the times, but that was because, in a defensive position such as his, the methods could not vary. He remained the representative of a past era which in 1847 had become the Napoleonic legend.

From the diaries of the Princess Mélanie—his adoring third wife whom he had married when he was fifty-eight and by whom he had five children—one can picture their life in the imperial city of Vienna. His portraits show him to be a keenly awake, heavily built old man of rather sarcastic expression, his blue eyes fairly wide open but shrewd, his nose curved, his hair close-curling, his lips cynically humorous, and his breast resplendent with orders. It is a distinguished face but not altogether pleasant.[3]

For this old man there still existed a deep respect, but especially throughout those senior generations of the German world, where anti-Napoleonic feeling remained a power. By them it was remembered that he had been in office since July 8th, 1809, when, after the disaster of Wagram, Count Stadion had resigned the ministry of foreign affairs, and he, Metternich, then only thirty-six years of age, had been called on by his Emperor to save the state. Austria was at its lowest ebb— compelled to surrender to the French armies for the fourth time within twelve years. Nevertheless he had never abandoned hope; from the first he had perceived that Napoleon's period of domination was probably only a passing phase, dependent on his avoiding defeat, and seriously imperilled during each fresh campaign. Metternich therefore had set himself to engineer his downfall; had bearded him in the historic interview during which (so Metternich tells us) Napoleon, in the true adventurer's spirit, had tried to "bluff" his opponents by hurling his hat into a corner and shouting

[3] When describing his personal appearance Beust speaks of "the truly great nature which showed itself in the illustrious appearance of the great Chancellor". Beust, *Memoirs*, 1, 18.

out that a million men were nothing to him;[4] and only two years later Austria had sent forth a triumphant army to occupy Paris, and to make peace in which she received a lion's share of the spoil.

Throughout his long life he had worked on a gigantic scale and had been, nearly always, the predominant figure in issues of European importance; but the letters of his later years show a profound consciousness that, in spite of his unceasing toil, the order which he had founded and so long sustained was nearing its end. Everywhere he saw the populations in that state of semi-suppressed discontent which usually pre- cedes a step forward in the march of Progress, and is nearly always accompanied by bloodshed. In this coming battle of the giants Metternich well knew that for the powers-that-be the prospect had never been so inauspicious. In reality his policy of universal negation, prolonged during forty years, had ended by combining and arraying against him all types of revolution; the Liberal, the social and the national. Liberal institutions were being demanded by the peoples; social un- rest was rampant—peasants and serfs were rising against their landlords; and, finally, the spirit of nationality was every- where calling aloud for freedom. This last influence was by far the most powerful in 1847. How truly did Radowitz[5] write, on November 20th of that year, to his sovereign King William IV of Prussia: "The most powerful force of the present time, that of Nationality, has become the most dangerous weapon in the hands of the enemies of rightful order."

[4] In view of this saying it is surely rather unreasonable of Napoleon's biographers to object to sentries being placed in the grounds of Longwood to prevent his escape. All Europe regarded him as a wild animal; v. d'Azeglio's *Ricordi*, etc.

[5] Born at Blankenburg, 1797. In 1823 passed from the service of Hesse to that of Prussia. In 1830 became Chief of Staff for Artillery. Was one of the friends of the Prince Royal (afterwards Frederick William IV). In 1842 Plenipotentiary at Carlsruhe; 1845, Major- General; 1848, Member of the Parliament of Frankfort; 1850, Minister for Foreign Affairs; died, 1853.

B. THE REVOLUTION

Here we have a wonderful phenomenon: the arising of the peoples who are of one race; or merely of one language; or merely of one will to be a nation.

1. *Austria*

This year of 1847 brought with it many anxious days and nights. Metternich realised that in Austria, in Germany, and in Italy, the ancient Habsburg Empire was shaken to its founda- tions by three great racial upheavals which threatened to break it into fragments—the Pan-Slav,[6] the Pan-German and the Pan-Italian movements; and that, over and above all this racialism, the Revolution in general was now considered to have received the benediction of the Catholic Church.

In German Austria democracy was stirring against absolut- ism; there was agitation for the freedom of the press, for equality before the law and for parliamentary guarantees. In the other units of the Empire the movements were national; the oppressed peoples were rising to claim their birthright of independence and unity.

In Hungary Kossuth's movement was in full blast, and the meetings of the Diet were becoming more and more tumul- tuous, but its cause was partly vitiated by its own domination over the subject populations of Roumans, Germans, Croats, Serbs and other Slavs. Metternich, of course, encouraged and inflamed these divisions: his remarks about the Magyars were characteristic.

---

[6] "Oh! If our Slav peoples were of gold, of silver, of copper, I would weld them all into one single statue. Of Russia I would make her hands, of the Poles I would make her body; the Czechs should be her arms and head, and the Serbs her feet. The secondary tribes, the Wends of Lusacia, the Silesians, Croats, and Slovaks should be her clothing and her weapons. All Europe would kneel before this idol, whose head would be above the clouds and each of whose steps would cross the world." Song by the poet Kollar (quoted in *Histoire Contemporaine*, Driault and Monod, p. 172). M. Ernest Denis gives a slightly different translation; *v. La Bohême depuis la montagne blanche*, II, 151; he speaks of "our dispersed Slav peoples".

The Hungarian character is rather given to Utopias. The spirit of the nation is one easily carried away by first impressions. It is always ready to be seduced by effective words without troubling about their degree of practical value.

All that was required to bring them to reason, he said, was some material development, and "government by a firm hand; then the menées of the parties, their hollow theories and their sterile polemics will vanish in smoke before the energetic attitude of the government".

In Bohemia the Czechs were reviving their national tradition: more especially their language, a matter sacred to every Bohemian—for while the language lives the race can defy conquest; their old songs were being sung once more, and their history studied in the schools. In 1847 their Diet under the influence of Count Frederick Deym passed a resolution that, legally, no taxes could be collected in Bohemia unless voted by the Estates; indeed they were rapidly working up to the moment (1848) when Palacky, on being invited to represent Bohemia at the Pan-German assembly at Frankfort, indited with passionate feeling his celebrated letter of refusal: "I am a Czech; by race a Slav; and I have dedicated myself entirely and for ever to the service of my own people. It is not one of the great peoples of the earth, but it has always been independent and self-governed...." [7]

Count Frederick Deym was, on account of his eloquence, known as the Bohemian O'Connell. Incidentally it is very interesting to see how closely the Bohemian movement followed the lines of the Irish. [8]

[7] Translated from the French of M. Ernest Denis, *La Bohême depuis la montagne blanche*, II, 261. *V.* also Maurice, *Bohemia*, p. 523; Lützow, *Bohemia*, p. 334. For the various phases of this movement *v.* also Nosek, *The Spirit of Bohemia*, and H. Jelinek, *Histoire de la littérature tchèque*. These five books are those very kindly recommended to me by the Czecho-Slovak Embassy in London.

[8] As in those days the "Censor-office" prohibited all allusions to the internal affairs of Bohemia, Havlicek used to publish his sharp criticisms of the government in the form of reports on the condition of Ireland. Thus, says Count Lützow, there originated the com-

It was the Polish sentiment of nationality, however, that had caused more trouble than any other. But in Galicia, Metternich was able to cope with it by making use of its internal discords. The discords were twofold; the peasants against their landlords and the Catholic Poles against the Greek-Church Ruthenians. In 1846 the unrest had culminated in the rising already mentioned, during which some of the revolutionary network had been discovered.[9]

In Austria, therefore, the government had never before been so insecure: and consequently the Austrian policy was weak both at home and abroad.

2. *In Germany*

In Germany, which was Metternich's "sphere of influence", matters were equally unsatisfactory: the Pan-German spirit was abroad. In 1815 he had organised the German Confederation, with its thirty-four states and four free towns, under a Diet of plenipotentiaries of which Austria was president. Germany was weak because it was divided, and Metternich had been able to dictate his will to the Diet. But the giant was awakening "to full consciousness of his latent power, to the foreknowledge of a great political future". In every state the people were calling for freer institutions.

But, more especially, they were calling for unity. The Zollverein (Customs Union)—originally formed during the years 1828 to 1833 between a majority of the German states under the leadership of Prussia—had now become a new

parison between Ireland and Bohemia which has since become one of the commonplaces of political controversy. It was also with reference to Ireland that the great patriotic association formed in Bohemia shortly before 1848 assumed the name of the Repeal Society. *V. Bohemia*, by Count Lützow, p. 329 *et seq.*

[9] These two acts proved the communications which existed between the conspirators in Galicia and the Directory Committee of Polish Emigration at Poitiers and Versailles; and also their affiliation to the conspiracy in the Grand Duchy of Posen, De Marescalchi to Guizot, August 14th, 1847, Paris Aff. Etr., Autriche, 1847–48.

factor in the situation. It had made commercial treaties with other nations, with Turkey in 1840, with England in 1841 and with Holland in 1842. In 1841 it had been renewed; and thenceforward it had felt the need of military power.[10] This Zollverein was purely German and refused to include Austria among its states because the Habsburg Empire was mainly composed of non-German peoples. It looked to Prussia as its chief. And in 1840 a true sentiment of nationality had been inspired into the call for Pan-German unity, by the aggressive attitude of the French statesman Thiers. Thiers' chauvinism had aroused throughout Germany the splendid patriotic reply which has been immortalised in the *Wacht am Rhein*—the same wave of national feeling which afterwards welled up into the countless endeavours of 1848, and continued to grow in strength until it reached its zenith in the triumphs of 1870.[11]

In this new ordering of Germany, Prussia was inevitably the rival of Austria.

3. *In Italy*

On April 3rd of the year 1847 Lamberti, secretary of the Giovine Italia, had written to a member named Lami,[12] expressing satisfaction with the national progress made under the Moderates but hoping soon to take their place:

[10] *V.* Debidour, 1, 403; Mowat, p. 170, and other authorities.

[11] This feeling is strongly expressed in the books of the time, as for instance in the Memoirs of Prince Chlodwig von Höhenlohe Schillingfurst, who was by birth a Bavarian but eventually became imperial chancellor. Writing in November 1847 he says: "When we study the map and see how the Baltic, the North Sea and the Mediterranean break upon our shores, and how no German flag commands the customary salute from the haughty French and English, surely the hue of shame will alone survive from the red, black and yellow, and mount into our cheeks. And must not all the whining talk about German unity and German nation remain woefully ludicrous...until we have the reality of a great United Germany?" But he had no illusions. "Progress leads to Revolution; a hard saying but a true one."

[12] *Protocollo*, v, 57.

The spirit and opinion in favour of nationality and independence are forming well in Italy from all points of view, and there is a general hatred of the Germans. If a favourable event occurs or one that will fire the mine, there will be a general rising there. This was helped by the discussions over the hopes aroused by Charles Albert and the Pope, in neither of whom I have any belief. The Moderate party is now the dominating power there, but it will not and cannot do anything. With the call of danger that party will be dissipated—and then we will come in to inspire them with confidence and push them to action. Soon I hope we shall have a vast European ball; already one can hear the tuning of its great orchestra.

"The word 'Italy'," said Metternich, "is a geographical denomination", and he was perfectly right.[13] But he said it without perceiving or wishing to perceive what an excellent argument this was for her becoming a nation. One might equally well say that "Great Britain" is a geographical denomination; and that is surely the main reason why the English and the Scots, who were at war with each other for centuries, are now a united people.

A tremendous situation! And how ludicrously inadequate seems the governing clique, the small Conference at Vienna. It was composed of the Emperor Ferdinand, who was half-witted, and of his regent the Archduke Louis. There was Metternich for foreign affairs, and his rival Kolowrath for internal matters, and several bureaucrats and members of the royal family. In fact, there was a great old man within a small council deeply divided by jealousies.

One dominating factor, however, we have not yet mentioned. We are writing about Italy and we have left out RADETZKY. True, he bears the marks of seven wounds; he can remember nine horses being killed under him[14] and he is eighty years of age; nevertheless it is he who will dominate the future. Only a year later the whole situation will be

---

[13] *Aus nachgelassenen Papieren*, VII, 388, April 12th, 1847.
[14] *Radetzky*, by A. Luzio. Quoted by Masi, *Nell' Ottocento*, p. 176.

summed up in the five famous words addressed to him by an Austrian poet:[15] "In deinem Lager ist Oesterreich."

C. METTERNICH'S DIPLOMACY

1. *The Situation*

In diplomatic skill, at all events, Metternich in 1847 might still be called first among the foreign ministers of continental Europe. His opinion was still the best worth reading: and on all sides of his Empire he was planning fortified outposts at important centres, in order to forestall the coming outbreaks. But he required an ally, especially when dealing with the Italian question. This is the period of his *rapprochement* with Guizot.

His usual friends no longer sufficed him.[16] In Russia, the Czar Nicholas was a true ally against the Revolution—as he was destined to prove to the world in 1849; but he was more interested in his own questions than in those of the Italian peninsula. Similarly Prussia; in Switzerland she was an ally over the Sonderbund question; but in Italy she was indifferent, and in Germany now she was the rival of Austria. England, whose foreign policy had been under the guidance of Palmerston since the middle of 1846, was frankly Liberal, to the point of sometimes inadvertently patronising revolutionists. There remained only France.

With Louis Philippe it was the very moment for arranging an understanding.[17] On the one hand France could not possibly unite her destinies to those of Russia or of Prussia, and on the other, her existing *entente* with England was on the verge of coming to an end. Both sides were tired of it. England was becoming more Liberal, whereas, now, Louis

---

[15] Franz Grillparzer: "Within thy camp is Austria"; because Vienna was seething with revolution; and the existence of the Austrian Empire depended on Radetzky's being victorious.

[16] Debidour, I, 443, and other histories.

[17] Debidour, I, 422; *Camb. Mod. Hist.* XI, 40; and other histories.

Philippe and Guizot were almost as much afraid of the Revolution as was Metternich himself. France was full of unrest: movements for reform (Odilon Barrot, Thiers, etc.); for universal suffrage and a republic (Ledru Rollin); for social revolution (the Labour leaders); besides which there was the attack on the Jesuits. At the same time a campaign of banquets was beginning, similar to that against Pius. In fact the situation in France was developing more and more towards its final crisis, the Revolution of 1848.

In the second half of the year 1846 the Anglo-French *entente* had come definitely to an end. On June 29th the Tories (Sir Robert Peel), after passing the Repeal of the Corn Laws, were defeated on a Coercion Bill for Ireland, and were displaced by the Whigs under Lord John Russell and Palmerston. With Palmerston, a true Liberal and an active, pushing minister, Guizot was already at daggers drawn—and their differences soon came to a head. On October 10th the Spanish Marriage question was brought to a conclusion by the double marriage of Queen Isabella to the Duke of Cadiz, and her sister to the Duc de Montpensier, fifth son of Louis Philippe. This caused the breach: firstly, because it was a diplomatic triumph for France over England, for it meant that in all likelihood Spain would pass into the hands of the French royal family; and secondly, because Palmerston and Queen Victoria felt that they had been grossly duped during the negotiations—and there seems to have been some justification for their resentment.[18] After that the Anglo-French *entente* soon came to an end.

From that moment, too, begins the *rapprochement* between Metternich and Guizot. Already Metternich had seized the moment of this breach between France and England to take

[18] "La Reine...blessée au vif par ce qu'elle qualifie d'indélicatesse de la part du Roi Louis-Philippe, qui sous les dehors d'une affection paternelle, aurait abusé de l'inexpérience d'une jeune femme...les caresses qui lui ont été prodiguées ont à ses yeux la valeur de griefs." Metternich to Apponyi, February 25th, 1847 (*Aus nachgelassenen Papieren*).

an important step forward. In concert with Russia and Prussia he had occupied Cracow, as already described.[19]

By this step the extinction of Poland was completed (November 11th, 1846), and the true value of the Treaty of 1815 was demonstrated. Yet Metternich regarded his work as a splendid success; in fact as the final suppression of a stronghold of conspiracy. From his point of view no doubt there was a good deal of truth in that accusation; but he was to learn that those conspirators were quite as dangerous when disseminated all over Europe, and far more bitter and reckless when they had nothing to lose at home.[20] Fifteen months later, during the convulsions of 1848, there were many Viennese rebels who took matters light-heartedly enough, but the Poles went straight to their goal.

Metternich's next project was also destined to failure. He meant to strike a blow at the Revolution in Switzerland: to arrange with France for the joint occupation of that country on lines similar to those at Cracow. He even proposed to Guizot that Austria and France, together with the other powers, should send a joint note to the Swiss Diet to say that "they will not allow the Cantonal Sovereignty to be violated". Guizot, however, felt that this step would lead to armed intervention and he refused to agree.[21] Meanwhile, the Swiss Federal Diet stood firm. So no invasion took place. And Count von Beust[22] has recorded his opinion—and recorded it

[19] Vienna Staats-Archiv, Rome, *Rapports*, II, January 10th, 1847.

[20] "In 1846 the Polish Revolution had indeed been overthrown but its fugitive germs had been scattered into many a region of future activity besides the hotbed of Paris." *Camb. Mod. Hist.* XI, 142. The influence of the Polish fugitives seems to be admitted.

[21] Paris Aff. Etr., Autriche, 1847–48, Guizot, June 25th.

[22] Count von Beust. Born 1809. By birth a Saxon. Saxon Minister in Paris, Munich, London and Berlin. 1849–59, Minister of the Crown in Saxony. Afterwards Chancellor of the Austrian Empire. He says, "When both France and Austria had encouraged by every possible means the resistance of the Cantons of the Sonderbund...the threat of armed intervention on which the Sonderbund party had the right to rely, ended in the powers merely

several times over—that it was this failure in Switzerland on the part of Metternich and Guizot which showed up the weakness of their governments in 1847 and thereby encouraged the Revolution to attack them in 1848.

By June 1847, therefore, Metternich had occupied Cracow and was still in the process of threatening the Swiss Liberals. In Italy he had made even more elaborate preparations against the Revolution.

The corner-stone of his plans, however, was not yet secured: namely a definite *entente* with Guizot.

2. *Metternich's preparations in Italy*

In Italy Metternich's military scheme was almost perfected : he had nearly completed his plans for getting a strangle-hold on the country. He meant to occupy positions which would enable him, if necessary, to keep down the whole peninsula.

But what were his actual plans? Were they aggressive? Was he preparing an advance? Many writers have thought so and that is the main problem before the historian, because it governs the whole situation, especially during the Ferrara episodes.

As far as one can tell, he meant to consolidate his defensive position into one of immense strength, for the time being. And it is difficult not to believe that he was also arranging the situation so that some day the ripe fruit might fall into his hands. But apparently he was not planning any aggressive action against the Liberals in the Papal State. Rather later in the year, on August 22nd, 1847, Metternich wrote to Graf Ficquelmont, the newly appointed Austrian adviser to the Viceroy in Milan, a letter of directions in which most probably he expressed his genuine views. These fall under four main headings: not to intervene in Rome or Naples, while

allowing things to take their course.... The recognition by the Revolutionary Party of the weakness of the European powers had the natural consequence that the February Revolution (in Paris) operated everywhere like an explosive." He speaks in the same strain elsewhere. *V.* also Herman, *Metternich*, p. 242.

retaining unaltered the right to do so if necessary; to try to win back Piedmont to Austrian alliance; to agree if necessary to a European concert over the affairs of Naples or the Papal State, but not elsewhere. If the Grand Duke of Tuscany, the Duchess of Parma, the Duke of Modena, should call on the Austrian Emperor for help, it must be remembered that these princes are agnates of the House of Austria; he is the head of their family, and "it is his duty to help them without consulting a concert".

It seems, therefore, that for the present he was not planning any advance of his frontiers, or any action in Rome. But he was consolidating his military position by occupying outlying positions, and this fact caused great alarm in the Papal State and in Tuscany. Before the end of the year people were heard to say: "First it was Cracow; then it was Parma, Modena, and Ferrara; next it will be Florence and Rome." Undoubtedly to live next an empire of this type is rather like living next a kleptomaniac.

The following are the items in his military programme in July 1847:

Venetia and Lombardy, already under Austria, were secured by the impregnable Quadrilateral, and he had seventy thousand loyal men to hold it (Fabris, 1, 72); Tyrolese, Croatians, Hungarians, Italians and Germans, under Marshal Radetzky. From that position he looked out westward upon Piedmont and southward upon the Papal State and Tuscany. Piedmont he could not attack without arousing France, but he had nearly completed his *entente* with Louis Philippe; as for the central states of Italy they were to be held in awe by his garrisons in the fortresses of Ferrara and Comacchio, two Papal towns beside the river Po.

Meanwhile he was establishing himself in forward protective positions in the Duchies—Parma and Modena—so as to cut off Piedmont from Central Italy. In the Duchy of Parma he had a garrison in the town of Piacenza, and, by the Treaty of 1815, had the right to keep it there until the death of the

Duchess Marie Louise (widow of the great Napoleon). As matters turned out she did not die until December 15th, 1847, and then—needless to say—the Austrians remained in occupation.

In Modena, on the death of Duke Francis IV, Metternich had sent in troops to keep order until the accession of the young Duke Francis V; and they had remained there as a garrison.

While dealing with this subject[23] we may perhaps be allowed to go a little beyond the actual date about which we are writing (July 1847), in order to complete the picture of Metternich's movements for forestalling the Revolution. On December 24th, 1847, he completed his scheme by signing an offensive and defensive "alliance" between Parma, Modena and Austria, whereby the two small states virtually disappeared. Their troops were henceforth under the orders of Field-Marshal Radetzky, and their fortresses became merely advanced posts of the Austrian frontiers in Italy.

3. *Metternich's understanding with Guizot*

Metternich had almost completed his vast programme of resistance. To some extent it had revived the Holy Alliance with Prussia and Russia: it included his negotiations with the German Confederation; his annexation of Cracow; his attempted overaweing of Switzerland; and his scheme of fortified positions and subservient princes in Italy. But there remained one predominant factor to be secured, perhaps the most important of all, namely the approval of France. Without that he could not be safe against the Revolution.

January 1847 was the date of the first *rapprochement* between Metternich and Guizot.

The moment was propitious. Guizot, now estranged from England, required an ally; moreover he wanted Austria to remain neutral over the Spanish question; and thirdly, he

[23] On all these matters *v. Aus nachgelassenen Papieren*, VII, 350, and a later despatch to Apponyi of December 24th, 1847.

was almost as much afraid of the Revolution as was Metternich himself.[24] Consequently he was in a generous mood. The position taken up by Guizot was that he wanted to see administrative reforms in the Papal State, but that he would not approve of any change of the territorial *status quo* throughout Italy: this amounted to a guarantee of Austria's hold on Lombardo-Venetia. Moreover, in case of Austria's intervening, he went so far as to say that there would not be a *coup-de-main* by France similar to the occupation of Ancona in 1831. France would intervene, but by mutual arrangement; and he hoped that no intervention would be necessary.

On the other hand Metternich was equally glad of an agreement. He regarded France as the permanent cause of disturbances. He attributed them to French newspapers, to Italian refugees in Paris, to Pellegrino Rossi. He felt that during this great crisis the rivalry with France must cease; he must get Guizot to join with him in repelling the Revolution.[25]

It is hard to say from which side came the first overtures: but by January 1847 Guizot, who knew German, had arranged a channel of communication through a secret agent called Klindworth—a German who, it is said, had already served Metternich. On January 9th, 29th, and on February 8th, 1847, Klindworth[26] conveyed the French views to Count Apponyi, the Austrian ambassador in Paris, and later he went on two secret missions to Vienna (apparently at the end of March and at the beginning of June). We need not go into every detail of the negotiation; probably it never resulted in a treaty, but it did result in an *entente*.

[24] Vienna Staats-Archiv, Frankreich, 1847; Apponyi's despatches of January 19th and 29th and February 8th, 1847. These are quoted by Stern, Part II, vol. III.
[25] *V.* Metternich's Exposé of April 12th, 1847, *Aus nachgelassenen Papieren*, VII, 391.
[26] Metternich's *Aus nachgelassenen Papieren*, VII, 307, 326–7, 383, 391, 395, 397, 399.

Undoubtedly the two statesmen came to a strong agreement as to leading principles.[27]

The Austro-French rivalry in Italy must cease: that was the prime creator of revolutionists.

They must avoid as far as possible one-sided intervention. Metternich retained his right to intervene. Probably he did not want to do so, but perceived that he might be very near intervention. Within a few months there might be in Rome either a Liberal constitution or a republic or a revolution and Metternich would not suffer any of the three.

Thirdly, they agreed on tendering joint advice to the Italian princes as to improvement of laws and administration; and joint warnings to them against setting up representative constitutions. This joint warning would apply mainly to the Pope and Charles Albert.

It is evident, therefore, that Metternich had secured the support of Guizot. They were no longer rivals but allies in maintaining the *status quo* in Italy.[28] They proposed to give joint advice to the Pope.

[27] Of German historians Hillebrand (1879) said that there was a written treaty and that he had seen it in the Turin Archives. (I am quoting Silva, *La Monarchia di Luglio*, p. 310 note.) Apparently no treaty has been found there. The only document to which he could have referred is a memo, not from the Piedmontese ambassador in Vienna but from a junior, Count d'Antioche: this, of course, may or may not be an accurate résumé of the treaty (if there ever was one).

The terms of the secret treaty as given by Hillebrand are as follows: Austria pledged herself to neutrality over the Spanish marriages; France agreed to join in putting pressure on Switzerland, though not to the point of going to war; France to allow Austria a free hand in Italy; France to help to deter Charles Albert and Pius from setting up constitutions.

The historian Stern (1922) does not accept the existence of a treaty. He takes the same view as mine. For the whole question of the secret treaty, *v.* Stern's *Geschichte Europas von* 1830 *bis* 1848, III, 435. Also Hillebrand's *Geschichte Frankreichs von der Thronbesteigung Louis Philipps bis zum Fall Napoleon III.*, II, 681 *et seq.* Also Silva, *La Monarchia di Luglio*, p. 310.

[28] Metternich, *Mémoires*, VII, 390–1, April 12th, 1847, the Exposé.

And the best advice to give to the Sovereign Pontiff at this moment is, beyond doubt, not to let himself be drawn into paths whose slopes are slippery and lead to an abyss.

This advice must certainly have seemed strange to Pius, as coming from his old ally France; rather tardy and self-contradictory; but apparently not much of it ever reached him.

In connection with the Papal State Metternich laid down in his secret instructions to Klindworth the joint aims of France and Austria under the following headings:

(*a*) To maintain the State of the Church on the conditions which form the present basis of its existence.

(*b*) To silence the agitation in that state.

(*c*) To assure the means of achieving the above, by strengthening the governmental authority, as may seem most reasonable.

(*d*) M. Guizot and I will consider the enterprise as successful if it results in maintaining peace in the State of the Church and consequently in the Italian Peninsula; as also in diminishing the chances of a material intervention by Austria for the purpose of smothering revolutionary outbreaks.

Metternich then adds that Guizot believed that peace could be restored to the Papal State if Pius would resolve to grant concessions on the lines of the Memorandum of 1831, and (in Metternich's phrase) to abstain "from any further advances in the sphere of a shallow and unpractical liberalism".

4. *Metternich and the Italian rulers*

At the same time Metternich was trying to smooth his way by overawing the Italian rulers: for everywhere in Italy he saw a growing tendency to subvert law and order—or at all events the existing laws and the established order. One or two extracts from his letters will illustrate this process.

On May 29th, 1846, he had written to Turin:[29]

King Charles Albert followed the flag of Liberalism in 1820; that flag is done with now; the colours of the Radicals have taken its place. If, therefore, we suppose that the King definitely wishes to leave Conservatism, he will not have the choice of two subversive lines; now there is only one—that of the *Revolution by Carbonarism*. What chances then can a Radical career offer him? The chances are plain: they consist in two elements—*civil anarchy and political war*. Can King Charles Albert wish to take these risks? I do not think so.

On April 24th, 1847, he wrote a striking letter to the Grand Duke of Tuscany warning him that Italian nationality meant an end of all the existing thrones in the peninsula, because the union of Italy could only be achieved in the form of an Italian republic; and he added:[30] "If this power (the power of Austria) were to fall, the Italian princes would fall too."

About the party of reform and the Revolution Metternich "let himself go" when writing to the Grand Duke of Tuscany:

Between a Balbo, a Gioberti, an Azeglio, a Pettiti—these champions of Italian Liberalism—and a Mazzini and his acolytes, there is no more difference than there is between poisoners and assassins in the open street; even if their wishes may differ, the difference disappears when they come to the field of action.

On August 2nd he sent a despatch to each of the five Great Powers asking them to state definitely what value they attached to their guarantees of the existing sovereignties in Italy. This was in fact raising again the Treaty of 1815 in defence of the *status quo*.[31]

5. *Metternich and Pius IX*

From our short review of France, Germany, Austria and Italy, it will be evident that everywhere throughout Europe

[29] *Aus nachgelassenen Papieren*, VII, 227.
[30] *Ibid.* p. 405.
[31] *V.* Lord Ponsonby's despatches to Palmerston, *London Corr.* pp. 73, 74.

men were on the verge of an immense shock between the existing régime and the forces of Revolution.

Certainly when Pius, at this terribly critical period, declared in favour of a Moderate Liberal policy, he must have seemed to many people rather like a man who, when two gigantic fleets are dashing at each other, suddenly launches a pinnace to try to keep them apart. But Metternich realised that Pius' movement was a serious danger. In his view the Pope was being used as a banner by the advanced-guard of the Revolution; but evidently he thought that he was dealing with it on the right lines.[32]

The occupation of Cracow in November 1846, he tells us, had reminded all these revolutionists that the three eastern powers did not intend to surrender to the Revolution. It had produced a similar effect on the moderate Liberal party in Italy. Cracow had been "the succursal of Polish Emigration, under French protection", and—he continues—a standing danger to the Holy Alliance. But since its occupation by Austria the members of the Italian reform party had moderated their language.[33]

"You will lose everything," say these meneurs of Revolution to the masses whom they have themselves aroused, "you are merely grieving the great heart of Pius and you will render abortive all his generous intentions.... Do you want to end like Cracow?"

For once Metternich was ill-informed. He did not know that the Giovine Italia had used the fall of Cracow as one of their trump cards. De Boni had compiled a documented history of it, and already on February 11th he had written to Lamberti: "The book will be of more use to Italy than to

---

[32] V. Metternich's *Coup d'œil retrospectif sur la situation d'Italie*, 1846. He sent out three copies: to Rome, to Florence and to Naples (*v*. Vienna Staats-Archiv, Rome, *Rapports*, II, February 21st, 1847). It is printed in Metternich's *Mémoires*, vol. VII; and also in his *Aus nachgelassenen Papieren*, VII, 293.

[33] These words were repeated almost verbatim in a despatch to Lützow, Vienna Staats-Archiv, Rome, *Rapports*, II, January 10th, 1847.

Poland.... In a few days Lombardy will be flooded with it"
(Protocol of the Giovine Italia, v).[34]

As to the Papal State, it has often been suggested that in
1847, especially during the Ferrara episode, Metternich was
engineering a crisis by means of secret agents and Gregorians,
in order to start some act of rebellion which would justify
armed interference: but on the whole it seems more probable
that—for the time being at all events—he wanted to keep the
peace.

In reality Metternich's letter of June 6th, 1847, is the best
and the most instructive of all. There is a certain tragedy about
it. It was written in German and addressed to a sovereign
outside the Italian arena, namely the King of Würtemberg,
and it sums up Metternich's views about Europe and the
coming revolution:

Where the evil appears it is unmistakable and Prussia has come
to grief. Already the King has been drawn into the path along
which he did not mean to go; he did not want central estates-
general (Reichsstände) and now he has got them in the shape of
combined diets (vereinigte Landtage).

After some further remarks about Prussia he continues:

In Switzerland the outlook suggests that, next thing, a volcano
will burst into flame. I do not know what will happen there.

In France the internal situation could not be more miserable.

That of England is little better; meanwhile English policy
applies itself to favouring all revolution.

Italy suffers from the disease of an unharmonisable nationalism
and from governments without weight.

Austria is standing on her time-honoured foundations. She
has only two undertakings before her: internally she must maintain those foundations for herself, and externally she must work
through them as far as possible to keep things peaceful.[35]

Russia, he ends, stands apart, shut off from the rest of the
world.

[34] Cf. also Guizot's opinion: "In that peninsula (Italy) there still
exists a considerable ferment which...has received fresh stimulus
from the deplorable episode of Cracow." Letter, January 11th,
1847, to Flahaut.   [35] Metternich, *Mémoires*, VII, 373.

This letter and many others show that Metternich was absolutely conscious of the dangers around him, and was warning all the other governments of the approaching revolution. Austria was to stand like a rock against a tidal wave. At home her policy was to be conservative even if this involved repression; abroad it was to preserve the peace even if that involved intervention.

In his eyes the whole order of civilisation was marching, nation by nation, into the abyss: straight into political, social and religious chaos. And he, in his old age, was condemned to witness this disaster simply because he could no longer get the governments to combine against it.

And the tragedy of the situation lay in the fact that Metternich was right, and his prophecies were very soon to be fulfilled. Before another eighteen months had passed the existing governments had been overthrown in France, Austria, Hungary, Bohemia, the German Confederation, Switzerland, Rome and most of the Italian states; and, when the tide turned, Charles Albert was driven from his country, Mazzini forfeited his republican presidency, and Metternich himself, who had seen the storm afar and had so clearly warned the whole world of the *débâcle* to come, was finally obliged to flee from Vienna and seek refuge as an exile in England.

And when during the fateful months of 1848 this vast revolution broke out, the sensitive conscience of Pius IX must have felt an appalling load of responsibility, for it was he who had unconsciously weakened the dykes. And as the news came that nation after nation had risen in arms and overthrown its ruler, until finally his own state rose and he himself was obliged to flee, and it seemed as if the temporal power of the Popes were gone for ever, then the immense weight of the responsibility overwhelmed his original beliefs and hopes, and left him disillusioned for ever, an old man, kindly and distinguished, but a mere spectator of progress for the rest of his days.

Chapter XII

THE AGITATION TO WIN THE
CIVIC GUARD

In this and in the next chapter it will be seen how the revolutionists managed to bring off a successful coup under the very eyes of Metternich.

Ever since the Manifesto of Rimini (1843) the Civic Guard had been a main demand of the agitators. Of course the winning of an armed force is always the crucial point in every revolution. But in this instance it would be not only a gesture of defiance to the Austrians, but also inevitably a danger to the pontifical government. The question was: Would Pius agree to grant it? Finally he did so: and, looking back on the scene now, one feels glad that the Italians were able to win an armed force to serve against the Austrians in 1848; but at the same time one cannot help feeling sorry for Pius.

By January 1847 this agitation was spreading rapidly through the state, and its progress was all the more insidious because it came from the provinces.[1] No sooner had Bologna won its night-patrols than demands for Civic Guards were made in other towns: Ancona[2] claimed a Civica; Ferrara claimed a Civica. Presently Forlì sent up a deputation to ask for one; and by the beginning of March the Amnistiati were collecting signatures for a petition[3] to Pius. Of the men connected with the movement perhaps the most influential were the Bolognese group, Minghetti, Silvani and several others, nearly all avvocati (barristers)—and with them was their Piedmontese friend, Massimo d' Azeglio. They were in touch

---

[1] Spada, I, 244.
[2] Vienna Staats-Archiv, Fasc. 76, Lützow to Metternich, January 9th, March 26th, June 1st and 5th, 1847.
[3] Minghetti, *Ricordi*, I, 227, 238, 244, etc.

with the sovereign. In a letter[4] of April 17th, Silvani says that he and two other lawyers, Giuliani and Pagani, had talked to Pius about the Civica: Massimo d'Azeglio had already done so,[5] and—even as early as April 20th—was expecting the edict to come out within a few days: but it did not come.

Pius was not opposed to setting up a Civic Guard; in fact it was he who had saved the Bolognese patrols; but evidently he was very anxious not to have it brought in at that moment. He knew that the times were perilous[6]—although probably he did not realise that this was the beginning of a great crisis in his fate.

In general there were two main classes of individuals who asked for the Civica; firstly, people who had no political aims; many of these were genuine law-abiding citizens who required it as a protection against crime and disorder. The police was inefficient, largely manned by old Gregorians who wanted nothing better than to see the Liberal régime a chaos. But, secondly, apart from these peaceful men, there were also the revolutionists who thought an armed force would be supremely useful for political purposes. In some places these two types coalesced: the revolutionists encouraged disorders in order to have an excuse for obtaining arms.

This movement, like all the others during these months, contained two elements, that of the genuine people and that of the revolutionary wire-pullers. In almost all the towns there was faction-fighting; ostensibly to prevent the export of corn, but in many cases this was a mere excuse. In some places the roughs were out for plunder, and in others it was a move to win the Civic Guard.[7]

[4] Minghetti, *ibid*. p. 249.
[5] Letter of April 1st, *v*. Minghetti, *ibid*. p. 243.
[6] Letters of Della Porta, Silvani, etc., *v*. Minghetti, *Ricordi*, 1, 244, 249.
[7] In the 1851 edition of Gualterio (in four large volumes) there is a government narrative which gives an account of all these numerous disorders during Pius' first year. *V*. Gualterio, vol. 1, *Le Riforme*, Appendix, Doc. XXXIV.

Thus in Rimini and in the Cesenatica, when some peasants —corn-rioters—suddenly invaded the streets, and the citizens formed Civic Guards to protect their shops, the Austrians suspected a ruse.[8] In that case perhaps they were wrong; but their documents give good information because they kept a constant watch on this movement, which they saw was a danger both to themselves and to the Papal government. And Cardinal Gizzi, as Secretary of State, entirely agreed with them and was continually holding conversations with his friend Count Lützow on the subject. One of the most important places mentioned was Ferrara.

The medium-sized town of Ferrara lies in the north-western district of the Papal State, two or three miles south of the Austrian frontier which is the river Po. Thus it was a Papal town, well within the boundary. But in 1815 the Austrians had obtained the right to keep a garrison in the "place" of Ferrara and also in that of Comacchio, a smaller town about fifty miles east of it, in order to cover the bridges over the Po and thereby secure their hold over Lombardo-Venetia; and also their path of intervention further south, so as to dominate Central Italy. These two towns were used as an advanced post; connected with each other by road, and each connected back with Lombardo-Venetia by a highway.

Here, as elsewhere, the Congress of Vienna had made a stupid arrangement. It had settled that there should be an occupation of two Italian Papal towns by foreign troops, entirely similar to the allied occupation of certain German towns after the Great War: and this Austrian occupation was to be permanent, not temporary.

In such a situation trouble was *sure* to arise—sooner or later.

At the beginning of January 1847, the Ferrarese, tired, no doubt, of seeing foreign uniforms in their streets, had tried to form a Civica; but to allow two sets of uniforms in the

[8] Vienna Staats-Archiv, Fasc. 76, January 28th, 1847.

streets seemed dangerous, and their demand was firmly refused by Gizzi, who hated the whole idea. Thereupon the
municipal officials resigned.[9]

Throughout all this episode they seem to have shown
remarkably little tact. Their next step was to send a young
Ferrarese, the Marquis Giovanni Costabile, to interview
Pius. At this interview, according to them, Pius spoke with
very great frankness to this young man. He said that the
magistracy ought not to have resigned; that they made it
impossible for the government to grant their request without
seeming to give in to force: that "these good Ferrarese had
been taken in by people who wish no good either to them or
to me", and ended up by saying: "Costabile, write and ask
them to return to good order: by right methods everything
can be obtained.... When they have returned let me know at
once and, here, you and I will see how we can fulfil the desires
of your fellow-citizens."

The Marquis Costabile wrote a full description of this
interview to his brother, and—incredible as it seems—
Costabile's letters soon afterwards were made public. Of
course, Lützow forwarded a copy to Metternich.[10] It looks
rather like a plot to force Pius' hand; if so, it was a very stupid
attempt and, for the time being, they gained nothing.

On March 20th[11] Lützow reported to Metternich a piece
of information which afterwards assumed a strange signifi-

[9] Vienna Staats-Archiv, Fasc. 76, Lützow to Metternich,
January 9th, 23rd, 1847.

[10] For this story I rely mainly on Lützow's despatch of January
23rd, 1847 (Vienna Staats-Archiv, Fasc. 76). It includes Costabile's
letter dated January 9th. I have no recollection of this episode being
mentioned in the Italian Archives. But on January 12th, 1847, Pius
told Bargagli (the Tuscan minister in Rome) that he had refused to
allow a Civica to Ferrara. And elsewhere Bargagli heard that the
Ferrarese were angry and insisted on forming a corps, and that they
patrolled the city at night simultaneously with the Austrians: that
Pius sent Swiss troops to take the situation in hand. V. Bargagli's
Despatch, January 14th, 1847, Florence Arch., Dip. Est.

[11] Vienna Staats-Archiv, Fasc. 76, March 20th.

cance. He said that some of the best of the police-agents formerly employed under Gregory XVI were asserting that "they have received word from the most faithful of their trusted men that the agitators are forming proscription lists; and that on these lists there appear the names of a certain number of Cardinals. The thing is possible. Masonic signs, and here and there the word 'Morte' (Death) have been seen on some house-doors." Lützow added that the police were trying to discover the authors of this plot against the citizens, "which is perhaps only a joke intended to alarm some one or other". Pope Gregory's secret service must have been surprisingly efficient.

The agitation to win the Civica was now rampant in many towns all over the state. Whether or not it was a campaign preconcerted between them is a point hard to decide. Certainly the Austrians thought so,[12] and spoke of it with a good deal of acerbity. On April 10th Lützow reported that there was trouble at Imola[13] over the young men's going about armed at night, and added that

the formation of the Civic Guards seems to be a pre-arranged plan which is being carried out with the greatest keenness. I have reason to believe that enrolment-lists circulate by the hundred; that thousands of names are already inscribed on them and that this Militia will be an already-existing formation when the Pope receives the petition.... It will be an accomplished fact, I fear, which then will be presented to the Pope to receive his ratification.

Gizzi, he says, had resigned, but the Pope had persuaded him to withdraw his resignation.

[12] As early as March 26th Lützow wrote: "Les nouvelles d'Ancône d'aujourd'hui sont infiniment plus inquiétantes que ne l'avait été celles de l'année 1831. Un mouvement général pour assister à la formation des gardes civiques est attendu très prochainement; on fixait déjà pour cet effet le dimanche des rameaux; il devait partir de Bologne à la suite d'une invitation à leurs frères dans les provinces...." This is a specimen of many Austrian despatches on the subject. Lützow to Metternich, March 26th, 1847, Vienna Staats-Archiv, Rome, 72.

[13] Ibid. April 10th, 1847.

This question was becoming a cause of division between Pius and Gizzi. It seems to show that they were both Liberals but that Pius had the greater spice of patriotic pride. Gizzi took no risks for the Temporal Power and had long talks with Count Lützow during which, to do him justice, he often tried to make Pius' Liberal measures seem more palatable to Austria; but during all this year he was a sick man, often ill with gout. Pius, on the other hand, was more closely united to Pellegrino Rossi (France), the exile of Murat's days, and it was with him that he discussed these questions. Pellegrino Rossi was believed by Lützow and others to have supported the Civica; but certainly in his despatch to Guizot he would not commit himself to approving of it.

On April 4th Lützow reported that there had been held an informal council of ministers at which Pius was able to congratulate himself on a cessation (temporarily at all events) of agitation in Ferrara, Ravenna and Ancona. Next, he had suggested setting up the Civica under government auspices. There was a dead silence.[14]

Lützow says[15] that the Marquis Potenziani (President of the *Contemporaneo* newspaper) had persuaded Pius that it was better for a sovereign to grasp a question that has become inevitable than to let it be imposed on him; that by getting the Civica into right hands it could be made perfectly safe. This had been done elsewhere, in Naples and in other places. If the officers were nobles and the muskets were in the hands of responsible citizens, the Civic Guards would remain loyal and orderly. Metternich, however, foresaw that very soon the muskets would pass into the hands of poorer and much more reckless men.

During all this period Count Lützow, and during his absence the Chevalier Ohms, and thirdly the Austrian consul-general in Ancona, Count von Welserheimb,[16] all three

---

[14] Vienna Staats-Archiv, Rome, Fasc. 76.
[15] *Ibid*. April 10th.
[16] " Diese Herren scheinen ihrer völlig gewiss und erwarten unter

continued to report most persistently about the widespread agitation for Civic Guards; and Lützow's despatches are valuable because they are often verbatim reports of his talks with Gizzi.

Nevertheless six months had passed and Pius had not made up his mind to grant it. In fact they were in the fourth week of June when suddenly there appeared Gizzi's Notificazione of June 22nd. This was a great blow: it was taken to mean that there would be no more Liberal concessions. And the Civica had not yet been granted: nor had the Consulta, though promised; nor had a hoped-for second reform of the Press Law!

Andern mit Nächstem die Bewilligung zur Errichtung der National-garde, wodurch sie die Waffengewalt endlich auf gesetzliche Weise in die Hände bekämen." Extract from Graf von Welserheimb's report to Lützow, Ancona, June 5th, 1847.

Chapter XIII

THE REVOLUTION OBTAINS FROM PIUS AN ARMED FORCE

(THE "CONGIURA")

I. THE GRANTING OF THE CIVIC GUARD

This was a triumph for the revolution, but for Pius it was destined to be disastrous.

It will be remembered that on June 22nd, 1847, Cardinal Gizzi published a Notificazione pointing out that although His Holiness intended to carry out reforms, his power of doing so was limited by the fact that he was Head of the Catholic Church. On p. 70, chapter IV, we quoted a salient paragraph, and pointed out the great importance of this Notificazione.[1] In the next paragraph Pius spoke even more plainly: it ran as follows:

Hence His Holiness has not been able to see without serious distress of mind that some restless spirits would take advantage of the present conditions to set forth and cause to prevail doctrines and thoughts entirely contrary to his maxims; and to push on or set up claims entirely opposed to the calm and peaceful disposition and the sublime character of one who is Vicar of Jesus Christ, Minister of the God of Peace, and Father of all Catholics alike— whatever be the part of the world to which they belong; or, similarly, to excite in the populations, by writing and by speech, desires and hopes of reform beyond the limits above stated.

But these restless spirits are few in number; and since the good sense no less than the rectitude which guides the thoughts and conduct of the great majority has hitherto been able to reject such insinuations and counsels, the Holy Father is quite convinced that they will never be favourably received.

---

[1] *V.* p. 70 (ch. IV), paragraph beginning "His Holiness is firmly determined". There are copies of this Notificazione of June 22nd, 1847, in the Vatican Archives, Viennese Archives and elsewhere.

This Notificazione of Gizzi on June 22nd is constantly quoted in histories because it is the turning-point in the story of Pius' Liberal movement. It states the dilemma in a few clear words; and it is the signal for the first outbreak of revolt. Liberals chose to see in it an intimation that the concessions were coming to an end, and at once it aroused a widespread and angry discontent. The Pope was going no farther: the Civic Guard was not yet in their hands, and without that nothing was safe. The Liberal institutions already granted could be revoked under protection of Austria, and new concessions could be refused. Gizzi's proclamation was nicknamed the Notificazione of Undeceiving.[2]

Perhaps the most impartial accounts of the weeks between June 22nd and July 14th, 1847, are those despatched to their respective capitals by the foreign ambassadors in Rome. They were watching the situation very closely so as to keep their governments forewarned of any coming trouble. On June 28th the Tuscan minister, the Cavaliere Bargagli, sent the following description to Florence:[3]

The first impressions of surprise and stupor felt by the public at the wise edict of the 22nd have been converted into silent but fairly eloquent manifestations of disapproval.

He adds that on the 27th when Pius had passed through the streets he had been received no longer with enthusiasm but amid silence and even indifference; that the Jesuits had been hooted and the Swiss Guard insulted; that on his return journey a letter[4] had been thrown into Pius' carriage; that the

[2] Gori, p. 192.
[3] Florence Archives.
[4] The Roman people loves in Pius IX the Father of the People, the Just and the Magnanimous, and places its trust in Him Alone. Most Holy Father—if anyone throws doubt upon our good faith and upon that affection which animates all of us for Your August Person; if Anyone dares to portray us as insatiable, restless, irreligious, or, in one word, as being unworthy of You: *distrust that man.* Most Holy Father! *that man* is more your Enemy than ours! *That man* is tending to precipitate both You and Us into the same abyss....

people were returning to clandestine methods: that at a meeting held by Sterbini it had been resolved to ask the Pope peremptorily for railways, municipal government and the National Guard.[5]

Pellegrino Rossi wrote a very similar description to Guizot.[6] "The public is out of temper", he added, "and is sulking at its sovereign."

Count Lützow went farther. On July 2nd he wrote to Metternich:[7]

The faction says that it wants deeds and not words. It insists on further concessions and for the last few days the word "revolution" is on the lips of everyone. The catastrophe is announced as imminent with a cynical impudence, as if it were merely the staging of a new opera.

It was during this period that the cry was raised of *Viva Pio Nono solo!* "Long Live Pius IX alone!" Some people believed that he was under the sway of the reactionary cardinals.

Incidentally Count Lützow tells us that Pius was "extremely downcast"; that he had been greatly disappointed at the cold reception of his Council of Ministers on June 14th and still more so over that of Gizzi's Notificazione of June 22nd; and that fears were entertained for his health:

The Pope looked ill. People who had not seen him for some time thought him ten years older. He is growing very grey now, though he had no grey hairs at the time of his election.[8]

But God is watching. That God Whom *Those People* have ever on their lips, but never in their hearts, that God who has Chosen You to be Father and Regenerator of the people. Most Holy Father! the other princes are responsible only for the present in the sight of God. But You are responsible for both the present and the future.

[5] The National Guard was what they really wanted; the other two headings were "window dressing". Railways were already being dealt with and a new Municipality for Rome was under consideration.

[6] Paris Aff. Etr., Rome, Rossi, June 26th, 1847.

[7] Vienna Staats-Archiv, Rome, Lützow, July 2nd

[8] Vienna Staats-Archiv, *ibid.*

Pius, no doubt, realised that he was on the verge of making a vital concession which would endanger the whole of his movement: and even the temporal power itself.

Nevertheless he was obliged to grant it. By June 30th he found himself almost alone. Many people on both sides wanted the Civica. His Liberal followers were out of temper because they had not got it, and at the same time his Conservative subjects were calling for some guards to keep order: for—worst of all—his police had failed him: Monsignor Grassellini and his men were unwilling to deal with the situation. On that evening, June 30th, popular feeling seemed so tense that a deputation[9] headed by Prince Borghese and including some of the richest and most Conservative people in Rome, waited on Pius and persuaded him to give in. "They prayed His Holiness to take such measures as might protect the lives and property of the inhabitants from possible violence...as the military and police did not think it prudent to interfere, and therefore this protection could only be afforded by a powerful national guard." So the concession was promised and at once the unrest subsided.

By a Notificazione of July 5th the Civic Guard was instituted. In Rome it was to include all citizens between the ages of 21 and 60 and was to consist of fourteen battalions, one for each *rione* in the city. Priests and soldiers were exempted, also men of certain trades, and those physically unfit. For the moment Rome only was to have the Civic Guard; but in case of special demand it was understood that the measure might be extended to other towns.

Recruiting offices were opened and the people were soon handing in their names in a quiet and orderly manner all over the town so as to be ready to answer a summons. "The government", said Pellegrino Rossi, "will thus have carried out what it did not want to do; or, rather, the contrary of

[9] Freeborn to Palmerston, *London Corr.*, I, p. 61.

what it wanted to do." He refused, officially, to have any
kind of connection with the matter.[10]

II. GIZZI'S RESIGNATION

It is reported that he said he could no longer work with a
man like Pius. But before resigning he took a step of considerable interest. On July 1st or 2nd (1847) he enquired
formally from his friend Count Lützow as to what reply
would be given by Metternich if Pius should find himself
compelled to call on Austria for intervention (meaning by
armed forces). Of course this was a hazardous question; it
might be interpreted to mean that Pius was considering this
step, or that Gizzi himself was a pro-Austrian. Lützow at
once referred the matter to Metternich.[11]

On July 5th Lützow had another conversation with Gizzi,
and reminded him of the great difficulties involved nowadays
in offering the material and active support of the Imperial
arms "to the Holy Father, as he was now asking". Gizzi
replied that hitherto the overture had come only from himself
(Gizzi), not from Pius. Lützow said he did not doubt it: and
again emphasised the great difference between the existing
position (1847) and the Austrian intervention of 1831; especially in view of the confidential communications with
Guizot.[12]

The despatches upon this subject are of the most confidential nature, all in cypher. They are important because they

[10] Paris Aff. Etr., Rome, Rossi, July 8th, 1847. In this despatch
he says to Guizot: "Le gouvernement pontifical se trouvera ainsi
avoir fait ce qu'il ne voulait pas faire...j'ai cru que nous devions
rester complètement étrangers à cette question." But Massimo
d'Azeglio says in a letter of July 6th to M. Doubet, that Silvani
had told him that Pellegrino Rossi had spoken to the Pope explicitly
in favour of the Civic Guard, and had even presented a despatch
from Guizot in this sense. It seems evident that one or other of
them or someone else concerned had been romancing.
[11] Vienna Staats-Archiv, Rome, Fasc. 72. Lützow to Metternich,
July 2nd, 1847.
[12] *Ibid.* Lützow to Metternich, July 6th, 1847.

reveal Metternich's mind. Hitherto it has been assumed by
many historians that he was thirsting for a chance of intervening in order to put an end to Pius' Liberal movement.
Many Italian and foreign writers, both then and since, have
thought that the two outstanding episodes which occurred on
July 17th, 1847, known as the Gran Congiura (Great Conspiracy) and the military reinforcement of Ferrara, were
arranged by Metternich in order to give him an excuse for
invading the Papal State. But the documents which we are
considering rather tend to show that that was not his purpose.

Firstly we may say that there is no question of Pius' having
ever thought of asking for Austrian protection. This enquiry
seems to have been a feeler on the part of Gizzi to find out
whether or not Metternich would intervene to prevent the
arming of the Civica—as might very well have been his
intention.

Metternich consulted the Emperor and then sent a formal
reply through the Papal Nuncio at Vienna, Mgr Viale-Prelà.
It is dated July 10th. He said that (if called on) Austria was
always ready to lend any kind of help to the pontifical government. But there were difficulties. If Austria decided to
intervene, when should her intervention take place? Before
the revolutionary outbreak? This would cause her to be
slandered all over the world as the suppressor of liberty.
After the outbreak? To wait until after an outbreak would
involve very grave trouble and bloodshed. The rising would
begin in Rome, and Austria could not march as far as Rome
with less than 25,000 men. Such an expedition would arouse
France, and, by her short sea route she might arrive first, "in
which case it would not suit Austria to remain in the provinces while the Tricolour waved over Rome". These, he said,
were the difficulties; but nevertheless the Austrian Court
would not hesitate to bring help to the Holy Father if it were
requested to do so.[13]

[13] Vienna Staats-Archiv, Rome, 72. Copy of Prelà's despatch.
Prelà to Gizzi, July 10th, 1847.

On July 29th Lützow wrote: "Mon Prince; the request for an Austrian intervention is, for the time being, both improbable and impossible. The Pope could not make it even if he wanted to do so."[14]

That was the last word of any importance on the subject; but on August 18th the Prussian envoy reported to Berlin that Austrian intervention was impossible because the Pope would never ask for it; and for other reasons as well.

These documents are of some help towards settling the vexed question as to Metternich's real intentions at this moment, July 1847.

To fill Gizzi's place Pius appointed on July 10th Cardinal Gabriele Ferretti, a man well known for his determined character, the same who had defended Rieti against the rebels in 1831. But Cardinal Ferretti was far away in his Legation at Pesaro, and five long days elapsed before his arrival on the 15th.

During these ten days of interregnum the city of Rome was virtually in the hands of the people, and it was due solely to their own good spirit that no looting occurred.

III. THE CIVIC GUARD CAPTURED BY THE REVOLUTION[15]

There still remained one chance for Pius, namely that of arranging the Civic Guard so skilfully that it would be a weapon to his hand. But here, too, the fates were against him.

July 17th, 1847 was the anniversary of the Amnesty, so it had been set apart by the people for the greatest rejoicings of the year. They had arranged that there should be festivities on that evening in the Piazza del Popolo; concerts by Roman philharmonic composers, and fireworks; also a cantata at the theatre. And an order had been given to the sculptor Am-

[14] *Ibid*. Rome, Fasc. 72. July 29th, and August 18th.

[15] Professor Montanelli (revolutionist) says: "The arms had been decreed for the citizens. Nevertheless, owing to the ill will of the employees, who knows when the people really would have had them if they had not taken them themselves?" Montanelli, *Memorie*, ii, 8.

brogi for a colossal statue of Pius to be executed in wood and
gesso. When accepting this order Ambrogi had refused all
payment either for his expenses or for his work; and, so great
was the enthusiasm of the time, that on July 11th when the
statue arrived, its very reception was turned into an improvised festival with illuminations. The whole world seemed to
be full of good-will.

But as the feast day came nearer, a strange atmosphere of
mystery and uneasiness began to pervade the town.[16] Curious
rumours were being circulated and believed: and it was noticed
that there was a large influx of strangers, many of them "of
grim and sinister aspect", who formed small groups together
and spoke to one another in low voices—the unmistakable
sign that there is plotting and counterplotting in progress—
who did no work, and paid their bills with foreign money.
At the same time on the walls there began to appear strange
signs, and writings in characters hitherto unknown; and these
we are told gave rise to fights among the populace, which also
attacked the Jews. Some people said that daggers had been
found with the name of Pius IX deeply incised upon them,
and that crosses of blood-red colour and large figures of S
had been seen on the houses of those citizens selected for
sacking and for slaughter;[17] on others there was an ominous
M (*Morte*). Manifestly these stories rather suggest the carrying into effect of the plot foreshadowed to Lützow several
weeks before, by the old Gregorian spies.[18]

[16] Spada, I, 249; Gabussi, I, 67, *La Bilancia*, July 21st, 1847.
[17] De Boni, p. 125, "Saccheggio e Sangue". He adds: "Moreover
in the houses of the most serious and earnest citizens red crosses and
other signs were found painted on the area-walls, and capital S's
to denote words of extermination. The Angels of Death had marked
their victims." De Boni does not tell us who first discovered that
the letter S stood for sacking and slaughter, or how he knew that it
was the Angels of Death who wrote it. It is just as likely that it
represented "Sancta Simplicitas" and that the "Angelo" was
Angelo Brunetti.
[18] It will be remembered that several weeks earlier Lützow had
received word from some of the best spies of the old régime, that

When a town is passing through a political crisis, scores of perfectly honest people repeat to each other stories for which there is no foundation whatsoever. In this case there was almost certainly a plot of some sort in existence, but the question is: who were the plotters? Even now no one can say absolutely for certain whether it was a revolutionary scheme to capture the Civic Guard, or whether it was a Sanfedist reactionary conspiracy; but most present-day writers, I think, would accept the first alternative. At the time, however, the Roman citizens were quite convinced that there was a widespread conspiracy among the reactionaries all over Italy to kill Pius' policy of reform: that the plotters proposed to take advantage of the crowds assembled on July 17th to provoke rioting and bloodshed, to murder the Liberal leaders, to imprison Pius, to effect a counter-revolution and to justify Austrian intervention in the interest of law and order; in fact, at any price to prevent any further Liberal concessions. And the whole episode has ever since been known as the *Gran Congiura* or Great Conspiracy.

At that moment there was undoubtedly some excuse for these ideas.

In Rome itself the Pope was now a Liberal, but the personnel of his government remained almost unchanged, and continued to hate new ideas and to be hated.

In the provinces the situation was far worse. The old Gregorian authorities were powerless and the new-come Liberals were not yet on strong ground. The country was lawless; dagger fights and shootings continued here and there between infuriated ex-centurioni and young Liberals: the following is the picture drawn by Farini:[19]

The horde of satellites which under Gregory had run wild to the top of its bent was now devoured with envy and mad with rage.

the revolutionists were preparing Masonic signs, accompanied by the word *Morte*, and other inscriptions: at that time their purpose was not declared. *V*. p. 194.

[19] Farini, I, 200.

The so-called Pontifical [Gregorian] volunteers who still possessed arms, and the Centurioni who still owned their privileges and patents...and various others who had won money, power, and infamy in the Military Commissions, in the Sanfedist groups or in the vexatious activities of the police—these men refused to submit to their present ill-fortune, and lived in a state of dissatisfaction with the Government and the Pope. In Romagna, where the civil discords were of old standing, where the factions were long-established and the hatreds were fierce, one might hear priests of high standing as Sanfedists, preaching sermons against Pio Nono ...at Faenza the Gregorians fired their arquebuses at young men who were singing their hymn in honour of the Pope.[20]

Such facts as these reached Rome—no doubt in an exaggerated form—and, as Farini tells us, gave rise to a not unnatural fear that there might be a combined action,[21] assisted by Austria, to crush the Liberal movement and its leaders in the capital. Such combined actions had occurred before now. To arms!

After all, these feelings were due to a subconscious knowledge of a very genuine danger; very genuine indeed: namely that the police force had broken down. In Rome there was no longer any force capable of protecting public life and property.

During these days it was said and believed that several of the most dreaded figures of the last reign had been seen walking the streets of Rome whither they had returned, no doubt for some fell scheme of their own: men such as Colonel Freddi, a Napoleonic veteran of the wars in Germany, Prussia and Italy; the man who for fifteen years had been the hated chief of repression in Romagna, and the head of the

[20] On the other hand Lützow reported that the lives of Gregorians were no longer safe: he said that the Liberals deliberately created disturbances in order to prove that the police were useless and thus to necessitate the arming of a Civic Guard.

[21] Various impartial observers—notably Pellegrino Rossi and Massimo d'Azeglio—thought that some such plot by Gregorian extremists was perfectly possible: Rossi thought that there might be a plot by the extremists on either side. He afterwards rather doubted whether there ever had been one.

execrated military commissions there; men such as Virginio
Alpi, the secret service agent of Gregory XVI, rightly believed to be in touch with the Austrians; men such as the
Cavaliere Minardi, commonly said to be an informer and
Alpi's best friend; or Nardoni who is described as an ex-
convict risen to high military rank under Gregory XVI, one
at whom "the poor people pointed with anger and terror".[22]
These descriptions may or may not be accurate, but they
represent the feelings of the time.

We now come to the important days. On the morning of
July 15th, two days before the great anniversary, the news
from Faenza was terrible: there had been a vast conspiracy
by the Gregorians:

in the very middle of the feast a large number of cut-throats,
mostly summoned from the Borgo of Faenza, had got to work with
the dagger and stabbed the amnestied men and the most influential
heads of the people; that amid the tumult and general alarm the
conspirators had shouted "Down with the Liberals and the new
reforms"; and to add to the terrors, many hired cabs, with
maddened cab-horses but without their drivers, had been stam-
peded into the crowd: people had been stabbed and the daggers
left sticking in the wounds bore, carved on their handles, the
inscription "Pius IX forever"; and finally, to add to the confusion, some of the troops which hastened up to restore order, had
increased the tumult beyond recall by beginning to arrest people
right and left, on the pretext of rebellion.[23]

This story was mere moonshine. But one feels that it was
likely enough to be believed because one or two episodes of
this type had occurred in other towns and other states. In
the city of Parma, for instance, only a month earlier, when

[22] So described by Gabussi, a republican; of course it by no
means follows that these descriptions are accurate. But in the
Vienna Archives there is a letter from Virginio Alpi to Lützow
(Austrian ambassador in Rome) received July 23rd, 1846, and
offering his services. He claimed (probably without many grounds)
that "among his kind masters were Cardinals Brignole, Bernetti,
Lambruschini, Gizzi and Castracane".

[23] Gabussi, 1, 70.

the people were celebrating Pius IX's accession, suddenly they had been set on by the police and had suffered about eighty casualties. If such a reactionist coup was possible in Parma on June 16th, was not a similar plot possible in Rome on July 17th? No one suspected Pius' good faith, but since June 22nd he was believed to be surrounded by Gregorians.[24]

But several real events occurred on the 15th.

It is on this day that Angelo Brunetti (Ciceruacchio) comes to the fore as a leader of armed men. He had—so Bargagli says in one of his despatches—a secret police organisation, through which he had discovered the plot and its authors. According to him Cardinal Lambruschini was the chief plotter for all Italy;[25] Monsignor Grassellini, head of the Roman police, was to be his right hand; its most active promoters were the Jesuits, and its executers were to be a horde of assassins in Austrian pay. The purpose of the plot was to organise "a public tragedy".

Ciceruacchio reported this discovery to Monsignor Grassellini as head of the police, but found him incredulous—as might be expected: for he himself was one of the accused. Moreover, as Lützow observed, it seemed unlikely that a cardinal of seventy-one would embark on a public tragedy.

But there are more ways than one of ventilating a plot. Early that morning (Bargagli says after midday) when the citizens went out, they discovered with misgiving that during the night there had been posted on the walls, along the Corso (the principal street) and in the squares, some hundreds of proscription lists, that is to say rough pen-and-ink notices giving the names of the authors of the plot "for carrying out

[24] Massimo d'Azeglio tells us that this was the cause of the Congiura. "One cannot altogether believe in this conspiracy, but there must have been something in it. Public reports said that a row was to be got up in Piazza del Popolo and the people were to be set upon, just as they were set upon at Parma; but we were prepared for this and the game failed." D'Azeglio, *Lettere a sua moglie*, July 20th, 1847.

[25] De Boni, p. 127.

a tragedy among the people ". Where these papers had come from, or who had put them up could not even be guessed. The names were all those of Gregorians or of reputed Austrian spies or of police agents.[26] The crowd rushed to read these incitements to vengeance. At the same time the Carabinieri arrived with orders to pull them down—for they contained the names of several of the most important people in Rome. But the crowd were not to be interfered with; amid shouts and imprecations, they drove away the carbineers and made themselves masters of the situation, and the notices remained up all day.

All authority had thus broken down. It was a moment of interregnum between two Secretaries of State, and Cardinal Ferretti was only expected to arrive that evening, so that the town was absolutely in the hands of the people and everyone lived in fear of rioting and looting.

It was evident that the amnesty celebration on the 17th could not possibly be held without danger of an outbreak. But Pius had given leave to hold it. The next problem was to get it cancelled without arousing anger.[27]

At this point the upper and middle classes certainly displayed some civic sense; and it was they who saved the situation. The Circolo[28] Romano, that is to say the most aristocratic of the clubs, deputed Prince Borghese[29] and Duke Massimo di Rignano to wait upon Pius and ask him, firstly, to postpone the amnesty celebrations until the Civic Guard were sufficiently advanced to be present: secondly, they called upon him to form and arm the Civic Guard immediately.

---

[26] One of these notices still exists in the Vatican Archives. It is written on one side of a double sheet of note paper: the writing is of large detached letters, as of an uneducated man who was rapidly writing notices; and it has several cabalistic signs at the top. That anyone should have taken this production seriously is astonishing. In Vienna there is a copy of another. *V.* Appendix.

[27] Paris Aff. Etr., Rome, Rossi's report.

[28] *V.* Notificazione, July 20th.

[29] Lützow says Prince Rospigliosi.

Pius agreed.[30] Indeed, there was no other course to pursue —even Pellegrino Rossi admits that. Princes Borghese, Corsini, Doria, Torlonia, Duke Cesarini and other rich men lent their palaces for barracks. Hundreds of young men came forward to join the corps, and some arms were served out to them; and that evening there was a patrol in every *rione* of the city. By these prompt measures, order was preserved, but the outcome of the situation was exactly what the agitators had desired; it had set up the Civic Guard; the officers were conservative nobles but the rank and file would all be Liberals; and during the next two days, they proceeded to capture the troops and the Carabinieri.

On July 16th the garrison of Rome decided to fraternise with their new comrades-in-arms, the Civic Guards; they embraced one another.

On July 17th the Carabinieri, who had been regarded as hostile to the popular cause, published a friendly address— in reality a grovelling apology—headed "To the Roman people".[31]

The new Secretary of State, Cardinal Ferretti, dismissed Monsignor Grassellini and appointed in his place Monsignor Morandi, a strong Liberal, who had defended Galletti.

[30] Notificazione, July 16th.

[31] Speaking of the tearing down of the notices the Carabinieri say: "We heard that thou [the Roman people], being moved to indignation about these matters, wert fulminating anathemas against us all, and wert laying the weight of infamy due to a few men onto our whole family of 3000 citizens of the state. We heard all this and we were profoundly grieved, all the more so because as soldiers in a subordinate position we were not permitted to raise our voice to the Throne to free ourselves from that corruption which infects our corps. Wouldst thou ascribe blame to us for the past calamities if we were compelled, against our universal wishes to behold in our ranks this sort of public infamy? How can we be blamed if they were invested with subordinate or superior rank?...What could we do? Stab them? That would have been a crime. Have resource to collective petitions? Military law forbids it...", and so forth. The use of "thou" makes the document sound far more stilted in English than in Italian. *V.* Vatican Archives, Fondo Spada, vol. VIII, No. 31.

On July 18th all was peaceful; the Carabinieri and Civic Guards were to be seen walking about the streets together, fraternising.[32]

Thus, within three days, all the chief elements believed to be Gregorian and hostile to the policy of reform, had been turned into its friends, but in reality they had also been captured by the agitators. All this fraternising was by no means to the interest of the government: it meant that in times of disturbance, its own armed men would side with the mob against it. At the moment Pius was immensely popular and was regarded as being the people's leader whom they had just saved from the reactionists, such as Lambruschini; but from this time onward, he was always in danger of becoming the tool rather than the leader of the people.[33] Henceforward they were masters. One may say that the revolution had begun.

At daybreak on the 19th a fresh alarm took place. New proscription lists were found unaccountably posted on the walls, this time containing the name of Cardinal Vannicelli. The people again became excitable. That afternoon, it was reported that one of the alleged conspirators, the Cavaliere Minardi, had been seen near the Church of Sant' Andrea delle Fratte, and the crowd at once started off in pursuit of him: their numbers were soon so great that the streets were blocked by people hunting for Minardi. Houses were invaded and the chase continued from roof to roof until the civic patrols were left far behind on the ground below. The foremost pursuers came to a check before a little oratory, and proclaimed that they had run Minardi to ground there, and that he was protected by the right of sanctuary of the Church. This right they would not violate, but they remained there for several hours, shouting that he should be given up. The authorities were powerless—or rather, helpless—but finally, at 10 p.m. they sent for Padre Ventura to deal with the situ-

[32] *La Bilancia*, August 24th; De Boni, p. 137.
[33] Pellegrino Rossi virtually said this to Corboli Bussi.

ation, and while Ciceruacchio held a lantern, the eloquent
padre harangued the crowd, assuring them that Minardi was
not in the oratory; after which, although still sceptical, they
agreed to march home in triumph. So the episode came to
an end.[34] It seems to be uncertain whether Minardi had ever
been there at all; however he was arrested soon afterwards in
Tuscany.

We are now in a position to ask: What were the results of
the Congiura?

Firstly the police and Carabinieri had proved themselves
absolutely useless to the government; secondly, the armed
force had now passed to the people in the shape of the Civic
Guard. Thirdly, the Civic Guard was already passing into
the hands of Ciceruacchio; but for the time being it remained
loyal.

It was a gigantic success for the democratic sections of the
movement. It meant that 12,000 muskets were being ordered
from France to put into the hands of the Roman people,
besides those already in the state. It meant that the idea of
the Civic Guard would spread to other unrestful states, and
that before the end of a year perhaps a hundred thousand men
would be armed throughout Italy.[35] It was a step forward in

[34] This description is taken from that of Pellegrino Rossi who was
a greatly amused spectator of the scene. Massimo d'Azeglio says
that Minardi was there and that he was allowed by Padre Ventura to
escape through a back door. D'Azeglio, *Correspondance politique*,
p. 17.
[35] Massimo d'Azeglio said that a hundred and eighty thousand
men would be armed in the Papal State alone. This was a great
over-estimate. *V.* d'Azeglio, *Lettere a sua moglie*, July 8th, 1847.

As to results: d'Azeglio said: "Whatever it was, it went well for
us. The Pope has opened his eyes and the Gregorians are broken
(*enfoncés*)", *ibid.*, July 20th. He wrote a letter to M. Doubs on
July 25th, but his letters to his wife probably represent his most
outspoken opinion.

Count Lützow wrote to Metternich: "The 17th and 18th of
July...approached, and at the same time there came news which
was said to be positive, indubitable—but of whose value I am still
very suspicious.... Vienna Staats-Archiv, Rome, 1847. *Rapports*,
I, July 16th.

the Risorgimento: only eight months later thousands of these men would be fighting against Austria; and it was a stage further towards the end of the Papal State; sixteen months later thousands of these men would be fighting against Pius.

So much for the winning of the Civica; but almost instantaneously we get the first result of that edict, one of supreme importance: namely, on July 17th, the Austrian military movement at Ferrara, which will now be described.

Chapter XIV

THE AUSTRIAN ACTION AT FERRARA

Metternich's system had produced the agitation for Civic Guards; and now Pius, when he consented to arm an Italian Civic Guard, was to receive a sharp retort from Radetzky's G.H.Q.; which in turn led, eight months later, to the war of 1848.

The military episode at Ferrara is the first definite *faux-pas* on the part of the Austrians; and virtually it marks the beginning of hostilities.

The towns of Ferrara and Comacchio—we have already said—were used by the Austrians as an advanced post in the Papal State. In spite of a protest by Cardinal Consalvi, the Congress of Vienna, in 1815 had granted them this right. Clause 103 of the Treaty ran as follows:

His Imperial and Royal Majesty the Emperor of Austria and his successors will have the right of garrisoning the "places" of Ferrara and Comacchio.

The word "places" is here printed in inverted commas because it is the French word *place*. Its exact meaning is disputed. It stands for *place forte* and Metternich claimed that it included the whole of those two walled towns; the Italians held that it included only the fortresses within them.

For thirty-two years the Austrians had restricted their occupation as far as possible to the fortress. During the risings of Gregory XVI's reign no doubt their troops had patrolled or occupied the streets as they pleased; and in those days they had done so unmolested, with the approval of the Papal government. But since Pius' accession, the people showed signs of being very tired of the foreign uniforms.

In such a situation trouble was *certain* to arise; and we hear that when the Ferrarese first formed their National (or Civic) Guard the Austrians refused to recognise it. But there was something to be said for the soldiers. Feeling in the streets was hostile to them, and the new Delegate, Cardinal Ciacchi, was reputed not to love them. Small incidents increased the irritation. During April, for instance, there had been an "insult" to the Austrian army; someone had put up "a dirty Papal flag" on their range: and on June 14th a really serious case had occurred. A well-known banker, Baron Baratelli, had been stabbed with a stiletto in the open street. He was the head of the Ferdinandea Society whose purpose was to bring the country under Austria—in fact he was a pro-Austrian of a "virulent" type. By some people he has been called a man of bad character, but it appears to be agreed that his murder was political.[1] Nevertheless, in spite of these episodes, the soldiers and townspeople continued to live on fairly good terms.

[1] *La Bilancia* of July 2nd, 1847, gives the following account of his life; it is written by Count Mamiani, a revolutionist. *V.* also *Carte segrete della polizia austriaca*, II, 278. Baron Baratelli was born near Ferrara, of very poor parents, and in his young days was said to have danced round the tree of Liberty. In 1813 he had joined the Austrians and English invading the Kingdom of Italy; in 1815 he had accompanied them in their pursuit of Murat; in 1821 he had returned with them to Naples, and in 1831 he had joined them in occupying the Papal State, had sat on their commission and signed proscription-lists in his native district of Ferrara. He was avowedly an agent of Austria. In the National archives in Rome there is an account of a trial in which his son appears to have got the family bank into very serious financial trouble. Rome, Archivio di Stato, Ministero del Interno, Busta 319.

Metternich's account is rather different. He says Baratelli was a well-to-do landowner who sided against the French invaders. That in 1813 when the Austrian armies advanced beyond the Alps, he got into touch with them. Since 1815 he had been a supporter of law-and-order, and a hater of the revolution. His murder was due to his opposing the formation of the Civic Guard. (Metternich omits all mention of the Ferdinandea Society.) *V. London Corr.* I, 51, Despatch of June 28th, 1847.

When, however, on July 5th, Pius granted the Civic
Guards, his concession filled the Ferrarese with triumph and
the Austrians with anger. They regarded this new armed force
as a danger to their interests all over Italy.

At this point the supreme importance of having an armed
force is proved to us—if proof is required—by the changed
demeanour of Field Marshal Radetzky.[2] As soon as he heard
of the Edict of July 5th he decided to reinforce his garrison
in Ferrara: the Ferrarese, he calculated, would raise three
battalions of Civica: so he ordered down from Lombardy an
infantry battalion, a half-squadron of cavalry and half a
battery of artillery. He meant his garrison to be secure from
insults due to the "fanaticism" of the people, because, in the
existing ferment, he felt that an insult might set all Italy on
fire—a fact of which he and Metternich were soon to have
abundant proofs.

It seems that he decided to make the entry of these reinforcements into Ferrara a kind of military demonstration.
Probably he thought that a display of armed force would
keep the natives quiet.

So far all seemed fairly regular. It was the manner of
their arrival, and especially the day selected for it which puts
them in the wrong. Their entry constituted a threat of the
most insulting kind, carried out by an armed force in an
allied country in time of peace; intended either to provoke or,
more probably, to terrorise the inhabitants.

On July 17th, amnesty day, when all the cities of Italy
were decked with flags and holding public rejoicings, and the
citizens of Ferrara were watching a parade, suddenly there

[2] There is no longer any doubt that this action at Ferrara was
due to Radetzky and not Metternich. He wrote to inform Lützow
of his decision to reinforce the garrison as stated in the text, and
apparently also to Metternich. Evidently he thought that a small
armed demonstration would keep the Ferrarese quiet. (V. Lützow to
Metternich, July 22nd, 1847, Vienna Staats-Archiv, Fasc. 82, Varia
de Rome.) Metternich says he knew nothing of the order, but was
ready to defend it if necessary.

appeared on the scene a body of Hungarian infantry about
600 strong with some cavalry and three guns. Their advance
is best described by the British Vice-Consul, Mr Macalister;
he was there and saw it:[3]

A circumstance which took place yesterday morning and which
has caused much ill-humour in this our peaceable town, is worthy
of notice, and I think ought to be communicated to the British
Government. Our citadel, as you know, is garrisoned by Austrian
troops, and for some years past by six companies of Tyrolese
sharpshooters, and a few artillery men, etc., together about 1200.
Everything has gone on in the best possible manner and in good
order, with the exception that somebody placed a small national
flag on a small edifice within our city walls, latterly made use of as
a rifle school for the soldiers. The Austrian commander here
insisted on satisfaction, declaring it a political and seditious insult
to Austria. However, all was apparently put to rest, and no one
thought any more on the subject. This took place about three or
four months ago. Yesterday morning arrived six companies of
Hungarian infantry, two squadrons of cavalry, and a small detach-
ment of artillery with three field pieces. After crossing the Po,
part at Ponte Lago Scuro and part at Francolina, they arranged
themselves in battle order. Orders were given to load their
muskets and field pieces and march on Ferrara. In place of directing their course, as customary, to the fortress, they paraded up and
down several of our principal streets with their artillery-matches
burning. After this, part were marched into the citadel and part
into the two barracks they hold in our city, San Benedetto and
San Domenico; thus augmenting the numbers to about 1800 in
all. There is a report that in a few days 2000 to 3000 more are to
arrive. Our Cardinal Legate sent off an express immediately to
Rome, to announce this circumstance, which in the present enthusiasm for the "guardia civica" and other concessions made by
the Pope, and aversion generally to Austria, might have had a
serious result.

Such a march as this on foreign territory could not have
been carried out unless previously planned and ordered by
G.H.Q.

On the previous day Cardinal Ciacchi, the Papal Legate in
authority in Ferrara, had received demands for billets for

[3] *London Corr.* 1, 65, Macalister, July 18th.

men and horses but, apparently, no formal notification of the troops' arrival, and, of course, no notice of this armed demonstration. He promptly reported the whole incident to Cardinal Ferretti, the new Secretary of State in Rome; and Ferretti indited a formal complaint[4] to Count Lützow. Thus the diplomatic incident was fairly started.

But in this connection Lützow told Metternich—and not without surprise—that it was Pius himself who wrote to Cardinal Ciacchi and ordered him not to find billets in the town. He said that the Austrians had no right to occupy the town; if they did so, he directed Ciacchi to report the matter, and said he would issue a formal protest to the Great Powers.[5]

Undoubtedly in this Ferrara episode Pius was justified in taking a strong personal line. In a general way the Papal State was a neutral institution, but, if attacked, it was Pius' duty to defend it. At this moment the Austrians were aggressors. They had not yet gone far, but it was the insult

[4] Ferretti complained (1) of the occupation of the town, not the "place" or citadel, under Act 103, and quoted Consalvi's protest. He also quoted a solemn promise of the Emperor Francis that he would never claim the right to garrison the town, (2) that the troops' arrival had not been previously announced, and that this had offended Pius, (3) the manner of the entry had been such that Pius had spoken of it as hostile. Lützow was so much struck by the personal action taken by Pius in this Ferrara affair that he wrote two cypher despatches dealing with that fact alone.

[5] Lützow to Metternich, July 22nd, 1847 (Vienna Staats-Archiv, Fasc. 82, Varia de Rome, 1847). Lützow says that Ciacchi had written asking for instructions as to the lodgings and stables that he had been asked to provide by the Imperial Commandant. Pius' reply had been as follows: "Instructions addressées d'ordre de Sa Sainteté au Cardinal Ciacchi. Il lui a été défendu d'adhérer à la demande du Commandement Militaire Impérial de loger des troupes, de quelques armes qu'elles fussent, dans l'intérieur de la ville de Ferrare, puisque sous la parole 'place', ainsi que dit l'acte du Congrès de Vienne, ne saurait être sousentendu la ville. Si cependant le Commandant de vive force voudrait soutenir sa demande, le Cardinal Légat devait en rendre de suite compte à Sa Sainteté qui ne tarderait point pour lors d'adresser des protestations aux cours étrangères contre cette atteinte portée à sa Souveraineté."

that he resented. The arrival of the troops had not been formally announced—on that part of Lützow's despatch Metternich has scrawled a note: "To announce them beforehand would have led to an outbreak"—and secondly there was the manner of the entry which, in conversation with an officer, Pius had even termed "hostile".[6]

In a very few days the news had spread far and wide and all Italy was afire; and at Ferrara the excitement on both sides had reached such a pitch that it was impossible to prevent further developments. For purposes of clearness we may classify the happenings of the next five weeks under three main headings: firstly, what may be called the Jankovich episode, and then the two formal protests by Cardinal Ciacchi.

On August 1st an Austrian captain named Jankovich complained[7] that when coming home from a café to the citadel at half-past eleven at night, he was followed in the dark by three men, one of whom waved a sword and another carried a fowling-piece, and that, when they whistled, other men appeared between him and the citadel; and that finally his way was barred by a crowd of fifty to eighty people, some of them carrying sticks and some of them armed, who shouted "Viva l'Italia! Viva la libertà!" and "Viva Pio Nono". That he was obliged to turn back and get a patrol, whereupon the crowd dispersed.

In consequence[8] of this alleged insult to one of his officers, the Austrian Commandant, Count Auersperg, on the following morning (August 2nd) informed Cardinal Ciacchi that he

---

[6] Lützow to Metternich, July 24th, *ibid*. He had discussed the whole matter with Ferretti and Corboli-Bussi. He ends up: "Les formes dont Sa Sainteté s'était sentie blessée au point de les qualifier, envers un officier supérieure de la Garde Civique nouvellement constituée, d'hostile."

[7] *V.* Jankovich's report. A copy is in Bargagli's despatch August 9th, 1847 (Florence Arch.); another copy in Vienna Staats-Archiv, Fasc. 82.

[8] *London Corr.* i, 103, Ferretti to Lützow.

meant to report the matter to G.H.Q. and at once to patrol those portions of the town which were near the citadel, and the esplanade, and also other parts of the city,[9] to protect officers who were returning late at night from inns or private houses. In order to prevent the Papal patrols with different pass-words from clashing with his men, he asked Cardinal Ciacchi to forbid anyone to pass from the "Corso della Citadella" to the esplanade. The Cardinal replied that, before taking any such steps, an enquiry should be held so that the Jankovich episode could be dealt with according to the law, and that in any case it was only an ordinary disturbance; that if special measures were taken (such as the patrolling) he should protest against them as being outside the treaty rights of the Austrians.

On August 6th,[10] Count Auersperg, who by that time had obtained fresh orders from Radetzky, again called on Cardinal Ciacchi and told him that he intended to patrol the town near the barracks, the officers' lodgings, the castle and the house occupied by G.H.Q. This meant, of course, patrolling a good deal of the town; most probably as much of it as they liked. So Cardinal Ciacchi drew up a statement before a notary, challenging Jankovich's story and protesting against the military occupation of a Papal town.

This was his first formal protest. After detailing the events already related above, he ended up:[11]

remembering that such an act is entirely illegal and contrary to agreements subsequent to the Treaty of Vienna and to long un-broken custom, and—in my position as Apostolic Legate of this city and province—wishing to preserve intact the sacred rights of

[9] Auersperg does not mention the other parts in writing, but Ferretti says that he did so by word of mouth. Bargagli also received the same information (Florence Arch., Dip. Est., Busta 2956.

[10] *London Corr.*, *ibid.*, also p. 85. Ferretti's Report. Bargagli gives a similar account. *V.* also Vienna Staats-Archiv, Fasc. 82.

[11] Farini, I, 215; and in Vienna Staats-Archiv, *ibid.* there is a full copy of the protest.

the Holy See, I do solemnly and in the most emphatic manner
protest against the illegality of such an act and of every ulterior
act which may be committed in prejudice of the said right, and
of these pontifical subjects entrusted to my administration and
guardianship.

This formal protest was printed in the *Diario di Roma* of
August 10th, where it was read aloud with the greatest enthusiasm in the piazzas and streets in Rome.[12]

On the nights of both August 6th and 7th there were many
Austrian patrols throughout the town.[13]   Ciacchi forbade
the civic patrols to go out, as they were not yet armed.

On August 8th Count Auersperg wrote to Cardinal
Ciacchi[14] to order the Civic Guards not to furnish the guards
at the piazza and at the city gates, otherwise his Austrian
troops would increase the strength of their detachments at
those posts.

On the following day the Cardinal replied that His Holiness
had full right to exercise his temporal power in his town of
Ferrara.[15]

On August 9th Cardinal Ferretti made an appeal to Europe;
he wrote a formal note of complaint to the Austrian ambassador in Rome, enclosing a copy of Ciacchi's protest; similar
notes and enclosures were addressed by the Papal government
to all the foreign embassies in Rome.   Count Lützow was
much astonished, especially when he was informed who had
written it.[16]   On the 10th Ferretti came to assure him that the
government guaranteed his safety and also that of his family.

---

[12] Farini, I, 216.

[13] According to the Italian newspapers. *La Bilancia* of August
14th says that on the 6th they terrorised the inhabitants by firing
shots and pointing bayonets, but that on the 7th they were peaceful.

[14] *London Corr.* I, 97; Bianchi, V, 21.

[15] According to Bianchi, V, 21, Auersperg warned Ciacchi that
Austrian troops were gathering along the Papal frontier ready to
cross it if any breach of law and order rendered this necessary.   I
have not seen that letter.

[16] "It was the Pope himself who dictated the note which the
Cardinal Secretary of State addressed to me.   It is merely another

On August 12th Cardinal Ferretti wrote a long letter to the Papal Nuncio at Vienna, in the course of which he said:[17]

I am eager to render conscientious service to my sovereign at every period of my life, but I serve Pius IX also in virtue of the affection inspired by his rare gifts of heart and mind which make him a model in private life and an excellent prince, and have made him the idol of his people. Nor shall I cease—because so deep an affection and one based on such reasoned motives must necessarily grow rather than decrease—from co-operating in the wise reforms that are universally desired, or from seconding, as far as is compatible with our situation and with the essential character of the pontifical government, the desires and tendencies of that Moderate party which undoubtedly forms the immense majority of our populations.

This was probably the last occasion on which it could be said that the Moderate party represented the majority of the population; for this struggle over Ferrara had the effect of turning hundreds of moderates into extremists. Cardinal Ferretti then continues:

Hence it is easy to understand the indignant surprise of the people of Ferrara at the carefully-planned entry of the Austrian reinforcements for H.I.M.'s garrison there; especially as it was carried out with every appearance of a hostile entry, the troops being preceded by vedettes, the cavalry carrying their carbines in their hands, the colours flying, and the longest way being selected for the march to the citadel.

On August 13th a fresh episode occurred.[18] At eleven in the morning Count Auersperg paraded all his men in front of the citadel; two infantry battalions, a troop of cavalry and several guns. He then sent the major of the infantry battalion, the adjutant of the fortress and three mounted men, to the

concession dragged from him." Lützow to Metternich (cypher), August 10th, 1847, Vienna Staats-Archiv, Fasc. 82. Lützow regarded himself as trying to save Pius from political suicide.

[17] Farini, I, 217.

[18] Vienna Staats-Archiv, Fasc. 82, Ferretti's note of August 16th to Lützow; v. also Farini, I, 222; *London Corr.* I, 96. *V.* also the *Diario di Roma*.

palace of Cardinal Ciacchi with a letter calling on him, by
Radetzky's orders, to hand over at once all the armed "posts"
in the city to the Austrian troops. This looks, of course, like
an attempt at intimidation; but, if so, Cardinal Ciacchi—as
Farini says—"a worthy wearer of the purple robe", proved
equal to the occasion; he received the major in his audience
room and met his demand by a formal refusal; adding
that if he were compelled by force to yield he would
make a solemn protest in the name of the Pontiff and of
international right. Count Auersperg allowed him an hour in
which to warn the Guard,[19] and, at the end of that time, proceeded in the most public manner possible to occupy all the
city gates and the other disputed points in the town. Some of
them were guarded by Papal troops. The Papal troops had to
be withdrawn from their posts in broad daylight before an
immense crowd. The citizens saw all these things and made
no resistance because none was possible; but they put up
their shutters, and here and there were heard shouts of "Viva
Pio Nono".

Then Cardinal Ciacchi drew up his second formal protest[20]
before a notary, and forwarded a copy to Rome. There it was
published in the *Diario di Roma* and aroused such enthusiasm
that soldiers were required outside the newspaper office, to
regulate the crowd of would-be purchasers.

One can imagine the difficulty of the situation for Pius. In
the midst of his schemes of reform he was suddenly inter-
rupted by these insults of an all-powerful enemy from outside.
With a very imperfect army of only twelve to fourteen
thousand men, and an inherited financial deficit of unknown
quantity, he was called upon to defend his unarmed people
against a first-class military power. In these conditions it was

[19] Cardinal Ciacchi, in his previous communication, had asked
Count Auersperg to delay the occupation until after dark, in order
to avoid the danger of bloodshed; but evidently Auersperg did not
agree.

[20] *V. Diario*, August 17th and *Contemporaneo*, August 21st.

difficult for him to know what to do, but in one respect at all events his line of action was already decided: he would refuse to be driven out of his policy of reform by any show of force from Vienna. When asked what means of defence the Pope would have, Cardinal Ferretti said that he would first return the Austrian ambassador his passport; he would then, if necessary, have recourse to the spiritual arm; and finally, if that went unheeded he would send out an appeal to all Italy.[21]

On August 16th the College of Cardinals met and ordered an observation camp to be formed at Forlì for 15,000 men. Meanwhile Pius urged his people to keep the peace.

At Ferrara, in fact, we have the first clash of arms, pre-announcing the campaign of 1848.

[21] Cardinal Ferretti told Bargagli this on September 2nd. *V.* Florence Arch., Dip. Est., Busta 2956.

Chapter XV

INDIGNATION OVER THE
FERRARA EPISODE

Having thus laboriously detailed the actual facts of the case, we may now approach the arguments and opinions on either side. Firstly, was Metternich responsible for this Ferrara episode? Secondly, how far were the Austrians within their rights? Thirdly, what were its political results?

Until quite lately Metternich has nearly always been made responsible for the Ferrara episode, and also for the Congiura. It was firmly believed that he had engineered them both in order either to terrorise the Italian people, or else to provoke them and thereby to justify an Austrian intervention. Nowadays, however, there are more documents available, and we may safely accept Metternich's statement[1] that the orders came from Radetzky, acting on his own responsibility. Radetzky himself wrote to both Lützow and Metternich that he gave those orders because he feared that, with the arming of the Civic Guard, there might be insults which would set all Italy on fire.

Moreover Metternich wrote to Lützow that Radetzky had not informed him of the order, but that nevertheless he was ready enough to defend it if necessary.

No doubt Radetzky considered the reinforcement advisable for the sake of safety; but most probably he also thought that by turning it into a military demonstration he would keep the people quiet. If so, he soon discovered his mistake. Times were changed since the occupation of 1831, when the sight of an Austrian corps would put an end to all resistance. The

[1] Vienna Staats-Archiv, Fasc. 82, Varia de Rome, Metternich to Lützow, July 25th, August 7th. Srbik, II, 131: "The military meddled with the political sphere." The Viennese documents put the matter beyond doubt.

Liberal movement had roused all classes, and the Progressives were calling for arms.

Secondly we ask: how far were the Austrians within their rights?

According to the strict letter of the law undoubtedly there is a certain amount to be said for them. Metternich contends: that Radetzky feared the Civic Guard would be a danger to his troops: that the reinforcements marched into Ferrara merely in the same order that had always been customary when entering that or any other garrison town, including even Vienna: that the word "place" means a fortified town, not merely the citadel—that the citadel and the walls are contiguous and that therefore he had a right to garrison the whole of the "wall-surrounded" town of Ferrara. In proof of this argument he urges that the word "place" could not have meant merely "citadel" because in 1815 the citadel of Ferrara was in ruins—practically negligible; and that he was also authorised to occupy the "place" of Comacchio where no citadel existed at all, but merely fortifications; so that the word "place" could not possibly refer to the citadel.

In support he quotes a letter of the Austrian commander Marshal Bellegarde, written in 1816 when the question first arose. In it Bellegarde claimed that, if their barracks, hospitals or other necessary establishments were found to be insufficient, some suitable ground should be assigned to them, for fresh buildings. Metternich added that, as the citadel had always been too small, two barracks had already been furnished by the pontifical government.

Of course his arguments are by no means unanswerable; for instance, one might retort:

As to the order of march: the fact that the troops adopted this order when entering Vienna gave them no right to do so in Ferrara; and their march struck outsiders—for instance Mr Macalister—as being highly provocative.

As regards the word "place". To apply that word to Ferrara was a misnomer. It was one of the ancient capital cities of Italy: if the diplomats in 1815 had meant the whole town to be occupied they would have used the word "city".[2]

As to Marshal Bellegarde's letter; that was merely an Austrian claim, and it might be interpreted so as to justify demanding barracks for twenty thousand men.

In this connection it must be remembered that Cardinals Ferretti and Ciacchi base their protest not only on the treaty itself, but also on agreements subsequent to it.

Finally one can say that the day selected was certainly intended to be provocative or menacing. If Radetzky was really afraid of setting all Italy on fire why did he choose amnesty day for his march over the frontier; a day on which all Italy was full of patriotic enthusiasm?

In any case, Metternich perceived almost at once that the action at Ferrara had been a serious mistake, for it had alienated the sympathy of nearly all the peoples in Europe. They saw plainly that, whether legally right or not, this was a menace on the part of Austria and intended to prevent a small nation from arming a Civic Guard to defend its Liberal reforms. Consequently Metternich soon found it futile to explain (as quoted above) to the Great Powers that the word "place" in reality meant a fortified town, because the replies of Palmerston and others were based on the rather irrelevant theme that the smaller nations had a perfect right to develop their own Liberal institutions.

The result was that there surged up a great wave of sympathy for Pius all over the world.

To the nations of Europe in the year 1847—at a moment when they were already quivering with the feverish passions of the coming revolution—it seemed that the drama before

---

[2] According to Bianchi, v, 30, when the Austrians first arrived in 1815 they tried to garrison the town as well as the citadel, but Cardinal Consalvi for the pontifical government denied their right to do so under the treaty and they agreed. Bianchi quotes a note of Consalvi of September 15th, 1815.

them was that of a small and weak people united, for defence, around its peaceful ruler whose only crime consisted in trying to inaugurate a happier and more civilised era; whereas on the other side there stood a colossus of reaction and oppression merely seeking an excuse to overwhelm them.

The cardinal's appeal had touched the right chord: "Let us draw close together as one family around the common Father...let us rely on the assistance of Heaven invoked by that Saint, on the justice of our cause, and on the sympathy which it receives from every honest and noble mind." These words had made generous hearts vibrate in every civilised country. In England, Palmerston took a stronger line than any of the continental ministers. Although himself a supporter of the Treaty of 1815, he spoke to the Sardinian ambassador of "this brutal and insulting way" of treating the Papal government,[3] and wrote to Metternich that "every independent sovereign has a right to make, within his own dominions such reforms and improvements as he may judge conducive to the welfare of the people whom he governs";[4] and that "no invasion of the Papal state could take place without leading to consequences of great gravity and importance." In another letter of September 11th he added that "Her Majesty's government could not but regret that the Austrian commander at Ferrara had thought it necessary to make such a change in the disposition of his troops", and hoped that the Austrian government would be able to return to its original military distribution.[5]

This was the second time within eighteen months that England had spoken out for justice to a smaller nation. In February 1846 when Metternich's troops occupied Cracow,

[3] Bianchi, v, 410 (Di Revel, September 3rd).
[4] *London Corr.* i, 115 (Palmerston to Ponsonby, September 11th, two letters).
[5] Cardinal Ferretti, Secretary of State, spoke in the most grateful tone to Mr Petre: "England has alone spoken clearly and frankly. Happy be that country. Providence and England are with us!" *London Corr.* i, 162.

Palmerston had not minced his words in the House of Commons.[6]

In France there were fiery speeches in the Chambers, and M. Guizot, whatever may have been his previous agreement with Metternich, saw that there was a deep sensation throughout Europe; he sent Pellegrino Rossi to express his sympathy to Pius and to offer his protection. On September 1st he wrote a very strong letter to Vienna;[7] and, in his memoirs, he claims that it was owing to his influence there that an agreement was finally arranged.[8]

In Germany it is harder now to gauge public opinion; but we know at all events that Mr Howard, the British ambassador at Berlin, wrote to Lord Palmerston: "I think I may say that great sympathy is felt among the public in this part of Germany for the present Pope....Equally strong are the regrets that the difficult task undertaken by His Holiness should be rendered still more arduous by the jealousy and conduct of a power like Austria, which ought to be his firmest support."

But it was amid the smaller Catholic peoples that there existed the most truly heartfelt sympathy for Pius; in the Catholic cantons of Switzerland and in Belgium the popular feeling welled up in his favour, and in Catholic Ireland the peasants offered to come and die for him.[9]

[6] He said that if the Treaty of Vienna did not hold good on the Vistula, it would not hold good on the Rhine or the Po.

[7] Paris Aff. Etr., Autriche, September 1st, 1847.

[8] Guizot, *Mémoires*, VII, 384.

[9] Metternich, *Mémoires*, VII, 315. The Princess Mélanie mentions this fact in her journal. "We invited M. d'Usedom to dinner, with the Nuncio, Arnim, Brassier de Saint-Simon who stayed a few days here, and Clanwilliam. The latter had an interview with my husband, by desire of the Duke of Wellington who begs Clement to make known to him his views on the general situation. In England we are being attacked with fury. The Irish are even offering themselves to protect the Pope against us." In Belgium King Leopold ordered his minister in Vienna, Count O'Sullivan, to keep him in close touch with Roman affairs. Bianchi, V, 398.

In Italy itself, patriotic enthusiasm rose to the point of being actually harmful; many people seem to have thought that, in Pius, they had found a condottiere to lead the national cause against Austria; his name, from being that of a reformer, became almost a war-cry—with disastrous results later on. But for the time being the movement swept all before it. Indeed Metternich must have been astonished to discover what very different effects were being produced by this intervention of 1847 from those produced in previous years. This was the result of the Liberal advance. He was now attacking not merely a ruler but also a people full of triumph in their newly granted emancipation; and, more especially, a free press.[10]

The press very soon got to work with considerable ability. Italian writers agree that, within a few days, more hatred was aroused against Austria than in the previous thirty-two years. Perhaps the best way of describing the situation is simply to quote a page or two from one of the best of their modern historians.[11]

The world was still quivering with anger at the Roman Congiura and the risks run by the Pope. On to this perilous state of public feeling there came the aggression in Ferrara. Not only Europe but also America was stirred by it. In the French Chamber the occasion was seized for fiery attacks on the servile Guizot; this

[10] When complaining of the way in which people were speaking about Austria, Lützow said: "The Cardinal especially begged me not to lose sight of the great difference between the position today and that in 1831." Vienna Staats-Archiv, Fasc. 82, August 18th, 1847.

[11] Gori, p. 249. See infra. Spada, I, 276, speaking of the anti-Austrian propagandists, says that "they did more in these few days than in the thirty-two previous years". In his opinion the revolution in Vienna some nine months later was due indirectly to this episode at Ferrara. Farini says (I, 232): "Prince Metternich and Marshal Radetzky succeeded by their ill-considered provocations in arousing spirit to an unusual degree; in leading the Roman court further perhaps than it wished or desired to go; and in drawing upon Austria the animadversion even of devout people who hitherto had taken no interest in politics; and the blame of civilised Europe."

afforded some gratification to our ancient pro-French sentiment.
The remonstrances made in the most open and public manner in
Rome, opened up a free and unbridled path for our own anti-
German sentiments which had hitherto been displayed with a
certain degree of caution. Those few days of supreme political
incitement created more enemies to Austria than all the time
before; the reactionaries were amazed, and they cursed their
imprudence. The protests of Ciacchi and Ferretti were printed,
were bought by the thousand, and were read aloud in the streets.
The press overflowed all censorial dykes, and dilated openly on
the questions of the union of Italy and national independence.
Even moderate men became the zealous proposers of fiery resolutions. The *Felsineo* spoke of "the imperial hordes". Massimo
d'Azeglio wrote a pamphlet which was read and approved by the
Pope, entitled *Sulla protesta pel caso di Ferrara* and containing a
warm defence of the national dignity and independence. Burning
appeals were circulated in the name of the citizens of Ferrara,
addressed to "the peoples of Pius IX", and to their Italian brothers.
The *Italia* and the *Alba* brought forward the question of the rescue
of Lombardy. Even Liberals advised the use of spiritual arms;
the *Bilancia* said that greater reliance should be placed on them
than on armies. Habitués of the Quirinal spoke of excommunication, and the Pope himself was considering the idea.[12] A protest
in the name of the Roman clergy contradicted the assertion that
they disagreed with the intentions of Pius IX, or that they disapproved of the Civic Guard, and promised that the clanging of
the church bells should mingle with the roll of the drums. In
order to signify the fusion of religion with patriotism, a com-
memorative service for the Bandiera brothers was held at Pisa and
elsewhere, even in Ferrara under the eyes of the Austrians; and
when the commandant complained to the Archbishop he merely
received the reply: "I cannot forbid prayers for the dead whatever
their politics may have been."

[12] Gori gives this only on the authority of Farini. Incidentally
one may say that, though right as regards popular enthusiasm, this
paragraph of Gori is perhaps a little exaggerated as to the newspapers. The clandestine press—the revolutionist leaflets—seems to
have become very violent, but responsible journals such as the
Contemporaneo and the *Bilancia* retained their common sense and
saw that though resistance was right, a war of liberation was not yet
possible. But this episode of Ferrara undoubtedly caused Pius to
be regarded as the anti-Austrian champion of Italy instead of merely
as the Liberal Pope.

It will be noted also that Massimo d'Azeglio submitted his *Protesta*, or strong defence of the national dignity, to Pius for approval before having it printed—this, says Minghetti, shows clearly how sincere was his (Pius') feeling at that time; not merely as to the necessity for internal reforms, but as to the national dignity and independence.[13]

But perhaps the most striking episode of these weeks is the fact already mentioned that, from Monte Video, Garibaldi wrote a letter to Pius offering his services in defence of the Holy See. It was a strange beginning of Garibaldi's connection with Rome where only a year and a half later he was to defend, not the Pope, but the Mazzinian republic; and for whose possession some twenty years later he was to adventure on his last great political campaign: O Roma o Morte.

And this offer of Garibaldi brings us to a more serious consideration, namely that Pius was henceforward regarded by many people as being virtually pledged to a war of liberation. On this point Gori speaks as follows:

In that leaven of Guelfism it seemed as if the Pope ought to proclaim a crusade against the Emperor. The kindly Pius IX appeared before the Italian imagination with the fierce lineaments of a warrior pope. It was said that the troops were starting for Forlì and that he like a new Julius II was to go there himself, so that his presence should increase the valour of his fighting men. In the cause of Pius' honour which they regarded as the symbol of the safety of Italy, the towns of Bologna, Forlì, Imola, Rimini, Cesena, Faenza, Osimo, Orvieto and Ferrara itself, declared through their municipal councils that they were ready to face any undertaking. In Rome a list which had been opened for citizens volunteering to march to Ferrara, was covered with signatures. The Swiss soldiers were not behindhand, and swore that the Austrians would have to cross their dead bodies before they reached Pius. From two different quarters the government received large and spontaneous offers of arming the Civic Guard, which was steadily improving and was drilling day and night so as to be ready to resist the foreigner.[14]

[13] Minghetti, *Ricordi*, I, 278.
[14] Gori, p. 250.

This description of the military enthusiasm is fully confirmed by Bargagli, the Tuscan minister in Rome at that time. In his reports he spoke of the enthusiasm with which the young men of all classes were drilling and manœuvring nearly all day.[15]

Certainly Austria, however unwittingly, had initiated a new stage in the advance towards the union of Italy: but also, by forcing the Pope's hand, had rendered a very great service to the revolution. It was this Ferrara episode that led to the war of 1848. And Pius' name was now rapidly becoming a war-cry; in Milan, for instance, during a clash with the Austrian soldiers the crowd would sing Pius' hymn and shout "Long live Pius IX, King of Italy."[16] In Rome, henceforth, the whole political atmosphere had become entirely unsuitable for preaching reforms or compromises: and even less suited for preaching the universal brotherhood of Christians which, of course, remained the first and the supreme duty of the head of the Church.

Here, too, there is another point well worth mentioning. On the reactionist side we notice a great bitterness among the old Conservatives, and it finds vent in vague talk against an inept and misguided Pope: it even goes so far as to whisper of a rebellion and schism. Simultaneously on the progressive side the Italian patriots begin to claim that Pius should excommunicate Austria. These two rival threats, namely those of schism and of excommunication, were destined to have great influence on Pius at the moment of crisis in 1848.[17]

At this juncture Metternich composed several despatches which show some signs of discouragement. On August 22nd, 1847, he wrote to his old friend Marshal Radetzky a letter in which there is more human feeling than in perhaps any other. He begins by introducing Ficquelmont and then says:[18]

[15] Florence Arch., Dip. Est., Busta 2956.
[16] *London Corr.* I, 138, Dawkins to Ponsonby.
[17] Predari, pp. 193–6.
[18] Metternich, *Mémoires*, VII, 476.

You and I, my dear Field Marshal, have been through difficult times, and we have accomplished some big things without our ever finding the slightest cessation in the perfect understanding that subsists between us: but we are destined by Providence not to spend our old age in repose. The past called for great efforts from us, but it was better than the present; for you and I know how to struggle against tangible bodies, but, against phantasms, material force is useless. Well, nowadays it is against phantasms that we have to fight. There actually has been reserved for the world the spectacle of a Pope who professes Liberalism!

May heaven preserve you a long time yet for your Emperor and State. You do not doubt, I know, that no one attaches a higher importance than I do to the realisation of this good wish.

Evidently Metternich felt that there was only one man who could help him to save the Austrian system in Italy.[19] He and his old friend were still efficient—the last living remnants of the coalitions against Napoleon. In reality he took a far truer view of the Italian situation than did Palmerston. He foresaw that Liberalism would be swallowed up by revolution; that hardly a throne in Italy would be left standing—Metternich was able to foretell all this ruin because he had been working the puppet show for thirty years. But Palmerston still believed that Liberal institutions could develop peacefully in each separate state, and entirely failed to perceive that this was impossible because of the presence in Italy of the Austrians. As long as the Austrians were there with their treaty rights of 1815, it was useless to expect peace. Palmerston, did not know—and nor did Guizot—that the Liberal spirit cannot co-exist with a suppressed nationality.

For about five months the negotiations continued. At one period the Prussian Minister M. d'Usedom intervened, but without being able to bring the matter to a conclusion. The Papal Nuncio at Vienna proved a failure; he was said to be

---

[19] Pius also realised this. A story is told that some of his entourage suggested to him to excommunicate the Emperor and Metternich. "And what about Radetzky?" asked Pius with a smile.

strongly opposed to Pius' Liberal policy. But Cardinal Ferretti showed a good deal of firmness and tact, and finally brought the matter to a successful issue. It was agreed that the question of national rights should be waived in favour of a simple working arrangement between the soldiers on either side. The guard and the gates were to be handed back by the Austrians, and henceforth to be occupied by Papal regular troops, not Civic Guards; but the Pope maintained his right to place Civic Guards there if he wished. The Porta Po was always to remain open, with two sentries without muskets stationed in it, one Austrian, the other Italian, to prevent desertion from their respective corps, and with a guard of pontifical Finanzieri or Customs officers. The Austrians were not to send out patrols into the town. Their soldiers were to have free passage between the barracks and the citadel; and they were allowed to have guards in the barracks, but the main body of their forces was always to be in the citadel. The pass-word each night was to be given by the Papal Legate. This last condition marked him out as the supreme authority.

The agreement was dated December 16th, 1847. On December 23rd, before a large concourse of people, the Austrian troops were withdrawn from the guard and from the four gates as publicly as when they had taken possession of them, and these posts were occupied by pontifical troops. This was a striking scene and marked a very definite success for the pontifical government.[20]

[20] Even Sterbini, whose creed was Pan-Italian and therefore disposed to overlook the success of any individual state, wrote an article full of genuine feeling at the first news of the coming success. He claimed, of course, that, primarily, it was a triumph for the peoples of Italy because of their united sentiment and orderly support of the cause: "To-day it is a glory to belong to this people." But then referring to Pius he says: "Every heart forms good wishes for him, every lip repeats his praise, every arm is ready to defend him. And why should it not be so? Wherever there exists an oppressed people he who speaks of justice in the name of God and sheds the light of his example upon his words, will always be

At this point we must leave Pius for a while. Henceforth, against his will, he is now regarded as the inspirer and leader of the coming war of liberation—a position impossible for him or for any other Pope.

It is time, however, to consider the influence of all these events on Charles Albert and on the other leaders in Italy.

listened to as a loving father and a liberator inspired by Heaven." *Contemporaneo*, October 2nd, 1847. As to the agreement *v. London Corr.* ii, 6.

Chapter XVI

ITALY AFTER THE FERRARA EPISODE
(1847, JULY TO DECEMBER)

This chapter covers the second half of the year 1847. During these six months each state passes through the stage of agitation and arrives at that of action; and that is a great advance.

We have already stated in chapter VIII that during the first half of the year 1847 the Liberals in most of the small states were trying to win a free press; whereas during the second half they agitated for a Civic (National) Guard and a Consulta.

The Ferrara episode aroused such widespread patriotic indignation throughout Italy, and so deep a sympathy for Pius, that it may be said to mark this new phase; the phase when the people are calling for arms and for an assembly— for the Civic Guard and the Consulta. Pius' movement has overflowed his frontiers and has become the principal dynamic force all over Italy. His name no longer represents Gioberti's reforming Pope. It is simply a revolutionary cry for winning reforms, and a war-cry against Austria. And—absurd as this seems—it is almost synonymous with rebellion. Wherever a crowd rises against anti-Liberal government or against Austrian soldiers, the people begin by singing Pius' hymn with shouts of "Viva Pio Nono!"[1] The documents of this period show an enthusiasm for Pius which can be paralleled

---

[1] The figure of "the great Pius, redeemer of his people and symbol of the Italian fatherland, was magnified and idealised in the hearts of all; it gathered their sentiments into a union which was both spiritual and patriotic; and it set on fire their fervent enthusiasms so that they broke out with greater or less intensity... according to the special conditions of each Italian state." Masi, *Il Risorgimento*, II, 159.

only in 1860 when, during the glorious days of the Thousand, every political demonstration began with shouts of "Viva Garibaldi!"[2]

For nearly two years his unsought hegemony remained an unquestionable fact; but it could not possibly be permanent. This ebullition of popular sentiment was placing Pius in a completely false position in every Italian state; and he realised this but he could not prevent it. On November 2nd, 1847, during his well-known interview with Professor Montanelli, he spoke of the matter at some length. "Would you believe it", he said, "in one of the Calabrian towns it was with cries of Viva Pio IX that they set free the prisoners in their gaol!" It is difficult for us now even to imagine what Pius' feelings must have been when he saw the revolution everywhere around him springing from the earth, called into life by the mere sound of his name—he who represented the Prince of Peace, and had hoped to cure the ills of Italy by means of mutual good will and good understanding! Nevertheless the beliefs of Gioberti were still his guiding influence: as yet Gioberti's plan had not been fully tried.

Here we have reached the first growth of the new nation; in almost every Italian state we see it—Rome, Piedmont, Tuscany, Parma, Modena, Lucca, Lombardo-Venetia. The seed that was sown by the Carbonari, by Santarosa, by Silvio Pellico and Confalonieri, by Mazzini, by Gioberti and latterly by Charles Albert and d'Azeglio, has now been fertilised by Pius IX, and is coming near to its ripening.

It was on November 25th of the year 1847 that Mazzini sent off his celebrated letter to Pius IX. This letter was written in England and twelve days later it was thrown into Pius' carriage by a Mazzinian agent in Rome; in the meantime many copies of it had been circulated. It was an appeal to Pius to join the revolutionary party and unify Italy. Its most

[2] *London Corr.* I, pp. 121, 124, 131.

salient sentence was the following: "Unify Italy your native land. To achieve this you will not be called upon to act, but merely to bless those who act for you and in your name". This assurance was not made good in practice. Five months later the crisis came and Pius was ready to bless, but the Revolution rose against him because he had not acted as well.

Undoubtedly Mazzini's letter contained some fine passages,[3] and it created a certain sensation in Italy, but at the same time it produced no definite results.

During this period Mazzini's *trafila* and the influence of his unceasing propaganda must never be forgotten: nor that of his own wonderful unchanging persistence. It was a period when he and Lamberti, in Paris, were often in low spirits, but they never lost confidence in their cause, although they were achieving very few definite results. This failure was due to the fact that now the Italian movement was constitutional; the Nationalists were working through Pius, through Leopold II, and through Charles Albert, so that they were not disposed to rise in favour of Mazzini's fused republic.[4] All the law-abiding Liberals—perfectly genuine nationalists— naturally preferred serving under an existing government. Nevertheless Mazzini's letters show such belief in the future —"the people will come back to us"—that, when opened and

[3] For instance the following appeal to the Pope urging him to throw himself into the Revolution. "Do not say to yourself, if I talk and work in this way the princes of the earth will dissent from me, and their ambassadors will tender me notes and protests. What are the selfish complaints of the princes or their notes in comparison with one single syllable of the eternal Gospel of God? Hitherto these phantasms have been of some importance because they have been opposed only by other phantasms. Oppose to them the Reality of a Man who sees the divine aspect of human affairs—which to them is unknown; oppose to them the reality of an immortal soul that is conscious of a high mission, and they will disappear before you like the vapours of the night before the sun at dawn. Do not fear their snares; the human creature that is fulfilling a duty is no longer of man but of God."

[4] Cf. Casati, Ant., *Milano e i principi di Savoia*, p. 144. Also *Arch. Triennale*, 1, 45 and 490.

read by Metternich they undoubtedly conveyed to him an exaggerated idea of the Mazzinian committee's resources.

On November 5th Mazzini travelled over to Paris for a conference, and took the opportunity to stir up his followers in some of the French towns. From France he sent fresh agents into Italy, to Piedmont, Tuscany (especially Leghorn), Rome and Naples; daring men such as Ribotti and one of the Fabrizis. They were to lead the crowds and thus to direct the Moderate movement into the way of the Giovine Italia; but more especially they were to urge forward everywhere the arming of the Civic Guard, so as to have a military force all over the peninsula.[5] Already in every town of central Italy the municipal authorities were buying weapons, and Mazzini tells us, before long the arming of the Civic Guard in Forlì and in Perugia (1000 muskets) was entirely in the hands of his agents.[6]

Meanwhile Metternich of course was trying to counteract this general movement for arms and Liberal assemblies, not only in the Papal State but all over the peninsula.

[5] They were to take advantage of the movement in vogue and turn it to the account of the Giovine Italia "which sets back all royalties while shouting at the same time 'The Grand-Duke of Tuscany for ever!' or 'Charles Albert for ever!' or 'Pius IX for ever!'" This was the description of the directions they received, reported by the French police. Mazzini, E.N. XXXIII, 41. It was during this period that there appeared in the *Osservatore di Ginevra* a celebrated article purporting to be Mazzini's directions to his agents. Spada and other Papal writers claim that it was written a year earlier, and that it proves Mazzini to have been the instigator of all the agitation against Pius from the very start. Gori believes the document to be genuine but written in 1847: I see however that it does not appear in the Edizione Nazionale of Mazzini's works. Yet it was evidently considered genuine by Minghetti for he gave (*Memorie*, I, p. 225) an analysis of it as representing Mazzini's principles.

[6] The Civic Guard, one must remember, had been won by agitation. Now neither Mazzini nor Guerrazzi had believed that agitation would ever win so valuable a concession. In this respect d'Azeglio and the Moderates were shrewder than the leaders of revolution.

PARMA AND MODENA

In Parma we have already described how, on June 16th, the crowd celebrating the anniversary of Pius' accession had been attacked by police and soldiers.[7] On December 17th, when Marie Louise died, she was succeeded by Carlo Ludovico, Duke of Lucca, who had lately found it wisest to resign Lucca to Tuscany, and was now an uncompromising reactionary; so thenceforth Parma was occupied by Austrian soldiers. In vain the Liberals drew up a petition asking for various reforms, for the Civic Guard, and for the entry of Parma into the Customs Union.[8] These demands were fruitless; Parma had fallen to Metternich.

The story of Modena is somewhat similar. Francis IV had been a strong Conservative; and when he died (January 1846) there were some hopes among the Liberals that his son Francis V would be less narrow-minded. The new duke, however, very soon proved himself to be more reactionary than his father. He greeted Pius' movements with undisguised indignation. "Many were the imprecations", says Gori, "against this intruding Pope, and the Duke Francesco distinguished himself above all others by the intemperance of his language." Nevertheless a Liberal party existed in Modena; and thousands of the peasants were wearing medals of Pius IX. But the duke had no fear of Liberalism, because he was protected, as he said himself, not only by his own

[7] Ranalli, *Le Istorie italiane*, p. 112. Bianchi, *I Ducati estensi*, says the Parmigiani hoped for better things of Carlo Ludovico (p. 203).

[8] The customs-union published November 3rd between Rome, Tuscany and Piedmont. Anent the occupation of Parma by hussars the following is a note sent by the Austrian Baron Neumann to Comm. Martini, Tuscan representative in Turin. "Quand aux hussards sur la présence desquels vous ne croyez pas devoir me féliciter, je vous dirai qu'elle est due à la démonstration inconvenante qu'il y a eue [sic] il y a 15 jours au moment de votre départ et de celui de Monsignor Corboli à la Porta di Bologna; un d'eux a crié Viva Mons. Corboli, l' indipendenza d' Italia, la lega dogànale [customs union], cris qui avaient été répétés à Reggio peu de jours après." Florence Arch. Cart. 2485.

army, but by "300,000 men behind the River Po".[9] Before
the end of the year, he and Metternich had signed a treaty
whereby his state was to be garrisoned by Austrian soldiers
and virtually to become an outpost of the Empire. When the
soldiers first appeared there was "the greatest consternation",
and the military entry into Reggio was met by a hostile crowd
which started singing Pius' hymn. But resistance was hopeless: Modena like Parma had fallen to Metternich.[10]

Metternich was thus consolidating his military position in
Ferrara, Parma, Modena and presently on the borders of
Tuscany: but meanwhile the Revolution was gaining ground
within his own dominions, and, there, it was far harder to
meet. The heart of the Austrian Empire was no longer sound.
Within the Conferenz at Vienna there were stormy discussions: Kolowrat and the civil party were not satisfied with
Metternich and his military policy. People realised that it
could not go on for ever. The day was not far distant when
the Princess Melanie would complain that her husband could
no longer get a journalist of any standing to write for him.

LUCCA

The first state, after Rome, to win the Civic Guard was the
small Duchy of Lucca, with its population of 123,000 under
a Bourbon duke, Carlo Ludovico (1824–1847). Of this duke
it was remembered that in his youth the Liberals had had
some hopes of him—in 1832 he had turned Protestant; in
1833 he had granted an amnesty to the prisoners of 1831; but
in 1842 he abjured his Protestantism, and became again a
strong Catholic. From that date his most favoured adviser
was an Englishman called Thomas Ward.

Ward was a Yorkshireman who had come into Italy with
the Graf von Loewemberg, employed in some connection with
horses. About Ward the accounts are very contradictory. It

[9] *London Corr.* I, 49; 251, 252; 287.
[10] Florence Arch. Carteggio col Min. A.E. Martini's despatch,
December 26th, 1847.

is said that he was a groom or a jockey, but the stories are more suggestive of a bookmaker or a trainer. Some writers tell us that his friendship with the duke dated from a race meeting at Florence, "because he made the Duke win"(!)[11] —which leaves the matter uncertain. "Of shrewd mind, engaging manners, with a noisy and flattering voice", he was said also to help the duke in his love affairs. Some writers allege that he was dishonest, but, on the other hand, we have an unexpected testimony in his favour from Professor Montanelli who says that personally he liked him "for his good sense, his politeness and his honourable behaviour": and certainly—groom or not—within five or six years he was created a baron.

The reforms of Pius IX were far from palatable to the Bourbon Carlo Ludovico. On July 18th the people claimed the Civic Guard. On July 21st he issued a motu-proprio to say that he would never allow the Civica; but he was not on safe ground. His family had suppressed the constitution of 1805, guaranteed by the Congress of Vienna, and several of his subjects began clamouring for it. On August 20th the duke retorted by imprisoning seven young citizens. Then there was an outbreak. On September 1st the people rose and marched out to the Duke's country-house; and from there he granted the Civica, and then took his family off to Massa.[12]

To his credit, be it said, he refused to call in the Austrians. On September 3rd he returned and was received with extravagant joy: but on the 15th, in order to avoid further con-

[11] Tivaroni, *Domin. Austr.* II, 99. Bianchi, v, 40, says that Ward was completely dishonest; that he made money out of the Lucchese finances, that he acted as an Austrian spy until it paid him better to do otherwise. Bianchi's account is little else but a tirade against the Duke of Lucca and all his following: he gives as his authority Carrega, the Sardinian Chargé d'Affaires in Florence. To find out the truth for certain would probably be very difficult now.

[12] *London Corr.* I, 117, Hamilton to Palmerston; *v.* p. 123 for Metternich's account; and p. 146.

cessions, he appointed a Council of Regency and again departed.

He was in a difficult position. Without Lucca he had not much to live on until the death of the Duchess of Parma (Napoleon's widow). He was her heir duly named and guaranteed by the Great Powers; but she was only fifty-five years of age. At this point the Yorkshire hard-headedness came to his assistance. By the advice of Baron Ward (who went to Vienna to negotiate the matter with Metternich) he sold his interest in Lucca to the Tuscan government for nine thousand francesconi[13] per month. This was merely anticipating matters because, by the Treaties of 1815 and 1817, his state of Lucca was to pass to Tuscany as soon as he became Duke of Parma. Owing to this new bargain it passed at once (October 5th, 1847) amid great Florentine rejoicings; and Ward must have felt that he had solved the problem of his master's leading a pleasant life and keeping his ducal title without possessing a state.[14] But, as matters turned out, the Duchess of Parma died on December 17th—only two months later.

[13] *London Corr.* I, 171, gives the text of the treaty; *v.* also p. 273. There was also a sum of 500,000 francs per annum, which the Duke drew annually out of his Duchy of Lucca, assigned to him by the Congress of Vienna. This sum Tuscany agreed to pay him as well as the 9000 francesconi: but both payments were to cease when he became Duke of Parma.

[14] Bianchi says that Ward's motive was to prevent his own peculations being discovered; that he thought it safest to retire with his master before the arrival of the Tuscan authorities. Surely these motives seem rather "far-fetched". Bianchi also says that Ward told the Austrian Minister in Florence nothing about this bargain until six days after the event; that, having previously been an Austrian spy, he was now changing over to the more popular side. But this hardly chimes in with the fact that it was Ward who went to Vienna to arrange about the bargain before it was signed. On the other hand Cantù speaks well of him: "ability he possessed most certainly, and he did good to the country... but his rapid rise offended the *amour propre*, one might say the national pride, of the Lucchesi." *V.* Cantù, *Cronistoria*, II, p. 735.

From that date Carlo Ludovico went off to be Duke of Parma, where he proved himself to be a strong Conservative; he lost no time in calling in the Austrians.

This tiny state of Lucca was the first to disappear and, indirectly, this was due to Pius' movement. The reason why we have given it so much space is because it gave rise to the Fivizzano episode which, for several weeks, seemed likely to set all Italy ablaze.[15]

The Fivizzano question arose as follows: under the settlement of 1815, when the Duke of Lucca handed over Lucca to Tuscany, Tuscany was bound by treaty to hand over the small district of Fivizzano to Modena; and also to give Pontremoli and other Tuscan parts of the Lunigiana to the Duke of Lucca—to go with him and eventually to become part of Parma.

Now these three districts—Fivizzano, Pontremoli and the rest of the Tuscan Lunigiana—were Tuscan territories, and they declined to be handed over like sheep; they refused to go either to Modena or Parma whose dukes were both pro-Austrian. They wanted to remain Tuscan. This difficulty had never been thought of in 1815, nor even in 1844 when the revising treaty was signed.

They protested; the peasants of Fivizzano began to arm themselves; and even sensible men, such as Massimo d'Azeglio, thought that this might be a beginning of resistance. The Tuscan archduke offered a money settlement. But on October 2nd the Duke of Modena's troops occupied the chief places of vantage, and on November 7th, at Fivizzano, the Modenese soldiers fired on the crowd, killing one man and wounding four others. In Tuscany this aroused the deepest sympathy for their fellow subjects. Florence was in tumult, and so was Leghorn: but the government could do nothing. It was bound by its own treaties.

[15] The Fivizzano question is extremely complicated; and, as it concerned only a few people and, in the end, produced no results, it has been relegated to the Appendix, where it can be fully described.

Eventually the matter was referred to Charles Albert and Pius IX for arbitration, and they decided in favour of the Duke of Modena. According to the treaties no other decision was possible.

TUSCANY

In chapter VII we left Tuscany on May 31st, 1847, when it had just won the promise of a reformed Consulta (nominated assembly); during the second half of 1847 it was destined to be busy—like most of the other states—in establishing the Consulta and also in securing an armed Civic Guard so as to prevent any revocation of the rights won, and also to facilitate a further advance: and after the Ferrara episode, this Tuscan agitation for internal reforms was reinforced by an angry national demand for independence.

Following at once on the new press law several newspapers had been founded: at Leghorn the *Corriere Livornese*; in Florence the *Alba* (Mazzinian), and the *Patria* (Moderate Constitutionalist); in Pisa *L' Italia* (enthusiastic for Pius IX; Montanelli's paper). This press movement of course encouraged the popular advance.

The Consulta, the first of the two popular objectives, was soon secured. Already there existed an old institution of that name; and on May 3rd a promise had been given of bringing it up to date. To get this promise fulfilled took several demonstrations, but the most serious outbreak of unrest was on the anniversary of Pius' accession, June 16th, 1847. The government had foreseen this, and on June 14th had forbidden assemblages and threatened to stop them by force. But at Leghorn (Livorno)[16] there was a *Te Deum* followed by a tumult and attack on the Governor's house. The government did nothing, and their weakness encouraged fresh outbreaks.[17] The population of Leghorn contained an element of rough,

[16] Livorno = Leghorn, cf. Edward Hutton, *Florence and the Cities of Northern Tuscany*, p. 129, note. "Livorno, in the barbarian dialect of the Genovesi, Ligorno; and hence our word Leghorn."

[17] Sir G. Hamilton, *London Corr.* I, 51 and 110.

seafaring, foreign type and there were more fights there than in any other town in Tuscany. Indeed *Il mondo va da sè* had for years been a motto of the Tuscan government, and now their individual towns were beginning to put it into practice.[18] On August 24th, after a great demonstration in Florence, the reform of the existing Consulta, already promised on May 31st, was definitely granted by motu-proprio. It was to have wide consultative powers—even that of discussing the question of the longed-for Civica—but by that time the people did not care about it. This Consulta was full of Conservatives, and government officials, and in any case by now, they wanted representation.[19]

The Civica was harder to win. The kindly Leopold II— who was by birth an Austrian archduke but by predilection an Italian prince of three generations standing—had always lived between two fires. Early in August, as already described, he had received a letter from Metternich forbidding him to grant the Civica on pain of having his state occupied by Austrian troops.[20] On the other hand the Tuscans, especially the people of Leghorn, kept demanding it with increasing exasperation. What a crucial moment was this for Tuscany, situated as she was in full view of Austria! And critical perhaps even for Italy. But, says Zobi, the Liberals kept on pointing out that "now the Pope has granted it and it has given splendid proof of its usefulness in Rome" (at the time of the Congiura),[21] and before long on September 1st the Duke of Lucca granted it in his small state. To clinch the matter, on September 3rd a deputation waited on Cempini the Tuscan minister, and threatened a rising in Leghorn. In that lively town there were now some firebrands of every type, such as Guerrazzi, La Cecilia and Niccolo Fabrizi; and they had planned a rising. Felice Orsini and

[18] *London Corr.* I, 109, 110; *v.* Zobi, v, 106.
[19] Tivaroni, p. 49; Gori, p. 255.
[20] Cf. *London Corr.* I, 157.
[21] Zobi, v, 98.

Ribotti were also to hand, with Montanelli. These were some of the most fearless physical-force men in Italy.

On September 4th the Civica was granted.[22]

At this point we reach the beginning of the next stage of Tuscan agitation which eventually led to a constitution (February 17th, 1848). The people were now captains of the situation, and hilariously triumphant. They organised a campaign of federal banquets (Montanelli); at Lucca, Pisa and Leghorn tricolours were flown, and on September 12th, at an immense reception by the grand-duke, there was a crowd "estimated at 70,000 and 24,000 volunteers". Some 6000 Civic Guards marched past the Pitti Palace under a tricolour banner: and the grand-duke replied by waving a tricolour.[23] That was a gesture of Italian nationalism; but Tuscany was federalist not Mazzinian, and had no desire to be fused.

In September Don Neri Corsini (Junior), Governor of Leghorn, sent in a report warning the grand-duke of the danger of revolution and advising him to grant a Constitution.[24] Certainly that would have been a more normal way of expressing his assent than by waving banners; but it was impossible, because Austria would have intervened. Consequently the grand-duke merely changed some of his ministers; and the Marchese Cosimo Ridolfi became his chief adviser. Ridolfi at once sought the support of the more advanced

[22] Zobi, *ibid.* p. 110; Gori, pp. 256–8, and 264–74; and other historians. For the constitution of the Civic Guard, *v. London Corr.* 1, 145.

[23] So says Tivaroni: but Sir George Hamilton says that as a tricolour passed him, he and his son pointed to and touched the Tuscan flag apparently to denote that it would be with the tricolour. *London Corr.* 1, 135. At this point Cempini resigned his position as chief adviser and was succeeded by Ridolfi; but Cempini remained in the government. *V.* Zobi, v, 128. Gori, p. 267, speaks of 50,000 people.

[24] Baldasseroni, pp. 239–40, says the Grand Duke consulted Gino Capponi as to setting up a Constitution. Capponi replied that Pius IX could not possibly do so and it would be the greatest mistake to force his hand: that all the Princes of Italy should stand together.

Liberals; Montanelli's price was three-fold—arm the country, enfranchise the communes, and take diplomatic steps to join the Italian league.[25] Good advice; but simultaneously Metternich was insinuating threats; so Ridolfi only carried through a measure of reform.

The result was discontent everywhere. Lawless Leghorn was dragging all the rest of Tuscany after it. On September 22nd the extremists there brought off a "Congiura" similar to that of July 16th in Rome; and Corsini was obliged to give arms to the Civica in order to preserve any sort of order. On October 25th, riots in Florence; and the year closed amid general fury over the Fivizzano question.[26]

In Tuscany now it was a case of *Il popolo va da sè*. The agitation was working up to the moment when the constitution would be granted. The existing conditions could not continue long.

There is a large party here becoming daily more disgusted with the present state of things; amongst these are the principal merchants and tradespeople of the City of Florence, as well as the nobility, and who would much more readily see the Austrians arrive here than that there should be a continuation of the present state of anarchy. The streets are patrolled at night by a Liberal junta, and all is kept quiet by them for the present.[27]

LOMBARDO-VENETIA

We left the Austrian-ruled provinces Lombardo-Venetia at the moment (January 14th, 1847) of the great funeral mass in Milan for Count Confalonieri. Already they had been touched by the new movement. In 1847 the peasants began to stir, says Cesare Correnti, and that was a wonderfully good sign.[28] During the next six months undoubtedly some progress was made; intellectuals published anti-Austrian

---

[25] Baldasseroni, p. 243. Tivaroni, *Domin. Austr.* II, 52; Gori, p. 273.
[26] The Fivizzano question is fully described in the Appendix A.
[27] Sir George Hamilton to Palmerston, *London Corr.* I, 146.
[28] C. Correnti, *Scritti scelti*, II, 6 and 10.

works at Capolago and society people boycotted the Austrian officers.[29]   Here, too, we must admire the courage of Cesare Correnti; though himself a government official he did excellent service to the cause by publishing a work called *l'Austria e l'Italia*, an anonymous but excellent little book from Capolago.   But it was the Ferrara episode on July 17th which was the chief cause of the great and tumultuous advance towards nationalism during the latter half of 1847. At the same time thousands of medals of Pius IX were distributed in the state, especially among the peasants.   The townspeople started various special emblems of their own. Presently several "unfortunate episodes" came to aggravate the situation.

In November 1846 Archbishop Gaisruck had died.   There had been no bitter feeling about him.   He was a good man; but he was an Austrian and the people wanted an Italian.   So on the arrival (September 4th, 1847) of the new archbishop called Romilli, who was a native of Bergamo, a great and openly nationalist demonstration was organised by the municipal authorities in honour of their Italian bishop sent to them by their patriot Pope; the streets were resplendent with the Papal colours and the tricolour, and enthusiastic crowds went to meet him.   On the next feast day, September 8th, there were fresh rejoicings for him, accompanied in the evening by shouts of "Viva Pio Nono", and "Viva l' Italia!" Arrests began; but the cries continued.   Thereupon the police, already much provoked, attacked the demonstrators with drawn swords.   In the melée many were hurt; but the people answered back with sticks and stones, and sang Rossini's

[29] Dawkins to Palmerston, June 27th, 1847, *London Corr*. 1, 59: "An Austrian is hardly ever seen at the house of a Milanese and vice versa. . . . Notwithstanding this feeling of dislike I do not think any outbreak is to be apprehended at present." *V*. also *Pensieri sull' Italia* by Un anonimo Lombardo, p. 236: "The Austrian soldier returns hatred for hatred and knows how to revenge himself at the first opportunity. . . this reciprocal hatred increases every day; so we may hope that, soon or late, we shall see its results."

chorus to Pius; and order was not restored until the following day. On the night of the 10th there was more disturbance, and the soldiers on duty were using both bayonets and swords. The total number of casualties amounted to one killed and nine in hospital; and it is said that there were about fifty others hurt.[30]

This collision of September 8th created irreconcilable hatred; and events marched rapidly.

Before the end of September there took place the seventh Scientific Congress, held in Venice with profound patriotic enthusiasm.

On October 8th at Varese there was a demonstration and banquet in honour of Pius. All the fashionable people of Milan were staying there for the season, and Pius' bust was carried in procession together with the national colours.

There was no longer the slightest prospect of accommodation with Austria; during August Metternich sent Count Ficquelmont to Milan as a kind of imperial adviser to the viceroy, and also to Radetzky. Whatever may have been Ficquelmont's abilities,[31] he did not arrive until too late—in

[30] Casati, C., *Nuove rivelazioni sui fatti di Milano*, 1, 87 ff. and 122 ff., gives the Municipality's protest and correspondence. The governor and chief of police said that the police had been told to be patient, but that there had been great provocation. *V*. also Gualterio (1862 edit.), v, 250, and Gori, p. 281. Helfert, *Geschichte der Oesterreichischen Revolution*, 1, 104, says that the police only used the flat of their swords and that the death was due to a man being trodden on by the crowd. *V. Archivio Triennale* (Capolago, 1850), Docts. 27–32; *London Corr*. 1, 134, Dawkins to Palmerston, September 11th, 1847; 137, Dawkins to Palmerston, September 14th, 1847. Of course there are many accounts of these Milanese demonstrations against Austria. Undoubtedly they were encouraged by the Municipality.

[31] Helfert, *Geschichte*, 1, 120. On p. 203 he speaks of Ficquelmont's ability as a soldier and quotes a letter of Nugent to Count Hühn: "I know him well; and, although of late years he has been better known as a diplomat, I still think that the military is his real sphere. And this was also Wellington's opinion; for he told me in Spain that Ficquelmont was one of the first officers in Europe."

October. He found himself ostracised. Nationalism was sweeping all classes. In Venice we are approaching the period of Manin, and in Milan we are nearing the Five Days. The Milanese were in a state of suppressed rebellion. The following short description of their condition strikes one as being extraordinarily true to nature.

Ficquelmont, an able supporter of the Austrian schemes in Italy, was in a state of consternation at his inability to deal with the Milanese. This unfortunate Count was heard to exclaim: "There is a police here stronger than ours." This great weapon of Torresani had snapped at the first serious test: the very spy system itself was powerless and spied upon. The police went about searching for a secret committee—and indeed most of the Milanese believed in the existence of such a committee. But it was the intimate relations between Liberals of all classes from the patrician to the popolano, and the banding together of all political groups which constituted, so to speak, a web including the whole of the city, and formed the most terrible of all known conspiracies, namely that of a whole people. After the events of September, a war of active and implacable hostilities had been declared between the Milanese and the Austrians.[32]

Gori then describes how in October the unfortunate viceroy retired to his villa at Pizzo on the Lake of Como, but only to find himself pursued by agitators; in the evenings they came out in boats to sing Pius' hymn:

on the walls, on the clay floors, on the dust of the road, on the quays for the boats, even on the bark of the trees was written Viva Pio IX; the whole of the big wall of the Villa del Pizzo was covered with it, with *Morte alli* [sic] *Austriaci* and similar inscriptions.[33]

In November the Archbishop of Milan, and the Cardinal Patriarch of Venice, and other bishops exhorted the parish clergy to condemn from the pulpit those who misused the Pope's name. Some obeyed, but the bulk of the parish

---

[32] Gori, p. 358. *V.* also Dr Carlo Casati, I, 164–9; Cattaneo, *L'Insurrection de Milan*, pp. 28–9; *London Corr.* I, 275–6, Dawkins to Palmerston.

[33] Confirmed by Dr Carlo Casati, I, 150.

priests took an independent line. They stood for their own people, because they believed that the dignitaries of the Church were overawed by Austria.

Finally during the last two months of 1847 we notice that the resistance becomes more systematised. Both rich and poor settle down to oust the Austrians, each in their own way. The educated people begin to plan a regular constitutional agitation for self-government, while the poor people supply the more violent elements without which agitation is useless. Anonymous writers begin to pester the central Congregazioni (assemblies) with letters calling on them to do something. On December 9th, 1847, a lawyer named Nazzari, member for Bergamo on the Central Congregazione of Lombardy, arose and proposed that that Assembly should name a Commission[34] consisting of nine members, one for each Lombard province, to examine and report on the existing conditions and discontent. "He seemed a Mirabeau." This was the first open protest for thirty years, and it would certainly go to the Emperor. But it was a perfectly legal suggestion, and the Congregazione received permission to deal with it.

Following on this, Nazzari and his colleagues drew up a petition[35] demanding fundamental reforms—notably a separate

[34] Tivaroni, I, 411; Correnti, *ibid.* p. 11 (Tivaroni says it was the 8th). Nazzari's proposal is given in full in *Carte segrete*, III, 131, and also in *Archivio Triennale*, Doct. 102.

[35] Gori, p. 364, gives its headings as follows: it asked for wider powers for the Congregazione; reform of education and criminal law; restriction of the authority of the police; a less severe censure; reduction of certain taxes; customs reforms; abolition of farming and taxes; revision of stamp law; lowering price of salt; publication of the condition of the Lombardo-Venetian state pawn-shop and restoration to its former conditions; shortening of the period of conscription (eight years); Lombardo-Venetians to be eligible for posts in the Aulic offices (Vienna), and those in their own country to be reserved for them. Last, and most important of all, a political

political existence for Lombardo-Venetia; and—a sign of the times—over 3000 people left their visiting cards on him.

In the same month a pamphlet appeared drawing up a regular list of grievances; the severity of the imposts; abuses of the courts and of the police; all legislative and administrative direction being concentrated in Viennese bureaux; the press censorship; the price of salt; various other complaints, especially the conscription of all their young men for so long a period as eight years. This pamphlet ended up with a call for autonomy.[36]

In this same month, December, Cesare Correnti published the *Nipote del Vesta Verde* which is still well remembered. It was nominally an almanack—named after the old Vesta Verde almanack—but in reality it was full of political allusions and sentiments.

On December 21st the Provincial Congregazione of Milan sent a special address to the Central Congregazione. Virtually it demanded a measure of Devolution. It claimed that the Aulic Dicasts (bureaucrats in Vienna), who were appointed for Italian affairs, should henceforward be distinct from the others, or attached to the sovereign representation of the kingdom (Lombardo-Venetia), which was to be held by the viceroy, with the help of Lombardo-Venetian subjects and no others. Various reforms were demanded, similar to those in the pamphlet.

On December 30th, 1847[37] the Provincial Congregazione of Pavia sent up a long detailed list of grievances ending with a demand for a central administration, on the spot, for Lombardo-Venetia.

So much for agitation by the educated classes: it seems

and individual existence for the Lombardo-Venetian Kingdom. Nazzari sent a copy to Manin and Manin to Tommaseo. *V.* Tommaseo, *Capponi Carteggio*, II, 601, note.

[36] For all this page *v. Archivio Triennale*, I, 141; Tivaroni, *Domin. Austr.* I, 412; Helfert, *Geschichte*, I, 117.

[37] Tivaroni, *Domin. Austr.* I, 412.

astonishing that they had not started earlier on this line of resistance.

In the streets this constitutional agitation was being supported by the more violent methods of the poorer classes. Every sort of hostile demonstration was being carried out— sometimes even absurdities on the spur of the moment. The walls were covered with seditious inscriptions "Viva Pio Nono", "Viva l' Italia!" "Morte ai Tedeschi!" The police were christened "pollin", turkeys, and were openly gobbled at while on their beat. Calabrian hats were fashionable because they recalled the Calabrian rising and—more serious—the organisers had borrowed an idea from the "Boston tea-party" and were about to cut off supplies by boycotting the game of Lotto which brought in eight million lire a year, and tobacco which brought in five millions.[38] The anti-smoking campaign however was not to start until January 1st, 1848.

In Venetia [39] the population was less quickly inflammable than the Lombards,[40] perhaps because the rich people gave less help,[41] but nevertheless from about 1840, off and on, there had been contentions over the railway question, during which Manin had come into prominence as a leader of the patriotic party who wanted to join Milan to Venice by the shortest railway possible.

In 1844 there came the tragedy of the Bandiera brothers, which, however, says Mr Trevelyan, "affected Italy and Europe more than Venice herself".[42]

[38] Dr Carlo Casati, p. 149; Ottolini, p. 26; v. also Gori.

[39] This Venetian agitation has already been described in English, and of course far more perfectly than can be attempted here, by Mr G. M. Trevelyan; v. *Manin and the Venetian Revolution of 1848*.

[40] Ficquelmont's opinion and that of various Italian writers: cf. also Consul-General Dawkins to Palmerston, December 3rd, 1847.

[41] *Ruggiero Bonghi*, p. 205.

[42] *V.* Trevelyan, *Manin*, p. 50. There have been so many descriptions of the Bandiera episode that it seems unnecessary to give one here. Mr Trevelyan gives two new points, namely that the brothers were influenced by the memory of their father's action in 1831, and that their destruction was not due to information supplied by the British government, as had hitherto been believed.

In June 1847 the Moderate movement was at its height and Manin was again to the fore, assisted by his friend Tommaseo, a well-known literary man. Manin's campaign was to prove that the Austrians had never observed the constitution which they had granted to Lombardo-Venetia in 1815.

On September 13th, 1847, came the Scientific Congress at Venice, perhaps the greatest of the series, an assemblage of 860 effective members and many supporters: "As it went on, it seemed gradually to inject life into that city", says the Milanese historian Cesare Cantù, who was one of the speakers. At first Prince Canino—the original founder of the Scientific Congresses—presented himself in the uniform of a private in the Roman Civic Guard to make a speech on zoology, and began a harangue about Pius IX; in politics Canino was "a brawler"—says Helfert; but, after he and Masi had been expelled from Lombardo-Venetia, the Congress took up the theme with more good sense. Cantù, especially, made the speech of his life on the railways question which had been handed on to him from the Congress of 1846. He began with references to Charles Albert and to Pius IX, the reconciler; he spoke of the Alps as "a barrier created for us by Nature—but created in vain"; and dealt with the railways as a means of uniting all Italians like brothers: every word of his speech was national and not provincial.[43]

Nazzari's protest of December 9th aroused emulation, and things began to stir in Venetia. One fine morning there appeared on the Vice-regal palace a notice: "This palace is to let for the year 1848. Venice 20th December 1847".

On December 21st Manin presented to the Central Congregazione (of which he was not a member) his Istanza or petition, in which he called on them to break the silence that they had kept for thirty-two years; and to let the government

---

[43] This account is taken from the Austrian secret reports on the Congress in Carte segrete, III, 347–60; from Cantù, Cronistoria, II, 764; Helfert, Geschichte, I, 104–7; Trevelyan, Manin, p. 56; and, of course, the general histories.

know that the people of Lombardo-Venetia are neither happy nor satisfied.[44]

On December 28th a provincial deputy for the city of Venice, bearing the ancient and noble name of Morosini, wrote formally to the Central Congregazione of Venice complaining that "the government was not Italian and the Viceroy was subject to the Aulic dicasts in Vienna, who are distant and can only with difficulty form a judgment on our conditions."[45]

In fact there was a campaign of petitions; but perhaps the most striking episode was that of Niccolo Tommaseo, a student, by birth a Dalmatian, who on December 30th was to read a paper to the Ateneo (the Athenæum of Venice) on the state of Italian literature and Austrian press censorship. He was a friend of Gino Capponi, of Manin, and other Liberals, but even so it came as a surprise to hear this quiet and rather ironical man of books read a speech full of patriotic fire:[46] in it he said that the Austrian censorship no longer commanded respect, and he called on the Imperial government to establish a local censorship for appeal cases. His speech was considered —says Sandonà—a great act of courage: indeed Tommaseo himself said "it meant giving up my beloved solitude". It ended with the words:

I have pledged myself [to other Italians] that the Venetians preserve the memory of their past...and already, thank God, my promises are coming true; for the conscience of nations may be asleep for years and years; but as long as they are not dispersed off the face of the earth it will never die.

He obtained at least 200 signatures on the spot and more later on.

[44] *Carte segrete*, III, 130, gives the document. Cantù, *Cronistoria*, II, 779; Helfert, *Geschichte*, I, 117; Trevelyan, *Manin*, p. 61; Tivaroni, *Domin. Austr.* I, 514, and other general historians.

[45] *Carte segrete*, III, 132; Cantù, *Cronistoria*, II, p. 780; Helfert, *ibid.* p. 117.

[46] *Carte segrete*, III, 135–48; Sandonà, *Il preludio*, etc. (*Rivista d'Italia*, January and February, 1927); Helfert, *ibid.*, p. 117; Trevelyan, *Manin*, p. 63.

Our survey ends with the year 1847: but we may add that only five days later, on January 5th, 1848, Manin read to the Central Congregazione his famous list of national demands.

It will be seen that during these two[47] years of agitation the Progressives in every state of Italy had achieved enormous gains in numbers, in political status and in boldness of conception; they were on the verge of turning agitation into action. They would no longer be satisfied without representative government, and in Lombardo-Venetia they would no longer be satisfied with Austrian bureaucracy. What an immense difference between January 1st, 1846, and January 1st, 1848!

[47] We may count the agitation as having been founded on the scheme preached by Gioberti in 1843: but probably Massimo d'Azeglio (March 1846) was the man who, more than any other, popularised the idea of working by means of agitation—on the lines of O'Connell; and finally, of course, the Liberalism of Pius IX (June 1846) was the making of the movement. Apparently it is not generally remembered that in September 1847, Tommaseo had had rather a touching interview with Pius, during which the latter had virtually laid upon him the task of writing this speech. "He urged me to write", says Tommaseo, "he urged me to speak words of moderation, and I replied 'That is my natural temperament and my duty'." *V.* Tommaseo-Capponi *Carteggio*, II, 605, and note; and also p. 532.

Chapter XVII

PIEDMONT AFTER THE FERRARA EPISODE

Thus the Ferrara episode had made war almost inevitable; and the fact that Pius was in the forefront of the resistance had produced a deep impression on Charles Albert.[1] To his dynastic and Piedmontese ambitions was now added his pride in being the defender of the Holy Church and in feeling that he and Pius, the only[2] two national sovereigns, might stand side by side against the foreigner. Most of his subjects, too, were thoroughly aroused; they were in that angry state of mind which often precedes a war. This episode of Ferrara had stimulated Piedmontese activities not only in Turin but also in Rome, Florence, Milan and elsewhere.

In Rome Massimo d'Azeglio had actually taken service under Pius, and had gone as a Papal agent to Ancona and Pesaro to organise popular resistance in case of an Austrian invasion. During his stay of about a month in those provinces he interviewed scores of important people and formulated many schemes—among others he sent out a definite plan of defence for the citizens of Ferrara.[3] Throughout this period, of course, he was in constant communication with Pantaleoni in Rome, and with Balbo in Turin. In September his Papal appointment came to an end, but instead of returning to Rome he passed on to Florence—then full of Liberals—to

[1] Bersezio says: "To his mystic character this seemed a promise of divine help." Bersezio, II, 401.

[2] *London Corr.* I, 99.

[3] Aurelio Saffi, *Arch. Trienn.* I, 52 (Mazzinian), was very scornful about this. He said d'Azeglio urged them to resist like Saragossa but no longer spoke of help from Piedmont; Saffi adds that Edward Fabbri was furious and said that the Piedmontese wanted to push others into the front of the battle and reap the profit themselves.

Lucca, and finally to Turin; in this way he was able to keep in touch with Liberalism everywhere. Meanwhile, in September, Charles Albert's nominee, Colonel (now General) Giovanni Durando had arrived in Rome to help the Papal authorities with military advice.

Not only was Charles Albert himself greatly stirred, but so also were Balbo, Predari and all the Liberal circle in Turin. It was on September 2nd that the king once more made known his true sentiment—this time in an open letter to Count Castagnetto, the now celebrated "Prince Schamyl" letter which was read to the Associazione Agraria during its annual meeting (September 1847) at Casale, and sent a thrill all over Italy.

Tell them that if God ever vouchsafes us a war of independence, I alone shall be in command of our army, and I am determined then to do for the Guelf cause what Schamyl is doing against the immense Russian Empire.

And as a postscript he added:

It seems that at Rome they have their spiritual arms in reserve. Let us hope so. What a magnificent day it will be when we can raise the cry of national independence.[4]

Turin. September 2nd, 1847.

That had always been his dream; a national war in which all Italy should take part under his leadership, and Pius should excommunicate the enemy.[5]

In August he wrote to Pius offering, in case of Austrian

---

[4] This is the version given by Bianchi, *Stor. Doc.* v, 58.

[5] Shortly afterwards he said, in an official letter to the Marchese Doria: "The King is determined to defend the independence of the State against any foreign aggression but equally decided never to compromise himself with the Great Powers by pushing his arms outside the state without being attacked; there is no truth in the report that he intends to make war for the independence of other states, unless the High Pontiff raises the Cross and proclaims a religious war...." He adds that he refuses to grant either the Civic Guard or the freedom of the Press, because they merely lead to disorder.

invasion, to send a warship to Civita Vecchia, to bring him safely to Piedmont.[6]

On September 8th there was a great demonstration in Genoa; crowds cheering for Charles Albert, for Pius IX, for the Line and the Piedmontese army, for the Independence of Italy. Abercromby remarks on the fact that it was quite orderly: that the people of Italy are now beginning to understand that they should give their rulers moral support and encouragement, but not increase their difficulties by excesses.[7]

Massimo d'Azeglio, however, had no great confidence in all this enthusiasm or in its producing any definite results. On October 23rd he wrote:

I have found matters in a very bad state at Turin.... The King is always the same man...now up and now down.

Early in October, he continues, there had been a crisis and at last Charles Albert had dismissed both his rival ministers, Villamarina (October 8th) and Solaro della Margherita (October 11th) "and I fear very much that the discontent here will end in some trouble which will mix up all the rest of our affairs".

Massimo therefore proposed to try and influence Charles Albert just as he had tried to influence Pius: in Turin the Liberals had reduced patriotic wire-pulling to a fine art.

He is very sensitive to praise and still more so to blame. We have sung enough hymns to him. It is time to speak in a measured and dignified strain, but with inexorable severity. I have passed the same word out to France, England and Florence; I now pass it to you [Pantaleoni] and will pass it to Bologna. Busy yourself with it seriously for it is important and urgent.

Massimo eventually returned to Rome; but he travelled via Florence, and did not arrive until the middle of November.

Meanwhile matters had become very serious in Turin. Pius' cause was sweeping the town. He was the centre of admiration—so much so that his popularity aroused some

---

[6] *London Corr.* I, 99, Abercromby to Palmerston, August 25th, 1847.　　　　[7] *Ibid.* p. 131.

resentment among the Conservatives. The hymn of Pius IX was being sung in the streets: the women had taken to wearing ribbons of yellow and white, the Papal colours; and, for men, cravats "à la Mastai-Ferretti" were now the fashion, and little buttonholes made of yellow and white flowers.[8] Finally the authorities posted up a prohibition: "For eight hundred years Piedmont has borne very different colours from these: that anyone should dare to change them will never be tolerated!" And on October 1st, the king's birthday, a great crowd which was singing Pius' hymn was broken up by the police with fixed bayonets, swords and pistols. In view of Charles Albert's avowed sympathy with Pius, this violent action aroused great resentment: it is said to have been the work of the municipal authorities—all reactionaries who wanted to set the Liberals against Charles Albert.

It was during this period that the name of *Il Re Tentenna*, the wavering or vacillating king, was fixed upon Charles Albert. Among the numerous letters circulating from hand to hand all over Italy there was one which consisted of a poem written by a young man named Domenico Carbone. It was an uncommonly able satire directed at Charles Albert's long-protracted policy of alternate encouragement and discouragement of the hopes of the Liberals. It told the story of a certain king called Tentenna (the waverer) whose chief joy in life consisted in being rocked to-and-fro in a swing, by his two ministers: one of them would rock fast and the other slowly, but in neither case, of course, did the king make any advance. The refrain of each verse ran:

> Ciondola, dondola
>   Che cos' amena,
> Dondola ciondola
>   E l' altalena.
> Un po' piu celere
>   Meno...di piu...
> Ciondola, dondola
>   E su e giu.

[8] *London Corr.* I, 140; Predari, and others.

Its gist is more or less as follows:

> Swinging and rocking
>   How pleasant it seems;
> Rocking and swinging,
>   A motion of dreams.
> A little bit faster!
>   Slower...now more.
> Pleasantly upwards
>   And down as before.

The poem was handed to Charles Albert by the old Count Michele di Cavour (father of the great Cavour), a hard Conservative who hoped to set the king against the Liberals.[9] Several of its verses are scathing and, for a day or two, they reduced Charles Albert to a state of the deepest despondency. When a friend pointed out to him that the author was not a Piedmontese subject he merely answered: "Indeed I see that the Italians have not yet begun to know me." But it produced the very last result intended by old Count Cavour; it helped to convince Charles Albert that he must hasten to grant some

[9] Bersezio (II, 405) says that this poem was written by young Carbone when he returned home furious after being maltreated by the police during the demonstration on October 1st. The verse about Rome must have touched Charles Albert to the quick; it ran as follows: "Quoth Martino [Villamarina], 'Turn to Rome: the Austrian shows symptoms of death-agony; shatter his bit and shake off his burden from you and kick him back the way he came'. Quoth Biagio [Solaro della Margherita], 'Rome is a boaster: wars are not waged with holy water; stand fast by the German; against cannons you require other things besides big crosses'. And then spake the King, 'I will see whether I can manage this. Long live the Pope! And the German for ever!'" Verses III and IV are about popular liberties and the censorship. Verse IV about the censorship was especially strong. "Quoth Martino, 'The censors are the warders of whosoever can best castrate thought; but thought though mutilated by the scissors will re-cross the mountains and return entire'. Quoth Biagio, 'Have them sharpened, dear Tentenna, if you wish to reign. Find sharpeners of a better school, for instance followers of Loyola'. Then spake the King, 'Let them be sharpened so that the blade may either cut or not cut, as may be preferred'. Swinging and rocking, how pleasant it seems, etc., etc."

drastic reform or else he would not have Italy behind him on the day of battle.[10] Fortunately he had by him a scheme of reform in process of completion; otherwise of course he could not have produced one for months to come.

As already recorded, on October 8th and 11th he dismissed "his ambidextrous government", but even this drastic measure did not bring him peace. Popular discontent was not allayed. On October 19th Balbo addressed a memoir to Charles Albert, in which he said that Piedmont was no longer the leading Italian state either internally or in her external relations. "Pius IX and Leopold have thrown themselves resolutely upon the path of liberty, and have placed between themselves and Austria an abyss such as befits the princes who are truly Italian."

On October 21st and 22nd Pius' hymn was sung in the streets: on the 23rd, 24th and 25th processions passed by in silence; it seemed as if revolution were coming near.[11]

Finally on October 30th, 1847, Charles Albert was able to announce his list of reforms, of which the following are the chief headings.[12]

Exceptional jurisdictions were abolished: a new penal procedure introduced, including publicity of trial.

A *Cour de cassation* (appeal court) was created; and important reforms introduced elsewhere into the legal procedure.

Police reforms (extensive): transferred from military to civil authority; and powers defined.

Administrative reforms (important):

(*a*) The communal councils were to be elected by the people within certain fixed categories and to settle their own affairs.

[10] Balbo pointed this out to him (October 19th); so did Lord Minto. *V.* Appendix.

[11] At this point the Comte de Sonnaz breaks out: "Nous y voilà, nous y voilà. L'arbre planté à Rome par Pie IX étend ses rameaux de Naples à Turin. Toute l'Italie peut en cueillir." Costa de Beauregard, *Les Dernières Années de Charles Albert*, pp. 65, 66.

[12] For full list of them *v. London Corr.* I, 212 *et seq.*

(*b*) Provincial councils were set up to administer each province. The councillors were to be chosen by the king from lists sent to him by the communes: and from among syndics of communes.

The press censure was entirely reorganised.

The above is a very short summary of Charles Albert's concessions: he did not propose to grant a Consulta and still less a constitution: "It is just because I desire the liberation of Italy that I shall not grant a constitution; for great enterprises one requires soldiers not lawyers."

They were good and far-reaching reforms: true, he did not grant any central assembly, but (perhaps for that very reason) he was able to introduce the representative system, to a limited extent, into the communal councils. This was advancing a little further than Pius had gone or cared to go in his parishes: however small, this grant might perhaps be the beginning of representative institutions. And the erection of permanent deliberative provincial councils was also an important advance. Such concessions, of course, were far less dangerous for Charles Albert than for Pius, because Pius had to consider the safety of his Church.

These reforms were genuine; and they were taken to be the first great Liberal step in Piedmont. Consequently they were received with the greatest joy and gratitude. On November 3rd, when Charles Albert started for Genoa, he was given an ovation such as never before had been seen in that grave city of Turin.[13] The whole population was out to greet him. The crowds cheered him enthusiastically, but they remained perfectly orderly and respectful, because they knew that that was what he thought right. As Charles Albert rode between them —a rather wan figure—he bowed right and left in the most formal manner, but he had turned very pale and as he dis-

[13] Organised by the Marquis Roberto d'Azeglio who was capopopolo and thence was named "the Ciceruacchio of Turin". He was Massimo's elder brother and had done a great deal of work on the Liberal side.

mounted to enter his carriage the spectators thought that
there were tears in his eyes. For twenty-six long years, ever
since 1821, he had felt himself regarded as a traitor and hated
by his people; he had been the king with the stain upon his
name; but to-day he was their hero. And yet it was not
possible for him to carry out their wish: the moment had not
come; but he was prepared to put his life in the balance.

In Genoa the scenes were similar. This was a great hour in
her history. Now for the first time "Genova la superba"
voluntarily joined herself to Piedmont. There was immense
enthusiasm; as Charles Albert rode between the cheering
crowds a youth seized his horse's bridle and shouted: "King
Charles Albert, cross the Ticino and we will all follow you."
This youth was Nino Bixio,[14] afterwards the celebrated
Garibaldian leader. But what struck Abercromby about
Genoa, as also about Turin, was that the people remained
orderly and respectful. And evidently they knew that Abercromby was their friend for, on December 5th, when they
passed the British Embassy they raised loud cries of "Viva
Victoria! Viva l' Inghilterra! Viva Abercromby!"

Even outside Piedmont, in many of the Italian towns there
were rejoicings and especially in Florence. There the crowd
filed past the windows of the Sardinian minister cheering for
the king, for the reforms, and for the independence of Italy;
the Tuscan colours, the Papal and the national tricolour
saluted those of Piedmont, and the Gonfaloniere of Florence
presented an address conveying the city's congratulations on
the concessions made by Charles Albert to "that fraction of
Italians who live under his rule". On November 10th Charles
Albert sent a courteous reply.

The Austrians of course were displeased at Charles Albert's
concessions: he had granted some of the very points—notably
the censure—which they had been refusing for weeks to the
Lombards. The concessions, therefore, came as a proof to the
latter of what they might gain by joining Piedmont.[15]

[14] *London Corr.* I, 217, Abercromby, November 5th.
[15] M. Vidal has made this point very clear, *v.* p. 392.

Finally, we may add, just as the Austrian coup at Ferrara had converted Pius' name into a popular war-cry, so now it was beginning to place Charles Albert in similar difficulties. The crowds were claiming a constitution and war with Austria. Yet Piedmont was not nearly strong enough to face such a war; in normal times it would be insane for him to attack Austria. Would Charles Albert be able to hold out against his own people until the great opportunity should arrive?[16] They had named him the Re Tentenna, but undoubtedly he was a far better judge than they were as to the right moment for declaring war.[17] In 1848 that fact was proved by the event.

In this volume, however, we must leave him at the end of the year 1847 when, at length, he had taken his first great plunge into Liberal concessions.

[16] On his return journey from Genoa he actually drove through the crowds at headlong speed in order to escape from the ovation.

[17] This had long ago been pointed out by Balbo.

Chapter XVIII

NAPLES

I. RECAPITULATION 1815–1847

The Kingdom of Naples and Sicily (the "two Sicilies") contained no less than 8,000,000 souls—about 6,000,000 in Naples and 2,000,000 in Sicily[1]—so that numerically it stood first of all the Italian states and might well have played a leading part in the Risorgimento; but history shows us that up to the year 1848 its share in the pan-Italian development was almost negligible.

The fact was that the two peoples of Naples and Sicily lived in a state of mutual hatred, and consequently neutralised each other's importance. The great majority of these extreme southerners cared nothing about the rest of Italy or the Risorgimento.

The two chief aims of the Neapolitan Liberals were to obtain a constitution for Naples and at the same time to maintain the union with Sicily.[2]

On the other hand the two million Sicilians had only one great enthusiasm—the longing to free their beautiful island from the loathed Neapolitan.[3] They had but little interest in

[1] The population of Sicily in 1815 was only 1,681,983 (Tivaroni, *Domin. Austr.* III, 236), but this would have made it the fifth largest state in Italy.

[2] Gualterio (1862 edit.), v, 253, says that in the revolutionary committee of the City of Naples there were many Italian nationalists; but that the strength of the revolution lay in the provinces and that there the unvarying programme was merely the Neapolitan constitution of 1820 which had been sworn by the King and then overthrown by the Austrians.

[3] Paladino, *Il Quindici Maggio del* 1848 *in Napoli*, p. 35, says of the Sicilians: "The Sicilian revolution differed from that of Naples which was exclusively the work of a faction of the Borghesia [middle class]. It (the Sicilian revolution) was carried out by a whole people united in one *fascio*, without distinction of social classes; united by

Italian unity and that only on federal lines; so that neither of these movements produced causes or effects—except incidentally—towards the building of the new Italian nation.

In no other state had the Congress of Vienna left such a deadlock of unhappiness. From the first day onwards it was impossible for any king to satisfy his subjects in either country. He was in a cleft stick. In Naples, if he granted a Liberal constitution his country would be invaded by the Austrians. In Sicily, if he gave back to the Sicilians their beloved separate parliament—their constitution of 1812 enjoyed under the English—the Neapolitans would be furious. They were all unionists and would not agree to any form of Home Rule. Consequently the King was constantly involved in a repression of either the Neapolitan Liberals or the Sicilian nationalists.

The names of the rulers during this period are: Ferdinand I (1759–1825); Francis I (Francesco) (1825–30); Ferdinand II (1830–59).

The only incident between 1815 and 1847 worth recording in a general history of the Risorgimento-development, is the rebellion of 1820. In that year there broke out, suddenly, a rising organised mainly by the Carbonari. Their aim was to

their hatred of the government of Naples. Such was the character of that revolution and it proved a complete success, at all events at first. But the Sicilian separatist movement did not find grace with those who directed the Italian movement of 1848." Both Gioberti and Mazzini deplored it. "Now, if Gioberti and Mazzini had no sympathy with Sicilian separatism, it was natural that—in order to preserve the territorial integrity of the Kingdom, and out of respect for historical tradition and for strategic and commercial reasons which had always compelled the dominators of the south to keep their foot on the island—it was natural, I say that the government of King Ferdinand should be a jealous defender of the unity of the state." Anent this difference of sentiment *v.* almost any of the authorities on either Naples or Sicily, e.g. Nisco, Nitti, Amari, Chiaramonte, Guardione, Palmieri, La Masa, Crispi; as well as the general historians.

secure a Liberal constitution; and, led by a fairly able general, Guglielmo Pepe, they set up the Spanish constitution, the most democratic of all.[4]

Apparently people hoped that if it were once in being, the Austrians would accept the *fait accompli*. But in December 1820 their old king, who had sworn to the Constitution, was summoned to the Conference of Laibach, and Metternich made him clearly understand that the Powers of the Holy Alliance would not suffer any free constitutions in Italy. In February the Austrian troops marched southwards and, on March 7th, defeated Pepe's half-trained Neapolitans at Rieti; and that was an end of the rising.[5]

Its chief importance lay in the fact that, firstly, it proved convincingly to the Neapolitan Bourbons, to Charles Albert, and to every other princeling in Italy, that Metternich intended to fight rather than permit a constitution; and secondly in its being a part-cause of Santarosa's mutiny in Piedmont. Incidentally, too, it showed that the Neapolitans, though they might want a parliament for themselves, entirely refused to grant one to Sicily.

The history of Naples (as distinct from that of Sicily) up to 1847 is simply a story of constant small conspiracies and repressions: but in reality they do not concern the Risorgimento. Sometimes they are due more to social than to political causes—for there existed in Naples a land question and a certain amount of nomadic brigandage—but even the most political risings aimed only at a Neapolitan constitution. Thus when we review the long struggle against Austria, it is

[4] P. Colletta, *Storia del Reame di Napoli*, i, 265. Pepe's report is not of much use except for the fighting. Nisco, *Storia d'Italia*, ii, and all the general histories, Tivaroni, etc.

[5] The old king has been held up to immortal obloquy because he broke his sworn oath to the Spanish Constitution; and certainly all appearances are black against him: but the Neapolitan Liberals were hardly in a position to complain, because at this very moment their Parliament showed no compunction whatever in breaking its contract with the Sicilian rebels. *V*. p. 307.

only fair to remember that the Italians received virtually no help from Naples or Sicily.

Certainly, we cannot but feel sorry for those of the Neapolitan Liberals who were genuinely in earnest. Most of them were middle-class men who wanted a constitution. But they were comparatively few in number and had very little grip on the nation; and—if the truth be told—during their short period of office they seem to have proved themselves entirely below the level of the task.[6]

One episode alone we need mention between 1821 and 1846: the "massacres of Cosenza" which led to the self-sacrifice of the Bandiera brothers. In 1843 the "Mixed" Committee in Paris (largely Mazzinian) tried to start a joint rising in Calabria (Naples) and Romagna (Papal State). This was an attempt at united action between southern and central Italy, but it failed. Each district waited for the other to start first.[7]

[6] Tivaroni, *Domin. Austr.* III, 149, 180, etc. On this point *v.* Paladino, *Rivoluzione Napolitana*, pp. 68, 72, 85 and 94. He says that the Liberal régime, itself inefficient, was overwhelmed by the mob of place-hunters. Nitti (revolutionist), in *Vita Italiana nel Risorgimento* (1846–9), III, 84–94, says: "No one knew whither they were drifting (p. 94). The state was a ship without a rudder, and if things were bad in the capital they were worse in the provinces. In the public mind there was far greater faith in the King than in the Liberals" (p. 105).

De Cesare, *La Fine d'un regno*, p. 95, says: "The Liberal institutions degenerated at once into turbulent anarchy." In 1848 Naples was not yet sufficiently developed to benefit by Pius' Liberal institutions. Thus a free assembly and a free press would be of use to Piedmont, and in a lesser degree to the Papal State and Tuscany. But in Naples, in 1848, the assemblies proved futile; the free press printed anything that occurred to it; and the place-hunters swept the capital.

[7] This Moto di Savigno is described in vol. I, p. 216 *et seq.* Simultaneously there was discovered a curious little plot by a professor called Granghi and a priest named Rizzo, to stop the King's carriage, kidnap him into a house and then by any expedient get him to sign a Constitution. By this means apparently they hoped to bind his conscience (Tivaroni, p. 150; Nisco, *Ferdinand II*, 61).

It led, however, to the "massacres of Cosenza" a year later. Revolutionary feeling had been aroused in Naples, and a rising was fixed for March 15th, 1844. Here was an attempt at united action between Naples (constitutionalist) and Sicily (separatist); and this also failed. Near Cosenza about a hundred people were implicated, but only about fifty took part in the fighting and they were crushed by the police. A captain of gendarmes was killed, and several civilians. Of the rebels five were executed, fourteen sentenced to long terms of imprisonment, and over twenty to lesser punishments.

This local rising was of no great importance in itself—but it led to the celebrated tragedy of the Bandiera brothers. That story of the Bandieras has been told a hundred times. Here we need only summarise its main points. It was the first really notable attempt by Mazzinians to raise their fused-Italy republican banner in Naples; and even in this instance we may notice that it was not planned or approved by Mazzini: and that in the course of their defence the Bandieras, though republicans, offered their support to the King of Naples if he would agree to become ruler of a united Italy. The expedition upon which they embarked was absolutely insane: with twenty-one men they invaded a kingdom where no one knew anything about them. They themselves realised that it would produce few material results. We are told, indeed, that their friend Ricciotti said that they expected to find the mountains full of rebels: but Emilio Bandiera stated that they came because people were saying that the exiles encouraged local risings, but then waited to see whether the movement would be a success before starting to join it. Perhaps their most heartfelt motive was the idea that they had inherited a dishonoured name; because in 1831 their father had captured General Zucchi and the other Italian leaders, and handed them to the Austrian authorities.

The results were divers. The fact that two young men in their position, Austrian naval officers and sons of a baron, should have made the supreme sacrifice, caused a deep sensation; it brought home to other believers in the unification of Italy that this was a cause and not merely a theory; a cause for which men would have to die. It formed a precedent of desertion for Italian soldiers and sailors in Austrian service; and—rather unjustly—it aroused hatred against Ferdinand II. On the other hand it discredited Mazzini's teachings because they caused young men to seek such useless destruction; and thus it strengthened the Moderate movement for several years to come.

Perhaps the best verdict on it is that so simply expressed by Tivaroni. "The Bandieras taught men to die, which is the most difficult virtue for an enslaved people to learn; but on the day that it learns that lesson it becomes free."

II. FERDINAND II: BEFORE 1848

King Ferdinand II (1830–59) has gone down to posterity as "Bomba" and as "the thrice-perjured King of Naples" and "the King-whose-prisons-were-shown-up-by-Gladstone", so perhaps it is best to begin by saying that these names do not concern us, because they date from the latter years of his reign. In 1847, although he had been seventeen years on the throne, he was not yet known by any of them. In fact, during his first period he had earned golden opinions,[8] and had even been looked upon by some Liberals as a possible leader of Italy instead of Charles Albert.

The view often taken by historians, that he was always a cruel monster, is certainly not that accepted by the best Italian writers nowadays, nor was it believed even by most of the revolutionists of his own time. Baron Nisco, for instance, had been imprisoned by him for eight years: "I still bear the marks of Ferdinand's despotism on my feet and on my wrists," he says. Yet he makes a point of telling us that up to 1837 the king was not a tyrant (this was the date of his first political

[8] Guardione, *Il Dominio dei Borboni in Sicilia*, 1, 73 (1907): "His administrative and political provisions earned Ferdinand the reputation of being an excellent prince, both in Sicily and in Naples." This is the accepted opinion.

executions): and that "his first years have been confused with those that followed, especially after 1848 when the Bourbon nature fully re-asserted itself and made him the aversion not only of Italy but of Europe".[9] Ferdinand seems to have shown a kindly disposition and good intentions, but he was gradually driven into opposite courses by the advance of the revolution in Naples and of the separatist movement in Sicily. To neither of these demands could he or would he listen. In Naples he was a Bourbon absolutist who (supported by Metternich) refused all Liberal institutions. In Sicily he was a unionist who believed in maintaining the union even at the price of shutting his eyes, at times, to cruelties. But it must be admitted that in Naples his administration was better than anything achieved by the Liberals when they seized the

[9] Nisco, *Ferdinand II*, pp. 7 and 22. By 1848 he had spent eighteen years in defending himself against rebellions and against several attempts on his life. After the strain of 1848 he was never the same man. In 1856, though only 46 years old, he looked 60. He died in 1859 at the age of only 49.

Nitti, p. 65: "He [Ferdinand] has passed into history as King Bomba, and nothing is remembered of him but the betrayal of the constitution, the persecution of the Liberals, the repression of Sicily, and the terrible letters of Gladstone. We have forgotten too soon that during two-thirds of his reign the Liberals themselves spoke of him as Titus [the best Roman emperor] and praised and exalted him for his virtues and his desire for reforms. We have forgotten too soon the relief which his financial reforms brought to his people and the ardour which he displayed in suppressing old abuses." Speaking of 1848, he says (p. 108): "How can he be called cruel who, after the events of May 15th, did not have any death-sentences carried out?"

Chiaramonte (historian of Sicily) says that good laws were promulgated by Ferdinand, but remained a dead-letter owing to corruption and ineptitude. "But if the Liberals had demanded an intelligent and rigid execution of the laws, and economic and administrative progress, everything leads us to believe that such demands would have received willing agreement from a monarch whom Raffaele, Nisco, De Cesare, Nitti and other impartial historians depict as not unprovided with good administrative qualities, and, during the first years of his reign, also with excellent intentions."

government; and in Sicily—although he sent an army of conquest which earned him the name of Bomba—that such an army would have been sent by the Neapolitans even if he had never existed.

In estimating his character it must be remembered that he was the chief target for political abuse, both before and after his death. But undoubtedly he became harder towards the end of his reign[10].

The Risorgimento, of course, had no advantages for him. To drive out the Austrians would merely aggrandise Piedmont, his natural rival. As to Italian unity—he was perfectly satisfied with the kingdom of Naples as it stood, so long as he felt that his throne was safe: as to Liberal institutions, he was not entirely without Liberal ideas, but wanted no organic changes.

So much for the king. Among the people of Naples there can only have been a very small percentage who cared for anything outside their own frontiers.[11] In spite of the Mazzinian efforts and in spite of the self-sacrifice of the Bandiera brothers, the idea of a united Italy had made very little progress.

[10] The worst accusations are those brought during the latter years of his life and are entirely outside the scope of this volume. It is impossible to say for certain how far he, personally, was responsible for the evils of those years, without spending many months in the Archives reading his own original letters and documents and specialising in the history of Naples. The present writers have not had time for this research which is outside their subject.

[11] In the Tuscan National Archives in Florence there is a packet of diplomatic reports which seems to prove this. In the summer of 1848, after the defeat of Custoza, the Tuscan government, with Pius' support, sent an envoy extraordinary, the Cavaliere Giuseppe Griffoli, down to Naples to arrange for a league or federation of all the Italian states. At the end of three months he got himself recalled because his mission was merely waste of time. He said that, not only the government, but "the highest classes of people who held very much by the international constitutional regime", showed great apathy as regards Italian nationality.

Florence Arch. Busta 2670 Lega politica, Carteggio col Cav. Griffoli.

At his accession Ferdinand, aged twenty, was a tall and stoutly built youth, whom some people called good-looking, in spite of his thick lips and "jowl of a Franciscan friar";[12] a fairly good rider and sportsman, and a keen amateur soldier very often in uniform. With the army he was excellent. He could handle a cavalry or infantry brigade with perfect efficiency[13]—on the parade-ground at all events—and had a wonderful memory[14] for the faces of officers and N.C.O.'s. He was a very hard worker; but he regarded the state rather as his estate, to be ruled by the king in council with the help of some of the aristocracy and his glorious army; and eventually, as the years went by and he was no longer so regular in his attendance at the council, this led to the complaint that important matters were often left waiting for months. He is said to have disliked the middle-classes, but he had a sentimental sympathy with the poor. As a general rule he spoke French or Neapolitan, not Italian.

He realised fully the importance of having sound finances; indeed—except for Del Carretto and one or two really able men—he seems to have been the predominant intelligence in his circle: a fairly clever man of a slightly coarse type. He despised "quill drivers" (writers) and hated doctrinaires, and —having no great education himself—believed in settling matters "by common-sense". On unofficial occasions he often addressed people with half-chaffing Neapolitanisms, although for strangers he could put on the most captivating manners. It is said that his vein of Neapolitanism could degenerate among friends into practical jokes which may have made him popular among the lazzaroni but enabled his enemies to say—falsely—that he had caused the death of his

[12] Nisco, *Ferdinand II*, 8. "Grugno" literally means a snout. Nisco, of course, was a hostile critic.

[13] So Pepe tells us. The Neapolitan army consisted of 36,000 (peace-strength) or 64,000 (war-strength): its best troops were 6000 Swiss. Equipment good. Gori (p. 18) says that in the Neapolitan, French and Spanish armies alone could an N.C.O. rise to be a commissioned officer.   [14] De Cesare, p. 94.

first wife.[15] Nisco and other revolutionists accuse him of deceitfulness, but all authorities admit that he was moral, a good and affectionate father, and genuinely, though narrowly, religious.[16]

During this first period he showed plenty of energy. His reforms, besides those in the army and navy, included the finances, the making of two small railways (the first in Italy) and of other roads, the encouragement of agriculture—in fact, all those reforms and improvements for which Charles Albert received so much credit.[17] We notice that he began by cutting down his expenses; and that during his first seven

[15] Mr Bolton King (1, 138) says of Ferdinand II: "His boorish brutality killed his wife, the gentle Christina of Savoy." He gives no authority for this damning accusation published in 1898 while the family of King Ferdinand was still alive. The incident to which he is referring is a story that she died because Ferdinand pulled a music-stool or chair away from under her, two days, or a few days, before the birth of her last child. It is entirely discredited; and has been so ever since 1867.

One of Ferdinand's contemporary biographers Mariano d'Ayala, a Liberal who hated the king, says that "it is related that by a very unbecoming joke" the king withdrew or moved her chair when she was with child and made her fall on the floor. But d'Ayala does not suggest that she died of it. In fact, he is writing about the year 1833 and she did not die until 1836, with her last child (v. d'Ayala, Vita del Re di Napoli, p. 29).

The other principal contemporaries, Nisco and Settembrini, both rebels, give a most sympathetic description of the saint-like Queen Maria Christina's death without including a word against her husband. The great historian Tivaroni says that the story of this practical joke was told against Ferdinand, but does not say that it was true: and says nothing about the queen's having been *enceinte* or of her suffering from the fall.

In 1867 Bianchi, the Piedmontese historian, went into the question and disproved it. Lately Signor Guardione, the distinguished Sicilian historian, has examined the question again and is satisfied that it is completely disproved.

[16] De Cesare, p. 99.

[17] Nisco; v. also Nitti, p. 64: "Between 1830 and 1848 few princes did as much good as he"; and p. 63: "For eighteen years he had given proof of great kindness and much shrewdness."

years he reprieved all the political prisoners condemned to death.[18]

These early efforts won approval. In 1832, after the attempt on his life, he pardoned the two would-be assassins;[19] and soon afterwards the Bologna Liberals sent him a secret offer of their support for the crown of all Italy. He was pleased, but refused the offer because, as a religious man, he could not encroach upon the Papal territories.

What doomed him to failure was the fact that he was a real Bourbon absolutist: a strong Conservative and an uncompromising unionist. Rightly or wrongly he would never grant a constitution to Naples and he would never grant self-government to Sicily. In the end it was this constitutional struggle in Naples which led to his being called a perjurer; and his suppression of Sicilian autonomy which left him permanently branded with the nickname "Bomba".[20]

It is fortunate that he was tied by these convictions, for, had he blossomed out into a constitutional king, there would have been two popular monarchies in the peninsula, and they might have caused division in Italy when the great chance came of accomplishing her unity.

[18] d'Ayala, *Vita*, p. 23, quotes his decree of December 20th, 1830, in which he not only reduced by half all the existing political sentences, but abolished certain criminal proceedings in such cases.

[19] *V*. Guardione, *Domin. Borboni, Sicilia*, 1, p. 97. And on p. 110 he says, quoting Bianchi, IV, 446, that Metternich feared Ferdinand might be aiming at the Crown of Italy.

[20] *V*. Signor Guardione's protest against modern historians who reproduce the "lies and jibes which were hurled at the Bourbons during the revolution". Guardione, *Domin. Borboni, Sicilia*, 1, pp. 41, 42. He speaks elsewhere of "the thousands of lies, circulated by patriots after Ferdinand's death". He says that people made the king a scapegoat for their own swindles (p. 117). Signor Guardione is, of course, the chief living Sicilian historian. Towards the end of his reign the king realised that many families had been ruined by him for political offences; so he used to help them tacitly. De Cesare, p. 102.

III. 1847. THE MODERATE MOVEMENT IN NAPLES

The advent of a Liberal Pope in 1846 was a misfortune for him because it meant that henceforth the Holy See would be more in sympathy with Piedmont than with Naples.[21] In any case Pius' movement in 1846 and 1847 was far from being welcome to a ruler so fanatically absolutist as King Ferdinand. Hitherto his chief supporters had been the army, the bureaucracy, the Church and the Plebs, but if Pius' tenets should enter the kingdom—more especially his reputed tenets—many of these stalwarts might gravitate towards Liberalism. From the very first, Ferdinand made every endeavour to close the door against the new Papal ideas.[22] His despatches to and from Baron Ludolf, his ambassador in Rome, show how much he feared the new movement. Very soon he took steps to prevent Roman newspapers from crossing the frontier, and by January 1847 he was refusing permission to Papal subjects —even to prelates and cardinals—until this treatment drew forth a protest from Gizzi.[23]

During the first year of Pius' reign Ferdinand succeeded in shutting out his movement; but after the middle of 1847 this became impossible. By then there were a great many Liberals among the educated classes; propagandist papers were being disseminated by an active secret press, and various committees had been organised; and Lord Napier, British minister in Naples, had begun to realise that the agitation for

[21] Gualterio (1862 ed.), v, 36, 254, and others.

[22] Signorina Irma Arcuno, the latest writer on the subject, says: "The trend which events in Rome were taking after the Indulgence [Amnesty], and the resulting hopes and enthusiasm among the Liberals, infuriated and frightened the Court of Naples, so that its attitude towards Rome became hostile, and sometimes even officially so." Arcuno, *Il Regno delle due Sicilie nei rapporti con lo Stato Pontificio*, pp. 9 and 12.

[23] Arcuno, *ibid.* p. 24 and note, quoting a letter of Ludolf's of January 23rd, 1847. Speaking of this period Settembrini says: "Woe to him who received letters or papers from upper Italy." Settembrini, *Ricordanze*, p. 147; *v.* also Gualterio (1862 ed.), v.

a constitution might become a danger because there existed no machinery for expressing the demand.[24]

It is said that King Ferdinand was wont to declare that in Naples there were better laws and institutions than elsewhere. He was right. Everyone is of the same opinion. The Neapolitan restoration had retained much of the French administrative and judicial orders: a council of ministers (presided over by the king), an armed Civic Guard, a Consulta, courts of justice, a court of appeal. The civil code was, with slight exceptions, entirely Napoleonic and the penal code and procedure were "worthy of the most perfect nations". In every commune there was a council, and from these were formed, by election, the provincial councils, whose duty was to control the administration of the province, and to report on it to the king; so that, after hearing the Consulta he should make suitable provision.[25]

In July 1847 a historic answer was made to these claims of King Ferdinand, in the celebrated *Protesta del popolo delle due Sicilie*, a pamphlet anonymously published by a man named Settembrini. His reply was that it is no use having comparatively good institutions if the whole personnel, from the king downwards, is rotten to the core, entirely corrupt and inefficient.

Settembrini intended the *Protesta* to pillory the Neapolitan government just as d'Azeglio's *Degli ultimi casi di Romagna* had been intended to pillory the pontifical government. He

[24] Napier to Palmerston, July 25th, 1847; *London Corr.* I, 76.

[25] This is copied almost verbatim from Gori, a lawyer (p. 16). Baron Nisco, a revolutionist, confirms almost all the above points and adds: No baronial or ecclesiastical jurisdiction; no class privileges; no trusts. But he ends up: "But all the institutions—the best that could be desired under an absolute monarch—were spoilt and corrupted in practice, with great harm to the nation. Thus the people had great reason to want a Statuto [constitution] that would bridle the power of the man [Ferdinand] who, so far from making good new laws, was assiduously spoiling the old which were excellent." Other writers say that his edicts for Sicily were good but remained a dead-letter.

draws a disgusting picture of the régime as "an immense pyramid of which the king is the apex" and in which every single man is corrupt. He gives every kind of detail about the king, the council, the ministers personally, and of each government office just as if he had lived in it. He says, for instance, that the king, when preparing his edicts, sends a friend out into the market beforehand, to buy or sell for him according to the probable results of the edict: that the ministers are so dishonest that on one occasion when the king was visiting a certain named department he advised the other ministers "to keep their hands over their pockets": that the council was a farce because all its members were either bribable or incompetent, and so jealous of each other that often the business before them had to be returned to its original department where, eventually, it could be paid for by those who wanted it put through: that the Consulta was rarely consulted, and was used chiefly to hang up any awkward proposals.

In most instances he gives names (which I suppress); so that it is a thoroughly libellous document. The pages which seem most heartfelt are those which describe the tyranny of the police, who, he says, have power to imprison without trial, or to flog or torture ordinary citizens; and he adds that they use this power openly and shamelessly to extort money. How far these accusations are true—if at all—is now very hard to say.

It is strange that so many historians have accepted this pamphlet as gospel, for Settembrini himself would hardly make such a claim. Most of it is merely a vulgar political diatribe extraordinarily bitter and unconvincing;[26] and to

---

[26] It is always regrettable to have to condemn the work of a man who has suffered so much for his cause; and the historians have great sympathy for Settembrini. But it is useless to deny that the *Protesta* is a document which would not carry conviction in a lawcourt. It reveals more about Settembrini than about his intened victims. It shows that he was a man who loathed the king, the nobles, the government, the ministers individually, the priests, the police and the army, and in fact almost everybody. The follow-

anyone who has read Settembrini's autobiography this is not surprising. He was a married man of thirty-four, the son of a lawyer; he had been a member of the Giovane Italia—not Mazzini's society but another—had affiliated several friends, and in 1839 had been imprisoned for three and a half years. Naturally he was bitter. Probably his political mentality was no longer quite normal. He tells us himself, with evident pride, that the reason why he wrote the *Protesta* was because he saw Del Carretto's servants rudely (*villanamente*) turn away a beggar woman and her little boys from his carriage-door. "I will avenge her!" he said. "I ran to my house, took my paper at which I was working, threw myself upon it with renewed ardour, and did not leave it until I had completed the *Protesta del Popolo delle due Sicilie*." This pamphlet swept the whole town; and he was much amused to find that people assumed that it was written with "inside knowledge" whereas he had merely collected and written what he heard said "by

ing specimens will illustrate what I mean: "*The king* has laboriously taken the trouble to select the most stupid, the most wicked, the most perverse and the most dishonest people, and has surrounded himself with them and given them offices and power. From him descend all our evils. From him all his ministers learn to tyrannise; from him they get that stupidity, that idleness, that bestiality which is to be seen in the actions of the government; he is the biggest and most disgusting worm in the sore which is eating into us. Worms too, are the Prince of Bisignano, the Duke of San Cesareo, General Salluzzo, the Duke of Ascoli and all the other nobles with livery, who form the Court. They are stupid and ignorant to the point of not being able to read; from which you would think they were like their ancestors, if, on looking them in the face you did not perceive that they were plebeians, and resemble the adulterous servants in their families. Among them there is not a single one who is good, not one who is pious, not one who has a little common-sense or can give good advice...." He then describes each of the ministers: "The Minister for Foreign Affairs, Prince di Scilla, is nothing else but a mass of shapeless flesh, which can only stammer and splutter you with saliva"; in one edition he adds a remark too vulgar for translation. In similar terms he describes the priests, the police, the army, etc., for forty-five pages, which to me are entirely unconvincing.

other persons worthy of trust". And he ends up in triumph: "That poor woman is avenged."[27]

As to corruption: undoubtedly, in a general way, the accusation is true.[28] That Naples was fearfully corrupt appears to be the opinion of everybody. But up to date there seems to be no proof that the king had been corrupt; and the head of the police, his chief minister Del Carretto, accused by Settembrini of peculation, took a noble revenge by dying poor.[29] In any case the remedy proposed by Settembrini was revolution; and when dealing with a cone of corruption there is very little use in turning it upside down—as he was obliged to ad ⸱ a few months later.[30]

The ⸱ef reasons for Settembrini's success were the existing desi. for a constitution and the fact that the Pope, Charles Al. ⸱t and Leopold II were on the path of reform, and every Li. ⸱al in Italy wanted to force the King of Naples to join them. ⸱ ⸱ Protesta marks a new phase of opposition which finally con ⸱elled Ferdinand to grant a constitution

[27] Settembrini, *Ricordanze*, pp. 147–9. Such an episode as he describes happened a thousand times a day in Naples. Even fifty years later the beggars were numbered by the hundred and many of them would follow a victim for five or ten minutes, determined, if he had not given them anything, to pay him out with insults and abuse. In these respects the town has improved beyond recognition. To-day it is a pleasant and beautiful place to be in.

[28] Gualterio (1862 ed.), v, 258 says: "The Neapolitans...knew by experience the difference between the written law and the law put into practice; the value of the safe-guards of the citizen where many of those laws were null by use and by abuse and where justice was in the hands of a corrupt magistrate and entirely dominated by the omnipotent police...."

[29] Nisco, p. 22.

[30] *V*. Napier's opinion July 25th, 1847, *London Corr*. I, pp. 75–6. Cf. De Cesare, *La Fine*, p. xviii. And even as late as 1895 he wrote about Italy: "This corrupt parliamentarianism is dying, despised and almost accursed: but what can one substitute for it? Twist it or turn it over, the primary material remains the same,—man: whatever be the form of government. Here we require an internal work of analysis and purification." Apparently this great work has been carried out since 1922.

(January 28th, 1848): but this phase produced few permanent results in the Risorgimento, because after a few months he was able to eliminate the Chamber of Deputies, which, indeed, had won little public sympathy. He simply ceased summoning it; and his being allowed to do so seems to show that there was very little driving-power behind the Liberal party in Naples—especially after its hopes had been damped by Pius' allocution of April 29th, 1848.

Already, however, in the summer of 1847, there were revolutionary committees at work, although it was a bad moment for a rising. The Liberals were divided: the Neapolitans wanted a constitution and the Sicilians wanted their independence from Naples. Moreover on August 13th Ferdinand had won some popular approval by abolishing a tax on flour, and also several other taxes. Nevertheless, a portion of the revolutionary committee headed by a gentleman named Domenico Romeo, of Santo Stefano, tried hard to combine, literally, Scylla and Charybdis. They arranged for a joint rising, to be started on either side of the straits by the Neapolitans in Reggio and the Sicilians in Messina; and on September 1st and 2nd some fighting took place in both towns, initiated with shouts of "Viva Pio IX! Viva Italia! Viva la Costituzione!"; but only with a short-lived success. By land the king sent a line regiment, a regiment of Cacciatori and two guns; by sea he sent two steam-frigates—his fleet was up-to-date—and according to General Pepe, the local Urban guards fought energetically for their king.[31] There were only sixty-five rebels in Messina and some hundreds in Reggio and Gerace, so resistance was overpowered; and for some time to come there were no further attempts at joint action between the Neapolitan Liberals and Sicilian separatists.[32]

[31] Guglielmo Pepe describes this rising and says that, when victorious, the rebels proclaimed Ferdinand as their constitutional sovereign; so perhaps it was fortunate for Italy that they were not finally successful. *V.* Pepe, *L'Italia nel 1847, 1848, 1849.*

[32] This account is based on Nisco's, which is accepted by Tivaroni. Its main points are confirmed by La Masa, *Documenti*, 1,

Nine of the insurgents were shot, and, in retaliation, during October an attempt was made to murder the king—"sangue per sangue". Many more were imprisoned. Carlo Poerio, the well-known leader, spent ninety days in prison, but, while there, he was allowed perfect freedom to see his friends; and, strangely enough, he continued, as usual, to direct the revolutionary movement.[33]

Meanwhile these executions had aroused the rebels to make plans of revenge. The Sicilians were to rise in Palermo on January 12th, 1848—a fateful day in history. At the same time the Neapolitans were to rise and claim the constitution of 1820.

"At this point", says Nisco, "it seemed, to a sensible man, that the moment had arrived to withdraw the country from desperate and fierce expedients, and to shepherd the Neapolitan people into the same method of progression as that of the others throughout the peninsula—namely, that of pushing on the princes, by means of applause, to greater things." So they organised street demonstrations similar to those in Rome, for November 22nd and 24th, but Ferdinand forbade any such troubling of public order.[34]

Nevertheless, on December 14th, there was another great demonstration "of a more resolute and menacing character", this time in honour of Pepe and Italian independence. There

20; also by Settembrini, *Ricordanze*, p. 150; and by Guglielmo Pepe. Lord Napier said that Ferdinand had "40,000 well-appointed troops and a steam flotilla of eight vessels", *London Corr.* 1, 166.

[33] Nisco, p. 83; Settembrini, *Ricordanze*, p. 158, and many other authorities. According to Signori Libertini and Paladino (*Storia di Sicilia*, p. 672) only one Sicilian was executed: "Times were turning towards clemency, and the Bourbon—who had refused to follow the policy of Pius IX, Leopold II and Charles Albert—once that the fury of the first moment was past, became kindly."

[34] Napier to Palmerston, *London Corr.* 1, 286. He says that "the object of the Liberals in continuing these nocturnal meetings and vociferations is to familiarise the common orders with the aspirations and watchwords which agitate the rest of Italy, and to offer that protest against their government which the laws forbid them to make in a more rational and tranquil manner".

were collisions with the police and a cavalry charge. Meanwhile Poerio, though still in prison, had got a secret messenger through from Palermo, a man sent to bring him word that the revolution would break out there on January 12th, 1848, "with the certainty of a bill of exchange". On receipt of this information it was arranged that Baron Nisco and another Liberal should slip away to Rome to consult with the agitators there.

This meeting in Rome is singularly interesting because it reveals the innermost feelings of some of the best-known men who were professing to be loyal subjects of Pius IX. Nisco received a solemn assurance from the Committees of the Circolo Romano and the Circolo Popolare, conveyed to him by Masi and Sterbini, that if the Austrians marched southwards to crush the Sicilian rising, their advance would be resisted by the people of Romagna. Apparently the people of Pius' northern provinces were to initiate war without asking him.

At the same time it was arranged that Pius' other subjects should send two armed forces to support the Neapolitan rising—one under the daring Nizzard officer Ribotti, to enter the Abruzzi; and the other to operate in Calabria and the Salerno district under Colonel Giacomo Durando,[35] brother of General Giovanni Durando the Piedmontese officer who was training the Papal army. It seems evident that the Piedmontese were redoubling their activities. By now the Papal army was virtually in their hands; some of the Tuscan officers were being trained by them, and the Neapolitan rebels, too, would soon have Piedmontese leaders.

There still remained more than a fortnight before January

[35] Coppola, p. 29, says that La Masa, on arriving in Rome, formed a committee to run this movement in the Abruzzi: that it was Luigi Masi, Caldesi, Pigozzi, De Andreis, Merighi, Beretta, Princess Belgioioso, Canino, two Neapolitans Primicerio and Beatrice [?]; that "General Durando became president, declaring that 'he was ready to dash off anywhere that could be of use, even if he had only 100 men'".

12th, 1848, the day which was destined to set fire to half of
Europe. Some last efforts were made to convert the King of
Naples. In December an address was published, signed by
thirty-two Piedmontese and thirty-four Romans—all the most
distinguished Liberals in Italy, from Balbo, d' Azeglio and
Cavour, down to Masi and Sterbini—calling on Ferdinand to
unite his policy to that of Pius IX, Charles Albert and
Leopold II. It produced no result; so finally they formed a plan
that Professor Montanari, of Bologna, and Baron Nisco should
travel down to Naples and hold an interview with King
Ferdinand, for the purpose, nominally, of persuading him to
join the Italian League, but mainly in order to sound the
state of his mind as to Italian independence. The nationalists
still had hopes of him.

On December 31st, 1847, King Ferdinand received them
in his library. It is rather a curious story. Nisco[36] says:

To Montanari's opening, he [King Ferdinand] replied with
evident frankness and truth: he showed that the reforms in
Tuscany and Rome were all things which the Neapolitans had
possessed for half a century; that in Naples there was a Civil
Guard better armed and trained than that of France. Concerning
the military relations with Austria he expressed such thoughtful
considerations that Montanari, in a moment of enthusiasm, said
"Sire! You be the King of Italy". But when we emerged from
the royal palace, and when the fascination of the king's conversation had ceased, Montanari perceived that, with great cleverness,
Ferdinand had let him lose sight of the objective of his mission,
that is to say, the League: and that the Neapolitans were right in
requiring constitutional guarantees for the very purpose of
maintaining those institutions that already existed, namely, the
laws, but not the arts or methods of the government which
constantly misused them with its over-riding power.

They had come there for the purpose of persuading him to
join them, and the sudden apostrophe "You be the King of
Italy", addressed to the most powerful monarch in the peninsula could hardly have been received by him as anything but

[36] Nisco, p. 88

an appeal to his ambition. But Ferdinand had no desire to tread in the footsteps of Manfred, nor even in those of Murat.[37]

To summarise the situation: Ferdinand II in Naples had shown more powers of resistance than any other Italian ruler except Metternich in Lombardo-Venetia: and, as to these two, their refusal of Liberal concessions had left them both face to face, henceforth, with armed rebellion.

[37] This is the view taken by Tivaroni.

Chapter XIX

THE CUSTOMS-UNION[1]

I. The greatest political project of Pius' life is undoubtedly his attempt to unify Italy by means of a confederation of states. It was the scheme which was to form his chief hope for a year and a half to come; and yet, strangely enough, it is seldom connected with his name—at all events to English readers.

The German Empire has been fashioned from a Germanic confederation developed out of the Zollverein (customs union). Similarly the modern Italian nation might have been fashioned from an Italic confederation developed out of the Lega doganale (customs-union). In 1847 this was the only form of union that was possible.

The idea was not new. It can be traced back to the eighteenth century or earlier, and it formed part of Gioberti's programme: but Pius was the first ruler who tried to carry it out; and had he succeeded in unifying Italy, or even in beginning its unification by this means, he would have added a very great achievement to the record of the Holy See.

There is no doubt that Pius addressed himself to this

[1] The principal authorities from which this chapter has been done are:

La Civiltà Cattolica, for 1879. Article "Pio IX e Carlo Alberto" by Ballerini.

La Civiltà Cattolica, for 1898 (last three months). Article "La causa nazionale" by Ballerini.

Rassegna storica, 1914. Article by Fernanda Gentili. She also has an article in the *Rivista d' Italia*, 1915. Between them they give most of the documents hitherto obtainable. Fernanda Gentili has had the privilege of reading those in the possession of Mgr Morichini's heirs. Manno gives some of the best documents of Corboli-Bussi. Besides the above there are of course various other authorities who give their documents, such as Bianchi, etc. Vidal quotes several letters of Charles Albert.

problem not merely from the nationalist but also from the Papal point of view. Firstly he saw, just as Charles Albert saw, that the revolution was a danger to every throne in Italy; and he hoped that a confederation of governments would be able to show a firm front to rebellion and to the consequent disorder and irreligion. But secondly, from the nationalist point of view, he saw that there were two possible ways to unity and independence. The first was to declare war upon Austria—with very small chances of success. The second was to form a confederation; and this became the chief aim of his policy in Italy.

He proposed to begin by a customs-union; this would mean that all the Italian states would have free-trade between them—except the Austrian provinces of Lombardy and Venetia. In such a situation Austria could hardly continue to isolate her subjects from all other Italians. But the other Italians would insist on setting up barriers against German imports. Consequently—so it was hoped—the Lombardo-Venetian kingdom would gradually be drawn away, right out of the German circle into the Italian circle. Most probably Austria would content herself (after negotiating terms) with setting up one of her archdukes as an independent ruler of Lombardo-Venetia[2]—just as in the eighteenth century Maria Teresa had set one up in Tuscany. Thus Italy would be united, independent and free from the Alps to Sicily: and this would be a peaceful solution.

II. The first occasion on which he spoke of the scheme was July 8th, 1847, when he mentioned it to some of his cardinals. It must be remembered that he had very few sympathisers among his ecclesiastics. Monsignor Corboli-Bussi is the man whose name is chiefly connected with the League, and, apart from him, there were only about five genuine believers in the

[2] This at all events was the hope of Mgr Corboli-Bussi, Pius' representative in the matter; v. Corboli-Bussi's letter of September 10th, 1847, quoted in the *Civiltà Cattolica* for 1898 (October to December) p. 284; and in his letter of January 8th, 1850 (Manno, p. 280).

idea: there was the old Abbé Graziosi, once Pius' tutor and now his confessor—a friend of thirty years' standing; Cardinal Gabriele Ferretti, his new secretary of state; Cardinal Antonelli; and the pro-treasurer Monsignor Morichini, his able financial adviser;[3] but before the scheme could take shape the Abbé Graziosi was dead, and his loss was regarded as a misfortune not only by Pius but by all the Liberals in Rome.

In August 1847 Pius selected for the work Monsignor Corboli-Bussi, a prelate of only thirty-four, refined, intelligent and still young enough to be enthusiastic about this great chance in his very short life. He was to go first to Florence and then to Turin to negotiate the customs-union for the three states. It was the right moment, because the Ferrara episode had awakened all Italy to the need of unity.

On August 24th Corboli-Bussi left Rome, and on the 26th he reached Florence. There he met with a joyful reception and found the government more than ready for some form of union. In the course of private conversation, the kindly old Grand-Duke, Leopold II, said that he boasted himself an Italian prince and the son of an Italian prince; and, after two days' discussion, he notified Corboli-Bussi formally that he was ready to join the customs-union himself, and undertook also to bring in Lucca, and—so he hoped—Modena and Parma as well. He authorised Monsignor to inform his own government of the fact and also to take the news with him to Charles Albert at Turin.

This was an excellent beginning, and evidently it caused great satisfaction in Rome. On September 6th Pius communicated the news to a congregation (committee) of cardinals, and they actually sent a despatch to Corboli-Bussi fixing Civita-Vecchia as the best meeting-place for the congress of delegates from each state, when the time came for them to discuss the scheme in detail.

[3] These are the five names mentioned by Signorina Fernanda Gentili in her excellent essay on this subject (*Rassegna storica*, 1914).

III. Meanwhile Corboli-Bussi had left Florence on
September 1st, and on Sunday, September 5th, he arrived in
Turin. There he was received with unrestrained enthusiasm,
which, however, was due to a complete misapprehension as
to the purpose of his mission. The people were still excited
over Charles Albert's letter to Castagnetto in which he spoke
of becoming the Prince Schamyl of Italy, and they thought
that this pale young prelate had come as an envoy from Rome
to negotiate an alliance against Austria; to call on an Italian
prince to defend Ferrara! And Charles Albert had the same
hope. Count Castagnetto, who was his A.D.C., tells us in his
narrative that:

His Majesty was full of eagerness over this visit; he hoped to
obtain very precise details as to the situation in Rome and the
intentions of His Holiness. The King still hopes for a rupture with
Austria, an excommunication and a war of Religion.

This vision, of course, was absurd; and it probably tended
to frighten Pius from making any political defensive alliance
with Piedmont for the time being, lest it should be used for
offence.

No war against Austria could be called a war of religion or
justify excommunication unless Radetzky's troops had first
deliberately invaded the Papal State in despite of a formal
protest by the Pope. It seems as if Charles Albert thought
that the Ferrara episode could be considered an invasion.
But it certainly would not have been regarded as such by the
Five Powers.

On September 6th Corboli-Bussi had a private interview
with the king. Charles Albert was all in favour of fighting,
and more than once he placed his hand upon the hilt of his
sword and declared himself the champion of the Pope. But
Monsignor held the same views as his master. He did no
believe that such a campaign could prove successful, a
inwardly felt a little scornful about the reference to Schar   .
He replied that His Holiness "while still hoping for ie
preservation of peace in Italy, had thought of a way wh eby

these offers might be given a practical significance even in peace-time: namely a customs-union similar to that which unites the states of Germany".[4] Charles Albert (we are told by Signorina Fernanda Gentili) was greatly disappointed.

His disappointment is not surprising. Pius' plan would have put an end to all the Piedmontese hopes and to the future of the House of Savoy. Charles Albert's dream was to fight as the defender of the Pope supported by an excommunication: if successful he would claim for Piedmont the Austrian provinces of Lombardy and Venetia, and perhaps Parma and Modena as well.[5] No doubt he believed, genuinely, that this accretion of territory was necessary for the safety of Piedmont, and he had, as we know, been at work for many months getting arms into Lombardy, and his agents into the rest of Italy.

If this new plan of Pius' took shape there would be no war; the boundaries would remain unchanged; Lombardy and Venetia would have their own separate government or governments instead of being joined to Piedmont; so would Parma and Modena. Naturally he was not pleased.

The first objection which he raised was that if Lombardo-Venetia came into the customs-union this would bring in Austria; and thereby would admit German goods to compete with those of Italy. But Corboli-Bussi assured him that, so far from admitting Austria, Pius desired that the treaty should be kept secret from her. After a fairly long discussion Charles Albert referred Corboli-Bussi to his treasurer Count di Revel, but before ending the interview he repeated his friendly assurances and said that "all his forces would be assembled at a sign from Your Holiness for your defence".

Corboli-Bussi's estimate of Charles Albert's motives shows

[4] Palmerston expressed his strong approval of this scheme, v. *London Corr.* i, 188.
[5] Vidal states this and quotes an old letter of Castagnetto's in 1842 in which he says: "The King thinks that Piedmont must enlarge her boundaries or she will be swallowed up by Austria and France." Vidal, p. 408 note.

some shrewdness.[6] In this letter of September 10th he summed them up as follows:

If I had to say what, to my small understanding, are the secret and intimate dispositions of this King, I should say they were two-fold. Firstly that he wants to avoid making any political concessions to his people, and that in order to avoid doing so he wants to preserve his reputation with the Liberal party by offering his arms to maintain the independence of your Holiness during the progress of your reforms. The second is that it would afford him great pleasure to enlarge his dominions at the expense of the small Austrian grand-dukes. Hitherto I see that, to the demand for a customs-union, he replies by offering a defensive league....

Here we get the fundamental difference between the policies of Charles Albert and Pius; and it is worth noting, because, without doing so, one cannot fully understand their long discussions over the confederation during a year and a half to come.

What Pius wanted was a customs-union; it might grow peacefully into a confederation; and it might then peacefully extract Lombardo-Venetia from the Austrian Empire. His aim was peace.

What Charles Albert wanted was in reality some sort of alliance whereby the Pope should preach a crusade against Austria and bring most of Italy in his train for a war of liberation. He called it a political league, or, sometimes, a defensive league, but in practice it would doubtless become aggressive;[7] what he wanted was "Italia farà da sè", and, at the right moment, war.

[6] This was the great chance of Corboli-Bussi's life—to be the man who negotiated the unification of his native land. He evidently made as good an impression at Turin as he had in Florence, from all points of view. Even the A.D.C. Castagnetto, though opposed to Corboli's peace-measure, tells us that during a conversation of two hours he "found the prelate very witty".

[7] Vidal, p. 410: "As to Charles Albert and the confidants of his political ideas, they wanted to conclude a military offensive alliance allowing Piedmont to attack Austria as soon as the opportunity arose, uniting to their own Sardinian military forces the moral

For Pius, war would be a fatal misfortune. As spiritual sovereign it was his duty to avoid it: as a temporal sovereign it represented a very foolish policy. In the existing conditions his state was absolutely safe, guaranteed by Europe: his foreign relations, as he himself said, were impregnable. From war he had nothing to gain and everything to lose.

Even by merely signing a *political* league with Charles Albert he might run into danger.

If war came upon him—if his people forced him to declare war against Austria—then indeed he might be anxious for a league, because it would regularise his position before the Five Powers and before the Catholic world. He could plead that as member of the league of Italian princes it had been impossible for him to refuse. This situation actually arose a year later.

Having interviewed the king, Corboli-Bussi proceeded to interview the Piedmontese ministers. After two hours of

---

power of Rome and the support of Tuscany." He confirms this with quotations.

As to the political views of Charles Albert, we may note that Corboli-Bussi urged Pius to write to him direct, in order to dispose of "the doctrine which the Piedmontese progressives profess rather openly, namely that we ought to avoid, for the present, every imprudent manifestation in which Austria could find a pretext for declaring war; we ought to prepare ourselves, with an internal league and by arming the civic guard, to undertake the war in two or three years' time, and then finally come into the field taking the opportunity of protecting a rising in Lombardy". Letter of September 21st, Corboli-Bussi to Pius. *La Civiltà Cattolica*, 1898 (October–December), p. 285.

Pius, of course, did not mean to go to war. His letter of October 9th, 1847, explains his position: "The political league, looking at it from the point of view of foreign affairs, raises some doubt in our minds, seeing that I consider the Holy See to be invulnerable on that side...and at the same time I feel that it should have a complete understanding with all the Potentates, so that I cannot persuade myself how and by what means this league can be formed without causing the Holy See itself to fall into distrust among the other nations...." Pius to Corboli-Bussi, October 9th, *La Civiltà Cattolica*, 1898 (October–December), p. 660.

rather fruitless talk with Castagnetto, he ended the discussion by laying stress on the good will of Tuscany, Lucca and the Duchies; and, as he saw that the Piedmontese Liberals wanted war, he actually went so far as to say: "Perhaps this secret league will cause Austria to decide on an attack; in that case the Pope will not give way, and we shall emerge at all events from a state of things which is no longer tenable."

He also interviewed the two lately dismissed ministers, and found that they both disapproved of his scheme though from opposite points of view: Solaro della Margherita, as a strong Conservative, regarded the plan as a covert Liberal and nationalist move; Villamarina, as a strong Liberal, disapproved of it on the ground that it was a substitute for a war of liberation; and, thirdly, there was the Count di Revel who, as Piedmontese treasurer, was unwilling to unite his financial organisation to that of any other state. In reality all these ministers were raising difficulties in the way of a plan which was unpleasing to their king. Di Revel insisted on financial details which caused delays.

On or about September 20th the Cav. Giulio Martini arrived from Florence,[8] sent by the Grand-Duke of Tuscany to support Corboli-Bussi; he took up his abode with Balbo. Corboli-Bussi was greatly pleased, for his previous assurance as to Tuscan goodwill had been received with some reserve.

IV. Meanwhile Pius was anxious. Abroad he feared Austrian aggression; at home the people were excited. From every point of view he wanted a customs-union.

On September 30th he wrote to Corboli-Bussi to get the customs-union agreed in principle; the details would have to be settled later. But Corboli was ill—destined to die three years later at the age of only thirty-seven—and he was discouraged.

[8] Incidentally a strange proof is afforded of Metternich's domination among the small Italian states by the fact that heretofore Tuscany had actually been represented at Turin by the Austrian minister.

On September 29th, though unable to see visitors, he had written a long letter to Rome asking to be made plenipotentiary. He hoped to persuade Charles Albert to accept the customs-union by offering, in exchange, to accept Charles Albert's proffered political league; he hoped to get Piedmont to agree to a customs convention in exchange for his agreeing to the defensive league, and thus settle the matter.

It was with this feeling in his mind that on October 5th he wrote to Pius saying that he proposed to send in a formal "ufficio" to the Piedmontese minister for foreign affairs, stating the case to him in such a way that he must either accept the customs-union or reveal the fact that its failure was due to Piedmont.

But Pius was not prepared to make him plenipotentiary. He felt that he might find himself let in for a political league which would lead to war.[9] So he wrote to Charles Albert to sound his intentions, and to explain that war was out of the question. He pointed out that the purpose of his customs-union was peace; that it would unite the Italian princes and enable them to avoid the "two rocks upon which some people intend to make us crash [*urtare*]", namely an Austrian intervention condoned by France, or else an onset of the Revolution.

This league [the customs-union] is an efficacious method of preserving the tranquillity of Italy. To this aim of tranquillity we direct Our thoughts, Our cares and Our prayers; for the Vicar of Christ can only desire peace.

From all the above Your Majesty will recognise how deeply Our heart has been wounded by the manner in which some people have abused Our name.

On October 8th Corboli-Bussi wrote that the political league proposed by Charles Albert was one of political

[9] Charles Albert had written him a somewhat bellicose letter on September 27th and Corboli's despatches of September 10th, 16th, etc., could not have left him any doubt as to Charles Albert's warlike hopes.

principles; namely a formal declaration that the Italian princes:

(1) Shall proceed in mutual agreement as to the institutions which they intend to grant to their peoples. (This was evidently an attempt to check Pius' Liberal movement which was becoming a danger to the other princes.)

(2) In framing these institutions or reforms they will follow our national history and character rather than foreign theories (not grant an English, French or Spanish constitution).

(3) In maintaining them afterwards and in preserving peace in their state they will lean rather on internal union than on foreign influences (not to call in Austria or France to keep order, but Piedmontese troops).

This league of political principles, as suggested by Charles Albert, would have justified a certain degree of Piedmontese interference in the Papal State as regards social, constitutional and military questions. Evidently it alarmed Pius and still more Monsignor Santucci, who was acting minister during a temporary absence of Cardinal Ferretti. Its acceptance might even become a step towards uniting Italy by fusion. Any such risk Pius was compelled to avoid. For him the preservation of the Papal State and of Papal independence were a sacred trust. He could only move towards unity by means of a confederation which should safeguard the Papal authority as it stood.

In this case Santucci was evidently startled; afraid lest Corboli, carried away by the warlike patriotism of Charles Albert, should bind the Holy See to terms incompatible with the spiritual side of the Papacy. He seems to have seen plainly that Piedmont was a greater danger to the Papal State than were France or Austria; he may, for instance, have reflected how easily a Piedmontese occupation of Romagna might become permanent. At all events on October 9th he wrote to Corboli-Bussi a letter urging him to go on with the customs-union, but filled with cautious restrictions concerning the political league. He said—

This proposal evidently aims:

1. At assimilating the governments of the states concerned.
2. At co-ordinating means of repression.

Assimilation. Is it desirable at a time when so many Italians are tending towards national fusion?

Papal independence. All Christendom desires that the Pope should be entirely independent of other princes. Much more, therefore, will it desire him to be independent of conformity with representative governments. That might be possible if he were ruler of a secular state.

As to joint repression of rebellion: is it better for the Holy See to bind itself to have recourse to one power, or for it to be able to select the power which it desires?

The Papacy is cosmopolitical [sic] rather than national. If it is ever bound to one state, will not this fact offend outside nations which are anxious and pledged to help it? And what advantage will it reap? It will be compelled to appeal for help to certain allies, with a reciprocal obligation to help them; whereas normally it can obtain help from any nation without any reciprocal obligation.

These were Santucci's ideas, but apparently Pius had seen them before they were sent. They represent the adverse side of the question. However they were not meant to be pro-hibitive; "they do not prevent your negotiating widely on this subject, but they put you on your guard and in a state of great precaution not to contract irrevocable pledges".

Pius was evidently unprepared to make a league on the principles suggested by Charles Albert because, for one reason, the Austrians were still in Ferrara, and a league might mean war: for another because he objected to the idea of fusion.

But this did not mean that he had abandoned the hope of uniting Italy by means of a confederation. On the contrary he is the indefatigable champion of the federal idea for an-other year to come, as opposed to the republic-by-fusion of Mazzini, and the north Italian kingdom-by-fusion of Charles Albert.

On October 14th Corboli-Bussi received the letters of the

9th from Santucci refusing him the post of plenipotentiary, and the possibility of achieving—as he believed—the great step towards the unifying of Italy.[10] He was profoundly disappointed. "I humbly bow my head," he wrote to Pius.

But the situation was changing: Charles Albert was now freed from his ministers Della Margherita and Villamarina, both of whom had been hostile to the customs-union; and he is said to have received a report in its favour from Genoa. Perhaps it was due to these causes that, on the 16th, suddenly the whole sky became clearer.

A baby daughter had lately been born to the wife of Prince Victor Emmanuel, the future King of Italy, and Pius had given his promise to be its godfather. The 16th was the day of the christening, so the Papal Nuncio held the child at the font.

After the ceremonies were over, Charles Albert called a special meeting of his council and in the evening sent a confidential note to Corboli-Bussi to inform him that he was very glad to crown so happy a day by adhering to the customs-union between the state of the Church, Tuscany, Modena and his own."[11]

It was a joyful moment for Corboli-Bussi! The longed-for customs-union was agreed in principle; and he himself might feel that he had done a great work for the unity of Italy.

[10] By agreeing to a political league with Charles Albert, if Charles Albert would agree to the Customs-Union (i.e. if Charles Albert agreed to give up the idea of annexing Lombardo-Venetia, the Pope would take the risk of accepting his three conditions, *v*. p. 12).

[11] "Although yesterday was not a council day and was one of a ceremony so important as that of the baptism of a princess borne to the font in the august name of His Holiness, nevertheless the King held a special council during the afternoon; and at seven o'clock in the evening a confidential note from the Minister of Finance announced to me that His Majesty was very glad to be able to crown so happy a day by his adhesion to the Customs-Union between the State of the Church, Tuscany, Modena and his own, with the exception of certain small clauses which should be explained to me." Letter of October 17th, 1847, Corboli-Bussi to Secretary of State. *V. Rassegna storica*, 1914, p. 621, Article by Fernanda Gentili.

The child was christened Maria Pia after Pius; she appears in history as the Queen of Portugal; and, a few days after the christening, Pius wrote to the mother, Princess Maria Adelaide, and sent her the golden rose which he had blessed—a present only given on special occasions. It is the traditional gift of the Popes to those whom they personally esteem.

Unfortunately it was impossible that the scheme should ever become more than an expression of mutual goodwill. The principle had been agreed but the negotiations continued as to preliminary conditions.

On October 3rd the difficulties were still threefold:

(1) As to place: was the convention to meet at Rome or at Turin?

(2) Difference of system. The policy of Tuscany was virtually free trade; that of Piedmont was protection; that of Rome was "mixed"; and in Piedmont the reputation of the customs-service was good, whereas in the other two states it was not so.

(3) As to the sharing-out of the proceeds of the customs. At first the two smaller states had suggested sharing the proceeds equally, on the basis of population, because their joint population was equal to that of Piedmont.[12] But Piedmont pointed out that her customs brought in nineteen million francs: Tuscan customs brought in only four millions and Roman only about eight millions. Thus the two smaller states, combined, totalled only twelve millions as opposed to nineteen million francs. On this point Corboli-Bussi was ready to compromise.

Finally on November 3rd, 1847, there was signed, not an actual customs-union, but a basis of customs-union.

It seemed as if this might be the beginning of Italian unity!

[12] Piedmont had about 4½ million people; the Papal State about 3 million, and Tuscany about 1½. On this basis the Papal State and Tuscany, jointly, could claim half the proceeds. Mgr Morichini (pro-Treasurer in Rome) wrote some extremely valuable letters about the relative financial positions of the three states. *V. Rassegna storica*, 1914, Article by Fernanda Gentili: she quotes the letters.

But in reality the divergencies between Piedmont and the Holy See remained unaltered. Moreover in Article III there was a stipulation that the meeting-place of the commissioners should await the decisions of the King of Naples and of the Duke of Modena as to whether they would join the league or not. The King of Naples, for the time being, of course, was certain to refuse. However, they might have done without him; but the Modenese territory, the Duchy of Massa and Carrara, extends between Piedmont and Tuscany: and the Duke of Modena, although he agreed to give "facilities" and "free transit" through his duchy, would never agree to join the union. This was unsatisfactory.[13]

So the basis of customs-union never became more than a basis; it was only a formal expression of the desire for national unity; and a clearing of the ground for future schemes of confederation. Still even that had its value. People realised that this was in reality a political document disguised as a customs-union; and it expressed in dignified terms the underlying principle of their hopes.

His Holiness Pius IX, Supreme Pontiff, His Imperial and Royal Highness the Grand Duke of Tuscany and His Majesty the King of Sardinia, being at all times desirous to contribute by their mutual accord, to the increase of the dignity and prosperity of Italy, and being convinced that the real and substantial basis of Italian union lies in the fusion of the material interests of the populations which form their states; and being persuaded moreover that such a union would in process of time most effectually enlarge the national industries and national traffic; and—being strengthened in those sentiments by their hope that the other sovereigns of Italy will likewise adhere to them—they have determined to form a Customs-Union between their respective dominions.

To this end the undersigned, in virtue of the authorisation conferred on each one of them by his own sovereign, make the following declaration:

[13] *V. Rivista d'Italia* for 1915. Article by Fernanda Gentili: she deals fully with the negotiation with the Duke of Modena; quotes documents. Vidal gives a good summary on p. 415; Gori also.

Art. I. A Customs-Union is agreed in principle between the States of the Holy See, of Tuscany and Lucca, and of Sardinia; it will be carried into effect by the nomination of commissioners especially delegated by the high contracting parties to draw up a common customs tariff, and to select an equitable principle for the distribution of the common proceeds.

Art. II provided for periodical revisions of the tariff.

Art. III. The time and place of meeting of the aforesaid congress of commissioners shall be determined as soon as His Majesty the King of the two Sicilies, and his Royal Highness the Duke of Modena shall have made known their intentions with regard to the Customs-Union.

In these clauses the people saw, for the first time, their inward hopes boldly adopted and publicly stated by the princes of Italy. The independence of the act aroused great enthusiasm for the rulers of Rome, Tuscany and Piedmont which henceforth were known popularly as "the three reforming states"; and especially for Pius who was recognised to be the originator of the movement. As opposed to the revolutionists his position was temporarily strengthened.

It was felt by both courts that Monsignor Corboli-Bussi was the person responsible for this success, so the Papal authorities bestowed the warmest compliments upon him, and Charles Albert presented him with "a golden snuff-box adorned with the royal effigy and enriched with diamonds" (Manno, p. 156).

Chapter XX

SICILY

The cause of the Sicilian patriots was different from any other: it was a purely Sicilian movement, a crusade to free their beautiful island from the hated Neapolitans. Consequently it has been accused of "municipalism".[1] But it gave evidence of an enthusiastic devotion often to be found among islanders. It came from the heart of the people; the wounded insurgents, for instance, upon whose head a heavy price had been fixed by government, were sometimes betrayed in Naples, but in Sicily they were safe even in the poorest cottages.

A beautiful island! Where the sky and sea are of an intensely soft blue; the true "land where bloom the citron bowers" and where the historic tradition is traced through Norman and Saracen castles to the temples of ancient Greece; and even to the days before history. No man born to such memories could be other than patriotic.

Thus the Sicilian movement was a romantic passionate story of self-sacrifice lasting forty years;[2] but its motive was purely local patriotism and had little or no effect on the main course of the Risorgimento until, by the strange hazard of fortune, on January 12th, 1848, suddenly it became a turning point in the history of Italy—one might almost say in that of Europe.

[1] *V.* Mazzini's letter to the Sicilians, February 20th, 1848. The following authorities are some of those used in this chapter: Amari, Calvi, Chiaramonte, Colletta, Coppola, Crispi, Gualterio, Guardione, La Farina, La Masa, Libertini and Paladino, *London Correspondence*, Martino Beltrani-Scalia, Nisco, Palmieri; and general historians such as Tivaroni. For details about them *v.* Bibliography.

[2] Chiaramonte, *Il programma del' 48*, pp. 5 and 15; *v.* also many other writers; but Chiaramonte's book is perhaps the best *short* work on these years up to 1848.

I. RECAPITULATION: 1815–47

The Sicilian grievance may be stated more or less as follows.[3] During the whole of the Napoleonic interregnum the Sicilians had remained loyal to King Ferdinand I. While Naples was successively transformed into the Parthenopean Republic, the kingdom of Joseph Bonaparte and finally that of Joachim Murat, they had never flinched, and on two occasions (1798 and 1806) they had received their king when a fugitive. His capital had been Palermo, his army the Sicilian army, and his flag the Trinacrian flag. At the same time under protection of the British fleet, and under the temporary dictatorship of Admiral Lord William Bentinck, their ancient constitution had been brought up to date, and was known as the Constitution of 1812.

The weak point in their case was that, at first, the Constitution of 1812 had not worked very smoothly; but in the short space of two years there was hardly time for it to reach a high stage of efficiency: and, in spite of faults, it has remained a beloved memory of Sicilian independence.

[3] *V.* Libertini and Paladino, p. 605 *et seq.* Also Palmieri—especially the introduction by Amari. In Palmieri one can find copies of the most important documents.

Such portions as I have read of Palmieri's work are well-documented and apparently thorough. He is a Sicilian patriot; but as a rule he is not carried away by his patriotism; except perhaps in his preface, addressed rather sarcastically to the British Parliament which he regards as responsible for the ills of Sicily. His irritation was due to a debate in which Lord William Bentinck, always a friend of Sicily, had urged that the British Government should endeavour to restore to the islanders their violated liberties. Lord Castlereagh had replied with "three of the most solemn lies" (Palmieri): that Sicily had never had a representative government before 1812; that in 1815 the Sicilian Parliament itself had asked the King to reform the constitution according to his pleasure; thirdly, that the complaint came too late because, since the Congress of Laibach, Sicily was to have a government separate from that of Naples.

V. also the many works by Signor F. Guardione, the present-day historian of Sicily. Also Gualterio, *Gli ultimi rivolgimenti.*

In 1815, suddenly they lost everything. The king, Ferdinand I, left them and returned to Naples. They ceased to be a nation, even a separate entity. They lost not only the Constitution of 1812, but with it their own ancient Sicilian constitution.[4] Palermo became a shadow of its recent self. Henceforward they were governed from Naples by the king and the chancellor; they lost their army, their navy and even their flag.[5] But there were certain things that could not be taken from them—notably the blue sea around them which made theirs a separate land, and their old Sicilian tradition, which recalled the days of the Vespers.[6]

Thus arose the Sicilian nationalist movement; but we need not follow it in detail because during this period the islanders took little thought of the Risorgimento or of anything except their own freedom from Naples.

Now Amari,[7] the patriot historian, tells us that already for a century there had existed between Neapolitans and Sicilians "the most rooted and most pernicious of the territorial hatreds that we have in Italy". We may imagine, therefore, the full measure of their bitterness after five years of Neapolitan domination.

In 1820 Naples took up arms against the king and won its Spanish Constitution; and instantly the Sicilians rose against their Neapolitan garrisons. The insurrection was not well organised and some of the towns, notably Messina, sided against their own fellow-islanders.[8] Nevertheless, the people of the capital, Palermo, after a desperate defence, succeeded in winning a definite agreement from Florestano Pepe,

[4] Palmieri, pp. xxvi, 242 *et seq.* and 281. For Ferdinand I's Decree of December 8th, 1816 *v.* Palmieri, pp. 245–7; *v.* also Guardione, *La Sicilia*, p. 247.

[5] Libertini and Paladino, p. 621; Calvi, *Memorie*, p. 3, quoting decrees of Ferdinand I.

[6] I mention these because they inspired Amari in 1848.

[7] Palmieri, *v.* Amari's introduction, p. xxx.

[8] F. Guardione, *Il Dominio dei Borboni in Sicilia*, 1836–61, I, 43; *v.* also *La Sicilia*, 1795–1860, by the same author, p. 247 *et seq.*

brother of the better known Neapolitan General Guglielmo Pepe, that if they admitted his troops into their fortresses, the island would be allowed to vote itself a parliament separate from that of Naples. On securing this Convention of October 5th, 1820, the Palermitans admitted the troops as agreed: but the Neapolitan House of Commons—the very same Liberals who had just won the Spanish Constitution—refused to allow the Sicilians to vote at all on the question of their autonomy.[9] They declared the Convention "essentially null, as though it had never taken place". So gross was the breach of faith that Florestano Pepe resigned his military appointments and refused to accept from government the Grand Cross of St Ferdinand—which was, so far, an honourable gesture on his part, but did not alter the position of the Neapolitan garrisons in the Sicilian forts.[10]

The accession of Ferdinand II in 1830 aroused fresh hopes. He had spent the first ten years of his life in Sicily and seemed to have some fondness for his birthplace. Very soon he inaugurated an era of purely political reforms under the viceroyalty of his brother the Count of Syracuse. But these were

[9] The gist of the Convention lay in the following two clauses (v. Palmieri, pp. 355–65 and 389–93):

"1. The troops will take up quarters outside the city.... All the forts and batteries will be handed over to them.

"2. The majority of the votes of the Sicilians legally convened will decide on the unity or the separation of the national representation of the Kingdom of the two Sicilies.

"Executed on board His Britannic Majesty's cutter *The Racer*; commanded by Mr Charles Thurtel in the roadstead of Palermo, October 5th, 1820."

There are various other clauses in a similar sense. Signor Guardione has found the Convention in the Palermo Archives; he confirms all the above: v. also Paladino, *Rivoluzione Napoletana*, p. 87; P. Colletta, *Storia del Reame di Napoli*, II, 269, 270; Nisco, *Storia d' Italia*, vol. II, chap. IV.

[10] On this subject v. Palmieri, p. 355; Tivaroni, *Domin. Austr.* III, 262; Rosi, p. 92; also Libertini and Paladino, and other writers. Palmieri gives the documents. *V.* also Guardione, *La Sicilia*, p. 253, quoting Gualterio.

not sufficient to satisfy the Sicilians: they wanted their own parliament of 1812. To this neither Ferdinand nor his Neapolitans—not even the Liberals[11]—would ever agree; so after the year 1834 there were no more concessions; and in 1835 he recalled his brother.

In 1837 there occurred the fearful epidemic of cholera, accompanied by rebellion. Ferdinand was a great believer in strong government. He punished the rebellion by a cruel repression; and thenceforth his policy was one of centralisation, designed to abolish all distinctive institutions in Sicily, and to make it merely a province of Naples.

This was a terrible period. The wave of cholera had swept all through southern Europe. Among those uneducated populations it caused terror, more especially in districts where the people seriously believed that it was due to poison disseminated by their government. This notion was very widely spread on the mainland of Naples, and both men and women became frantic.

In Sicily everyone believed it: the following is Nisco's description:

The rumours of poison spread far and wide and were believed as certainties throughout the whole island, to the point that even the most expert doctors and chemists spoke of it; the Archbishop of Palermo, Cardinal Trigona, died refusing all relief, repeating: "There is no remedy for this poison"... a highly-placed magistrate died exclaiming "I thought this thankless government had some regard for me"...[12]

The Sicilians believed that the fountains and the flour were poisoned. They went delirious. They rose in rebellion at Palermo and elsewhere. In the trading city of Syracuse a well-known lawyer, Mario Adorno, brought an action against the sprinklers of poison, and harangued the people, calling

[11] Chiaramonte, pp. 13 and 14. Speaking of the Liberals of Naples he says that "this dislike of the independence of the Island was never a secret" and writes two pages on the subject.

[12] Nisco, pp. 42–8: confirmed by many other writers including Tivaroni, *Domin. Austr.* III, 278.

on them to rise. "Then the bells rang out to storm, the cry of Viva Santa Lucia! went up with fury, and the populace gave itself up to every kind of excess."

In other towns similar scenes occurred; and nameless horrors, says Nisco, were committed by the maddened people. Then a provisional government was set up, and a manifesto signed, declaring Sicilian independence. But it was only a flash in the pan. In August 1837 the Neapolitan troops landed under Del Carretto and there was no serious resistance.

Here we reach the first of the chief episodes which have branded Ferdinand II with the name of cruel. According to Nisco and others Del Carretto decided to emulate and surpass the insurgents in their worst moments. His use of tortures is described as horrible[13]—men were hung up by the arms, beaten, and sometimes tortured in obscene manner. This was Del Carretto's work: but from previous reputation the king must have known him to be a very hard man.

To us it is plain that the Sicilians had reached the stage of hatred when every misfortune and everything bad can be attributed to government agency.[14]

Ferdinand II had been seven years on the throne but, most probably, he did not yet realise that this bitter hatred of his rule by the islanders was by far the most serious and most permanent danger in his position. It was this movement of 1837 which first marred his good name with the stigma of cruelty. In 1848 it was the Sicilian rebellion—and not that

[13] The latest authorities, Signori Libertini and Paladino, say nothing about tortures. Guardione says that there were 1000 rebels condemned, but that the use of torture was not so bad as that in Charles Albert's repression of 1833; and that it was retribution for previous cruelties by the populace; he forgets that Charles Albert was acting against a mutiny, v. Guardione, *Domin. Borboni Sicilia*, p. 169. Others say definitely that the tortures were horrible; v. for instance, Chiaramonte, p. 11, Nisco, *Ferdinando II*, p. 48 *et seq*. It is only fair to add that in the following year, 1838, Ferdinand granted a wide Amnesty.

[14] Cf. Martino Beltrani-Scalia, 1, 247.

in Naples—which compelled him to grant a constitution; and it was after the bombardment by his troops of the Sicilian town of Messina that—although 350 miles distant—he was branded forever with the name of Bomba. Finally, in 1860 it was from Sicily that the Bourbons were attacked and driven into exile by Garibaldi.

II. IN 1847[15]

The importance of Pius' movement had been less definitely realised in Sicily than elsewhere, but towards the middle of the year 1847 the islanders began to feel its influence in their midst. Hitherto their conspirators had aimed purely at winning Sicilian autonomy, but now, owing to these new doctrines, we find that some of them are ready, if they win an autonomous Sicily, to bring it into an Italian league or federation. Thus, in the middle of the year 1847, the Sicilian patriots were not entirely of one mind. The majority remained purely Sicilian, but, during a short period, a few thought of bringing Sicily into a united Italy on a federal basis.

This wider view produced another attempt at united action with Neapolitan Liberals—the joint rising in Reggio and Messina on September 1st and 2nd, already described. At Messina a tricolour[16] was raised, and that was a recognition of the idea of unity.

In some of the Sicilian towns there were attempts at agitation similar to that employed against Pius and the other sovereigns. At Trapani a statue of Pius IX was erected and a Civic Guard was raised. But on November 30th Ferdinand definitely

[15] Between 1837 and 1847 there were some events of interest, but they concern the history of Sicily, not that of Italian unity.

[16] The tricolour was regarded as the flag of a federated Italy; v. La Masa, *Documenti*, p. 31. La Farina's stories as to the existence of important revolutionary committees in Sicily from 1840 onwards seem now to be discredited. *V*. Martino Beltrani-Scalia, 1, 242. And Crispi evidently did not believe that Pius' movement had any deep hold in Sicily, any more than did that of Mazzini. *V. La Vita italiana*, 1846–49: III. Crispi's essay, "La Sicilia e la rivoluzione".

refused to allow a Civic Guard. In Palermo there resulted some bloodshed, and that episode marked the end of the Moderate party. Thenceforth the Esaltati were to the front and were working for revolution. We come now to the celebrated rising which in Sicily was named the "sfida a giorno fisso"—an open challenge to government to fight on a day previously named. The boldness of this Sicilian defiance is unparalleled in the history of revolution. For some time previously the organisers had been informing their own partisans that January 12th, 1848, was "the day", and that the fighting would start then "with the certainty of a bill of exchange falling due". But, two days before the end, one of them boldly placarded the date on the walls of Palermo for their enemies to see; and in spite of that piece of bravado they rose at the hour previously advertised. In fact they were challenging the king to fight on his birthday, because on that day there was to be a review of troops in Palermo![17]

On the mainland, too, rebellion was brewing. It will be remembered that Nisco went to Rome and arranged for Ribotti to lead the Neapolitan rebels in the Abruzzi, and for Colonel Giacomo Durando to lead them in Calabria and in the Salerno districts. Among the Sicilians there was no idea of getting leaders from outside.

At that date there was living in exile in Florence a young Sicilian who was already in the act of laying the train which presently would explode in Sicily and from thence would spread until it had shattered half the thrones of Europe. This was La Masa, only twenty-three years of age, blond, long-haired and fearless.[18] His plan was as follows: Palermo was to start the fighting, so he would go there; but there was to be a revolutionary committee in Florence with Professor Montanelli as president. And in order to keep Palermo and

[17] On that day they could be sure of the position of the troops before attacking them.

[18] La Masa, *Documenti*, p. 35. Also Coppola, *La Vita di Giuseppe La Masa*, first 35 pages.

Florence in touch with each other, he proposed to found another committee in Rome, where it would also maintain communications with Naples and the Abruzzi.

Lord Minto[19] was then in Florence on his official mission, and with him was a General Adham or Adam, apparently a relative of his. On October 29th La Masa, with a Sicilian deputation, seized this opportunity of calling on a representative of England, and presented a memorial of their grievances. Minto refused to receive the deputation because his commission did not extend to Naples. However, he referred the matter to Palmerston, and he was authorised then to go to Naples if invited to do so by the king, and if he thought it advisable.

By this time the young La Masa was engaged to the daughter of the Duke of Bevilacqua. But the duke was a patriot and an old Napoleonic veteran; so on December 20th La Masa, armed with a Tuscan passport as Eugenio della Valle, started for Rome, on the way to adventure his life in a desperate struggle within the enclosed spaces of an island, from which, in case of defeat, escape would be almost impossible. This wonderful expedition of his has been compared with that of Garibaldi in 1860, in which, also, La Masa was destined to play an important part.

While in Rome he was told by Lord Minto that there had been no satisfactory reply from King Ferdinand, so he asked General Adham for advice. He states that General Adham—who was a friend of Sicily, where he had served under Lord William Bentinck—"suggested to me to hold a council of a few distinguished Italians in the house of Pantaleoni before rushing into the enterprise".[20] Consequently La Masa went off to the house of Dr Pantaleoni where he met several of the Piedmontese group and some others as well: Massimo d'Azeglio, Minghetti (deputy for Bologna), Pietro Ferretti,

[19] *London Corr.* 1, 193 and 211—Minto's despatch of October 29th and Palmerston's of November 9th, 1847.
[20] La Masa, *Documenti*, p. 35 and Coppola, p. 16 *et seq*.

General Durando (Giovanni),[21] Dall' Ongaro and Pantaleoni. It was this rather impromptu gathering which started the revolution of January 12th, 1848.

At this meeting d' Azeglio, of course, was the most important of the Moderates, and—as was to be expected—he spoke at first against any idea of rebellion; but, before the end, La Masa carried the day. "The government of Naples is Austrian", said La Masa, "and while that king is there Italy will never be free." Eventually Massimo not only agreed that rebellion was necessary, but promised to write to the Principe di Scordia and other important Moderates in Sicily. Thus, for the first time, Massimo d' Azeglio was committing himself to a rebellion.

Before leaving Rome La Masa formed a revolutionary committee[22] of which General Giovanni Durando was president. This seems the most extraordinary position for a regular officer who had been appointed from Turin to be chief instructor of the pontifical army. He was now blossoming forth as a Sicilian revolutionist against the friendly government of Naples!

Certainly La Masa was of a wonderfully sanguine temperament. His hope was that if the Liberals of the Papal State and of Tuscany threw themselves into Naples and helped to oust King Ferdinand, they could then unite the whole southern half of Italy and follow Charles Albert in a war of liberation. He was a gallant young man, always ready to risk his life, but this plan was a mere hallucination.

On December 26th La Masa left Rome for Naples, where he established a committee[23] so as to form another connecting link in the chain to Sicily; and then, with a Swiss passport, as

[21] Coppola, p. 29, says that it was Giacomo Durando.
[22] The committee consisted of Masi (Secretary); the Princess Belgiojoso (Treasurer). There were six other members including Canino.
[23] The Marchese Ruffo, Gennaro Belelli, Mariano D'Ayala; and the Sicilian lawyer Crispi had charge of the correspondence between Naples and Sicily, with Basile and Castiglia.

"Vincenzo Pazzo" he slipped across the strait, and went secretly on to Palermo[24] to await the fateful January 12th. On January 10th the placards were posted on the walls. "C'est peut-être le seul cartel de ce genre dans l'histoire."[25]

Sicily was only a small island—too small to be a separate nation. But Metternich would have been wiser not to treat as negligible its constant demands for autonomy; because these islanders had a genuine sense of injustice, and that is never negligible. It was they who, only a fortnight later, were to start the *débâcle* which drove him into exile.

[24] Visitors to Palermo can see the house of La Masa and his committee in the square then called Piazza della Fieravecchia, but since La Masa's rising known to everyone as the Piazza della Rivoluzione. On that house is a plaque recording all their names.

[25] Amari, *La Sicile et les Bourbons*, p. 67.

Chapter XXI

PIUS IX GRANTS THE CONSULTA

During the last three months of the year 1847 Pius continued his programme of reform with the hope of saving his Papal State to be a unit in the new Italy. He was a good Italian; but his own brother has left it on record that he was first of all things a priest.

This final period of 1847 centres round the erection of a Consulta (consultative assembly) for the state. Pius is coming to the end of his tether: he is granting a Consulta as his last possible concession; but by this time the people have begun to think of having a Pope who will be a constitutional monarch and who will make war on Austria.

On September 11th the distinguished writer, Count Mamiani della Rovere, returned to Rome after sixteen long years of exile. In 1831 he had been a rebel in Bologna; he had offered to organise a house-to-house resistance against Papal troops and he had been one of those exempted from the amnesty of that year, but now he was allowed to re-enter the state, and—to save his face—without signing the oath prescribed in Pius' amnesty of 1846. He wrote a touching letter to Cardinal Ferretti, Secretary of State, thanking him for permission to see again his family and the friends of his childhood, and he repeated a promise already made to Cardinal Gizzi, that he would not raise disturbance in the Papal dominions; adding "To respect the laws...has become an obligation which is natural, necessary and common to all, since, owing to the miraculous wisdom of Pius IX there now exists true law and order, hitherto unknown." It was a strange turn of fortune whereby only nine months later this newly returned exile was called upon by Pius to serve as his Minister of Internal Affairs.

Other and less distinguished revolutionists were also to the fore. Prince Canino was being prosecuted because, on the occasion of a formal celebration in honour of Gioberti, he had arrived dressed in the uniform of the Civic Guard, had made a fiery speech, and had afterwards led a band of young followers to cheer the Tuscan and Piedmontese embassies;[1] and while there, had made another speech from the balcony. This was by no means his only recent exploit, and no sooner was this episode over than he and Masi departed from Rome to attend the Scientific Congress at Venice. On the way they spent some hours with Massimo d'Azeglio who afterwards complained that, amid such a hurricane of words, he could not quite discover their meaning. At Leghorn they had a "frenzied" reception. At Venice they attended the Scientific Congress in the manner already described, were warned off by the Austrian police, and consequently returned to Rome in triumph to receive the enthusiastic ovations of their fellow citizens. So great was the excitement at that time that exploits such as these were considered natural expressions of joy over the Civic Guard, and of hatred for Austria. The Civic Guard was at the height of its popularity—"faceva furore"—just then; everyone wanted to be in it and to wear its uniform on all possible occasions. It was their way of preparing for the coming war of liberation. Almost every day a banquet was given to one or other of the battalions, speeches were made, and poems recited by Masi or by some other patriot. As yet these people in Rome had everything to learn—and much to unlearn. This generation had been brought up between the over-paternalism of the Popes and the silly catch-phrases of the French Revolution. They were heading straight for the disasters of Cornuda and Treviso. At the same time, on hundreds of the ancient slabs around them, were still to be seen the letters S.P.Q.R., the hall-mark of a heroic era. Un-

[1] Vienna Staats-Archiv, Lützow, 1847, *Rapports*, 1, September 14th. *V.* also Bargagli's description in the Florentine Archives. These accounts have some value as coming from outside.

doubtedly they bore a message to the living Romans:[2] for the *débâcle* of 1848 was destined to be followed by the Defence of 1849.

On October 1st, 1847, in the midst of all this turmoil Pius introduced his next reform—a municipal government for the city of Rome. Strange to say, of all the Papal towns Rome alone did not possess a municipal government; and in ordinary times its inauguration would have created a permanent sense of satisfaction.

Pius' measure was as follows:

Rome was in future to be ruled by two bodies:

I. *The deliberative Council* of 100 members[3] over twenty-five years old; only four of whom were to be clerics. At first all were to be nominated by the Pope, but after that they were to be co-opted by the Council itself.

II. *The Senate* or magistracy of the city of Rome. To consist of nine members elected by the Municipal Council, namely one *Senator* (its chief) known as the Roman Senator, and eight Conservatori.[4]

---

[2] They inspired even Sterbini to write a fine hymn to Rome: "Arise, mother of so many heroes."

[3] Consisting of 64 property-owners:

   (a) 15 with income of over 6000 scudi per annum.
   (b) 34 with income of over 1000 scudi per annum.
   (c) 15 with income of over 200 scudi per annum.

     32 public employés of importance: professors of liberal arts, or belonging to literary, artistic or scientific institutions.

     <u> 4</u> representing ecclesiastical bodies or public institutions.

Total 100 These were named by the government.

One-third of this body was to retire every two years. These members could be re-elected. But after one re-election they were to stand out for two years.

[4] All to be over 30 years of age. These nine were elected by the municipal council.

   3 members from the most distinguished of the Councillors. From among these three the Roman Senator was to be appointed by the government.

One important clause—important, that is, from the point of view of the modern tourist—was the fact that Pius recommended to his municipality the care of all public monuments both ancient and modern.[5]

This municipal scheme was the product of several months of hard work by one of Pius' commissions, and it handed over to the new municipality so many duties hitherto performed by government, that Pius had been compelled also to re-organise his whole administration; and shortly afterwards he re-grouped all the great offices of state, by his motu-proprio of December 29th.

Moreover it involved a very important innovation, namely the placing of the municipal authority in the hands of laymen.

The concession was received with rejoicings. On October 3rd there was held a great demonstration of thanks attended —we may note—by about 4000 of the Civic Guard.[6]

But the people, of course, were not thinking of municipal reforms, they were thinking of Ferrara. The state of political

3 members from the Councillors who had over 1000 scudi per annum.

3 members from among the remaining councillors.

One-third of the Senate retired every two years, on the same principle as the Councillors.

In this motu-proprio of Pius, some twelve pages are given to classifying every imaginable species of municipal duty, some being assigned to the Senate and others to the whole municipal authority.

Until the details of finance could be finally regulated the government undertook to hand over to them 500,000 scudi per annum, or about £100,000 sterling.

[5] It will be seen that the administration was to be mainly in the hands of the richer type of bourgeois: and no longer in those of the aristocracy (Vienna Staats-Archiv, Lützow's despatch of October 2nd, 1847). He regarded this measure as democratic.

[6] "Is it to be wondered at if the contemplation of so many benefits included in that sovereign act aroused in the hearts of the Romans a joy that can hardly be described?" *Contemporaneo*, October 5th, 1847. The first meeting of the Municipal Council was ordered for November 24th amid fresh rejoicing. (Notificazione of November 19th, Vatican Arch., Fondo Spada, *Documenti storici*, vol. 1.)

excitement can best be judged by giving a short list of the demonstrations that took place during these weeks.

On October 6th Verdi's opera, *Ernani*, was performed at the Argentina Theatre. At the point where Charles V says: "Pardon I grant to all. Ye are free; love one another"; and the reply comes: "To Charles the Great be glory and honour"; for "Charles the Great" was substituted: "To Pius IX give glory and honour" amid tremendous applause and waving of handkerchiefs. And this demonstration was repeated on the succeeding nights.

On October 7th there occurred a far more important event. A joint field day was held near Ponte Molle by the soldiers and Civic Guard. They manœuvred among those flat fields beside the Tiber, while many thousands of spectators stood watching them from the curving slopes of Monte Mario. When the manœuvres were finished, General Zamboni gave the order to present arms, and, with uplifted sword, shouted: "Viva Pio IX!" "Long live Pius IX!" a cry which was taken up by the soldiers, Civic Guard and spectators "with frenzied enthusiasm"; and at a given sign the soldiers advanced towards the Civic Guard and both corps threw themselves into each other's arms shouting with one voice: "One force only are the arms of Rome, just as their head is one, and their Father one. We will all live and die for Pius IX." The people then joined them, and they all returned together in one triumphal throng to Rome, cheering and singing all the way.

This fraternisation meant that the soldiers as well as the carbineers had now been captured by the Civica, and that the government was virtually in the hands of its own volunteers.

On the same evening the 9th Battalion was entertained at the beautiful Villa Doria Pamphili by their colonel, Prince Doria. At the end of the banquet, Masi, who was now a captain, improvised in prose and verse, and was presented with a wreath. He little knew that only twenty-one months later he would be a Garibaldian colonel desperately defending that villa against the French.

On the 12th there was a banquet at Monte Mario, the mountain overlooking Rome; after which Masi again improvised.

On the 17th an entertainment was given for the 5th Battalion; there were political speeches and poetry. And the 7th Battalion was entertained elsewhere.

On the 18th a company of the 2nd Battalion was entertained at the Ponte Molle, an ancient bridge across the Tiber, just outside Rome.

On the 27th the scene was at La Caffarella, a Civic Guard camp of about 3000 men; military manœuvres until midday; then tables and a banquet. Dr Sterbini, of the *Contemporaneo* newspaper, turned up and tried to make a political speech: but the colonel, Prince Aldobrandini, who was an old soldier, gave orders to beat the big drum until Sterbini abandoned the attempt.[7] This latter detail, however, was not reported in the *Contemporaneo*.

This list of petty incidents, by no means exhaustive, shows that the population of Rome was in that febrile condition which, unfortunately, can very seldom be relieved except by blood-letting. It shows also how completely unmilitary were the people, and more especially the government. But both were conscious of their lack of preparation for war, and the people were burning to remedy it, especially since the incident at Ferrara.

On October 14th, amid all this tumult of banquets and speeches, Pius introduced his *Consulta* (consultative assembly); the supreme effort of his internal reforms.

On December 29th he completed this new scheme by setting up a reorganised Council of Ministers to act as a sort of upper committee of nine.

Together these two bodies form the scheme of government proposed by Pius as a solution of his difficulties. He was a spiritual ruler, with his Church to protect: he proposed a Consultative government.

[7] According to Spada.

This is the last item of his considered programme of reforms. It is interesting because it shows us the governmental system which would have been set up in a modernised Papal State, had times been normal.

It consisted of:

I. *The Consulta:* a consultative assembly of state, composed of:

A cardinal as president, named by the sovereign.

A prelate as vice-president.

Twenty-four Consultori or councillors from every part of the state; all to be Papal subjects at least thirty years old; none of them need be an ecclesiastic.

A general secretary and a capo contabile (head accountant).

The method of election for Consultori (members of the assembly) was as follows: each commune throughout the Papal State drew up a " terna " or list of three names: all these were sent to the local provincial council which in turn formed a terna by selecting three names from among them. All the provincial lists were then forwarded to the Secretary of State who selected the twenty-four members of the Consulta.[8]

The communes were not restricted to choosing local men. They could send up the name of anybody in the whole state provided he were eligible.

Those eligible for election were (1) members of provincial or governmental councils; (2) gonfalonieri; and anziani of places presided over by a gonfaloniere; (3) property owners with 1000 scudi a year, or whose property was valued at 10,000 scudi; (4) lawyers inscribed on one of the three courts of appeal; (5) learned men belonging to the best scientific institutions; (6) merchants or proprietors of great industrial enterprises.

The term of office was to be for five years; one-fifth to

---

[8] Four for Rome and the Comarca; two for Bologna, and one for each of the other provinces.

retire each year, but they could be re-elected once; after which they were to stand out for five years.

Attached to the Consulta was a service of uditori, or young graduates at universities, specially selected from those who had taken good degrees in philosophy and law.

Members of the Consulta were removable by the sovereign after a hearing in the Consulta and Council of Ministers. This safeguard, as Pellegrino Rossi pointed out, regarded them as though they were members of a council of state.

II. *The Council of Ministers* (*v.* motu-proprio of December 29th, 1847). This was in reality a committee of the nine heads of departments.[9] By thus bringing together the chiefs of the great offices of the state he obtained a Council which could act partly as an upper house, partly as a cabinet.

The Secretary of State was to be a cardinal: about the other members nothing was stipulated; they might be laymen.

[9] At first of only seven, according to Pius' earlier scheme of June 12th (*Atti*). But when he completed his constitution on December 29th, he set up nine departments. This involved a complete reorganising of his administration, rendered necessary by the grant of the municipality to Rome whereby many duties hitherto carried out by the state were handed over to the town. It must have been an arduous task with so many people clamouring at him. The Council of Ministers consisted of:

1. President and Secretary of State—to be a cardinal; his substitute to be a prelate. The Minister for Foreign Affairs: represented abroad by nuncios and other diplomatic or consular agents.
2. The Minister for Home Affairs.
3. The Minister for Public Instruction.
4. The Minister for Pardon and Justice.
5. The Minister for Finances.
6. The Minister for Commerce.
7. The Minister for Public Works.
8. The Minister for Arms.
9. The Minister for Police.
   A secretary of the Council of Ministers.

The Minister for Foreign Affairs is President of the Council of Ministers. He is also Secretary of State for the whole kingdom, and is always a cardinal. He is, in fact, by far the most important man in the state.

The Council of Ministers was to meet once a week.

Its duties were to discuss all affairs of state before they were laid before the sovereign: also those sent down to it by the sovereign; and various named departmental matters.

We must remember that these ministers were permanent officials responsible to the sovereign and not to the people. But this new scheme rather curtailed their independence.

The great point of interest about Pius' constitution is the question of popular liberty; to see how much freedom he really allowed to his people, and how he reconciled it with the preservation of Papal authority: in fact, what were the powers of the Consulta or lower chamber.

The Consulta was primarily a consultative chamber, intended only to give its opinion when asked. It had no legislative power. But it had certain rights which added immensely to its importance. It had the right of claiming that all matters of state should be laid before it, before going to the Council of Ministers or being sanctioned by the Pope. It had the right of discussing, making suggestions, pointing out abuses and voting on all these important matters.

The right of actually initiating a measure seems to have lain with the ministers. But, by Article 26, the Consulta could make any *suggestions* that it liked arising out of the matters that came before it (a very wide privilege, and a certain basis for agitation). Though it was not allowed to make a law, it could express desires which would then be placed before the ministers or before the College of Cardinals.

The ordinary procedure seems to have been that if a minister wished to make changes involving legislation, he was not allowed to deal with them himself, even though they concerned his department alone, but was obliged to lay the matter before the Consulta.[10] When the Consulta had discussed it, made suggestions, and voted on it, then (and not earlier) it went before the Council of Ministers. When the ministers had deliberated on the measure, it was handed to the Pope

[10] For an analysis of the Consulta *v.* Spada, I, p. 374.

for sanction.[11] It was accompanied by *procès-verbaux* (minutes of the transactions) giving the votes, names and arguments in each chamber.

It is impossible to say how the constitution would have developed, because it was so quickly superseded. But one cannot help thinking that very soon the people would have had a considerable say in the management of their own affairs; and this was the opinion of Pellegrino Rossi, perhaps the best contemporary judge of the situation.[12]

To take, for instance, the true test of all constitutions, namely the passage of a money bill.

Supposing that the Minister of Finance wished to impose a new tax on the state. He must first lay it before the Consulta. Suppose that the Consulta voted against his tax. The proposal would then go before the Council of Ministers. The Council of Ministers might perhaps approve of it in the teeth of the Consulta. Theoretically, then, the Minister of Finance had the power of imposing that tax on the state, if the Pope sanctioned it. But, in practice, one doubts whether he would have attempted to do so. The Consulta was in a strong position. Being originally elected by the communes, its members would have a considerable power of agitation: they could appeal to the influence of the press which was now formidable; also to that of the clubs. And they possessed,

[11] The Pope had the right, if he desired to use it, of laying the measure before the College of Cardinals, presumably as a safeguard for the interests of the Church. But this right did not apply to the annual estimates. These were presented to him after being discussed by the Council of Ministers, by the President of the Consulta, whose duty it was to give all necessary explanations to him.

[12] "The sovereign power which has hitherto been absolute, will find itself in presence of bodies set up by itself, but supported by public opinion; bodies of which it will have to make use, or with which it will have to reckon." P. Rossi, Despatch October 18th, 1847. Paris Aff. Etr., Rome, 1847–8. Count Lützow's opinion was: "The College of Cardinals will be reduced to an influence so small and so rarely employed that it may be considered a nullity." Vienna Staats-Archiv, Rome, *Rapports*, 1, October 16th, 1847.

moreover, under Article 26, the right of suggesting any alternatives that they preferred.

In this case we have an instance of a quarrel between the two houses. In England of that day the matter would have been referred to the people (or, more accurately, to the voters). But in the Roman state the decision was to be given by the Pope. This was obviously a bad arrangement, because it might bring the sovereign into direct conflict with the people. But in practice it seems unlikely that Pius would have quarrelled with his people except about questions concerning the Church. Unfortunately for him the only vital question of this time was war, which did, of course, concern the Church.

Attached to the Council of Ministers, as also to the Consulta, was a corps of uditori, young men specially selected from graduates who had taken a degree in philosophy or law, and desired to enter government service.

Pellegrino Rossi's opinion of the Consulta was that it was workable; but he was despondent. He thought that the authorities were now too weak to stand by it: they had let all the power slip out of their hands and their position would be stormed by the Revolution; but he became far more cheerful after the second (December 29th) edict, setting up the Council of Ministers, which had his entire approval.

This Consulta of October 14th did not introduce the principle of popular election in local bodies, but it went far enough to set a good example; and in this respect Charles Albert, though in 1847 he did not venture to set up a central Consulta, was able to advance a little farther than Pius: when he granted his reforms he allowed the communal councils to be elected by the people within certain fixed categories. Of course, the representative system was less dangerous for him than it was for the Pope.

One great advance Pius had made: all the Consultori could be laymen except the president and vice-president: and in the Council of Ministers, too, every post except that of

Secretary of State could be filled by a layman. These changes might place the State of the Church under lay administrators. In the eyes of the old ecclesiastics they amounted to a revolution.

The Gregorian view is represented in Lützow's despatch to Metternich.

I am informed that this time the Liberals...are satisfied and have no criticism to make: and it would need a considerable dose of self-assurance, it seems to me, to claim more than the Pope has already given them by this law. To despoil himself of the whole of his sovereignty he would—in my opinion—only have to promulgate the secularisation of the government, or else to proclaim a republic.

Pius, no doubt, felt that he had made a great plunge and did not want to go any farther, at all events for the time being. He had no intention of becoming a constitutional monarch. He was merely a reforming Pope. From his point of view this was a very generous measure. The Consulta was a far more liberal concession than any outlined by Gioberti, and no doubt would have been accepted with joy at the time when Gioberti wrote. Pius probably had foreseen fairly accurately the form which it would have assumed in normal times: namely an assembly of loyal gentlemen such as Count Pasolini, who would spend their days in studying state problems and meet to discuss matters, especially finance, to give their advice, to make suggestions and to express their wishes and those of the people. That was rather the form which it took—that of an assembly slightly academic in character but capable of useful work. Owing to the political excitement, however, it never became more than a stepping-stone to greater concessions.

It was received with the most enthusiastic demonstration of the year. People felt that Pius was voluntarily endangering the authority which had belonged for a thousand years to his predecessors and had hitherto been regarded almost as a sacred charge: and this fact was appreciated.

The demonstration of thanks for the Consulta needs little description; it was one of the greatest, but similar to the others. That evening the crowds met in the Piazza del Popolo; each had its banners upon which were inscribed Pius' concessions. They then moved off as usual along the Corso and wended their way, a huge crowd, up to the piazza outside the Quirinal Palace. As they sang Pius' hymn, lights were seen moving inside that great and sombre building, and Pius appeared on the balcony and looked down on them for a few moments. Then he made the sign of the cross, and all fell upon their knees and remained in dead silence. It was only when he pronounced the words *Sit nomen Domini benedictum* that thousands of voices replied *Ex hoc nunc et usque in saeculum*. This demonstration seems to have been as genuinely heartfelt as any since his accession.

Chapter XXII

THE END OF PIUS IX's PROGRAMME OF REFORM

Thus Pius had set up his new form of government, the centre of much hope for the future. This was his solution of the supreme problem, namely that of combining Papal supremacy —to ensure security for the Church—with democratic advance; it was a compromise.

I. THE CONSULTA

He had no intention of making any further concessions, at all events for the time being. But already the doubt existed; had this concession arrived too late? Had the democratic agitation gone so far forward that the people would no longer regard the Consulta as worth having? Pellegrino Rossi approved of this Moderate assembly, but rather doubted whether it would be accepted as a great institution, and thus become sufficiently popular to form a centre of loyalty against the Revolution. And Rossi foresaw that if the Consulta proved a failure the whole Papal State would be imperilled. From the very beginning of the Liberal movement his feeling had been: faster, faster, before the Revolution gets in ahead of you! He perceived that in these stormy times the Papal authority could be saved only by establishing itself on a rock of Liberalism, in fact by founding institutions so democratic as to counter-attract its people away from the agitators.[1] With this end in view he urged Pius to take another forward step by appointing laymen to the Council of Ministers. As matters stood, although the members of the Consulta itself were all

[1] Montanelli, who was in Rome for the first fortnight of November 1847, tells us that the revolutionists regarded the Consulta merely as a means of getting further concessions. Montanelli, II, 64 and 69.

laymen except the president and vice-president, yet on the upper Council all nine ministers (heads of departments) were ecclesiastics. To popularise this Council by appointing three laymen to be ministers was the advice which Rossi urged upon Pius, and to which Pius very soon agreed.[2]

As to the Consulta, in normal times it could certainly have done useful work. This is proved by the good beginnings that it made. And it is remembered in history as an assembly of cultivated gentlemen, perhaps rather academic in their ideas, but earnest and patriotic students of the problems of their country.[3] They consisted of a president (Cardinal Antonelli) and a vice-president, who were both ecclesiastics; but of the remaining twenty-four members only one was a cleric, thirteen of them being nobles, and eight lawyers, and the remaining two also laymen. On November 15th they held their first meeting amid great popular rejoicing.

The line followed by Pius when thanking them for their address is worth noting: on this occasion, as on several others during these weeks, he took the opportunity of impressing on

[2] Guizot in his *Mémoires pour servir*, p. 392 *et seq.*, quotes a letter from Pellegrino Rossi describing the scene in the following terms: "He (Pius) had decided that by the new *motu proprio* of which he had spoken (that of December 30th, 1847), the Department of War could be entrusted to a layman, and he gave it to General Gabrielli; moreover he had laid down that of the 24 auditors attached to the Council of Ministers there should always be twelve laymen: 'Well, Signor Conte', he said to me with a gracious smile and a kindly bantering expression, '*l' elemento è introdotto*', the element is introduced. I must tell you that I had often made use of the gallicism *l' elemento laico*. You can guess my reply. But my compliment was accompanied by a respectful insistence on the introduction of two other laymen." To this insistence Pius agreed.

[3] "The great majority of the deputies to the Consulta were men of Liberal and generally temperate opinions: and the importance of a good understanding and concert with the government is strongly felt by them, both as necessary for the steady prosecution of measures of reform and in order that the Government may acquire strength in support of its influence and authority." Lord Minto to Palmerston, November 18th, 1847, *London Corr.* 1, 246.

them two facts; firstly that their duties were only consultative,[4] and secondly that the new institutions were intended to
be used for administrative work and not merely as a means of
revolutionary agitation for gaining further concessions. He
was aware that among the Consultori whom he was addressing
there were several extremists, notably Sterbini, so he inserted
in his speech two passages for their special benefit. He said
that he thanked them all for their goodwill; that by the
Divine help he hoped to do all that was possible in the future,
but "without ever diminishing, even by one iota (*apice*), the
pontifical sovereignty which he had received full and entire
from God; it had come to him from his predecessors, and he
must hand it on as a sacred deposit to his successors". He
ended up by telling them that the Consulta had been summoned so that he should ask its opinion when necessary, and
thus have the benefit of it in his sovereign deliberations when
he consulted his conscience and conferred with his ministers
and the Sacred College. At that point he fixed his eyes on the
assemblage before him, and in a more commanding voice he
spoke some phrases which have been remembered: "Greatly
deceived is anyone who thinks that his duties are different
from these; greatly deceived is anyone who sees in the Consulta thus set up, some Utopia of his own, and the seeds of an
institution incompatible with the pontifical supremacy."

Pius uttered these last words with marked emphasis. He
did not intend to resign any more of his authority, for it was
the only defence left to the Church.[5]

The Consultori then proceeded to vote their resolution of
thanks to the sovereign. It was cleverly drawn up so as to
include nearly all the existing grievances and to suggest
remedies for them, without actually seeming to interfere with
the administrative authority.[6] They wished to avoid any ap-

---

[4] They had the right also of making suggestions, etc., *v.* p. 323.
[5] *Diario di Roma*, November 16th; Spada, I, 395; *London Corr.*
I, 249, Petre to Hamilton, November 17th, 1847.
[6] Gabussi, I, 108, gives the text.

pearance of overstepping their limits as a merely consultative assembly endowed with the right of making suggestions.

Far more important, however, was the next step which they took, namely the passing of two "articles" relating to the following points: firstly, that the vote of each member should be made public; secondly, that their debates should be published in the press. These were extremely important from the democratic point of view.[7] They subjected each member to criticism by the people, and the pontifical government itself to popular fury if it did not carry out the suggestions of the Consulta.[8]

II. THE REVOLUTION

Unfortunately for the Consulta it was not destined to enjoy either the leisure or the internal peace necessary for its success. The revolution was hard at work; and the people were in a restless and excitable condition, ready to take up any popular cry, and easily manipulated by the systematic agitators and the clubs. A good instance of their excitability is their demonstration over the Sonderbund question (December 3rd); and a proof of the ease with which they could now

[7] Gabussi, I, 110; Farini, I, 324.

[8] In connection with the second article we have an interesting opinion from no less a person than Lord Minto, who was then in Rome as a semi-official representative of the British government. He had arrived in Rome on November 3rd and had taken a very Liberal view of the situation. In Rome he was less successful than in Florence and still less so than in Turin. We feel that, very naturally, he had thrown in his lot with men who were more extreme than they would admit; with Sterbini, Masi, Canino, d'Azeglio and even Ciceruacchio. Evidently he still thought the danger came from Austria, and did not perceive that in the Papal State matters were rapidly slipping down an inclined plane which would land Pius in disaster. About this matter of the publicity (of debate) he gave good advice, namely to allow it: if Pius had refused to do so, most probably there would have been trouble. So strong on this point was Minto, that on hearing that Pius was seeking advice in Florence and Turin, he (Minto) wrote to both places urging the authorities there to advise acceptance.

be controlled by the systematic agitators was afforded by the three great festivals of November 15th (opening of the Consulta), December 27th (Pius' birthday), and January 1st, New Year's Day, 1848.

Firstly, as to the Sonderbund; it was a purely Swiss question—but naturally all Pius' sympathies were on the side of the Catholic cantons: that was inevitable; and so were those of Metternich, of Louis Philippe, and secretly, of Charles Albert. But the Radical cantons were backed by Liberal opinion all over Europe, including of course that of the Liberals in Rome.

In November 1847 the civil war broke out in Switzerland. The Federal troops were superior in number and after two engagements they occupied Lucerne. The struggle which had been in progress off and on for three or four years had ended in the defeat of the Catholics, and consequently the Jesuits were expelled from Switzerland.

The news reached Rome on December 3rd, 1847, and naturally it came as a disappointment to Pius; and one would have supposed that, in view of his generous reforms, the Liberals in the town would have abstained from unseemly rejoicings. But so far from sparing the feelings of their ruler, some of the Roman crowd seized the opportunity that evening to march through the Piazza S. Ignazio raising shouts of "Down with the Jesuits"; "Out with them"; "Death to the Jesuits"; and then held a joyful demonstration outside the Swiss consulate. These people no doubt regarded the Society of Jesus as representing the old Gregorian gang. But Pius was deeply hurt at their conduct. He publicly deplored this demonstration in his Allocution of December 17th, and moderate men sympathised with him; even two years later when Farini wrote his history, he was still furious at the recollection of that evening.[9]

Secondly, as to the festivals above named.

Among the leading articles in praise of the Consulta there

[9] Farini, 1, 282; *v.* also Spada, 1, 426.

had been one which was positively enthusiastic, namely that of Sterbini in the *Contemporaneo* of October 19th. It is filled with eulogies. He speaks of the difficulties of Pius' position and expresses deep gratitude to him. He has no doubt that the new machine will work well and that the Consultori will be able to get their suggestions carried out. Moreover he says that the Consulta is better than the Prussian Diet about which, for many years, there had been so much strife.

Nevertheless the grant of the Consulta was seized upon by Sterbini and the agitators in the Circolo Romano to initiate their next activities. During these weeks there were held three political demonstrations, each one bolder than the last; they were the opening of the Consulta on November 15th; Pius' birthday on December 27th; and New Year's Day, January 1st, 1848.[10]

On November 15th (1847), in honour of the Consulta, there was a brilliant procession through the streets, and arrangements were made for foreigners of each nationality to march in one body under their own national banner. But the harmony of the day was rather marred by an attempt to make all the small states of Italy (including Lombardy and Venetia) march in one body with their banners grouped together, and thus turn the whole festival into a united-Italy demonstration. This scheme had been previously arranged by Sterbini, Montanelli and others at the Circolo Romano.[11] But it was forbidden, says Montanelli, at the request of the Russian, French

[10] I omit several other festivals of minor importance; during this period Rome did little else but hold festivals, as was noticed at the time. Spada, vol. I, chap. XXI.

[11] This is the account given by Spada (Papal) and Montanelli (revolutionary). Gabussi (republican) explains it in a different way. But Montanelli's evidence seems conclusive. He says that he himself was at the Circolo Romano, and saw Sterbini "excited and rhetorical, calling out Gruppo, Gruppo, 'Group, group', and heard the words 'Group, group', repeated in chorus by his 'bollenti'—boiling-hot supporters". This narrative is quoted and accepted by Spada, I, 398. Apparently Pius was annoyed with Sterbini. Montanelli, II, 64.

and Austrian ambassadors. This was a prudent order; for the
Lombard and Venetian banners would have constituted an
insult to Austria; and the Ferrara incident was not yet closed.

The next opportunity for agitation occurred on December
27th, Pius' birthday. Ciceruacchio seized this chance of con-
gratulating the Pope and at the same time of presenting to
him a long list of thirty-five popular demands claimed by the
people. There are various versions as to how he carried the
list. According to some accounts he himself presented it at
the head of a deputation of popolani; according to other
writers he had the demands written large on cards, sent them
to the secretary's office and distributed them far and wide.
The headings of his claims were the following:

Liberty of the press; expulsion of the Jesuits; civilian armament;
railways; abolition of the summary jurisdiction of the police;
codices with useful and impartial laws; public education; a poly-
technic school; encouragement for the arts; abolition of mono-
polies; an Italian league; emancipation of the Jews; a revival of
commerce; reform of provincial municipalities; reform and
guaranteeing of postal correspondence; a school of public economy;
civic artillery; publicity of the acts of the Consulta;[12] secularisation
of certain offices; reform of the charitable asylums for infants;
industry reanimated; farm settlements in the Agro Romano;
reorganisation of the military forces; individual liberty guaranteed;
a reserve to be organised for the Civic Guard; the navy to be
encouraged; abolition of the game of lotto; amnesty for the
twenty-four political prisoners in Civita Castellana; trust in the
people; a checking of constant summary judgements; abolition of
appalti camerali[13]; abolition of entails; reform of mortmain; the
imposing on the priests and religious corporations of what is due
to Pius IX and to the Church, namely love and respect.

This list[14] was obviously intended for purposes of agitation
and did not contain genuine demands of the people. It was

[12] This had been voted, but apparently Pius had not yet agreed
to it.
[13] Certain government contracts: it is hard to say exactly what
they included.
[14] Spada, I, 442, 443. If one takes them one by one, there is hardly
a single case that had not been already dealt with or was already

manifestly the work of the clubs, perhaps intended to show that they were not satisfied with the Consulta: perhaps a hit back by Sterbini for the words addressed to him on November 15th. In any case the presentation of such a paper to Pius by a man of Ciceruacchio's limitations—and more especially of the last clause in it—was certainly a piece of insolence.

This was the greeting for Pius' birthday.

Finally we come to the New Year's festival of 1848, which produced an episode of considerable importance. For that day of rejoicing the most careful political preparations had been made by the revolutionary party, but on the other hand the government had decided to try to assert itself. Now that the Consulta was at work, Pius' administration felt itself backed by an assembly of patriotic men who—though this first batch were merely nominated—represented after all a very large body of public opinion throughout the state.

The political demonstration[15] had been arranged by the

under consideration, or else amounted to little more than a vague generality. For instance; *the liberty of the press*; the press had already been freed as far as possible. It had taken advantage of this to run wild over the Austrian question and to attack the government on many other subjects. *The expulsion of the Jesuits*; there was no kind of definite accusation against them. *The summary jurisdiction* of the police; *the codices*; these were being already dealt with by Commissions to which legal experts were attached; and so forth. In any case these were all obviously matters for the Consulta to examine and suggest upon, and not to be laid before the Pope for summary decision on his birthday.

Evidently this was felt to be the case even by the writers who support Ciceruacchio; some of them pass quickly over the subject. Gabussi, though a republican, speaks of "demands, some of which could not be made good and of which others required time and mature counsel, evidently reveal as great confusion in the mind of the person who conceived them." Even he evidently did not believe that Ciceruacchio was the real author, as indeed was self-evident. Gabussi, I, 113, 114.

[15] All the facts of this demonstration are taken from Gabussi (republican). He is more or less confirmed by Farini (moderate), and Spada (Papal), all contemporaries. Farini says that Rome was full of agents sent out by Mazzini to lead the crowds: "to make use

agitators as follows: at nine o' clock in the morning there was
to be a reunion in the Piazza del Popolo consisting of the
officers of the regular forces and the officers of the Civic
Guard, with bands, and accompanied by members of the
Circolo Romano. They were to march to the Quirinal palace,
amid applauding crowds, to interview the Pope. In fact it
was proposed to show that the Circolo Romano, of well-
known Liberal tendencies, had got the soldiers on its side.

For once the government took some shrewd steps to counter
the revolutionary plans. On the evening of December 31st it
ordered all troops to be under arms on the following morning,
and summoned the officers of the Civic Guard to their
quarters. It also directed the Carabinieri to prevent any
assemblages of the people.

At 7 a.m. on New Year's morning the assembly sounded
and all the troops were confined to barracks; and patrols of
Carabinieri were sent out through Rome. At 9 a.m. two
officers called at the house of Ciceruacchio, but he was not at
home, so they simply warned the people there that any
assemblage would be suppressed by force. Meanwhile many
people had run to the Piazza del Popolo, the place of assembly,
but there were met by Colonel Cavanna with thirty Carabinieri who politely asked them to disperse. They did so.
During the day the report was spread through the cafés that
the Pope was unwell, and could not receive demonstrations.
So far the government's action had been entirely successful:
the demonstration had been checked. But the people were
angry. The popular heads of the Rioni met and decided to
apply to the Senator of Rome, old Prince Corsini, and ask
him to inform the Pope that they had been calumniated; that
evidently a perfectly peaceful demonstration had been repre-

of the present agitation for the benefit of Young Italy which is
against all monarchies; and to do this with shouts of Viva the Grand
Duke of Tuscany. Charles Albert for ever. Pius IX for ever."
Farini of course was a moderate: but his opinion is worth having.
V. Farini, I, 319; Gabussi, I, 129–32.

sented as dangerous. And undoubtedly in most of the people this was a genuine feeling; they had only wanted to thank Pius for his grant of the Council of Ministers, and they had been met by soldiers and Carabinieri. But simultaneously the agitators were at work.[16]

A great crowd now ran to the senator's palace, with shouts of rage. They found three Carabinieri at the door, so they told them to go away or there would be bloodshed; and "the Carabinieri did not need to be told twice". Prince Corsini, a venerable man of eighty years, seems to have kept his head well. He discussed the matter with Ciceruacchio and with Masi; it must have been an anxious time for the agitators, for if the demonstrations were stopped their chief weapon was gone. Finally Prince Corsini promised to go and see the Pope; he did not start until one o'clock, but on his return he assured the people of the Holy Father's goodwill, adding that he would give them proof of it on the following day. Order was thus restored.

The government, therefore, had succeeded in stopping the demonstration. But it is very hard to know what was really in progress; because even the chief people concerned did not know. Pasolini, for instance, believed that it was a perfectly harmless demonstration, and that the government did wrong to stop it; Lord Minto thinks that the ministers were frightened by the old Gregorian clique—though he admits that there existed revolutionists who were trying to take advantage of them. Farini's account is unconvincing either way. But it is certain, at all events, that hundreds of the people were very genuinely hurt and angry because they believed that they had been calumniated to their beloved Holy Father. It was necessary to dispel this idea.

At three o'clock on the following afternoon, therefore, accompanied only by four officers of the Noble Guard—and this certainly shows good courage on his part—Pius drove slowly out from the Quirinal by the Gesù, the Church of

[16] Spada, II, cap. I.

S. Luigi dei Francesi, and the Fontanella dei Borghesi into the Corso—which is the main thoroughfare of Rome.[17] He was received with unparalleled enthusiasm. It is described as "a joy, a transport, cheering, clapping of hands, a crowding forward which is beyond all description". Some of the crowd jumped on to the back of the carriage: others on to the steps. "Anyone who could touch the sides of the carriage felt himself a happy man; and happier still if he could touch the clothes or even the hand of the Pontiff." Pius was so deeply moved that he began to feel faint, and asked for some restraint of the enthusiasm. And when this was told to the people, at the word "Silence! the Pope is feeling unwell", in an instant everyone was silent. It must have been a striking moment. The crowd then assembled in the square of the Quirinal, under downpours of rain, awaiting the benediction, and departed sadly and in silence when it was announced that the Pope was indisposed and could not show himself. The reason given was genuine; he was temporarily overcome.

All this description is taken mainly from the book of a republican, so as to obtain the revolutionist's account of the episode. But the question remains: was it a rejoicing or was it another political demonstration? It was both. The opportunity had been too good to miss. Ciceruàcchio had followed the Papal carriage in one of his own (or, some say, on the back of the Papal carriage), with a large banner on which was displayed the motto: "Justice, Holy Father, for your people which is on your side."[18] With the cries of "Viva Pio Nono" had been mingled angry shouts of "Down with Savelli" (Monsignor Savelli was governor of Rome), "Down with the Police", "Down with the Carbineers", "Death to the Blacks", "Death to the Jesuits". The agitators were furious. The people had been told that there was a reactionary plot to prevent Pius from seeing his subjects, and they intended to

[17] Farini says he drove down the Via Ripetta into the Piazza del Popolo and then along the Corso. Gabussi says he went into the Trastevere, where the poor people live.
[18] Spada, II, 10.

win him back. Many of them joined in these cries with perfect good faith. But in the faces of some of the excited Traste-verini who sprang on the carriage step and grasped at his clothes, there was rage as well as affection. They evidently thought that he was weakening; this ruler whom for a year and a half they had been pushing forward and onward from position to position, until finally they had set him up as their national leader, whose name was now a war-cry all over Italy —at the critical moment he was weakening, overpowered by bad advisers; but he was theirs and he must not be allowed to falter. Perhaps it was the realisation of their sentiments which had proved too much for Pius. He must have seen that he had come to the parting of the ways between the friends of the Church and the leaders of the populace. His own feelings as to his treatment by the people we can only conjecture.

From among the crowds there had arisen shouts of fury: and yet these were his own partisans, the men whom he had tried to serve. And everywhere it was the same. Even in Sicily, La Masa and his Palermitans would rise against Ferdinand with shouts of "Viva Pio Nono!" "Long live Pius IX." The times were too hard for him.

It was an ill-omened opening of the terrible year 1848. He had come to an end of his Liberal concessions; he had no more to give. Still, so far, he had been able to carry out his two-fold duty: he had inaugurated a great Liberal advance both in his own State and also in Italy, the beginning of unity; at the same time the Church and its belongings were still safe; for he retained his supreme authority with which to protect them.

The risings of 1831 had been the work of municipalities. The coming war of 1848 would be the work of the small states, temporarily united owing to the Liberal peace-movement initiated by Pius. The war of 1859 would be an appeal to every Italian to follow Piedmont.

But now the period of agitation was very near its end. The train of revolution was laid in Sicily, timed to explode within twelve days.

22-2

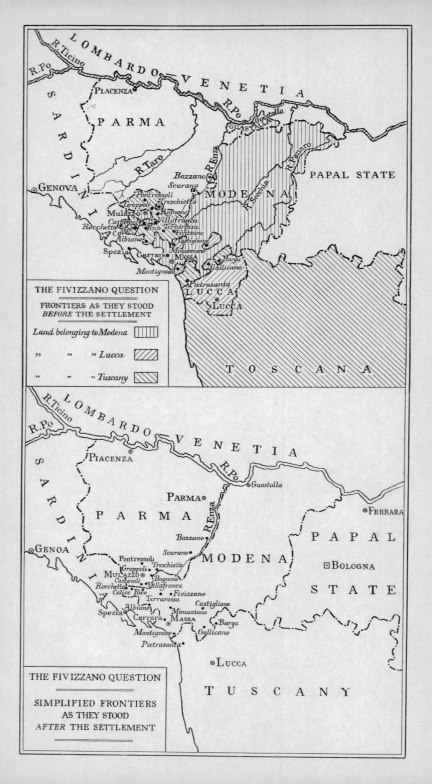

THE FIVIZZANO QUESTION

FRONTIERS AS THEY STOOD
BEFORE THE SETTLEMENT

Land belonging to Modena

" " " Lucca

" " " Tuscany

THE FIVIZZANO QUESTION

SIMPLIFIED FRONTIERS
AS THEY STOOD
AFTER THE SETTLEMENT

Appendix A

THE FIVIZZANO QUESTION

In the years 1814 and 1815 the Great Powers were rather hard put to find territories for all the Hapsburgs and Bourbons and other legitimist claimants. There was, of course, Napoleon's widow to be provided for; for, after all, by birth she was the Austrian Archduchess, Marie Louise, daughter of the Emperor. So they gave her the Duchy of Parma.[1]

This meant, however, that the Bourbons of Parma—another Marie Louise and her son Louis (in Italian, Ludovico)—were deprived of Parma, to which they had better claims than those of the newly installed Bonaparte Duchess. So they were allotted the small Duchy of Lucca, to be held by them during the lifetime of Marie Louise (widow of Napoleon). At her death Ludovico de Bourbon would become Duke of Parma. He would have to resign Lucca to Tuscany.

By the Congress of Vienna in 1815 and the Treaty of Paris 1817, it was provided that on the death of Napoleon's widow, the Archduchess Marie Louise, Duchess of Parma, an entirely new settlement should be made. On her death

1. The Duke of Lucca, Ludovico (it applied only to him, for his mother died in 1824), was to become Duke of Parma, Piacenza and Guastalla (belonging to Modena).

2. His duchy of Lucca was to go to Tuscany.

3. Tuscany, in compensation, was to resign to Modena the Tuscan territories of *Fivizzano*, Pietrasanta and Barga,[2] because Modena was to give up Guastalla.[3]

4. Austria, in compensation for Lucca, was to receive the Bavaro-Palatine fiefs.

---

[1] *V.* Rosi, p. 52.

[2] And Modena also got the Lucchese districts of Castiglione, Gallicano, Minucciano and Montignoso, which were inside the Modenese boundaries or near them. (*London Corr.* I, 227, Metternich to Dietrichstein, November 5th, 1847.)

[3] Austria had a right of reversion on Guastalla; but she agreed, in 1844, to transfer this to the territories of Pontremoli and Bagnone. She had a right of reversion on Parma—and Metternich used to claim rights on Tuscany.

This arrangement, however, was never considered satisfactory, and on November 28th, 1844, a secret treaty[4] was signed called the Treaty of Florence, between the four powers concerned, arranging for a complete re-shuffle. They agreed that on the death of the Duchess of Parma:

1. The Duke of Lucca was to give up his Duchy of Lucca to Tuscany.[5] In exchange for it he would become Duke of Parma and Piacenza; but, by this new arrangement, he was not to become Duke of Guastalla. He was to give up his claim to Guastalla, and also to the land east of the Enza, and leave them to Modena. The Enza was to be the boundary between Parma and Modena.

As Duke of Parma he would receive from Modena the border villages of Bazzano and Scurano.

2. Thus Tuscany was to get the Duchy of Lucca: and also Barga and Pietrasanta (already in her possession) on which Modena had claims. That gave her a nice accretion of territory and a clean frontier.

But on the northern side of the debated lands she was to resign to Parma various of her outlying possessions: in the Lunigiana she gave up Pontremoli, Bagnone, Groppoli, Lusuolo (just south of Villafranca), Terrarossa, Albiano and Calice.

Thus Parma under its Duke Ludovico would receive not only the border villages of Bazzano and Scurano (from Modena) but also from Tuscany the seven territories above-named, Pontremoli, etc.

But under this treaty Duke Ludovico agreed to exchange three out of these seven villages to Modena, namely the three southern places (Albiano, Calice, Terrarossa) and the village of Rico[6] in exchange for the Modenese villages of Treschietto, Villafranca, Castevoli and Mulazzo.

3. In reality Modena was the chief gainer in all these bargains.[7] From Parma she had got the Duchy of Guastalla, and some territory east of the river Enza.

Under the original Treaty of Vienna 1815, she was to get from Lucca the territories of Castiglione, Gallicano, Minucciano and Montignoso, as well as *Fivizzano* from Tuscany.

By acquiring this solid central block she obtained access also to her isolated district of Rocchetta (on the Piedmontese frontier).

[4] For copy of this treaty of 1844 *v. London Corr.* 1, 264.
[5] Clause II of treaty.
[6] These were handed over by Treaty of December 9th, 1847.
[7] All she resigned was the villages of Bazzano and Scurano, and her claims on Barga and Pietrasanta.

In fact Modena, by incorporating the Duchy of Guastalla, would now stretch from the river Po to the sea; and would cut off Piedmont from Tuscany. As Modena was considered an advanced guard of Austria, this caused great indignation.

This Treaty of Florence remained a secret for nearly three years: but then, in the summer of 1847, the Duke of Lucca began to encounter the political difficulties described in the text, and he decided to abdicate and to allow the sovereignty of his state to pass at once to the Grand Duke of Tuscany, on terms of receiving an income of nine thousand francesconi per month until such time as he should succeed the Duchess Marie Louise (Napoleon's widow) and become Duke of Parma. This treaty[8] between the Duke of Lucca and the Grand Duke of Tuscany was signed on October 4th, 1847. It altered nothing, but it meant that some of the clauses of the Treaty of Florence (1844) had to be carried out at once. Now that Tuscany was getting Lucca she had to hand over Fivizzano to Modena and Pontremoli and the outlying parts of the Lunigiana to the Duke of Lucca, eventually to become part of Parma.

Here the trouble began. The people of those districts were good Tuscans and they refused to go. Apparently this was a difficulty that had never occurred to anyone three years earlier when they signed the Treaty of Florence.

The above is a brief sketch of the Fivizzano question—an analysis of the treaties. As to the resistance there is nothing to add to what has been said in the text.

[8] For copy of treaty *v. London Corr.* 1 (1846–47).

Appendix B

LORD MINTO'S MISSION

In the middle of the year 1847 Lord Palmerston hit upon the rather curious idea of sending out to Italy Lord John Russell's father-in-law, Lord Minto, to go from state to state as Minister Plenipotentiary.[1] The duties assigned to him were to discover the truth about the situation and to advise and encourage the Italian sovereigns to continue their Liberal reforms, in fact, to tell them that in spite of the Ferrara episode they need not be afraid of Austria; that they were within their rights as independent rulers, and that England was there to protect Liberalism.

What originated the idea of this unusual English mission? Hostile critics have given as the real reason that because England had been left out of the Austro-French agreement, which was true, she sent out Minto to stir up revolution all over Italy, which is absolutely false.[2] Palmerston did not want revolution.[3] Indeed

[1] In Rome, according to English law, he could not properly be Minister Plenipotentiary; he went merely as "a member of Her Majesty's government...and entirely possessing the confidence of your sovereign and your colleagues". *London Corr.* i, 129.

[2] The Russian ambassador virtually said this to Palmerston himself. *V.* Bianchi, v, 96–9.

[3] Palmerston's views were as follows: "Her Majesty's government are of opinion that the stipulations and engagements of the Treaty of Vienna ought to be adhered to in Italy...and that no change can properly be made in the territorial arrangements that were established by that Treaty, without the consent and concurrence of all the Powers who were a party to it." Palmerston to Lord Ponsonby, August 12th, 1847, *London Corr.* i, 81.

And to the same (August 13th, 1847): "The accounts which Her Majesty's Government receive from Italy...show that the apprehensions of Prince Metternich are extremely exaggerated; and whatever may be passing in the minds of a few enthusiasts nothing has yet happened that can be called a revolution, or which can indicate any probability of an attempt to unite Italy under one authority.

In fact, the reforms which have been made or are in contemplation in Rome and Tuscany would naturally tend to counteract any such design, because in proportion as grievances are removed and nations

one French writer has stated that it was not Minto but his private secretary who aroused rebellion: and it is an interesting suggestion but so far without proofs. However, this much may be admitted: undoubtedly Minto, in encouraging Liberalism, unwittingly encouraged various people who were secretly revolutionist, and many more who afterwards became so; for within a year almost everybody was a revolutionist. In this respect Minto was in the same position as Pius IX: but his Liberalism was less moderate, and what he said was often claimed as an "English encouragement".

Besides the above-mentioned duties he had a secret mission to perform with Pius IX:[4] he was to ask His Holiness to "interpose his authority" to forbid priestly agitation in Ireland; and, to make a strong case, Palmerston had supplied him with material from the Irish newspapers.

Already there was under discussion in Rome the question of the Irish colleges; these Queen's colleges had been set up by the English government on the basis of their providing no religious education. Consequently, they had been refused by some, though not by all of the Catholic hierarchy, and when Minto arrived in Italy the case between these two sets of Prelates was still before Propaganda for decision.[5] On November 5th, 1847, however, Mr Petre, the British representative in Rome, was officially informed that the colleges had been condemned, so that they never became a concern of Lord Minto. Apparently Mr Petre, though presumably a Roman Catholic, took a very strong line against the Irish bishops, and against Padre Ventura's funeral oration; and had very little opinion even of the Papal government itself.[6]

A short sketch of Minto's Mission[7] forms the most fitting close

become contented with their existing condition, in the same proportion each man among them devotes his mind to the improvement of his own individual condition, and ceases to think or to wish for any great alteration in the political state of the country to which he belongs, be that country great or small." *London Corr.* 1, 82.

[4] F.O. 44, vol. 11 (Private).

[5] Bianchi, v, 103; F.O. 43, Rome and Italy, vol. XL, W. Petre.

[6] Judging by several letters of his at the time.

[7] Minto's Mission: First week in October 1847, arrived in Turin. October 23rd, arrived in Florence. November 3rd, arrived in Rome. February 3rd, 1848, started for Naples, and April 9th, returned to Rome.

Authorities. By far the best, of course, is F.O. 44, containing copies of all the letters to and from the Foreign Office and Minto. *London Correspondence* prints the most important of these. Other authorities

to this volume, because here we have an impartial impression of the whole moving panorama, by a distinguished Englishman, a Liberal peer. We can picture his well-known features, side whiskers, top hat and air of unmistakable gentility as he went from one court to another, meeting and discussing politics with most of the characters described in these pages; even with some of the most unlikely.

On October 9th, when he had been some days in Turin, he reported to Palmerston,[8] concerning the two chief dangers, that the peril of Austrian invasion was past, while, on the other hand, revolution seemed improbable unless the sovereigns were too timid about making Liberal concessions. He was all in favour of Liberal concessions:

Something approaching the blind subjection of military discipline has so long been thought, in these countries, necessary for security of Government, that the slightest abandonment of arbitrary right is contemplated with alarm; and I fear that both here and in Tuscany it was rather the irresistible impulse given by Pius IX than their own wisdom which inspired the Liberal policy on which they have embarked.

He dined with Charles Albert; it was a most friendly meeting. Apart from personal considerations Charles Albert must have felt that, after the *rapprochement* between France and Austria, England was his only friend; and before leaving Turin Minto advised him to grant the Consulta and the Press Law, and to join the League. Bold advice on so short an experience, but sound: as we have seen, Charles Albert carried out a good deal of it.

At Florence, after a week of civilities, he reported on October 29th:

There is no reason to apprehend any undue pressure on the government for larger measures than it has already given. The only point of danger is the Fivizzano position.

And he adds:

It is reliance upon British support which gives confidence to the governments of Central Italy and encourages them to proceed with the great reforms upon which they are engaged.... In my various conversations with the Grand Duke he has constantly assured me of his confident reliance upon the good sense and moderation of his subjects.

worth consulting are *Camb. Mod. Hist.* vol. xi; Tivaroni, Masi, Raulich, Rosi and the other general histories. Farini, i, 274; Bianchi, v, 82; Spada, i, 379 *et seq.*

    [8] *London Corr.* i, 165.

This last phrase was a fine effort on the part of the Grand Duke. However, Minto's advice to continue granting Liberal reforms in order to avoid revolution must have fallen pleasantly on his ears, for he could no longer do anything else. And he, at all events, might continue his concessions until he became a constitutional ruler: but this was impossible for the Pope.

On October 29th "a Sicilian gentleman called on me". This was the young La Masa. He represented a deputation of Sicilians and brought a memorial; but Minto refused to receive the deputation as that was his last day in Florence. However, he forwarded the memorial to Palmerston; it was a claim for the complete autonomy of Sicily, for the Constitution of 1812 whose existence England had guaranteed. "The cry raised by the insurgents is 'Long life to the Constitution', 'Long life to Pius IX', 'Long life to Italy'; and in this cry they seek to embody a claim for Sicilian public right and for Italian nationality."

This meant revolution; and, as we know, La Masa was busily preparing the revolution which he carried out with such extraordinary success only ten weeks later. Possibly it is this document which has caused it to be said that Minto spread rebellion. In reality he remained perfectly correct; but when the Sicilians had won their freedom he went to Naples and worked with great assiduity at the draft constitution for Sicily.

As to his private secretary "stirring up revolt", it is hard to say what this means. La Masa says that there was in Florence a friend of Minto, a certain General Adham or Adam, who was very nice to him (La Masa). Possibly that explains the statement.

At Rome, apparently Minto's position was not quite so satisfactory as in Turin and Florence, which, no doubt, was due to his no longer being Minister Plenipotentiary. Except about the Sonderbund there is little information in his letters. Moreover, he seems to have been too prone to accept the Liberals at their face value, which, however, was almost inevitable. Evidently this caused irritation to the authorities, for it finds an outlet in Spada's history; but we must remember that Spada wrote after the event, after the period of revolution and suffering and exile. He is angry because Minto encouraged men who, before long, became ardent revolutionists, but he forgets that this was impossible for an Englishman to foresee.

Minto had several interviews with Pius. He had brought with him a copy of the Memorandum of 1831 because Palmerston advised that its provisions should be carried out.

Spada complains that he threw himself into the arms of the

Esaltati. Minto evidently did not realise that throughout all Italy
—except perhaps in Piedmont—the Liberal movement was running away with the governments, just as untrained horses may
run away with a coach. He thought that the revolutionists could
be checked by a grant of Liberal institutions; whereas by this time
it was the very thing which would encourage them to ask for more.
He thought that the governments were hesitating because they
feared Austria, whereas now in reality they were afraid of the
people. Every single one of them except Piedmont was in fear
of annihilation. It was a necessary stage to go through before Italy
could be unified; but the danger in which they stood was not
realised by Minto.

Spada tells us that the people to whom Minto showed most
favour in Rome were Ciceruacchio, Canino, Masi, Sterbini and
d'Azeglio. If so, it is not surprising. After all, they were more or
less representative Liberals, each in his own way, and no doubt
they sought his acquaintance at the Circolo Romano. One rather
absurd slip he did commit. By way of civility to Ciceruacchio he
presented his second son Lorenzo with a copy of Macaulay's *Lays
of Ancient Rome*, in which he had written the following verse with
his own hand:[9]

> (Presented by Lord Minto to Lorenzo Brunetti)
> "These be but tales of the olden days.
> The patriot bard shall now his lays
> Of charming freedom pour.
> And Rome's fair annals bid the fame
> Of Ciceruacchio's humble name
> In deathless honour soar."

In this selection of a protégé Minto was far from fortunate. It
was this boy's brother who stabbed Pellegrino Rossi only eleven
months later, a murder to which Ciceruacchio himself was almost
certainly accessory. Naturally Minto could not foresee this; but
it rather justifies the Papal authorities' complaint, that he had very
little realisation of the type of extremist whom he encouraged.

In connection with Ireland he spoke to Pius about the Great
Famine that was raging and the desire to relieve it,[10] and, in
pursuance of his mission, as to Pius interposing to prevent the
priests from taking part in agitation. For this purpose he prepared a short memorandum on the nature of priestly agitation
prevailing in Ireland, accompanied by "a statement by way of
example of some of the cases detailed at length in the Irish news-

[9] Spada, I, 382; Martinengo, p. 276. [10] Spada, I, 379 *et seq.*

papers which you [Palmerston] had sent me, and the whole of which were added as an appendix with translations of the more important articles".[11]

Then, however, he decided that it was better not to ask the Pope to forbid priestly agitation in general (which would be disregarded), but to issue commands only in those cases "undoubtedly within the sphere of ecclesiastical authority". So he drew up a second memorandum.

To cut a long story short, on November 19th he handed all these documents to the Pope. Pius read them and, Minto tells us, expressed strong disapproval of political activity on the part of his clergy: and Minto ended by handing him a statement in French, asking him to issue a "défense Pontificale de prendre part à l'agitation politique". Apparently the matter had no sequel.

What probably led to his departure from Rome was the fact—which may as well be noted though it does not come into this volume—that the Sicilians had temporarily thrown off the yoke of Naples, and he went to try to devise a compromise which should prove acceptable both to them and to the King of Naples: obviously this was a noble task and one that would have saved an infinity of suffering: but although he worked out constitutions that were little or nothing short of separation, and actually persuaded Ferdinand to agree to them, the Sicilians proved unreasonable;[12] and this was a pity because it led to the celebrated bombardment of Messina[13] in the following August and to the reconquest of the island.

The following is an extract from the most interesting of the Minto letters during this period. It was written just after the occasion when Minto had communicated with Turin and Florence asking them to advise Pius to allow the Consulta's proceedings to be made public.

The Earl of Minto to Viscount Palmerston. Rome, January 23rd, 1848:

I had to-day some conversation with the Pope on the affairs of his own government.

[11] F.O. 44, vol. II (Private), December 30th, 1847.

[12] *V.* Bianchi, v, 147–57. They were unreasonable in refusing the most extreme terms that Ferdinand could offer. Of course they had a right to do so, but if so, they should have made war preparations; it meant a renewal of war; and they did nothing to prepare for it.

[13] It was from this bombardment that Ferdinand obtained the name of Bomba.

The subject was introduced by himself, in consequence, I imagine, of a communication which I had conveyed to him a few days ago, of the steps I had taken to let the King of Sardinia know my opinion of the great mischief and danger likely to ensue from a rejection of the demand of the Consulta di Stato for the publicity of their proceedings; upon which subject I knew a reference had been made to Turin for advice.

I had said in my message that I wished him to be informed of my proceeding, because it would serve to prove to him how strongly I was convinced of the necessity of this concession, if any terms were to be kept with the Consulta di Stato. I received a very gracious and flattering answer to my message, and I presume that he had it in his mind to-day, when he turned the conversation on his own affairs.

He said that he felt the necessity for free and constant intercourse with the Consulta and the Government, and that he desired that the influence of the Consulta should be felt in every branch of the Government.

I said this gave me great pleasure and that he knew I looked upon the Consulta as the chief strength and only support of the Government. He said yes: but that still there was a peculiarity in the nature of his government which did not admit of so free an expansion of Liberal institutions as was admissible in others. I said that in an important feature his government was not only unlike, but the reverse of all others. That elsewhere the Church was subservient to the State, and here the State was subject to the Church; but that after all this need not necessarily affect the character of action of his government.

I said I looked upon the Church (represented by the Pope) as the sovereign of this country. It matters not who or what is sovereign, the duties of sovereignty are the same in whatever hands. In most countries the civil and ecclesiastical administration is distinct. The State manages its affairs; ecclesiastical affairs are conducted by Ecclesiastics; and if the Queen interferes with them in England, it is only as head of the Church.

Why should not the same separation exist here? The Pope retaining his position as head of the State. In other states we say that it is the duty of the Sovereign to govern for the benefit of the people, not for his own advantage. And so it is the duty of the sovereign Church to have in view the public prosperity, and not the separate interest of the Church, in its civil administration. And there can be no reason why it should not introduce in its dominions any institutions or form of institution calculated to produce good government.

The Pope assured me that Cardinal Bofondi is of thoroughly Liberal opinions....

In fact Minto and also Palmerston believed that a Liberal Papacy was perfectly possible.

But, what about declaring war? That was the rock on which the scheme broke within seven months. Queen Victoria could declare war because hers was a national Church; the Pope cannot declare war because his is an international Church. And England would certainly have dissuaded the Pope from declaring war, as she tried to dissuade both Naples and Piedmont. Moreover there were many other difficulties.

Bianchi, the great Italian historian, quotes the chief paragraph of this letter of Minto and ends as follows:

In saying these things, Lord Minto was touching very lightly on very grave problems both religious and political. Presently it will be for us to relate the means used to try and solve them, and the effects that resulted.[14]

[14] Bianchi, v, 84.

Appendix C

AUSTRIAN ADMINISTRATION IN LOMBARDO-VENETIA.

The Viennese administrative machine shows surprisingly good returns. Of course one traces all through them the desire to make the Italian provinces a contented and submissive portion of the Empire. The Austrians wanted to justify their presence as rulers and their appropriation of authority over Italians. Still their machine can claim some administrative success. The population for instance showed a steady increase:

	1817	1832	1847
Lombardy	2,167,000	2,469,874	2,734,244
Venetia	1,856,000	2,073,832	2,311,627

In 1818 they established compulsory primary education with the following results:

In Lombardy	1818	1822	1832	1842
Boys' Schools	900	2127	—	—
Girls' Schools	300	503	—	—
Total of schools	1200	2630	3535	4021
Pupils		107,765[1]	166,767	201,277

But according to Sandonà about half the boys and four-fifths of the girls did not attend:

In Venetia	1831	1841
	1,597 schools	1,923 schools
	80,151 scholars	85,431 scholars

These schools, Sandonà says, were given over entirely to the parish clergyman. No doubt the Austrians felt that the priests would be very unlikely to permit any dangerous doctrine; and they introduced a compulsory political catechism enjoining the most rigid obedience.[2]

Next above these schools came the Ginnasi, of which there were a large number (divided into first and second classes); those in the capitals of the provinces were paid for by government.

[1] 81,241 boys and 26,524 girls. Sandonà, *Regno Lombardo-Veneto*, pp. 88–9, gives the totals for every year.
[2] Gori, p. 8.

Above these were the Licei; seven in Lombardy and seven in Venetia (1815–16).[3] It is very difficult to say for certain how far all these institutions were efficient.[4]

Lastly there were the two Universities, one at Pavia and one at Padua. Of these the Paduan soon became by far the bigger. In 1816 it had 559 students; in 1818 there were 826; and in 1847 there were nearly 2000, which was considered too many.

As to Lawcourts; the general verdict seems to be that their justice was good except in political cases: or in cases when the judge did not know the language of those whom he was trying.

The most unpleasant institution was probably the Austrian conscription; eight infantry regiments and one of cavalry were set apart to receive Italian recruits: the man who drew an unlucky number would have to spend eight years serving probably in Hungary or Bohemia, sent there to hold down other nationalities[5] or sometimes to defend the Austrian fortresses in Italy against attacks from the Piedmontese side.

In the streets there were foreign soldiers: Germans, Hungarians, Czechs, Poles and others; and their officers were manœuvred about the Lombard plain until they knew it better than did the natives; and everywhere the Police. "The Austrian Police is

[3] Two in Milan; one in Como, Bergamo, Brescia, Cremona, Mantua, Venice, Verona, Vicenza, Udine, Treviso, Padua, Belluno.

[4] Gori says that the primary education was good; the secondary only mediocre.

[5] A vivid idea of the hardship resulting from this conscription was conveyed to me by an old peasant living at Varenna on the Lake of Como. He related how he had been obliged to go across to Bellaggio. There he had drawn an unlucky number, No. 3, and had spent the next four years serving in a cavalry regiment in Hungary. He still remembered some German words of command such as "Link-schau, Rechtschau", etc. But then came the year 1859: on the eve of the Battle of Magenta he and three other Italian troopers found themselves riding out as a patrol against the French and Piedmontese armies. He described to me how, at the right moment, they looked at each other, and simultaneously put spurs to their horses and galloped into the Piedmontese lines. They were arrested as spies and sent to Turin; but before arriving there, had cleared themselves and were given a great ovation. He was allowed to enlist in the Royal Guards, and accompanied the King down to Naples where he was so lucky as to be present at the great scene when Victor Emmanuel shook hands with Garibaldi. All this he told me in Lombard dialect of which every word had to be translated into Italian by his son. His name was Anghileri, and his son Francesco was a well-known boatman.

present everywhere and you cannot see it or touch it. The public only knows that there is a great net stretched out there", says Count Torelli.[6] And Metternich was much piqued when the Piedmontese government refused to join him in establishing a central office for opening private letters. He said that he had already had such an office in Frankfort and that it had produced most satisfactory results.[7]

But the grievance which would supply a very genuine case against Austria was that she extracted an Imperial Contribution from Italy amounting finally to about two and a half millions sterling a year. The following is the case as stated by Sandonà, who gives his documents:

Up to 1823 the Lombardo-Venetian kingdom contributed 35 million lire annually to the Empire; in 1823 the sum was 45 millions of Austrian lire, in 1825 it was 59 millions, in 1826 it was 61 millions; from 1828 to 1836 it was 62 millions a year, in 1837 it was 67 millions and from 1837 to 1848 it amounted to 66 millions.[8]

In return for that sum, of course, the Lombards and Venetians had the protection of the Austrian army and fleet, the imperial family, their diplomacy, their government offices and all other imperial services.

That they should have paid more, and even more in proportion than some of the poor Austrian provinces was inevitable: but in such a case as theirs there should be a limit to the amount. They were actually giving up more than half their income; and to an empire which they had begun to hate.

At the same time the Austrians aimed at being popular, at

[6] Un anonimo Lombardo, *Pensieri*, p. 223.

[7] Sambuy, Confidential despatch, November 11th, 1843: "M. de Metternich a été piqué de notre refus de contribuer à établir en Italie un centre d'information."

[8] Sandonà, p. 321. Sandonà's tables show that Lombardo-Venetia paid about 82,000,000 lire in taxes (years 1816, 1821); and of that sum only about 46,000,000 lire was spent in Italy—the remainder was her imperial contribution; and that in later years the contribution became almost twice as great. To give a final opinion on this grievance would be impossible: the actual totals will be a matter of dispute, but, in his main general contention that the Italians paid too much, Sandonà appears to make a strong case: and Gori and Tivaroni are of the same opinion. He says also that the bureaucracy debited huge sums against Lombardo-Venetia in order to make out that there was a deficit.

encouraging material prosperity and making Milan a bright and pleasant town full of amusements, where people would not bother about politics. And they were successful. The best judge of a régime is one who has lived under it. Let us take the opinion of the celebrated Massimo d'Azeglio who hated Austria, but elected to spend ten long years of his life in Milan rather than in Turin. As we know, he was a man very much alive; popular, a Marquis, a soldier, an artist, a writer, a politician and soon to be a distinguished officer and Premier of Piedmont. His opinion runs as follows:

I, who was a professional hater of the foreigner, am compelled with shame to admit that, if I wanted to breathe, I had to return to Milan. And why? Owing to the subtle acts with which the Austrian authorities—who perhaps were bent on establishing comfortable quarters in a pleasant, rich, fat and cheerful city—succeeded in obliterating or softening the orders received from Vienna, and allowing the Milanese the fullest freedom to grumble, to ridicule the *pollini* (police) and to give them our final opinion not only on the play at the Scala theatre but likewise on politics; we weren't supposed to shout these things on the house-tops, but with ordinary prudence you could say anything.[9]

And again:

During my stay in Milan the usual occupations of the young generation were drinking and ballet-girls (whom it often married). It declaimed against the Germans from whom it kept itself apart. It lived in idleness and the most profound ignorance....

Nevertheless it produced good men during the Five Glorious Days.

[9] Massimo d'Azeglio, *I miei Ricordi* (3rd edition), II, 393.

Appendix D

THE "CONGIURA"

The Congiura. Who started it? There are two opposite views:

On the one hand, contemporary Papal writers such as Spada insist that the Congiura was a pretext got up by the Revolutionists in order to capture the Civic Guard: and various contemporary Moderates such as Pasolini[1] and Farini admit that there was no actual conspiracy; so do some of the leading historians, notably the republican Tivaroni. So do some of the diplomats: Bargagli, the Tuscan Minister to the Pope, seems to have accepted the first-named view of the situation. And, in any case, the idea of Austria's being concerned in it does not appear to have occurred either to him or to Pellegrino Rossi.

On the other hand, there were various contemporaries such as De Boni who believed in the Congiura; and so do several of the best modern historians, including Gori and Masi; they hold that the "occupation" of Ferrara gives us the clue to the true originator of the Congiura, and that it was Metternich. They say that the Ferrara episode and the Congiura were all part of one scheme, simply a repetition of the time-honoured device of stirring up strife in a smaller nation, in order to have an excuse for intervening to restore law and order.[2] Their reasons for this opinion are the following: firstly that it was not in Rome alone that the Congiura made its appearance; simultaneous disturbances occurred in nine or ten other Italian towns (including Ferrara) and afforded opportunity for Austrian repression; they hold that these were all obviously part of a concerted movement by Metternich now that he had an understanding with France. Secondly, they point out that on July 14th, the English Ambassador in Vienna stated to Lord Palmerston, that Metternich had spoken to him of the great alarm felt by the Papal Government, and had said that Austria had been asked to make preparations for sending armed protection; that, as no such demand had ever come from Pius,[3] most probably this story had been concocted by Metternich in order to pave the way

[1] *V*. Pasolini, 1, 86.

[2] Gori, pp. 238 to 242; Masi, *Nell' Ottocento*, p. 191, and *Il Risorgimento*, 11, 138.

[3] Since the publication of Masi's work two letters have come to light in the Viennese Archives; they show that although Pius had

for intervention. Moreover (Masi adds), an offer to occupy the
four Legations (Romagna) had lately been made by Metternich
to the Papal Nuncio in Vienna, and it had been confirmed by
Count Lützow, Austrian Ambassador in Rome.[4]

Thirdly, Massimo d'Azeglio says that there were several men
arrested who were known to be ex-Centurioni from Faenza; that
they had arms and Austrian money, but were in Rome without
any kind of written authorisation; that they were probably
Austrian agents.[5]

not asked for intervention, Cardinal Gizzi had sounded Lützow on
the point. This action of his, however, was taken entirely on his own
personal account, at a time when he was proposing to grant only
a limited number of the expected Civic Guard, and feared
popular resentment. It seems self-evident that Pius did not ask for
help from Metternich; any Austrian intervention would have
wrecked his Reform movement instantly. But Gizzi, apparently,
was trying to find out Metternich's intentions as to intervention.

Count Lützow, in reply, pointed out the great difficulties that lay
in the way of Austrian intervention; and reminded Gizzi that the
situation was quite different from that in 1831; Austria was now
acting in conjunction with Guizot. V. Lützow's letters of July 2nd
and 6th, 1847. Vienna Staats-Archiv, Rome, 72.

These Viennese letters seem to be confirmed by a letter in the
French Archives. De Marescalchi, the French chargé d'affaires in
Vienna, wrote, on July 10th, to Guizot a letter in which he says that
Metternich had expressed great alarm about the coming revolutions
in the Papal State and Tuscany, but had not said one word which
would suggest that he was thinking of the possibility of an armed
intervention in the states threatened. Yet Metternich could hardly
have intervened without informing France. From this letter it
seems probable that on July 10th Metternich was not proposing to
intervene. V. Paris Aff. Etr. Autriche, Marescalchi's letter, July 10th,
1846.

[4] I cannot find that any such offer had been made by Metternich;
Masi gives as reference the British official correspondence and
Bianchi, but I have not been able to find in them any proof of an
offer from Metternich to occupy the Legations. On the contrary
the Viennese documents show that he did not want to do so, at all
events for the time being.

[5] To his wife d'Azeglio wrote that he did not altogether believe
in the existence of a plot, although it was true that there had been
strangers, apparently Austrian agents, in Rome. Later, to Doubs,
he wrote that the various episodes could hardly be attributed to
anything but Austrian machinations.

In reality it is impossible to say for certain who was the originator of the Congiura. Of course the Ferrara episode was undoubtedly either a threatening or a provocative gesture on the part of Radetzky or his officers; but the Viennese documents seem to show that it had no connection with the Congiura.

It is even conceivable that not merely one, but both sides of the extremists within Rome itself had prepared a coup for the day of the anniversary of Pius' Amnesty.[6] Both parties were thoroughly aroused over the crucial question of the Civic Guard, and their opportunity lay before them. Amnesty Day was the very moment that Sterbini would seize for a political coup: and similarly, if the more reckless of the Reactionists wished to raise riots among the crowds in Rome, there could be no better opportunity for their secret agents and their money.

To the present writers the explanation all centres round the supremely important question of the Civic Guard. This concession meant that there was a chance of arming the people; and, to the leaders of revolution, that fact just makes the whole difference between power and helplessness. In this case they had won the bare concession on July 5th; but that concession of arms was intended to be only a partial and gradual measure; therefore—one is inclined to believe—the agitators meant to turn it into a force in being, and seized the interregnum as a good moment for doing so.

They felt it necessary for the Liberals to be armed. They believed that Metternich and his satellites were at work: and that Pius' movement might be overthrown by a police-Austrian plot in Rome just as it had been in Parma.

The Notificazione of June 22nd had been taken as a warning that they would not be allowed the Civic Guard; and since then they genuinely believed that their own beloved Pius was being surrounded and dissuaded by Cardinals such as Lambruschini, by Gregorians, Jesuits, Austrians and the like. That was why they shouted "Pius IX *alone*"; that was why Ciceruacchio carefully noted the names of the guests at Lambruschini's dinner; and that

[6] Pellegrino Rossi, the French ambassador, remarks that there had been a conspiracy and that it had been the work of the extremists on either one side or the other. But in his despatch of July 18th to Guizot he expresses himself rather differently. He merely says that on either side there are some visionaries and some men without principles who might do anything. Paris Aff. Etr., Rome, 1847–48, Despatch of July 18th.

was why Lambruschini and Grassellini (head of the police) and other reputed Gregorians or Austrian agents were pilloried as having formed a reactionary plot against Pius' movement, in fact against the people. It will be remembered that the spies of the Gregorian régime had previously reported that they expected a plot with proscription lists, daggers and Masonic signs, etc., just as actually occurred (*v.* p. 194 of the text).

It is hard to say for certain, but, in the opinion of the present writers, the Congiura was the work of the Esaltati.

Appendix E

THE NOTICES PLACARDED ON THE WALLS DURING THE "CONGIURA"

The following is the copy of the notice as sent by Lützow to Vienna. It is longer than the original in the Vatican Archives, as it contains two more names, Pieralti and Bedini.

Notice

Instruction of Incarico Lambruschini and Nardoni sent to the individuals mentioned below for carrying out a tragedy among the people.

The Governor (1)
Colonel Freddi (2)
Captain Nuzzarelli (3)
Lawyer Benvenuti (4)
Vincenzo Moroni (5)
Count Bertola (6)
Spy Partini (7)
Spy Minardi (8)
The three sons of Spy Galanti (9)
Fioravanti (10)
Lieut. Sangiorgi (11)
Lieut. Giannuzzi (12)
Pieralti (13)
Bedini (14)

Let anyone who tears this notice beware.
To the public and eternal shame of these scoundrels
the public indignation
has placed this notice
Vertatus.

Observations by Lützow.

(1) Mgr Grassellini, a Sicilian, believed to be agent to the Neapolitan police.
(2) Colonel of Carabinieri, and one of the principal members of all the military commissions which were held in Romagna.
(3) Captain in the Mounted Cacciatori and brother of Mgr Decacio of the Rota Court.
(4) Assessor-General of Police.

(5) Brother of the noted Gaetano Moroni, first Papal Chamberlain of the late Pope.

(6), (7), (8) Publicly known as spies.

(9) Their father was head of the police agents or spies.

(10) Maresciallo of Carabinieri.

(11) Lieut. in the Carabinieri, arrested in the evening of July 16th last, in the street, by a patrol of the new Civic Guard, which at that time seized a pack of cards and a dagger which Sangiorgi threw into a cantina when he saw the patrol coming towards him.

(12) Lieut. of Carabinieri who has been on leave for several weeks at Anagni, his home.

(13) and (14) Marescialli of Carabinieri specially told off for service in the Police dicastery.

INDEX

CAMBRIDGE: PRINTED BY WALTER LEWIS, M.A., AT THE UNIVERSITY PRESS

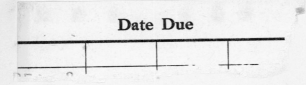

Date Due